SMOKING and CULTURE

The Archaeology of Tobacco Pipes
in Eastern North America

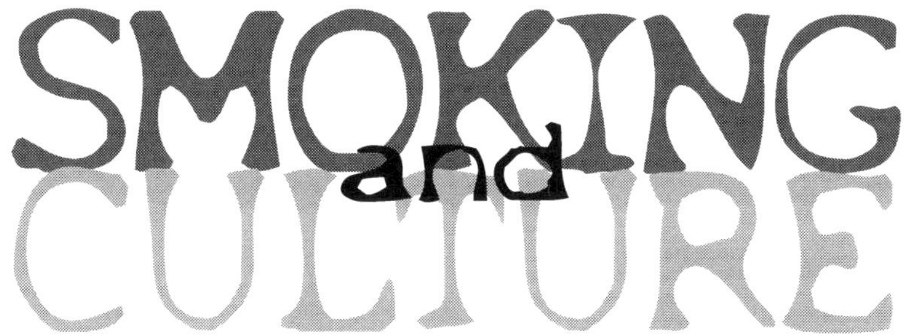

Sean Rafferty and Rob Mann

The University of Tennessee Press / Knoxville

Cloth: 1st printing, 2004.
Paper: 1st printing, 2016.

Library of Congress Cataloging-in-Publication Data

Smoking and culture : the archaeology of tobacco pipes in eastern North America / [edited by Sean M. Rafferty and Rob Mann].— 1st ed.
p. cm.
Includes bibliographical references and index.
ISBN 978-1-62190-232-4

1. Tobacco pipes—East (U.S.)
2. East (U.S.)—Antiquities.
3. Indians of North America—Tobacco use—East (U.S.)
4. Indians of North America-East (U.S.)—Antiquities.
5. Smoking—East (U.S.)--History.
I. Rafferty, Sean M. (Sean Michael)
II. Mann, Rob.

E159.5.S64 2004
394.1'4—dc22 2004010582

Contents

Illustrations

Figures

Maps

Tables

Introduction

Smoking Pipes and Culture

Sean M. Rafferty and Rob Mann

The papers collected in this volume were adapted from presentations given at the 2001 Society for American Archaeology annual meetings, held in New Orleans in a symposium entitled "The Sot Weed Factor: Recent Developments in the Archaeology of Smoking Pipes." The symposium, organized by the editors of this volume, was organized in reaction to a trend in the archaeological treatment of smoking pipes and of studies of single types of material culture in general. Until relatively recently, such research has tended to be descriptive and still largely reminiscent of the culture-history paradigm, with overriding concerns on typology and chronology. Studies of artifact types, when set in this perspective, can tell us a lot about the archaeological record but not nearly as much about the people who ultimately created it. We view previous studies of smoking pipes (for example, Rutsch 1973), as especially exaggerated examples of this tendency. While smoking pipes have been used by both prehistoric and historic archaeologists as cultural and chronological markers, there has been comparatively little research into what role smoking pipes played in the societies that used them, and through studying smoking pipes, what we can learn about culture. The authors in this collection have all attempted, in various ways, to overcome these limitations.

A Brief History of Smoking in North America

Smoking pipes have long been recognized as significant artifacts in prehistoric Native American contexts. Numerous smoking pipes have been recovered from Late Archaic period burial contexts (Walthall 1980:77), indicating that smoking in ritual contexts clearly has ancient roots in North America. These earliest pipes were generally tubular in form and made of ground stone. One of the earliest known smoking pipes was recovered from the Eva site in Tennessee from a component dated to approximately 2000 B.C. (Lewis and Lewis 1961:66). Tubular smoking pipes continued to be used during most of prehistory, but they are most commonly associated with the prehistoric cultures of the Ohio River Valley during the Early Woodland period, from approximately 1,000 B.C. to A.D. 200 (Rafferty, this volume).

The shift from the Early to Middle Woodland period saw a radical change in the style of smoking pipes in the Eastern Woodlands. While tubular pipes dominated the Early Woodland, the Middle Woodland is characterized by platform pipes (Gehlbach 1982; Irwin, this volume). In their simplest manifestations these pipes take the form of a flat or curved base platform that contains the pipe bore, with a cylindrical bowl located in the center. Rarer and much more elaborate were the effigy forms in which the plain cylindrical bowl was replaced by some form of animal figure. Numerous species are represented but avian forms dominate. Platform, or "monitor" pipes (so called for their resemblance to the Civil War Union ironclad gunboat of the same name), are generally associated with the Ohio Valley Hopewell, where the largest numbers of these pipes are found. Platform pipes were included in the repertoire of items traded throughout the Hopewell interaction sphere. Specimens are found throughout the northern Eastern Woodlands.

The Late Woodland and Mississippian periods are dominated by the form most associated with the idea of a pipe today: the elbow pipe. While elbow pipes had existed as minority styles in the preceding Early and Middle Woodland, they became the most common form of smoking implement from the eleventh century A.D. onward in eastern North America. While elbow pipes dominate in terms of raw frequency, figurine pipes and effigy forms are also important during later prehistory, especially during the Mississippian. The most famous of these is the so-called Big Boy pipe found at the Spiro site in Oklahoma (Brown 1985:102). The Mississippian effigy pipes often include stylistic elements that relate to the constellation of motifs known as the Southeastern Ceremonial Complex, commonly referred to as the Southern Cult (Brown 1985:127). The symbolic associations and ritualized contexts of smoking pipes continue, although in forms and contexts specific to the areas and periods in question.

The Northeast during the Late Woodland period is similarly dominated by relatively simple elbow-style pipes. Stone and clay elbow pipes with obliquely angled bowls characterize the beginning of the Late Woodland, with pipes from the Owasco period being prime examples (Bradley 1987:17–19). Pipes became increasingly angled in the Northeast through time, and by the beginning of the Iroquoian period, around A.D. 1300–1400, most smoking pipes had nearly right angle bowls (Bradley 1987:30; Noble 1992:42–43). This is not to say that elbow pipes in the Northeast lacked variability. Plain, decorated, and effigy forms existed. Effigy forms usually featured outward-oriented faces on the bowl area of a pipe. Designs included numerous abstract motifs, including incised zigzags and circles. Miniature forms also were manufactured, not as juvenile artifacts but probably as exchange items to cement personal relations (Kapches 1992). Pipe bowl morphology varied over time, including barrel, square, flaring, and trumpet styles among others; these changes have been found to be chronologically more sensitive than decoration (Noble 1992:41).

There is evidence of change in pipe use in the Northeast during the Contact period, with some areas around the Great Lakes preferentially using native pipes rather than the increasingly available Euramerican clay or pewter trade pipes

(Trubowitz 1992, this volume); other areas, such as the Onondaga territory, show a hiatus in native pipes followed by a resurgence (especially in effigy forms) during the 1600s, possibly some form of nativistic response (Bradley 1987:122). In addition, some areas saw a decrease in the use of durable materials, with perishable wooden pipes replacing clay or stone pipes, as observed for the protohistoric Seneca (Bradley 1987:61).

The references to the central importance of tobacco smoking and smoking pipes among Native Americans from the late Contact period through historical and modern ethnographic research are too numerous to summarize here. Several of the pioneers of American ethnology in the nineteenth and early twentieth centuries were aware of the role of smoking in Native American culture (for example, Lowie 1919; Morgan 1972). Tobacco smoking and sacrifice play important roles in a wide variety of Native American rituals, such as the sweat lodge ritual documented by Black Elk (Brown 1953) and still practiced today (Bucko 1998). Tobacco plays a central role in many Native American myths, generally myths that focus on origins or cosmology. For instance, among the Lakota, the origins of smoking are associated with one of the central mythical figures, the White Buffalo Calf Woman (Furst and Furst 1983:12–3; Steinmetz 1984:34–36). This myth associates the origin of smoking and the sacred pipe with the origin of corn, bean, and squash agriculture and the origin of horse riding and buffalo hunting—essentially the entire Siouan resource base from the sixteenth century through the Contact period (Furst and Furst 1983:13; Kaiser 1983:2–3).

Perhaps no other form of Indian pipe has received as much attention by researchers of the Contact period as the calumet and the rituals associated with it (Hart 1980). Simply stated, the calumet was a widespread practice in the Plains and Eastern Woodlands where stemmed pipes were used to facilitate intergroup interactions through participatory ritual involving references to shared cosmology (Brown 1989:311). The calumet's role as a facilitating device led to the misleading colloquial term *peace pipe*. This slang tells only half the story of the calumet, as not all social interactions that the calumet ritual enabled were peaceful; there was a calumet of war as well (Thwaites 1959:59).

Smoking and Culture

It is useful at this point to ask ourselves why pipes are such fascinating objects, why they have drawn the attention of archaeologists, and why they lend themselves so well to anthropological study. First, it must be kept in mind that smoking pipes are essentially drug delivery devices and that smoking instills varying degrees of altered states of consciousness (Joniger and Dobkin de Rios 1973, 1976). Their function is in no way utilitarian, which makes them very different from other artifacts that archaeologists habitually deal with. This by itself is probably what is responsible for the lack of previous interpretive studies of smoking pipes. The archaeology of the 1960s and 1970s, with its emphasis on positivism and functionalism, simply did not know what to make of artifacts that served to satisfy no physical needs whatsoever amongst their users in the past, relegating them to cultural and chronological markers to facilitate the study of other issues.

However, the nonutilitarian functions of smoking pipes make them ideally suited for addressing a host of ideational issues that are becoming more and more significant to archaeologists today. Smoking pipes often incorporate effigies or other design motifs (Brasser 1980; Irwin, this volume; Veit and Bello, this volume), facilitating the study of past symbolism. Ethnohistoric accounts of smoking various substances (for example, Brooks 1937; Catlin 1841) show that pipes were often integral tools in shamanic practices, which lend themselves to the study of ancient religious practices (Furst 1972; Furst and Furst 1982; Hall 1997; Harner 1973; Ripinsky-Naxon 1993).

With respect to historical archaeology, the ubiquitous clay pipe has long been considered a sensitive chronometric tool. Oswald (1951, 1960, 1961), for instance, developed the basic seriated pipe bowl typology still used today (see also Noël Hume 1991:Figure 97). White clay pipe stems have also proved to be useful temporal indicators. The pipe stem dating formula, developed by Harrington (1954) and refined by Binford (1961) and others (for example, Heighton and Deagan 1972; Noël Hume 1991:297–301), provides quite accurate results for sites occupied prior to circa 1780 (Cook 1989:226). Decorative motifs and makers' marks on stems and bowls can be used to derive secure dates for pipes made during the nineteenth century and the McKinley Tariff Act, which required that the country of origin be stamped on imported pipes, provides a convenient *terminus post quem* date of 1891 for late-nineteenth-century deposits (Cook 1989:226). This has created a "sizable blind spot in the analysis and interpretation of archaeologically recovered clay pipes" (Cook 1989:216). The emphasis on the chronometric aspects of clay pipes has been at the expense of behavioral and cultural studies of tobacco use. For instance, the often corporate and class-based characteristics of the practice of smoking presents fertile ground for study. Smoking pipes were most commonly associated with working-class populations historically, and the act of smoking was often practiced in groups. The very act of smoking facilitates interaction within groups and was often a means of expressing ideological concepts of working-class identity, gender, or ethnic affiliations during the eighteenth and nineteenth centuries (Dallal, this volume; Reckner, this volume).

We have organized the volume in broad chronological order. The chapters by Sean Rafferty and Jeff Irwin are both concerned with prehistoric case studies. Rafferty's article looks at some of the oldest pipes in North America, consisting of a sample of blocked-end tubular pipes from Early Woodland period contexts in the Ohio Valley and Northeast. While noting that these artifacts are useful diagnostic artifacts for the Early Woodland period, especially for demonstrating associations with the Ohio Valley Adena, his approach to these artifacts looks beyond taxonomy to see how these artifacts were active parts of Early Woodland cultural practices. Specifically, Rafferty outlines the prominent role that smoking pipes played in Early Woodland mortuary practices across a large portion of the continent and presents a model of how these artifacts were involved in ideological messages projected during burial rituals.

Irwin's chapter instigates Late Woodland period pipes from coastal North Carolina. Irwin first presents a valuable typology of elaborate stone smoking pipes from Late Woodland sand mound sites, focusing on both pipe morphology and on the range of incised iconography they often feature. He goes on to emphasize several of the points raised by Rafferty, focusing on the ritualized use of smoking pipes in facilitating social interactions as part of a burgeoning interregional trade network during late prehistory in the Mid-Atlantic region. Irwin explores how increasing territoriality, political boundedness, coupled with the development of an agricultural subsistence base, fostered increased intercultural contact and how smoking rituals may have served to mediate those interactions. Another common theme that links Irwin's and Rafferty's interpretations is that both emphasize the importance of a multiscalar approach in the study of cultural practices that transcend temporal and taxonomic boundaries to such great degrees as is the case for smoking pipes.

The chapters by Penelope Drooker, Neal Trubowitz, Rob Mann, Michael Nassaney, and Richard Veit and Charles Bello all deal with contexts that fall into the Protohistoric period and, in several cases, with situations where Native Americans and Europeans first met, defined, and redefined themselves and the new "Others." Smoking pipes were integral items in the varied interactions, negotiations, and conflicts that characterized the period. Drooker first offers a summary of the distribution of Late Prehistoric and Protohistoric Native American pipe forms in the Great Lakes, upper Mississippi Valley, and Northeast regions. Then, based on pipes recovered from the Madisonville site and a sample of related Fort Ancient sites, Drooker builds a compelling picture of the structure of interactions among Native Americans during the Protohistoric period. Drooker's analysis, as was the case with Rafferty and Irwin for prehistoric contexts, highlights the role that pipes often played in ritual practices that mediated interaction between Native American groups—as status indicators, ritual tools, and as gifts between the interacting parties.

Trubowitz presents a preliminary synopsis of his ongoing research program based on the prodigious pipe collections of the Peabody Museum of Archaeology and Ethnology at Harvard University. His summary of the distribution of pipe styles and ethnic affiliations across eastern North America during the Protohistoric and early historic periods (circa 1500–1850) will provide a valuable resource for pipe researchers. Trubowitz address the role of pipes as ethnic markers, differentiating pipe use among Native American, European, and African contexts. With respect to

Native American pipes specifically, he offers a picture of how smoking pipes, more than any other type of material culture, was resistant to change in the face of transculturation during the Protohistoric period. Pipes were not just recreation tools but also cultural symbols of considerable durability and were possibly a means of maintaining cultural survival during a very turbulent time in Native American history.

Mann revisits the theme of smoking pipes facilitating social interactions, but in this case the gulf between the interacting parties was vast. Participants in the fur trade during the seventeenth, eighteenth, and nineteenth centuries came from very different cultures—one European, the other native. The very cultural definitions of the nature of fur trade transactions differed fundamentally between them. While Europeans saw trade as divorced from social relations—in what Mann, drawing from Marx's perspective of commodity fetishism, associates with the expanding capitalist world system—the social relations of trade were at the core of the Native American perspective. To overcome this contradiction, avoid conflict, and foster profitable trade, rituals became basic parts of the fur trade. Stone tobacco pipes were central to these rituals. Mann's exploration of these artifacts from a nineteenth-century trading station along the Wabash River in Indiana provides a valuable case study to show how tobacco and smoking pipes had the symbolic power to make strangers into temporary kin and cover up the inherent cultural contradictions between fur trade participants, if only on a temporary basis.

Nassaney also investigates the role of tobacco and smoking pipes in Native American cultures undergoing transculturation during the Contact period. Looking at a case study of a Narragansett cemetery in Rhode Island, Nassaney traces the use of pipes with regard to changing gender relations and ritual practices. During the seventeenth century, the Narragansett culture was beset with a host of disruptive forces, including pandemic disease and dispossession at the hands of English colonists. Ritual practices, formerly controlled by spiritual specialists whose authority was called into question in light of their impotence to better Native life in the face of cultural dissolution, became increasingly personal and less corporate. Hence, pipes, with their integral role in Native American ritual practices, became much more prevalent. Furthermore, Nassaney notes that the increasing prevalence of personal smoking was not limited to males, as had been the case through the Protohistoric period, but was also indulged in by women, who themselves sought to strengthen their position in Native American society within the Contact world.

The last chapter to deal with Contact period contexts is written by Richard Veit and Charles Bello, who investigate a truly remarkable class of pipe. Pipes of base metals (lead or pewter) are found as rare specimens in museum collections or archaeological sites in eastern North America dating to the eighteenth or nineteenth centuries. Such was the skill with which these artifacts were rendered that they were commonly attributed to European manufacture. However, Veit and Bello provide compelling evidence that the majority of these pipes were of Native American making and that all of them were likely used by Native Americans. In addition to describing the pipes' form and distribution, they also present an analysis of the role symbolic iconography played in smoking practices in general and, specifically, with relation to the base metal pipes.

The last section of the volume comprises chapters by Diane Dallal, Paul Reckner, Anna Agbe-Davies, Patricia Capone, and Elinor Downs, and all are concerned with historic period, Euramerican contexts. Dallal's analysis of seventeenth- and eighteenth-century clay tobacco pipes from sites in New York City illustrate several interpretive realms in which smoking pipes can lead to valuable insights beyond the traditional chronological assessments based on bore diameters. She uses documentary evidence to illustrate ways in which female pipe makers manipulated the pipe-making industry in the Netherlands as a means of empowerment in a male-dominated culture. Additionally, she illustrates how several classes of pipe iconography were active elements in negotiating ethnic and gender tensions within the societies that made them.

Reckner's chapter also looks at a historic period data set of clay tobacco pipes from an urban context—in this case, late-eighteenth- and nineteenth-century Paterson, New Jersey. His focus is on a specific group of pipes excavated from a working-class neighborhood of Paterson, those with iconography related to Irish nationalism. While previous interpretations of similar assemblages have looked at Irish nationalist symbols as simple ethnic markers, Reckner draws on a host of documentary evidence to investigate how the very nature of ethnicity is fluid, changeable, and continually reproduced. Material culture, in this conception of ethnicity, is not a passive reflector but an active constituent, and smoking pipes are no exception, as Reckner demonstrates.

The final two chapters are similar in several respects. Both are largely methodological studies. They are included in this volume since, while methodological in content, both are critical of the more traditional methodological studies of pipes (for example, Binford 1961; Harrington 1954) and seek to revitalize studies of smoking pipe typology and materials analysis. Both deal with similar data sets: red clay pipes from Mid-Atlantic and New England contexts dating to the seventeenth century. Most important for the purposes of this volume, even though they are essentially pilot studies, both chapters move beyond the methodological realm to address important anthropological questions through the medium of smoking pipes. Agbe-Davies, for instance, critiques traditional typological analyses of smoking pipes on the grounds that the hierarchical nature of such typological schemes privilege some attributes over others, to the extent of sacrificing representativeness of the resulting taxonomies. In place of this, she proposes a modal analysis, which she finds far more amenable to artifacts that are so seldom found as complete specimens. Agbe-Davies then extends her analysis to address the relations of production and consumption within the study area, as well as the creation and reproduction of social identities. In a similar vein, Capone and Downs present a petrographic approach to the study of smoking pipes and conclude that traditional typological approaches that might lump together red clay pipes from New England and the Chesapeake regions based on similar exterior appearance are misleading, as, internally, the pipes from the two regions are in fact distinct, indicating local production rather than a centralized manufacture in the Mid-Atlantic area. The authors use this conclusion to question core versus periphery economic models that characterize seventeenth-century New England as economically dependant on the Chesapeake Bay area.

It is our hope that the researches of prehistoric as well as historic North America will find this volume useful. Our intent is to demonstrate that studies of specific types of material culture, be they pipes or something else, can be far more than typological or chronological tools providing base line data. Such studies can provide interpretive windows into a host of anthropological issues.

We would like to thank all of the authors who contributed to this volume, as well as the University of Tennessee Press staff. Their enthusiasm for the project made this volume possible.

References Cited

Binford, L.

1961 A New Method for Calculating Dates from Kaolin Pipe Stem Samples. *Southeastern Archaeological Conference Newsletter* 9(1):19–21.

Bradley, James W.

1987 *Evolution of the Onondaga Iroquois: Accommodating Change, 1500–1655.* Syracuse Univ. Press.

Brasser, Theodore J.

1980 Self-Directed Pipe Effigies. *Man in the Northeast* 19:95–104.

Brooks, Jerome E.

1937 *Tobacco, Its History, Illustrated by the Books, Manuscripts, and Engravings in the Library of George Arents, Jr.* Vol. 1, 1507–1615. Rosenbach Co., New York.

Brown, Ian

1989 The Calumet Ceremony in the Southeast and Its Archaeological Manifestations. *American Antiquity* 54(2):311–331.

Brown, James

1985 The Mississippian Period. In *Ancient Art of the American Woodland Indians,* edited by David S. Brose, James Brown, and David W. Penney. 93–145. Harry N. Abrams, Detroit Institution of Arts.

Brown, Joseph Epps

1953 *The Sacred Pipe: Black Elk's Account of the Seven Rites of the Oglala Sioux.* Univ. of Oklahoma Press, Norman.

Bucko, Raymond A.

1998 *The Lakota Ritual of the Sweat Lodge: History and Contemporary Practice.* Univ. of Nebraska Press, Lincoln.

Catlin, George

1841 *Letters and Notes on Manners, Customs, and Conditions of the North American Indians.* Catlin, London.

Cook, Lauren J.

1989 Tobacco-Related Material and the Construction of Working-Class Culture. In *Interdisciplinary Investigations of the Boott Mills Lowell, Massachusetts, Volume III: The Boarding House System as a Way of Life,* edited by Mary C. Beaudry and Stephen A. Mrozowski, 209–229. Cultural Resources Management Study No. 21. North Atlantic Regional Office, National Park Service, Boston.

Furst, Peter J., and Jill Leslie Furst

1982 The Sacred Pipe as Artifact and Prayer. *Terra* 22(2):11–17.

Furst, Peter T. (editor)

1972 *Flesh of the Gods: The Ritual Use of Hallucinogens.* Praeger, New York.

Gehlbach, Donald R.

1982 Ohio Pipe Chronology Chart. *Ohio Archaeologist* 32(4):8–9.

Hall, Robert L.

1997 *An Archaeology of the Soul: North American Belief and Ritual.* Univ. of Illinois Press, Champaign.

Harner, Michael (editor)

1973 *Hallucinogens and Shamanism.* Oxford Univ. Press, Oxford.

Harrington, J. C.

1954 Dating Stem Fragments of Seventeenth and Eighteenth Century Clay Tobacco Pipes. *Quarterly Bulletin of the Archaeological Society of Virginia* 5(4):9–13.

Hart, Gordon

1980 Calumets and Their Pipes. *Prehistoric Art* 15(1):22–29.

Heighton, Robert F., and Kathleen A. Deagan

1972 A New Formula for Dating Kaolin Clay Pipestems. *Conference on Historic Site Archaeology Papers* 6:220–229.

Joniger, Oscar, and Marlene Dobkin de Rios

1973 Suggestive Hallucinogenic Properties of Tobacco. *Medical Anthropology Newsletter* 4(4):6–11.

1976 Nicotiana an Hallucinogen? *Economic Botany* 30:149–151.

Kapches, Mima

1992 "Rude but Perfect" (Beauchamp 1989): A Study of Miniature Smoking Pipes in Iroquoia. In *Proceedings of the 1988 Smoking Pipe Conference,* edited by Charles F. Hays III. 71–82. Rochester Museum and Science Center Research Records No. 2.

Lewis, Thomas M., and Madeline Kneberg Lewis

1961 *Eva, an Archaic Site.* Univ. of Tennessee Press, Knoxville.

Lowie, Robert H.

1919 Tobacco Society of the Crow Indians. *Anthropological Papers of the American Museum of Natural History* 21, pt. 2.

Morgan, Lewis Henry
1972 *League of the Iroquois.* Citadel Press, Secaucus New Jersey.

Noble, William C.
1992 Neutral Iroquois Smoking Pipes. In *Proceedings of the 1988 Smoking Pipe Conference,* edited by Charles F. Hays III. 41–50. Rochester Museum and Science Center Research Records No. 2.

Noël Hume, Ivor
1991 *A Guide to Artifacts of Colonial America.* Vintage Books, New York.

Oswald, Adrian
1951 English Clay Tobacco Pipes. *Archaeological News Letter* (London) 3(10):154–159.
1960 The Archaeology and Economic History of English Clay Tobacco Pipes. *Journal of the Archaeological Association* 23:40–102.
1961 The Evolution and Chronology of English Clay Tobacco Pipes. *Archaeological News Letter* (London) 7(3):55–62.

Ripinsky-Naxon, Michael
1993 *The Nature of Shamanism: Substance and Function of a Religious Metaphor.* State Univ. of New York Press, Albany.

Rutsch, Edward
1973 *Smoking Technology of the Aborigines of the Iroquois Area of New York State.* Fairleigh Dickinson Univ. Press, Rutherford, N.J.

Steinmetz, Paul B.
1984 The Sacred Pipe in American Indian Religions. *American Indian Culture and Research Journal* 8(3):27–80.

Thwaites, Reuben Gold (editor)
1959 *The Jesuit Relations and Allied Documents: Travels and Explorations of the Jesuit Missionaries in New France 1610–1791.* Pageant Book Co., New York.

Trubowitz, Neal
1992 Thanks, but We Prefer to Smoke Our Own: Pipes in the Great Lakes–Riverine Region during the Eighteenth Century. In *Proceedings of the 1988 Smoking Pipe Conference,* edited by Charles F. Hays III. Rochester Museum and Science Center Research Records No. 2.

Walthall, John A.
1980 *Prehistoric Indians of the Southeast: Archaeology of Alabama and the Middle South.* Univ. of Alabama Press, Tuscaloosa.

1. "They Pass Their Lives in Smoke, and at Death Fall into the Fire": Smoking Pipes and Mortuary Ritual during the Early Woodland Period

Sean M. Rafferty

In 1634, Father Paul Le Jeune, the Jesuit Superior of the Quebec Mission in New France, wrote: "The fondness they have for this herb is beyond all belief . . . Let us say with compassion that they pass their lives in smoke, and at death fall into the fire" (Thwaites 1959:7:137). Le Jeune had been living among the local Native Americans for three years and was at the time the foremost expert in Native American spirituality and ritual life. This quotation is one of the most telling observations made by any European of a central Native American practice—their fondness of tobacco and the central place that tobacco smoking played in their culture. Numerous European observers as far back as Columbus had recorded Native American smoking; smoking and tobacco were seen to play a crucial role in Indian cosmology, spirituality, and ritual across a vast area of the continent from the earliest interactions between the peoples of the colliding "Old" and "New" Worlds.

The prehistoric underpinnings of this widespread phenomenon are at present poorly understood. There has to date been comparatively little insight into the early history of smoking. The earliest evidence for the ingestion of nicotine in the form of *Nicotiana* spp. tobacco comes from the Middle Woodland period Smiling Dan and Meridian Hills sites in Illinois, dating as early as 20–70 B.C. (Asch 1994:45; Butler and McGimsey 2000; Haberman 1984:271; Stafford and Sant 1985:356; Winter 1991). Dates for the Great Plains, Southwest, Southeast, and lower Great Lakes fall between the fifth and eighth centuries A.D. (Asch and Asch 1985:196; Haberman 1984:272–273; Wagner 1998:840). The oldest known dates for tobacco are from the North Coast of Peru, with dates ranging between 2500 and 1800 B.C. (Pearsall 1992:178).

However, there is ample indirect evidence in the form of smoking pipes that the use of tobacco significantly predates the Middle Woodland period. This class of material culture represents the earliest physical evidence of smoking in North America. Smoking pipes in eastern North America first appeared during the Late Archaic period and were associated with the development of complex mortuary ceremonialism in the Eastern Woodlands (Concannon 1993:73; Custer 1987; Dragoo 1963:241; Salkin 1986:92). This mortuary behavior increased in scale and distribution during the Early Woodland (circa 1,000–0 B.C.).

The Early Woodland period has long been considered enigmatic by American archaeologists and is still poorly defined in comparison to preceding and succeeding periods. Despite ongoing debate, we can list some general traits that are shared widely during the period. Ceramics first became part of Native American material culture during the Early Woodland, or at least this is when they first became widespread (Brown 1986). While some researchers have hypothesized that Early Woodland cultures engaged in limited horticulture to augment their subsistence resource base (Snow 1980), the majority of Early Woodland societies were still engaged in a hunter-gatherer lifestyle, although possibly with a greater degree of sedentism than was the case during the Late Archaic (Gardener 1982:61; Otto 1979). The body of Early Woodland sites currently known to archaeologists is heavily biased toward burials, with known habitations components generally being relatively small and ephemeral and often part of multicomponent sites. The large numbers of mortuary sites are evidence of what has been termed a "cult of the dead" (Dragoo 1963:243) involving the widespread practice of elaborate mortuary ritual with the use of numerous grave offerings, often of exotic materials, supported by an extensive regional trade network (Stewart 1989), although there is also evidence that the participation in this practice may have been differential, with some societies "opting out" (Versaggi and Knapp 2000). One of the most elaborate examples of an Early Woodland mortuary complex is the Adena phenomenon.

The term *Adena* refers to a constellation of archaeological traits that characterize some Early Woodland period sites in the central Ohio Valley. Adena sites are best known by their conical burial mounds and geometric earthworks. Adena sites tend to date between 500 B.C. and A.D. 200 based on radiocarbon dates. Dragoo (1963) defined Adena based on the burial regimen itself; primary burials and cremations of individuals at the base of mounds constructed in stages, often over the location of a previous charnel structure; and the addition of secondary burials in additional layers of the mound. Other, material traits for Adena included characteristic artifacts, including ovate and rectangular-stemmed points; blades; other lithic tools; grit-tempered ceramics; bone tools; gorgets of both stone and copper; copper tools; copper and shell bead decorations; objects of uncertain function, such as barite and galena cones or hemispheres; artifacts such as pallets and paint cups that may be pigment processing tools; and finally the stone and ceramic smoking pipes that are the topic of this investigation. These artifacts are almost always associated with mound burials or features. Habitation and other nonceremonial sites remain extremely rare for the Adena complex, as is the case with the majority of Early Woodland phases (Clay 1998).

Tubular smoking pipes are widely known as characteristic Early Woodland period artifacts (Salkin 1986). Their "classic" form is a parallel-sided tube with a wide distal opening and a narrow-bored proximal end, possibly blocked with a pebble (Gehlbach 1982; Meuser 1952; Stephens 1957) (Figure 1.1). Earlier pipes predating this blocked-end tube form included conical or cigar-shaped tubes; contemporary forms to the blocked-end tube included flared tubes, tubes with beveled ends, and compound "modified tube" forms, as well as the earliest platform and elbow pipes as minority forms. They are made from a variety of materials, including clay or sandstone, but the most famous examples are made from Ohio fire clay. This material is actually a fine-grained limestone from the central Ohio River Valley, although other sources are known to exist in Mid-Atlantic states (Stewart 1989; Thomas 1971:77). When found in primary contexts, smoking pipes tend to occur in burials and, less often, in caches. Tubular smoking pipes often show signs of intentional destruction or sacrifice, which has implications for their ritual context.

FIG. 1.1. ▸ *Typical Adena smoking pipes. Courtesy of the Smithsonian Institution.*

Early synthetic works on Adena treated tubular smoking pipes as indicators of Adena occupation (Webb and Baby 1957; Webb and Snow 1974) or as evidence of Adena migration east and northeast (Ritchie and Dragoo 1960). Later research elaborated on the central Adena trait list and developed the period's chronology (Dragoo 1963). Dragoo, in his seminal volume, *Mounds for the Dead* (1963), was the first to speculate on the cultural significance of smoking pipes as Adena burial furniture beyond their role as culture-historical markers. Dragoo speculated on the possible social implications of smoking pipes in Adena mortuary contexts, signaling some form of craft specialization (with pipes identifying a pipe maker's burial), tribute to the deceased by the "men of the clan," or some indeterminate form of "ceremonial significance" (Dragoo 1963:211). He also raised the issue of the social significance of the presence versus the absence of pipes in burials, noting that available evidence was insufficient to address the issue at that time. While discussing the similarity and relationship of Adena with neighboring complexes, including Red Ocher and Glacial Kame, Dragoo hypothesized that the role of pipes as grave offerings was central to all of them and that smoking had taken on a central role in the "Cult of the Dead" that had developed out of Archaic period antecedents (Dragoo 1963:245).

Despite the associations of smoking pipes with Adena and with the Early Woodland period (for example, Bense 1994:129), they have a much wider distribution in time and space. As Dragoo stated, "tubular pipes had a long history that began late in the Archaic and continued through Adena with a number of changes" (Dragoo 1963:194). Numerous smoking pipes have been recovered from Late Archaic period burial contexts (Walthall 1980:77), indicating that smoking in ritual contexts clearly has Late Archaic roots along with the rest of the Early Woodland mortuary phenomena (Concannon 1993:74; Custer 1987:42; Dragoo 1963:241, 1976). One of the earliest known smoking pipes was recovered from the Eva site in Tennessee from a component dated to approximately 2000 B.C. (Lewis and Lewis 1961:66). Webb and Baby (1957:22) noted that "prototype" tubular smoking pipes were recovered from Late Archaic shell mound sites in Alabama and Kentucky; current reinterpretations of Archaic shell mounds indicate that they were also ceremonial contexts (Claassen 1991, 1996; Sassaman 1995:189), suggesting that the ritualistic contexts of pipes have deep temporal roots.

During the Early Woodland period, the spatial distribution of tubular smoking pipes is much wider than the central Ohio Valley Adena. (See Map 1.1.) Tubular smoking pipes were recovered from Middlesex complex burials in northern New York, New England, and southeastern Canada, well outside of the Adena heartland (Fitting and Brose 1971:33; Haviland and Power 1994; Heckenberger, Peterson, and Basa 1990; Loring 1985; Ritchie and Dragoo 1960; Spence and Fox 1986:32). The Boucher site in northern Vermont, one of the few Middlesex sites excavated by modern techniques, contained a sizable assemblage of blocked-end tubular pipes (Concannon 1983; Heckenberger et al. 1990a, 1990b; Loring 1985).

MAP 1.1. ▸ *Approximate distribution of Adena, Middlesex, and Delmarva cultures.*

One of the most spectacular Middlesex finds was a large mass of smoking pipes cremated in place in a burial from the Rosenkrans site in Sussex County, New Jersey (Carpenter 1950; Kraft 1976), presumably an example of the ritual destruction of the artifacts during the burial program. Middlesex sites contain artifact assemblages distinct from Adena assemblages, including numerous traits found in the contiguous Meadowood complex (Snow 1980:264), but contain characteristic Adena-like artifacts, including tubular smoking pipes and copper artifacts.

Smoking pipes that are more or less identical in style to the Adena and Middlesex pipes have been recovered from burial sites from the Delmarva Peninsula and Chesapeake Bay area (Dent 1995:231–235; Thomas 1971). The Delmarva Adena complex, found primarily in Delaware, Maryland, southeastern Pennsylvania, and southern New Jersey, consists of both living and cemetery sites, most of which have been destroyed by twentieth-century development. Despite their close association with the Ohio Valley Adena, the largest numbers of pipes found in any one context have in fact come from Delmarva sites. Delmarva Adena assemblages are

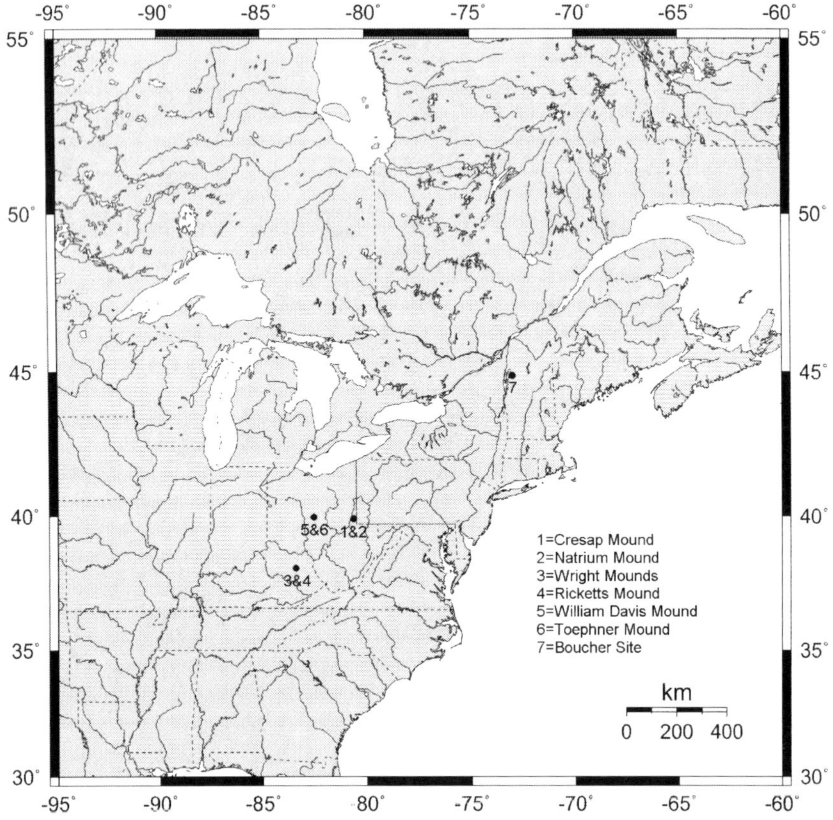

MAP 1.2. ▸ *Locations of sites used in analysis.*

also similar to other local complexes, specifically the Wolfe Neck complex (Custer 1987, 1989:173) with the addition of Adena-like artifacts, and show a similar settlement pattern, analogous to Middlesex's relation to Meadowood. Regrettably, many of the Delmarva Adena sites were disturbed, looted, or nonprofessionally excavated (for example, Cubbage 1941). Map 1.1 shows the general distribution of these archaeological complexes, overlaid by the geographic boundaries of this study.

The presence of characteristic Adena artifacts in areas far removed from the central Ohio Valley has been explained by several models, ranging from migration of Adena populations (Ritchie and Dragoo 1960) to theories of interregional exchange (Stewart 1989). The form and function of these exchange relations is beyond the scope of this project. My point here is that smoking pipes transcend taxonomic boundaries between archaeological cultures across the eastern Woodlands from as early as the second millennium B.C. The predominantly mortuary contexts in which these artifacts occur indicates that the practice was both sacred and ritualized. Burials, while subject to a variety of differing interpretations by archaeologists over past decades, can be viewed as the remains of death-related rituals, and both symbolize and legitimize the perceived relations within society and between society and a perceived spiritual realm.

If one opts for an even wider scale of analysis, it becomes apparent that smoking pipes are characteristic artifacts of a large number of archaeological complexes in the Eastern Woodlands that are otherwise distinct from Adena or Adena-related assemblages (compare Dragoo 1963). All of these mortuary complexes, which range from the Late Archaic through Early Woodland periods, included smoking pipes (Dragoo 1963; Fitting and Brose 1971:44). As described above, pipes characterize Middlesex as well as Meadowood complexes in New York and New England (Ritchie 1980). Smoking pipes characterize Point Peninsula sites as well (Ritchie 1980) and have been found in Pennsylvania (Smith 1978), Connecticut (Thomas 1971:63), New Jersey (Kraft 1976), and the Chesapeake Bay Delmarva complexes already mentioned.

The point behind this general survey is that smoking pipes, far from being specific to Adena, or indicative of Adena-related complexes engaged in regional trade, can also be viewed as a form of material culture that was minimally variable in form and function and was present over a wide area for a long time period. While there are numerous differences between these archaeological complexes, they all engaged in at least one common practice. The interesting question at this point is not what makes these complexes distinct, but what did they share? Viewed in this way, the importance of Adena "culture" is not so much in terms of its distinctive characteristics but rather in its relation to the numerous other Early Woodland period mortuary complexes and its role as the most elaborate of them (Dragoo 1976:1).

Extensive investigations of archaeological, ethnohistoric, and ethnographic evidence of Native American smoking practices reveals several common themes that are of great importance for my study.[1] Based on the historical outline of Native American smoking and smoking pipes, it is possible to derive a series of common themes that are repeatedly encountered both prehistorically and historically. One common theme that can be drawn about smoking from the Early Woodland period right up to modern times involves animal symbolism. These symbols can be integral to the material culture of smoking, such as the bird-shaped tubular and platform effigies or feather decorations of historic calumets. Additionally, they can be based on association, such as the correlation of smoking pipes and faunal remains found in at least one late prehistoric Iroquois site (von Gernet and Timmons 1985, 1987). This animal-related and probably totemic symbolism is very often avian in nature but not universally so. As discussed in the section on Late Woodland/Mississippian pipes, the differences in the animals featured can be interpreted as providing information on Native American cosmology, with bird forms relating to upper spiritual worlds, and other terrestrial, aquatic, or amphibian forms (such as bears, lizards, or frogs) acting as symbols of an underworld. Particularly with reference to bird-related symbols, it is important to note that while the basic referent of the symbolic association (that is, a bird) remains present across the continent and over three thousand years of history, the manner in which that referent is expressed (as a realistic effigy, or as abstracted elemental forms, or as associated faunal material) varies widely over time and across space.

Second, there appears to be a general association of smoking pipes with some kind of psychoactive agent, implying the alteration of reality or hallucination. This is partly functional in that oral or nasal inhalation is easily the most efficient means of ingesting a drug, far more so than oral consumption or enema (tobacco has historically been consumed by all of these means). Only intravenous injection is more effective. We know based on pharmacological research that tobacco, or rather nicotine, is not just a mild over-the-counter stimulant with unfortunate cardiopulmonary side effects, but a potent psychoactive in sufficient doses (Joniger and Dobkin de Rios 1973, 1976). The other two most widely documented substances smoked cross-culturally in pipes, cannabis and opium, also have psychoactive properties (Sherratt 1991:52–53).

In the Native American context, numerous other plants besides tobacco have been documented as having been smoked in pipes (Yarnell 1964), most notably the blend of tree barks known generically as "kinnickinnick." These were often used as a tobacco additive (tobacco itself being called by the same term in some contexts) as well as smoked alone, but there has to date been no comprehensive research on the possible psychoactive effect of these plants. On the whole, however, we can assume from documented evidence that psychoactive effects were a primary component of the use of smoking pipes, especially for those periods of prehistory where the use of tobacco was widespread.

Finally, the most important aspect of smoking shown in this historical overview is the overwhelming tendency for smoking to be a ritualized act. Smoking pipes from the Early, Middle, and Late Woodland periods are often found in archaeological contexts that are clearly not associated with secular life, such as mound burials or caches. Notably, these are all the remains of death rituals, which have the most overt material remains and are therefore most observable archaeologically. Ethnohistoric and ethnographic information on tobacco smoking from the late fifteenth through twentieth centuries shows smoking as a formalized ritual behavior, at both corporate and individual scales. These observed rituals have relevance to cosmology, social regulation, and spiritual purification beyond the death ritual associations that dominate the archaeological record. Tobacco smoking, sacred pipes, or abstracted smoking material culture (such as calumet stems) play central roles in many of the central religious rites of Native American societies across the continent. The ritualized nature of smoking is central to the theoretical orientation behind this analysis of smoking pipes for the Early Woodland period.

We can find common themes running through the treatments of ritual in cultural anthropology and the archaeology of ritual and mortuary behavior.[2] I have arbitrarily categorized these into themes relating to culture, themes relating to practice, and themes relating to material culture. These are not, of course, distinct zones, but they are deeply interrelated. The first of these themes relates generally to culture and specifically to the concept of ideology. Ideology can be defined for the purposes of this analysis as subliminal understandings that model and legitimate perceived social reality. Whether one adopts a Marxist conception of ideology as the "opium of the masses" that conceals social inequities or the "common sense" religious definition of Frazier (1980), ideology has almost always been expressed by anthropologists as having a regulatory and guiding function in society. In the sense adopted by such researchers as Bloch and Barth, which underlies this project, ideological understandings tend to support as well as reproduce the established social order that constrains and enables human behavior. Ideology has been observed by cultural anthropologists to vary at the local level, with nearby neighbors often finding the ideological structures unintelligible to each other, but it also can show long-term regional stability over time, with common elements present across huge areas of space.

Ideology has until the postprocessual movement been of relatively little interest to archaeologists as too ephemeral a phenomenon to approach through material culture. However, bridging the conceptual gap between culture and material culture is human action, and this project focuses on ritual practices as a window to prehistoric ritual, the second common theme in the theoretical concerns discussed above. Ritual is conceived of as an active expression of ideology. Several of the modern conceptions of what ideology is and how it operates, such as those adopted by such researchers as Bloch and Barth, were in fact based on observations of ritual practices rather than on trying to get at the ideological conceptions of the inhabitants directly. Ritual not only recapitulates a societal ideology but also acts to reproduce it and to reinforce, or even transform, basic conceptual foundations. This basic reproductive function for the relationship between ideology and ritual itself conforms to the stability/variability model and can in some contexts exhibit broad regional homogeneities, evidenced by continuous repetition of symbolic elements (Merrifield 1987:4; Renfrew 1994b:49), while at the same time showing local-scale variation within the broader conformity (Barth 1987:14; Bloch 1986, 1989:131).

Since ritual has been proven to have a variety of archaeologically observable correlates, it follows that ideology can be traced archaeologically. This has been the general conclusion of postprocessual treatments of mortuary rituals—that ideology can be analyzed from an archaeological context. This brings us to the realm of material culture and the third common theme in the theoretical underpinnings of the project. At the most basic level, the material culture in question here are smoking pipes; the generally mortuary context of these pipes commands that a broader approach based on mortuary theory be taken. The analysis of mortuary-related material culture has undergone a similar theoretical trajectory as anthropological treatments of ideology and of ritual practices. Early approaches drew simplistic assumptions regarding the social implications of mortuary assemblages; Early Woodland and Adena period smoking pipes were accordingly viewed as the deceased's direct possessions, indicating a shaman or pipe maker (for example, Dragoo 1963:210). More sophisticated approaches have focused on the complex ideological web in which burial material is set, as well as the ritual behavior that created it, which is itself a behavioral reproduction of ideology and is only sufficiently apparent at broad regional levels. Accordingly, the theoretical framework for this project focuses on the ideological implications of smoking pipes as burial furniture, both at local scales and in a broad regional context.

The necessarily broad scale of analysis presented a methodological problem. The sort of perspective I felt was required to sufficiently address the issue of pipe smoking presented the question of how to compose a manageable project while still adequately considering the research problem. A detailed analysis of smoking pipes across the entire Eastern Woodlands throughout the Early Woodland period would be unmanageable, especially since pipe smoking as a practice intersected with far wider-reaching facets of prehistoric lifeways. What was required was to narrow the focus of the study while still maintaining a broad scale of analysis. The only way to accomplish this was to undertake two separate but related research programs.

The approach I have adopted for this project addresses the research topic simultaneously from a broad regional scale of analysis by focusing on general trends. In addition to the regional-scale approach, there are a series of case studies focusing on specific sites for which good contextual data exists. The first stage of the analysis will provide a general picture of the nature of pipe use on the scale of the northern Eastern Woodlands and will investigate macroscale similarity and variability in the material remains of smoking. The second stage of the project, with its focus on individual sites, will examine the local-scale variations that would likely be concealed in a project with a solely regional scope. This dual approach represents a compromise between scales and focus: the broader the scale at which data are gathered, the less focus is possible, while highly focused case studies necessarily have limited applicability in a regional scale. Such a compromise will overcome the methodological problems of each scale of analysis, allowing me to keep track of the big picture of regional patterns while maintaining attention to local area variations.

Data sets for the project were derived from two general sources. I first drew on published sources of two general types. First, there are published studies that focus specifically on prehistoric smoking pipes themselves (for example, Rutsch 1973; West 1970). While relatively easy to isolate in literature searches, this was a minority category, with most sources pertaining specifically to smoking pipes dealing with single finds or to periods of prehistory much later than the Early Woodland. The second and dominant category of published material were synthetic studies of the Early Woodland period (for example, Farnsworth and Emerson 1986) or individual reports on Early Woodland period sites (for example, Dragoo 1963). While these general sources required more effort to accumulate, they tended to produce more detailed contextual data than those that focused on smoking pipes themselves, which were generally stylistic in focus. The second general source of data for the project was a survey of a number of museum collections. Metric and contextual information was recorded for Early Woodland and Adena pipes at ten museums and archaeological research institutions.[3] The collections survey was a vital source of data, without which I would not have been able to sufficiently investigate any of the local-scale case studies.

The data for the regional-scale analysis was drawn from the entire database of smoking pipes identified in both written sources and museum observations. In total, 478 specimens were recorded in the data base. Of these, 365 were complete or identifiably individual pipes and 113 were fragments. Pipes were identified from eighteen states and two Canadian provinces. A minimum of eighty-nine archaeological sites are represented in the database, although seventy-five specimens (or 16 percent of the total data set) were not identifiable as from any individual site, as they were initially in private collections. Of those sites that were identifiable, sixty-seven (75 percent) functioned either wholly or in part as interment sites for the dead.

The greatest number of smoking pipes was found at Mid-Atlantic sites in Delaware, New Jersey, and Maryland, accounting for a minimum of one hundred specimens, or 28 percent, of the total sample of smoking pipes with known proveniences. This is all the more interesting because the pipes from Mid-Atlantic states originated from only eight sites out of the approximately eighty-nine total sites in the database, meaning that more than a quarter of the total tubular pipe assemblage was recovered from only 9 percent of the total number of sites. These sites all correspond to the Delmarva Adena complex and are summarized in Table 1.1 on the following page; six are known cemetery sites.

The next concentrations of smoking pipes are from the Ohio River Valley and adjacent regions, including Ohio, Kentucky, and West Virginia. The majority of these are Adena burial mound sites, summarized in Table 1.2. These Adena sites account for eighty-three pipe specimens, roughly equal to the Delmarva Mid-Atlantic sites, although the average number of pipes per site is much smaller (2.7 pipes per site for the Ohio Valley sites versus 11.3 for the Mid-Atlantic sites), with the notable exception of a single site, the Beech Bottom site from West Virginia, which alone accounts for nearly half the total for the Ohio Valley Adena sites.

Table 1.1 ▸ Mid-Atlantic Site Sample

Site	State	Township/County	No. of Pipes
Bridgeport	Delaware	Bridgeport	1
Frederica	Delaware	Frederica	32
Killen's Pond	Delaware	Dover (12 Mi S)	1+
St. Jones River	Delaware	Lebanon/Kent	6
Unknown Prov.	Marland	Davisonville	1
Sandy Hill	Maryland	Combridge/Dorchester	30
West River	Maryland	Anne Arundel County	18
Unknown Prov.	Virginia	Barksley	1
Total			**90**

Given the lower average number of pipes per site for the Adena sites, this anomaly stands out all the more.

The final regional concentration of smoking pipes includes those located in the northeastern United States and southeastern Canada, including Connecticut, Maine, Massachusetts, New York, Vermont, Rhode Island, and the provinces of Ontario and New Brunswick. These sites are summarized in Table 1.3. Several trends are apparent in these pipes. First, there are more sites in general, and also there is a far greater variety of taxonomic phases represented than was the case in the Mid-Atlantic region or the Ohio Valley Region. This may be at least partly due to sampling bias in the database, as several of the repositories visited during the collections survey were dominated by northeastern sites, which could have increased the apparent diversity of site types for that region. Second, there is a large number of sites with comparatively poor provenience information, many of which were recovered by private collectors rather than by professional archaeologists.

A third trend that is not apparent in the table is that there is a far wider variety of pipe styles represented. While the majority of pipes from the Mid-Atlantic Delmarva sites were blocked-end tubes, and similarly so for the Ohio Valley Adena sites, the northeastern pipes include blocked-end, open-end, and conical tubes, as well as elbow pipes. This is likely related to the greater variety of archaeological cultures represented. Finally, it is apparent that despite the large number of sites, the diversity of archaeological phases, and the variety of pipe styles, a disproportionate number of pipes among the northeastern sites come from a comparatively small number of sites. Sites of known or suspected Middlesex Complex affiliation account for 144 specimens (pipes and fragments) out of 478, or 30 percent of the total. The majority of these Middlesex pipes are blocked-end tubes largely indistinguishable from similar pipes from the Ohio Valley and were manufactured of exotic raw materials from that same region.

TABLE 1.2 ▸ Ohio Valley Site Sample

Site	State	Township	No. Pipes
Cato	Indiana	Pike County	1
Mound Camp	Indiana	Brookville	1
C&O Mds	Kentucky	Paintsville	1
Fischer	Kentucky	Lexington (8 Mi N)	3
Ricketts	Kentucky	Mt Sterling (5 Mi)	3
Robbins	Kentucky	Big Bone (2 Mi NW)	1
Wright	Kentucky	Mt Sterling (3 Mi N)	4
Unknown	Ohio	Newark Locale	1
Unknown	Ohio	Unknown Provenience	6
Adena	Ohio	Chillicothe	3
Clyde Jones	Ohio		1
Davis	Ohio	Columbus	3
Englewood Md	Ohio		1
Greenbrier	Ohio	Columbus	1
James	Ohio	Delaware County	1
Sayler Park	Ohio		2
Sites Grove	Ohio	Madisonville	1
Thomas Bros. Md	Ohio		1
Toephner	Ohio	Columbus	1
Unknown	Pennsylvania	Unknown Provenience	1
Crall Md	Pennsylvania	Monongahela City	1
Hennery Island	Pennsylvania	Boekkel's Landing	1
Kinzua	Pennsylvania	Kinzua	6
Mathes Mine Md	Pennsylvania	Monongahela	1
Unknown	West Virginia	Unknown Provenience	2
Beech Bottom	West Virginia	Wheeling	25
Cresap Md	West Virginia	Moundsville	2
Grave Creek	West Virginia	Moundsville	3
Natrium	West Virginia	Moundsville	4
Welcome	West Virginia	New Martinsville	1
Total			**83**

A final point to make based on Table 1.3 is that there is a large gap in the distribution of pipes between sites. Most sites have only one or a few pipes, but a handful of Middlesex sites in Vermont include several dozen among them. This could be due to several factors. For instance, these sites could simply have been in use longer than others, allowing for more burials and more artifact deposition. Alternatively, this could be evidence that the use of pipes was taking place at a much greater level in that region than in the rest of the Northeast.

Table 1.3 ▸ Northeast Site Sample				
Site	State/Province	Township/County	Component	No. Pipes
Unknown	Connecticut	Avon	Middlesex	1
Unknown	Connecticut	Danbury	Middlesex	1
Unknown	Connecticut	Old Sayerbrook	Middlesex	2
Congarnond Lake	Connecticut	Suffield	Middlesex	1
East Windsor Falls	Connecticut	East Windsor Falls	Middlesex	1
Unknown	Massachusetts	Unknown Provenience	Middlesex	1
Unknown	Massachusetts	Grotton	Middlesex	1
Unknown	Massachusetts	South Hadley	Middlesex	2
Holyoke	Massachusetts	Holyoke	Middlesex	2
Tobin's Beach	Massachusetts	Brookfield	Middlesex	2
Mason	Maine	Orland	Middlesex	2
Augustine Md	New Brunswick	North Umberland County	Middlesex	2
Rosenkrans	New Jersey	Flatbrookville	Middlesex	7
Unknown	New York	Unknown Provenience	Early Woodland	1
Unknown	New York	Unknown Provenience	Middlesex?	1
Unknown	New York	Cataraugus County	Early Woodland	1
Unknown	New York	Saratoga County	Early Woodland	1
Unknown	New York	Amber	Middlesex	3
Unknown	New York	Cato	Early Woodland	1
Unknown	New York	Clay Locale	Early Woodland	1
Unknown	New York	Grenville	Middlesex?	1
Unknown	New York	Hoffmans	Middlesex	1
Unknown	New York	Lysander	Early Woodland	1
Unknown	New York	Onondaga	Early Woodland	1
Unknown	New York	Polksville	Early Woodland	1
Unknown	New York	Queensburry	Early Woodland	1
Unknown	New York	Van Buren Locale	Middlesex?	1
Unknown	New York	West Rush	Early Woodland	1
Bradt	New York	Hoffmans	Middlesex	1
East Branch Delaware	New York	East Branch	Middlesex?	1
Kipp Island	New York	Montezuma	E Point Penin	6
Long Sault Island	New York	Massena	Middlesex?	4
Morrow	New York	Ontario County	Meadowood	1
Muskalonge	New York	Jefferson County	Meadowood	1
Muskalonge	New York	Hammond Area	Middlesex	3

Site	State/Province	Township/County	Component	No. Pipes
Oberland 2	New York	Lakeland	Meadowood	1
Palatine Bridge	New York	Palatine Bridge	Middlesex	4
Riverhaven 2	New York	Grand Island	Meadowood	1
Rogers Island	New York	Greenport	Middlesex?	2
Scaccia	New York	Cuylerville	Meadowood?	1
Scaccia	New York	Cuylerville	Middlesex	1
Toll Clute	New York	Scotia	Middlesex	1
Vine Valley	New York	Middlesex	Middlesex	7
Vine Valley Local	New York	Middlesex	Middlesex	1
Walsh	New York	Fayette	Middlesex	3
Wray	New York		Meadowood	1
Hind	Ontario		Early Woodland	1
Karnery Bay?	Ontario		Middlesex?	1
Kb-1	Ontario	Killarney	Middlesex	2
Sillery	Ontario		Middlesex?	5
Kinzua	Pennsylvania	Kinzua	Adena	2
Unknown	Rhode Island	Unknown Provenience	Middlesex?	1
Bennett	Vermont		Middlesex	4
Boucher	Vermont	Highgate	Middlesex	19
East Creek	Vermont		Middlesex	27
Swanton	Vermont	Swanton	Middlesex	12
Total				**155**

My analysis of the range of metric variation, decoration, and raw materials within the sample of smoking pipes leads to the following characterization of stylistic variation among Early Woodland and Adena smoking pipes. The sample was divided into ten formal categories based upon generally similar morphology: blocked-end tubes, modified tubes, open-end tubes, conical tubes, biconical tubes, distally rounded tubes, elbows, curved-base, platform pipes, and pipe fragments. Of the nine complete pipe categories, three (open-end tube pipes, elbow pipes, and conical tube pipes) were found to contain substantial internal metric variation, as well as a greater range of decoration and raw materials. These categories are not considered to be archaeological "types" in the specific sense, only general morphological categories—common material solutions to the general practice of smoking. Modified tube pipes, biconical tube pipes, and distally rounded pipes exhibited far less formal variation, and can probably be considered as types, but were only present in small amounts within the sample of complete pipes.

Blocked-end tube pipes, by contrast, exhibit a singular morphology (despite the occurrence of distinct subtypes late in the Adena sequence), a narrow range of metric variability, a common low incidence of decoration, and characteristic raw materials with specific local origins. By any account, blocked-end tube pipes are an archaeological type. They were traded widely throughout the northern Eastern Woodlands in conjunction with the Early Woodland burial cult ideology, probably as completed artifacts due to the high degree of formal similarity within the sample. The coeval categories of open-end and conical tubes were likely developed as local analogs of the exotic blocked-end tubes, which would explain the greater degree of variation within those categories.

It has been understood by archaeologists that smoking pipes for the Early Woodland and Adena period were generally found in burial contexts, and this assessment is amply supported by this analysis. Burials and cremations account for over 80 percent of smoking pipes in the sample for which contextual information was available. Furthermore, many of the remaining pipes not directly associated with burials were recovered from other contexts, most of which functioned as cemetery sites. The sacred contexts of some smoking pipes documented ethnohistorically and ethnographically do seem to have ancient roots, as evidenced by their widespread association with sacred, otherworldly contexts of death some three millennia earlier. However, while pipes are commonly found in burial contexts, the local-scale analysis of specific sites (see below) also indicates that they are comparatively rare at any one site and may show preferential associations with specific social categories.

The assessment of pipes as predominantly burial furniture is incomplete without some comparative reference to nonmortuary sites. The Early Woodland and Adena period is, however, notoriously lacking in such contexts. There have been several interpretations put forward to explain the dearth of Early Woodland habitation evidence, including the comparative short time depth of the period (Concannon 1993) and depopulation (Fiedel 1992), as well as the ephemeral nature of small habitation sites left by a transient, hunter-gatherer population (Clay 1998).

There are a handful of known and well-documented Early Woodland period and Adena sites that have been interpreted as open-air, nonmound habitation sites (Clay 1998:13), as well as nonmortuary task-specific camps. In referring to site reports and secondary references to several of these sites, I have come across little mention of any ritual artifacts, including smoking pipes.[4] A single pipestone tube from the Leimbach site in Ohio (Shane 1975) was interpreted not as a pipe but as an atlatl weight, due to its unconstricted bore. A minute fragment of fireclay stone was interpreted as a possible smoking pipe fragment from the No. 2 Crawford-Grist site in western Pennsylvania (Grantz 1986). A complete but intentionally broken blocked-end tube recovered from an Adena context at the Hopewellian Philo Mounds site in Ohio (Carskadden and Morton 1989:47) originated from a burial context at the site. While Clay (1989) includes this site in his discussion of Adena habitations, the excavators describe it as a probable mortuary camp structure that never was covered by a mound, so it should probably not be considered as a domestic context. For the Northeast, few smoking pipes are known from Early Woodland habitations as well. These sites are generally small camp sites in New York State. The Brown Knoll Complex at the confluence of the Susquehanna River and Schenevus Creek contained no ritual artifacts (Versaggi 1999); a single pipe was recovered from the Meadowood Phase Riverhaven No. 2 site on the Niagara Frontier (Granger 1978), while no ritual artifacts were found at the Narhwold No. 2 site, another Meadowood context from the Schoharie Valley (Ritchie 1980:xviii).

While the available sample of habitation sites for the period is admittedly small (although many smaller, ephemeral sites that could have served as camps have been ignored), if there were pervasive use and disposal of smoking pipes at these sites, then one would still expect some evidence to have been recovered. This does not mean that tobacco or other plants were not smoked at habitation sites, only that high-investment material culture, such as stone pipes, were not used as often in comparison to mortuary sites.

Demographically, the analysis was hampered by a much narrower archaeological window, as few of the known burials had secure age or sex data. There is the appearance of an association between smoking pipes and adult individuals, especially for Adena contexts. Where sex data was available (for only eleven out of sixty-one individuals), Adena pipes were associated with male burials only. Middlesex examples in the sample presented a different pattern of associations from Adena contexts. Here we see, in addition to the adult male associations common to cultures in regions to the south, pipes buried with young individuals, including children and infants, as well as with female individuals, also of immature age. This is discussed in more detail in the discussion of individual sites below.

The inclusion of pipes, which are interpreted as associated with the spirit world, as a means of communication to spiritual beings, with these individuals, tells us more about the ideology of those societies than it does about the individuals themselves. Simplistic assumptions that artifact associations in burials inform on the social roles of the deceased would lead me to an interpretation that the pipes were the possessions of those they were buried with and that these were possibly individuals associated with spiritual interaction—"shamans," for lack of a better term. More sophisticated theoretical treatments of mortuary contexts, however, indicate that burial furniture tell us more about the people doing the burying, and that artifacts are more aptly seen as offerings rather than possessions, and that "the dead do not bury themselves" (Parker Pearson 1999:84). Seen in this perspective, I interpret the demographic evidence as pointing to statements about the spiritual associations of interest groups within society. These associations are presented as being the prerogative of mature, adult individuals among the Adena and their Delmarva neighbors, and possibly exclusively adult males. This has been referred to as a "sacred ordering" rather than as a statement of hierarchy (Parker Pearson 1999:94). This agrees with the majority of the ethnographic and ethnohistoric accounts. While the data set is small for Middlesex burials, there could have been some contestation of this association among the Middlesex cultures in the Northeast, with young and female individuals being accorded the same spiritual associations as adult males during graveside rituals involving the use and disposal of smoking pipes. Alternatively, this could simply have represented a regional "interpretation" of Early Woodland mortuary ritual.

A preponderance of intentionally broken blocked-end tube pipes in the sample appears to be related to both cultural and geographical factors. Pipes from the Mid-Atlantic region were far more likely to be intentionally destroyed than those from the Northeast or the Ohio Valley. If unknown cases are discounted, destroyed pipes for the Mid-Atlantic region account for 95 percent of the sample, while even including probably and possibly destroyed specimens, destroyed pipes for the Northeast and Ohio Valley pipes account for 23 percent and 26 percent respectively. As it happens, the regional figures for destroyed blocked-end tubes are similar to the treatment identified for other components, with Mid-Atlantic matching Delmarva, Northeast matching Middlesex, and Ohio Valley matching Adena, which is presumably due to the dominance of the blocked-end pipe style for those three complexes.

The apparent preponderance for pipe destruction among some archaeological cultures was evaluated using a chi-square calculation. In this case the null hypothesis was that the mode of pipe disposal was unrelated to the component from which the pipe originated. For this analysis, general Early Woodland and Early Point Peninsula contexts were dropped due to low sample size, and the probable and known positive cases of pipe destruction were combined, while the possible case was dropped. The chi-square calculation in this case clearly disproves the null hypothesis, indicating that the observed differences in pipe destruction frequency between the components is statistically significant and not due to chance.

The figures for intentionally destroyed pipes indicate that while the practice was shared widely across the study area, it was differentially expressed between regions, presumably as a result of cultural differences between the archaeological complexes that included pipes in their burial programs. The Ohio Valley Adena and Northeastern Middlesex samples indicate that smoking pipes were destroyed upon interment slightly more than half the time, while among the Delmarva Adena sites in the sample it was a nearly universal practice. Other contexts, including Meadowood and Glacial Kame, while featuring the practice of pipe sacrifice, may have done so at a much lower rate than the Adena, Middlesex, and Delmarva sites, but small sample size makes it difficult to make absolute assessments.

It is also worth noting that while the intentional breakage of smoking pipes is a characteristic of the Early Woodland sites that are my focus, this practice persists into later time periods. The Tremper Mound site in the Scioto River Valley and Mound City in Chillicothe date between 200 B.C. and A.D. 1000 (Brose 1985:62–3; Otto 1992). Both contain large caches of platform pipes that were intentionally broken and cremated in place, perhaps a continuation (at a vastly greater scale) of the Early Woodland tube-pipe cremation seen at the Rosenkrans site in New Jersey and other similar instances of pipe sacrifice during the Early Woodland. The cache at Tremper contained a minimum of 136 pipes, 80 of which were effigy forms; the Mound City cache consisted of more than 200 pipes, also including large numbers of effigies.

What is far more interesting than the distribution of intentionally broken pipes is what ideological beliefs the practice could have represented. Several lines of evidence have lead me to the interpretation that what is occurring in the intentional destruction of smoking pipes is the dissolution of intrinsic power, a power that is closely related to animist beliefs, eschatology, and the concept of soul. The Native American concept of the soul differed markedly from that of Europeans. History of religion researchers such as Mircea Eliade (1964) and Åke Hultkrantz noted two key differences: multiplicity and alienability. Where European cultures tend to believe in a single soul rooted in the mortal body until death's release, Native American cultures tend to believe historically in multiple souls, at least some of which can travel free of the body and interact with supernatural entities during the life of the individual (Eliade 1964:216; Hultkrantz 1997; McElwain 1985). Furthermore, tobacco and tobacco pipes are intimately related to the Native American soul, with tobacco, for example, being used as a lure to return an errant soul to the ailing body in cases of soul loss (Eliade 1964:217). Another relation to smoking pipes is that Native American cultures, which tended toward an animistic ideology, applied the concept of soul not only to humans but also to animals and to what we would call inanimate objects, but which were in their cultural context anything but. Pipes and tobacco were no exception and were imbued with souls as well (Steinmetz 1984:69; von Gernet 1995:74). McElwain (1985) associates the inclusion of pipes in Adena burials as evidence for the antiquity of the ethnographically documented duality of Native American souls, citing both their use as communicative instruments with a "sky-world" and their testament to an "alienable," traveling soul. Pipes, as destroyed, killed artifacts, also indicate an "inalienable" soul rooted in the world of the dead (McElwain 1985:42).

The idea of smoking pipes as items imbued with spiritual power has been forwarded by archaeologists, both ethnohistorically (Bucko 1998:71) and archaeologically for periods as early as the Middle Woodland (Hall 1977). A pipe, with its associations with smoke, ethnographically associated with the spirit world (Bradley 1987:123; Furst and Furst 1983:12; Penney 1985:194), and with tobacco, a sacred plant desired by spirit beings (Bucko 1998:42; von Gernet 1995:70), was a supernaturally empowered object on many levels. The symbolic association of pipes with life-taking weapons such as the atlatl dart (Hall 1997:110) enhances this identity of power. This weapon/pipe symbolic conflation is supported by the fact that weapons, in the form of points, are another category of Early Woodland artifact that is often intentionally destroyed.

The dissipation of this power was achieved, in some places, at some times, through the physical destruction of the pipe. The occasional practice of pipe cremation, separate from but related to the practice of corpse cremation, is interesting in this respect. Simple breakage is a satisfactory way of destroying something inanimate, but it is possible that one burns something because it was alive and therefore combustible and consumable by fire. If pipes were given the same soul attributions as humans, then the breaking and cremation could have served to release their alienable souls to travel freely in death (McElwain 1985:43). Such a sacrifice, in the literal sense of the willful destruction, or “killing,” of a living thing would have had a powerful psychological and spiritual effect on the participants in the ritual wherein it was effected, contributing to a renewal of group purity in the face of the polluting effect of proximity to death (De Vos and Suarez-Orozco 1987).

In order to investigate the roll of smoking pipes at a local scale, I conducted a comparison of a sample of Early Woodland affiliated sites in the upper Northeast. The sample includes six Adena sites, including the Cresap and Natrium sites in West Virginia, the Wright and Ricketts sites in Kentucky, and the William H. Davis and Toephner sites in Ohio (Map 1.2).

Cresap Mound is a typical conical burial mound located on a wide terrace approximately 330 meters from the Ohio River. The site was not an isolated example of Adena in the area; two smaller and disturbed mounds were located approximately 800 meters south of Cresap, and the Moundsville area is a major locus of Adena sites, including the Natrium Mound (see below) and the Grave Creek mound (Townsend and Narona 1962). The site was excavated under the direction of Don Dragoo of the Carnegie Museum of Natural History in 1958. The subsequent site report (Dragoo 1963) included the most substantial interpretation of the Adena phenomenon at that time.

The Natrium Mound site was located in a similar region and geographic context as the Cresap Mound. The mound is located in Natrium, West Virginia, 20 kilometers south of Moundsville, on the second terrace of the Ohio River, approximately 330 meters from the east bank. There are several other mounds in the vicinity.

The next major concentration of Adena sites in my sample is located in central and western Kentucky, south of the West Virginia cluster and east of the Ohio River from the Ohio cluster. Many of the Kentucky Adena sites were excavated by William S. Webb in the 1930s and 1940s, and the results of those excavations led to the earliest conceptions of Adena settlement pattern and social structure (Webb and Baby 1957; Webb and Snow 1974). There are differences in the material culture of the various Adena site clusters, especially in the quantity of artifacts, the feature composition of the sites, and the temporal affiliation. The Kentucky sites often include very well-endowed burials, as far as artifacts included; they tend to feature log tomb burials rather than pit burials, and they tend to be later in the Adena time period, dating after 300 B.C. The log tombs in these sites are interpreted as multiple-use ossuaries that were periodically reopened, cleaned out, and interred with new burials (Clay 1998; Mainfort 1989). This leaves the later Kentucky sites with fewer but more elaborate burials, although it is impossible to say how many individual burials a given tomb contained over time. These differences in the site composition and material assemblages have been argued as representing real social differences between populations. R. Berle Clay proposes that "there were broad Adena 'breeding populations,' for example north and south of the Ohio River. This is an indication that Adena is hardly the monolithic 'culture' and 'peoples' it was once supposed to be" (Clay 1998:16).

Next to Cresap Mound in West Virginia, the Wright Mounds site is probably the best known and most thoroughly discussed Adena site currently known. The site is located approximately five kilometers from the town of Mount Sterling in Montgomery County, in north-central Kentucky. There are actually three mounds at the site (and possibly a fourth very small mound), numbered Mm 6, 7, and 8; two of these, 7 and 8, are very small, and 8 was not excavated. All three mounds are situated on a bluff that rises over forty-five meters above a small creek. Mound 6 was one of the largest Adena mounds on record at the time of its excavation, over nine meters in height (and had originally been higher and steeper before erosion) and up to fifty-seven meters in basal diameter. This is nearly twice the height of the Cresap mound.

The Ricketts Mound site is also located in Montgomery County near the town of Mount Stirling, in the vicinity of the Wright Mound site, discussed above. While there are structural similarities between the two sites, there is a major difference in scale. Whereas Wright Mound 6 was so large upon its completion as to be classified as an aberration by Adena researchers (Clay 1998), Ricketts is within the normal range of other recorded Adena mounds. When recorded, the mound was approximately three and a half meters in height and thirty meters in diameter, half the size of Wright Mound 6 and similar in scale to the Cresap mound. The site was excavated largely under WPA funding by William S. Webb with the assistance of W. D. Funkhouser in 1934 and 1939 (Funkhauser and Webb 1935; Webb and Funkhouser 1940).

The central Ohio region has long been recognized as one of the primary areas of Adena occupation. The Adena concept itself was first conceived based on excavations in Ohio, and the entire cultural complex is named for the Adena site located in Chillicothe. Many of the key Adena sites excavated in Ohio were investigated in the 1950s under the direction of Raymond Baby of the Ohio Historical Society, a collaborator of William Webb. Some of the most impressive of these sites were located within the Scioto River Valley (see Hays 1995) in the vicinity of Columbus. On average, these sites tend to be younger than the Kentucky sites and include fewer grave offerings with the burials. Two of these, the William Davis Mound and Toephner Mound, were analyzed for this project.

The William H. Davis Mound site was excavated in 1959 by Raymond S. Baby under salvage conditions with personnel provided by the Ohio Historical Society. The site is located approximately sixteen kilometers east of the city of Columbus in central Ohio and is situated on top of a gravel ridge within a half kilometer of a minor stream. When excavated, the mound measured six meters in height and twenty-four meters in diameter. The mound was sited directly on top of a Terminal Archaic period cemetery including numerous multiple interment burials.

The Toephner Mound is one of the largest and most complex mounds in the Scioto River Valley. The site was excavated by Baby in 1953, again under salvage conditions, although documentation was better for Toephner than was the case for Davis. No site report was ever published for the site. Hays (1995) and Norris (1985), however, made detailed analyses of Baby's original field notes and assembled descriptions of the mound structure.

The local-scale analysis investigated several of the same issues covered in the regional-scale analysis, but in greater detail based on a sample of sites for which high-quality data was available. The first topic discussed in the local-scale analysis was demographic associations. Analysis of the demographic associations in a regional framework within the Eastern Woodlands raised the possibility that smoking pipes were preferentially associated with adults, adult males especially, although the data for age and sex were fragmentary. Therefore, the analysis of specific sites was intended to determine if this preliminary demographic characterization holds up for more detailed data sets.

Table 1.4 presents summary data that compares the relative demographic proportions of burials containing pipes as burial offerings in comparison to the overall burial population for each site. Entries for "pipes" represent the proportions of pipe burials for each demographic category, while entries for "all" indicate the total proportions of those categories within the burial population of each site. This table shows first that while the Adena sites are dominated by adult individuals overall, there are small numbers of subadults, children, and infants present as well. However, when pipes are associated with human remains at these sites, they are universally associated with mature adults, adults, or young adults, and never with children or infants. Also, while the sex data are fragmentary, whenever sex is identified for an Adena pipe burial, it is male. Females, while forming significant minorities of several of the Adena burial populations, are never associated with pipes in the sample.

Therefore, reference to the entire burial populations for the Adena sites show that adults were preferentially interred in burial mounds, but that immature individuals, including subadults, children, and infants, were present as minority categories. Males outnumber females as well. However, burials that contain pipes are almost always adults and, when sex data are available, males, confirming at a local scale the regional demographic patterns.

The next topic addressed at a local scale was the mode of burial. Early Woodland period mortuary programs are characterized by a wide variety of burial treatments, including extended and flexed fleshed burials, disarticulated bundles and skull burials, and cremation burials. There does not appear to be any social significance to the different burial modes beyond the fact that some of the skulls or disarticulated burials appear to have been intended as animistic offerings to other, intact burials rather than as individual interments. Fleshed burials were the preferred mode for all demographic categories. There does not seem to be any obvious patterning in the orientation of the burials themselves. We are left with the picture that burial mode was a matter of logistics rather than any kind of status-oriented practice, with fleshed burials preferred but cremations or bundles perhaps used in cases where a person had been dead for some time or died far from the final interment site. Burial mode is interpreted as determined by pragmatic concerns, with cremations and disarticulations only being used when the fleshed burial mode was not possible due to the time and place of death. The only possible pattern in the burial modes when the data are aggregated in this manner is that adult males appear to have been interred as bundles somewhat more often in comparison to other categories.

Not surprisingly, given this lack of demographic patterning in burial mode choices, there is also no obvious association of pipe burials to any one burial mode type, beyond the obvious preponderance of fleshed burials, which seems to have been the dominant Adena burial mode overall, pipe or no pipe. Smoking pipes are most often associated with extended burials, but that is the case with most artifacts in the Early Woodland burial program. There is the possibility of some common locations of pipes within graves in relation to the corpses they are buried with. For instance, of the fifteen smoking pipes from Adena burial contexts in the sample, I was able to determine specific locations within the burials for five, all of which came from one of two locations within the grave in relation to the skeleton: next to the face or in the pelvic region. I would hesitate to draw symbolic conclusions from so small a sample, but the point should be made that these locations are proximal to key orifices in the human body, which Parker Pearson (1999:46) and Leach (1977), note as possessing widespread if not universal symbolic significance.

The analysis of artifact associations was able to place the assemblages of pipe burials in the broader context of the entire burial population of each site in the local-scale sample. This was aided through the use of clustering statistics. Pipes in the Adena sample did not exhibit any statistically significant associations with other artifact types,[5] and burials containing pipes either did not exhibit strong similarity to other burials or were most similar to other pipe burials. This

TABLE 1.4 ▸ Summary of Demographic Associations of Smoking Pipes

		Mature Adult			Adult			Young Adult		
Site		M	F	?	M	F	?	M	F	?
Cresap	Pipes (2)				50					50
	All	2			26	6	30			4
Natrium	Pipes (4)			25			75			
	All			2	2		38			
Wright	Pipes (2)				100					
	All	19			19	19	5			
Ricketts	Pipes (2)				50		50			
	All				18	10	33			
Davis	Pipes (3)						66			
	All						66			3
Toephner	Pipes (2)						50			
	All		2		12	8	40		1	
Adena	Pipes (15)			7	33		33		7	
	All	<1		3	13	7	36	<1	1	1
Boucher	Pipes (13)				8	8		23	15	
	All	8	1	1	2	1	13	7	4	4

indicated that smoking pipes tended to be isolated in their symbolic relevance rather than part of a constellation of traits. In general, the pipe burials for Adena contained anomalously high amounts of other artifact types in comparison to the rest of the burial population from the site, primarily from burials that were mature adults, though there was no obvious statistical patterning in the other artifacts contained with pipes. This was interpreted as evidence that smoking pipes for the Adena were one type of material correlation that differentially marked certain categories of people—adults and possibly adult males—in comparison to the rest of the burial population. Other similar correlations may be present for tools/weapons and ritual artifacts, but these correlations are separate from pipes.

Opposed to this specific distribution of pipes, ritual artifacts, and tools/weapons is the distribution of adornment artifacts. These artifacts, especially

Subadult			Child			Infant	?
M	F	?	M	F	?	?	
					8		25
					2		58
			5				28
					3	5	25
							33
		7			3		24
							50
					11	2	24
							20
		<1	<1		5	1	31
		8			8		31
	1	1			13	14	29

copper jewelry and shell beads, showed a distribution that crosscut social categories, including immature and female individuals. One difference in artifact associations was the Ohio Adena sites, which appear to have had few adornment artifacts, although I have presented the argument (Rafferty 2001:262) that the very paucity of the burials from those sites itself acted as a means of social inclusion or that the material culture that symbolized inclusion was perishable. The statistical analysis of artifact associations calls into question the possibility that smoking pipes are associated with other artifact types to any significant degree; pipes among the Adena samples tend to be set apart from other burial furniture. The burial assemblages exhibit a high degree of variability, with few formulaic associations beyond the absence of any artifact at all or the general distribution of adornment artifacts. Pipes, other ritual artifacts, and tools/weapons tend to be statistically anomalous inclusions, which indicates that they were significant markers of difference rather than of inclusion for the burials with which they were associated.

An additional indication of the statistical analysis relates to the ethnohistorically documented conflation of pipes and weapons noted by Hall (1977, 1997). If this symbolic congruence was in operation at the Early Woodland sites I have investigated, it is not statistically evident in any direct associations of pipes with tools/weapons. Possible explanations include the absence of the symbolic congruence during the Early Woodland (or at least in the sites I investigated); that it was present but not preserved in material form (much of an atlatl would probably decay, for instance); or that the very congruence that Hall argues for means that one would be less likely to see them co-occur, as that would be symbolically redundant.

The primary issue of context to be considered is the nature and function of the site itself. With respect to Adena mound sites, there has been much speculation as to their function in the Adena societies that built them. On the most obvious level, they functioned as repositories for the dead. However, in no way were they the primary means of corpse disposal. Only a small and nonrepresentative fraction of the population ended up in Adena mounds. They contain comparatively small numbers of bodies in relation to the length of time they were in use—most of the burial population of these societies was disposed of by other means. In some of the few known Adena habitation sites, burials were found in house floors, for instance (Grantz 1986). Also, the mound burial populations are dominated, as already noted, by mature, adult individuals, with more males than females, when the entire burial population of small-scale societies were female in equal proportion and also included a high percentage of children and infants due to the high levels of infant and child mortality (Parker Pearson 1999:103).

While it is important to consider the context of pipes within the site at which they are found, it is also vital to look at these local contexts in terms of the nature of the sites themselves and their place in the social landscape in which they existed. If these sites were not the primary means of burial for the Adena, then what were they? Part of the key is their monumental nature—the fact that they are mounds. However, the significance of their monumentality takes a different form than has been conjectured elsewhere. Much postprocessual archaeological research has looked at monumental mortuary facilities as legitimating social inequality in hierarchical societies, particularly in times of political uncertainty (Garwood 1991:10; Parker Pearson 1992, 1999:40). While this would make sense for a sedentary chiefdom, it is less than appropriate for a more mobile and small-scale hunter-gatherer society such as the Adena (Mainfort 1989), not to mention the fact that for most of their existence even the largest Adena mounds were not terribly monumental due to their incremental construction, and most of the mounds were not really that large even when completed.

While not all Adena mounds were sizable monuments on the scale of Wright Mound 6, Cresap Mound, or Grave Creek (probably the largest Adena mound to survive to historic times [Townsend and Narona 1962]) they were still noticeable alterations of the natural landscape. Furthermore, the general absence of any habitation remains around most Adena mounds indicates that they were made at some remove from domestic space, in what may have been viewed as "liminal space"—not part of the everyday world but still part of the natural world, as opposed to the spirit world. This possibility is enhanced by the interpretations of Clay (1998), who notes that mound sites were not centrally located but were formed at the fringes of territories of loosely knit Adena societies and marked social boundaries between neighboring and interacting groups. Similar arguments have been made for other Early Woodland complexes. Loring (1985), for example, notes that the four Middlesex cemetery sites along the shores of Lake Champlain (Boucher, East Creek, Swanton, and Bennett) were not central sites, but they were active in boundary maintenance at the margins of socially distinct populations. Such a boundary-marking role has been hypothesized for mound sites in Neolithic Scotland (Parker Pearson 1999:134). As with Adena, the Scottish Neolithic sites had originally been thought to be centrally located (Renfrew 1973), drawing on the writings of Mircea Eliade (1964, 1965), which interpreted focal locations as metaphorical centers of the world, or of the "worlds," forming an *Axis Mundi* where the worlds of spirit beings and the world of everyday life are joined at one point. Parker Pearson takes the basic idea of a cemetery mound forming a spiritual center of the world and notes that it can just as easily fulfill such a purpose at a social margin as it can at a social center. In fact, the very liminality of such marginal areas makes them more amenable to the presence of such sites.

Researchers investigating monumental burial sites such as earthen mounds have also raised the point that they represent a separation of the community of the dead from that of the living, not only in terms of geographic space but also in terms of time. Parker Pearson points out that when such sites were in intermittent use for periods of time greater than human lives, as is the case for the Adena mounds, the interment of people at such sites represents an association of the dead with the past and a disassociation with the present, possibly representing a reference to spiritually powerful ancestors (Parker Pearson 1999:126). Koji Mizoguchi, coming at the same issue from a structurationist perspective, argues that mortuary rituals in general, and specifically those conducted at prominent ancient monuments (for example, linear long barrows in Britain), inherently represent references to the past, to history as well as memory. Furthermore, rituals at such sites afford an opportunity for contestation of the meaning of that past by participants in the ritual as part of the ongoing reproduction of society (Mizoguchi 1991, 1993). "Time," Mizoguchi (1993:232) argues, "is not an empty box. Time was marked by human practices." The fact that Adena mounds were constructed incrementally implies a cyclicity in the rituals associated with them, a cycle that may extend beyond human life spans given the length of time over which some of these sites were used.

It should also be noted at this point that Adena mound sites meet all of Renfrew's (1994b:52) criteria for the archaeological determination of religious rituals. These include attention-focusing settings or architecture, a purpose that would have been amply served by the mounds themselves, as well as the mortuary camp structures that preceded them. The mounds, with their peripheral location, also comprise "evidence of a perceived boundary between worlds," Renfrew's second criterion. Pipe effigies, while rare, could be seen as depictions of supernatural figures or deities. The burial offerings, and the burial rituals themselves, could represent "evidence of human participation or offerings." Smoking pipes specifically, with their function as mind-altering tools, would have made ideal "devices for inducing religious experience." The destruction of artifacts, including the pipes, was also a criterion predicted by Renfrew. Finally, the "documentation of repeated actions of a symbolic nature" is met by the cyclical nature of mound construction and Adena burial rituals.

Which brings us to the question of what role smoking pipes would have played at such locations. How do the practices of smoking pipes, and interring them with the dead, relate to the nature of the sites themselves as spiritually significant focal points at social margins that may represent the intersections of spirit world and natural world, and of present and ancestral past? As already discussed, both Clay (1998) and Loring (1985) have interpreted Adena burial mounds and Middlesex cemetery sites as having been located at societal margins in order to maintain those boundaries and also to aid in the interaction across the boundaries and thereby reproduce relations of interdependence between egalitarian, dispersed hunter-gatherer populations. The dead at any one site may represent not one social group but two, commingled in death. As stated by Parker Pearson (1999:114), "the community of the dead may well be very different from the communities of the living."

Clay explains the negotiation and interactions taking place at these sites as primarily economic in nature (and I do not dispute that this was a major component), with the individuals buried being active in or symbolic of that negotiation/interaction. I would add that the evidence from this study indicates that it was also *spiritual* in nature and that pipes were a major conduit in these spiritual interactions. Pipes, which a wealth of ethnographic and ethnohistoric evidence indicates are ideal for spiritual sanctification and communication, could have played a role in mound ceremonies that mediated between these interacting societies in Clay's model, in a similar fashion to later Native American use of smoking pipes, such as the calumet ceremony documented historically. In previous writings on Adena ceremonial practices, Clay (1986, 1988) has argued that some of the material culture (especially ceramics) found in mound fill at Adena sites were due to ritual feasting taking place during burial ceremonies. Such feasts, if they involved not just one social group but two neighboring groups, would be ideal venues for the negotiation, mediation, and reproduction of social relations between those groups, as well as for the contestation of power relations between the influential members of each group. And, it is only a small leap to see that smoking pipes, and the ritual taking of tobacco or other plants in smoke, would have likely played an important role in these graveside rituals.

Aside from the natural inclusiveness of sharing smoke, possible associations of tobacco with the creation of the world noted in ethnographic cases, and the physiological effect of tobacco that give the sensation of an out-of-body experience, could have allowed for the manipulation of time in a communal ritual act, bringing the present literally into the ancestral past that the mounds represented. Following their use in such rituals, some pipes were apparently sacrificed by inclusion in the burials that were the focus of the rituals taking place, sometimes being destroyed first to kill their innate animate spirit or being left as sanctification offerings to the mound location itself.

I propose that there were two primary roles that smoking pipes played in burial rituals among the Adena and Middlesex societies during the Early Woodland period. The first of these, which I will term an *operational role,* relates to the mortuary ritual practices in which they were used. These rituals in which pipes were smoked I will term *rituals of inclusion* among groups of adjoining territories. This is an analogous function to the calumet (Brown 1989). But, unlike the historic calumet ceremony, these rituals centered around mortuary practices, with group codependence (as hypothesized by Clay) being symbolized in death. The most likely explanation of the operational role for pipes was as a conduit to communicate with spiritual beings who might have sanctioned or even been seen as active participants (as something akin to clan totems) in the codependence between neighboring groups.

The second role pipes played I will define as a *symbolic role,* which relates to the ideological statements about social relations being forwarded in burial rituals. The inclusion of pipes with certain classes of burials served as marking criteria in a symbolized ideology in a two-tiered scheme. First, other Early Woodland researchers (for example, Heckenberger, Peterson, and Basa 1990; Heckenberger et al. 1990) have identified what I would call an *ideology of social equality.* This sort of statement of an egalitarian ideology is what one might expect from a comparatively loosely organized and egalitarian foraging society. For the Adena, this was symbolized with mortuary treatments that crosscut demographic categories, such as the formulaic associations of adornment artifacts in West Virginia and Kentucky or the general absence of any (durable) burial goods in Ohio. As stated previously, these artifacts symbolized equal membership in horizontal social divisions and may have extended these divisions to neighboring social groups. This was probably a factor in the operational role of pipes in rituals of inclusion—the expressing of an ideology of equality for individuals of different groups.

However, to say that the Adena were generally egalitarian societies does not mean that power was not an issue (Aldenderfer 1993), and the burials at these sites also put forward what I term an *ideology of sacred order* (Parker Pearson 1999:94), in which smoking pipes were key symbolic elements. The inclusion of certain key artifact classes, including pipes, tools/weapons, and certain ritual or faunal artifacts, expresses and legitimizes the association of some social categories with the spirit world that coexisted with the natural world, and the naturally accruing achieved status of those social categories. These artifact classes among the Adena are associated primarily with adults and possibly with adult males. This is probably symbolic of their role as hunters and warriors and the status and influence that age, experience, and actions can provide an individual even in an egalitarian society. It is in the expression of the ideology of sacred order that some of the differences between sites arise. The artifacts that legitimized achieved status appear to have been different between regions, with numerous ceremonial artifacts, especially those related to pigment processing, being found in adult burials in the two West Virginia sites but generally absent in Kentucky and Ohio; the tools/weapons association is also absent at the Wright Mounds site.

The use of smoking pipes in rituals of social inclusion most likely had its origins in the mortuary behavior of the Late Archaic, becoming increasingly developed and elaborated as the "burial cult" spread. The spread of these mortuary practices was supported and facilitated by trading networks, with raw materials and finished artifacts being traded within the Eastern Woodlands. The blocked-end pipe style that was such an integral part of the burial rituals during this period probably had its origin in the central Ohio Valley, in proximity to the sources of the most common raw material, a fine-grained limestone known as Ohio fireclay, although sources farther north and east are also possible contenders. While the artifacts themselves may have had an Ohio Valley inception, their use and the ideology they communicated was differentially accepted within subregions in the Eastern Woodlands. In some areas, such as the Delmarva Peninsula, pipes of fireclay limestone were present in even greater frequency than is found nearer to the source area. Other areas seem to have included only small numbers of such artifacts, such as southern New York, southern New England, northern Ohio, or Virginia. While this could be at least in part due to sample bias, as the availability of data in the museum collections I investigated may not have been representative, this should have been partially counteracted by the literature survey, which was more inclusive. It seems that there were some regions that included smoking pipes in their ritual practices, coeval with other sites that did not, or did to a lesser degree.

The application of a gas chromatography/mass spectroscopy technique determined that nicotine, the active agent in tobacco, could be recovered from archaeological contexts from pipe residue (Rafferty 2002). One Adena pipe from my local-scale sample from the Cresap Mound in West Virginia presented characteristic chromatographic decay signatures for nicotine, as well as mass spectrum matches for the alkaloid. This was interpreted as evidence that whatever plant was smoked in these pipes contained very high levels of nicotine and was therefore most likely a species of tobacco. This demonstrates that smoking pipes in the Early Woodland were used as drug-delivery devices and that the rituals in which they were used featured altered states of consciousness. This is also possible evidence that the use of tobacco predated the currently accepted Middle Woodland period dates by several centuries.

Two possible, and not necessarily mutually exclusive, explanations for this variation are possible. First, there is the issue of agency and the possibility that societies in some regions made active decisions not to participate in the regional trade or to refuse to practice the same sorts of rituals as other populations (Versaggi 1999). Second, there is the possible explanation for differential acceptance of the use of smoking pipes that is contingent: the ability to participate. Within the Eastern Woodlands there is considerable ecological diversity, and populations in some areas may simply have lacked the resources to participate in the regional trade relationships that underlay the pipe ritual complex (Hays 1995; Tiffany 1986).

I will finish by referring to the quotation from Father Le Jeune with which I opened. While early European observers of Native Americans using smoking pipes viewed the practice incredulously and condescendingly, an anthropological perspective shows that pipes were every bit as vital a component in the ritual and social experience as was the crucifix that the missionaries wanted to put in its place. Furthermore, this spiritual significance of the pipe has an even deeper history than its Western counterpart. When he noted that his charges "pass their lives in smoke," Le Jeune struck upon a primary foundation of their spiritual world. I have attempted in this project to unravel some of the history of that foundation. I have also tried to demonstrate that ritual practices, and the ideology that they symbolize, can be approached from the perspective of material culture. Far from the icing on the interpretive cake, the analysis of ritual practices, such as the use of smoking pipes during the Early Woodland, strikes at the core of anthropology's mission—to seek meaning in the ways other cultures viewed themselves and the world around them.

Notes

1. Brookes 1937; Brown 1989; Brown 1953; Catlin 1841; Goodman 1993; Haberman 1984; Hall 1997; Heiser 1992; Kaiser 1984; Lowie 1919; Paper 1987, 1988, 1992; Pego et al. 1995; Steinmetz 1984; Trubowitz 1992; von Gernet 1992, 1995.

2. Barrett 1990, 1991; Barth 1987; Bloch 1971, 1986, 1989; Bloch and Parry 1982; Garwood 1991; Härke 1997; Lewis 1980; Mizoguchi 1991, 1993; Nielsen 1997; Parker Pearson 1999; Sherratt 1991; Thomas 1991.

3. New York State Museum; Robert S. Peabody Museum of Archaeology; Carnegie Museum of Natural History ; Glen Black Laboratory of Archaeology; University of Kentucky Museum of Anthropology; Springfield Science Center; Ohio Historical Society; Smithsonian Institution; Yager Museum at Hartwick College; Peabody Museum of Anthropology. Collections research was supported by the National Science Foundation (Grant #SBR-9812751).

4. References to these sites include the following: Abrams 1989, 1992; Black 1979; Bush 1975; Carskadden and Morton 1989; Grantz 1986; Harn 1986; Markman and Kreisa 1986; Morgan, Asch, and Stafford 1986; Shane 1975; Shane and Murphy 1975; Theler 1986. Many of these are site reports for diverse Early Woodland phases in the Eastern Woodlands contained in Early Woodland Archaeology (Farnsworth and Emerson 1986).

5. This statistical analysis used the Jacquard Coefficient, a nonparametric measure that uses presence/absence of traits to look for patterned associations between paired categories.

References Cited

Abrams, Elliot M.

1989 The Boudinot #4 Site (33AT521): An Early Woodland Habitation Site in Athens County, Ohio. *West Virginia Archaeologist* 41(2):19–26.

1992 Woodland Settlement Patterns in the Southern Hocking River Valley, Southeastern Ohio. In *Cultural Variability in Context: Woodland Settlements in the Mid-Ohio Valley,* edited by Mark F. Seeman, 19–23. Midcontinental Journal of Archaeology Special Paper No. 7.

Aldenderfer, Mark

1993 Ritual, Hierarchy, and Change in Foraging Societies. *Journal of Anthropological Archaeology* 12:1–40.

Asch, David L.

1994 Aboriginal Specialty-Plant Cultivation in Eastern North America: Illinois Prehistory and a Post-Contact Perspective. In *Agricultural Origins and Development in the Midcontinent,* edited by William Green, 25–86. Univ. of Iowa Press, Iowa City.

Asch, David L., and Asch Nancy B.

1985 Prehistoric Plant Cultivation in West-Central Illinois. In *Prehistoric Food Production in North America,* edited by R. I. Ford, 149–203. Univ. of Michigan Press, Ann Arbor.

Barrett, John C.

1990 The Monumentality of Death: The Character of Early Bronze Age Mortuary Mounds in Southern Britain. *World Archaeology* 22(2):179–189.

1991 Towards an Archaeology of Ritual. In *Sacred and Profane: Proceedings of a Conference on Archaeology, Ritual and Religion, Oxford, 1989,* edited by Paul Garwood, David Jennings, Robin Skeates, and Judith Toms. Oxford Univ. Committee for Archaeology.

Barth, Frederick

1987 *Cosmologies in the Making.* Cambridge Univ. Press, Cambridge.

Bense, Judith Ann

1994 *Archaeology of the Southeastern United States: Paleoindian to World War I.* Academic Press, New York.

Black, Deborah B.

1979 Adena and Hopewell Relations in the Lower Hocking Valley. In *Hopewell Archaeology,* edited by David S. Brose and N'omi Greber, 19–26. Kent State Univ. Press, Kent, Ohio.

Bloch, Maurice

1971 *Placing the Dead: Tombs, Ancestral Villages, and Kinship Organization in Madagascar.* Seminar Press, London.

1986 *From Blessing to Violence.* Cambridge Univ. Press, Cambridge.

1989 *Ritual, History, and Power.* Athlone Press, London.

Bloch, Maurice, and Jonathan Parry

1982 Introduction: Death and the Regeneration of Life. In *Death and the Regeneration of Life,* edited by M. Bloch and J. Parry, 1–44. Cambridge Univ. Press, Cambridge.

Bradley, James W.

1987 *Evolution of the Onondaga Iroquois: Accommodating Change, 1500–1655.* Syracuse Univ. Press, Syracuse, New York.

Brooks, Jerome E.

1937 *Tobacco, Its History, Illustrated by the Books, Manuscripts, and Engravings in the Library of George Arents, Jr.* Vol. 1, 1507–1615. Rosenbach Co., New York.

Brose, David S.

1985 The Woodland Period. In *Ancient Art of the American Woodland Indians,* edited by David Brose, James Brown, and David W. Penney, 43–91. Harry N. Abrams, Detroit Institution of Arts.

Brown, Ian

1989 The Calumet Ceremony in the Southeast and Its Archaeological Manifestations. *American Antiquity* 54(2):311–331.

Brown, James

1986 Early Ceramics and Culture: A Review of Interpretations. In *Early Woodland Archaeology,* edited by Kenneth B. Farnsworth and Thomas E. Emerson, 179–190. Center for American Archaeology, Kampsville Seminars in Archaeology No. 2, Kampsville, Illinois.

Brown, Joseph Epps

1953 *The Sacred Pipe: Black Elk's Account of the Seven Rites of the Oglala Sioux.* Univ. of Oklahoma Press, Norman.

Bucko, Raymond A.

1998 *The Lakota Ritual of the Sweat Lodge: History and Contemporary Practice.* Univ. of Nebraska Press, Lincoln.

Bush, Deborah E.

1975 A Ceramic Analysis of the Late Adena Buckmeyer Site, Perry Co., Ohio. *Michigan Archaeologist* 21(1):9–22.

Butler, B. M., and C. R. McGimsey

2000 Features and Postmolds. In *The Old Runway Site (11J-1009): A Late Woodland Settlement on the Big Muddy River,* edited by B. M. Butler, 59–144. Technical Report 00-4. Center for Archaeological Investigations, Southern Illinois Univ., Carbondale.

Carpenter, Edward S.

1950 Five Sites of the Intermediate Period. *American Antiquity* 15(4):298–314.

Carskadden, Jeff, and James Morton

1989 Excavation of Mound E at the Philo Mound Group, Muskingum County, Ohio. *West Virginia Archaeologist* 41(1):42–53.

Catlin, George

1841 *Letters and Notes on Manners, Customs, and Conditions of the North American Indians.* Catlin, London.

Claassen, Cheryl P.

1991 Gender, Shellfishing and the Shell Mound Archaic. In *Engendering Archaeology,* edited by Joan M. Gero and Margaret Conkey. 276–300. Basil Blackwell, Oxford & Cambridge.

1996 A Consideration of the Social Organization of the Shell Mound Archaic. In Archaeology of the Mid-Holocene Southeast, edited by Kenneth E. Sassaman and David G. Anderson. 235–258. University Press of Florida, Gainesville.

Clay, R. Berle

1986 Adena Ritual Spaces. In *Early Woodland Archaeology,* edited by Kenneth B. Farnsworth and Thomas E. Emerson, 581–595. Center for American Archaeology, Kampsville Seminars in Archaeology No. 2, Kampsville, Illinois.

1988 The Ceramic Sequence at Peter Village and Its Significance. In *New Deal Archaeology and Current Research in Kentucky,* edited by D. Pollack and M. Lucas Powell, 105–113. Kentucky Heritage Council, Lexington.

1989 Peter Village: An Adena Enclosure. In Middle Woodland Settlement and Ceremonialism in the Mid-South and Lower Mississippi Vallye, edited by Robert Mainfort, 19–30. Mississippi Department of Archives and History, Jackson, Mississippi.

1998 The Essential Features of Adena Ritual and Their Implications. *Southeastern Archaeology* 17(1):1–21.

Concannon, Mary

1993 Early Woodland Depopulation: A Review of the Evidence. *Bulletin of the Massachusetts Archaeological Society* 54(2):71–79.

Cubbage, William O.

1941 Killen's Mill Pond. *Bulletin of the Archaeological Society of Delaware* 3(4):23–24.

Custer, Jay
1987 New Perspectives on the Delmarva Adena Complex. *Midcontinental Journal of Archaeology* 12(1):33–53.
1989 *Prehistoric Cultures of the Delmarva Peninsula.* Univ. of Delaware Press, Newark.

Dent, Richard J., Jr.
1995 *Chesapeake Prehistory: Old Traditions, New Directions.* American Univ., Washington, D.C.

De Vos, George A., and Marcello M. Suarez-Orozco
1987 Sacrifice and the Experience of Power. *Journal of Psychoanalytic Anthropology* 10(4):304–340.

Dragoo, Don
1963 Mounds for the Dead. *Annals of the Carnegie Museum.* Pittsburgh.
1976 Adena and the Eastern Burial Cult. *Archaeology of Eastern North America* 4:1–9.

Eliade, Mircea
1964 *Shamanism: Archaic Techniques of Ecstasy.* Princeton Univ. Press, Princeton, N.J.
1965 *The Sacred and the Profane.* Galimard, Paris.

Farnsworth, Ken, and Thomas E. Emerson
1986 *Early Woodland Archaeology.* Center for Archaeological Investigations, Kampsville, Illinois.

Fiedel, Stewart
1992 What Happened to the Early Woodland? Paper presented at the annual meetings of the New York State Archaeological Association, Orange County, N.Y.

Fitting, James E., and David S. Brose
1971 The Northern Periphery of Adena. In *Adena: The Seeking of an Identity,* edited by B. K. Swortz. 29–55. Ball State University.

Frazier, James
1980 *The Golden Bough: A Study in Magic and Region.* Macmillan, London.

Funkhouser, William D., and William S. Webb
1935 *The Ricketts Site in Montgomery County Kentucky.* Reports in Archaeology and Anthropology, vol. 3, no. 3. Univ. of Kentucky, Lexington.

Furst, Peter J., and Jill Leslie Furst
1983 The Sacred Pipe as Artifact and Prayer. *Terra* 22(2):11–17.

Gardener, William M.
1982 Early and Middle Woodland in the Mid-Atlantic: An Overview. In *Practicing Environmental Archaeology: Methods and Interpretations,* edited by Roger W. Moeller, 53–86. American Indian Archaeological Institute Occasional Paper No. 3, Washington, Conn.

Garwood, Paul
1991 Ritual Tradition and the Reconstitution of Society. In *Sacred and Profane: Proceedings of a Conference on Archaeology, Ritual, and Religion, Oxford, 1989,* edited by Paul Garwood, David Jennings, Robin Skeates, and Judith Toms, 10–32. Oxford Univ. Committee for Archaeology.

Gehlbach, Donald R.
1982 Ohio Pipe Chronology Chart. *Ohio Archaeologist* 32(4):8–9.

Goodman, Jordan
1993 *Tobacco in History: The Cultures of Dependence.* Routledge, London.

Granger, Joseph
1978 Meadowood Phase Settlement Pattern in the Niagara Frontier Region of Western New York State. Anthropological Papers, Museum of Anthropology, Univ. of Michigan, Ann Arbor.

Grantz, Denise
1986 Archaeological Investigations of the Crawford-Grist Site #2 (36FA262): An Early Woodland Hamlet. *Pennsylvania Archaeologist* 56(3–4):1–21.

Haberman, Thomas W.
1984 Evidence of Aboriginal Tobaccos in Eastern North America. *American Antiquity* 49(2):268–287.

Hall, Robert L.
1977 An Anthropocentric Perspective for Eastern United States Prehistory. *American Antiquity* 42(4):499–518.
1997 *An Archaeology of the Soul: North American Belief and Ritual.* Univ. of Illinois Press, Champaign.

Härke, Heinrich
1997 Material Culture as Myth: Weapons in Anglo-Saxon Graves. In *Burial and Society: The Chronological and Social Analysis of Archaeological Burial Data,* edited by Claus Kjeld Jensen and Karen Høilund Nielsen, 119–127. Aarhus Univ. Press, Aarhus, Denmark.

Harn, Alan D.
1986 The Marion Phase Occupation of the Larson Site in the Central Illinois River Valley. In *Early Woodland Archaeology,* edited by Kenneth B. Farnsworth and Thomas E. Emerson, 244–279. Center for American Archaeology, Kampsville Seminars in Archaeology No. 2, Kampsville, Illinois.

Haviland, William A., and Marjory A. Power
1994 *The Original Vermonters: Native Inhabitants, Past and Present.* Univ. Press of New England, Hanover, N.H.

Hays, Christopher T.
1995 Adena Mortuary Patterns and Ritual Cycles in the Upper Scioto Valley, Ohio. Unpublished Ph.D. dissertation, Binghamton Univ., Binghamton, N.Y.

Heckenberger, Michael J., James B. Peterson, and Louise A. Basa
1990 Early Woodland Period Ritual Use of Personal Adornment at the Boucher Site. *Annals of the Carnegie Museum* 59(3):173–217.

Heckenberger, Michael J., James B. Peterson, Ellen R. Cowie, Arthur E. Speiss, and Louise A. Basa
1990 Early Woodland Mortuary Ceremonialism in the Far Northeast: A View from the Boucher Cemetery. *Archaeology of Eastern North America* 18:109–144.

Heiser, Charles
1992 On Possible Sources of the Tobacco of Prehistoric Eastern North America. *Current Anthropology* 33(1):54–56.

Hultkrantz, Åke

1997 *Soul and Native Americans.* Spring Publications, Woodstock, Conn.

Joniger, Oscar, and Marlene Dobkin de Rios

1973 Suggestive Hallucinogenic Properties of Tobacco. *Medical Anthropology Newsletter* 4(4):6–11.

1976 Nicotiana an Hallucinogen? *Economic Botany* 30:149–151.

Kaiser, Patricia

1984 The Lakota Sacred Pipe: Its Tribal Use and Religious Philosophy. *American Indian Culture and Research Journal* 8(3):1–26.

Kraft, Herbert C.

1976 The Rosenkrans Site, an Adena-Related Mortuary Complex in the Upper Delaware Valley, New Jersey. *Archaeology of Eastern North America* 4:9–49.

Leach, Edmund

1977 A View from the Bridge. In *Archaeology and Anthropology: Areas of Mutual Interest,* edited by M. Spriggs, 161–176. British Archaeological Reports Supplementary Series 19, Oxford.

Lewis, Gilbert

1980 *Day of Shining Red: An Essay on Understanding Ritual.* Cambridge Univ. Press, Cambridge.

Lewis, Thomas M., and Madeline Kneberg Lewis

1961 *Eva, an Archaic Site.* Univ. of Tennessee Press, Knoxville.

Loring, Stephen

1985 Boundary Maintenance, Mortuary Ceremonialism and Resource Control in the Early Woodland. *Archaeology of Eastern North America* 13:93–127.

Lowie, Robert H.

1919 *Tobacco Society of the Crow Indians.* Anthropological papers of the American Museum of Natural History 21, pt. 2.

Mainfort, Robert

1989 Adena Chiefdoms? Evidence from the Wright Mound. *Midcontinental Journal of Archaeology* 14(2):164–178.

Markman, Charles W., and Paul P. Kreisa

1986 Early Woodland Adaptation along the Lower Rock River, Illinois. In *Early Woodland Archaeology,* edited by Kenneth B. Farnsworth and Thomas E. Emerson, 179–190. Center for American Archaeology, Kampsville Seminars in Archaeology No. 2, Kampsville, Illinois.

McElwain, Thomas

1985 The Archaic Roots of Eastern Woodland Eschatology: A Soul-Dualism Explanation of Adena Mortuary. *Cosmos* 1:37–43.

Merrifield, Ralph

1987 *The Archaeology of Ritual and Magic.* B. T. Batsford Ltd., London.

Meuser, Gordon F.

1952 Tube Pipes. *Ohio Archaeologist* 2(3):14–15.

Mizoguchi, Koji

1991 A Historiography of a Linear Barrow Cemetery: A Structurationist's Point of View. *Archaeological Review from Cambridge* 11(1):39–49.

1993 Time and the Reproduction of Mortuary Practices. *World Archaeology* 25(2):223–235.

Morgan, David T., David L. Asch, and C. Russell Stafford

1986 Marion and Black Sand Occupations in the Sny Bottom of the Mississippi Valley. In *Early Woodland Archaeology,* edited by Kenneth B. Farnsworth and Thomas E. Emerson, 92–120. Center for American Archaeology, Kampsville Seminars in Archaeology No. 2, Kampsville, Illinois.

Nielsen, Karen Høilund

1997 From Society to Burial and from Burial to Society? Some Modern Analogies. In *Burial and Society: The Chronological and Social Analysis of Archaeological Burial Data,* edited by Claus Kjeld Jensen and Karen Høilund Nielsen, 103–110. Aarhus Univ. Press, Aarhus, Denmark.

Norris, Rae

1985 Excavation of the Toephner Mound. *Archaeology of Eastern North America* 13:128–137.

Otto, Martha Potter

1979 Hopewell Antecedents in the Adena Heartland. In *Hopewell Archaeology,* edited by David S. Brose and N'omi Greber, 9–14. Kent State Univ. Press, Kent, Ohio.

1992 A Prehistoric Menagérie: Ohio Hopewell Effigy Pipes. In *Proceedings of the 1988 Smoking Pipe Conference,* edited by Charles F. Hays III, 1–14. Rochester Museum and Science Center Research Records No. 2.

Paper, Jordan

1987 Cosmological Implications of Pan-Indian Sacred Pipe Ritual. *Canadian Journal of Native Studies* 7(2):297–306.

1988 *Offering Smoke: The Sacred Pipe and Native American Religion.* Univ. of Idaho Press, Moscow.

1992 The Iroquoian and Pan-Indian Sacred Pipes: Comparative Ritual and Symbolism. In *Proceedings of the 1988 Smoking Pipe Conference,* edited by Charles F. Hays III, 163–170. Rochester Museum and Science Center Research Records No. 2.

Parker Pearson, Michael

1999 *The Archaeology of Death and Burial.* Texas A & M Univ. Press, College Station.

Pearsall, Deborah M.

1992 The Origins of Plant Cultivation in South America. In *The Origins of Agriculture: An International Perspective,* edited by C. W. Cowan and P. J. Watson, 173–205. Smithsonian Institution Press, Washington D.C.

Pego, Christina M., Robert F. Hill, Glenn W. Solomon, Robert M. Chisholm, and Suzanne E. Ivey

1995 Tobacco, Culture, and Health among American Indians: A Historical Review. *American Indian Culture and Research Journal* 19(2):143–164.

Penney, David W.

1985 The Late Archaic Period. In *Ancient Art of the American Woodland Indians,* edited by David S. Brose, James Brown, and David W. Penney, 15–41. Harry N. Abrams, Detroit Institution of Arts.

Rafferty, Sean

2001 They Pass Their Lives in Smoke, and at Death, Fall into the Fire: Smoking Pipes and Mortuary Ritual during the Early Woodland Period. Ph.D. dissertation, Binghamton Univ., Binghamton, N.Y.

2002 Chemical Analysis of Early Woodland Period Smoking Pipe Residue. *Journal of Archaeological Science* 29(8):897–907.

Renfrew, Colin

1973 Monuments, Mobilization, and Social Organization in Neolithic Wessex. In *The Explanation of Culture Change,* edited by A. C. Renfrew. Duckworth, London.

1994 The Archaeology of Religion. In *The Ancient Mind,* edited by Colin Renfrew and Ezra B. W. Zubrow, 47–54. Cambridge Univ. Press, Cambridge.

Ritchie, William

1980 *The Archaeology of New York State.* Harbor Hill Books, Harrison, N.Y.

Ritchie, William, and Don Dragoo

1960 *The Eastern Dispersal of Adena.* New York State Museum and Science Service. Bulletin no. 379.

Rutsch, Edward

1973 *Smoking Technology of the Aborigines of the Iroquois Area of New York State.* Fairleigh Dickinson Univ. Press, Rutherford, N.J.

Salkin, Phillip H.

1986 The Lake Farms Phase: The Early Woodland Stage in South-Central Wisconsin as Seen from the Lake Farms Archaeological District. In *Early Woodland Archaeology,* edited by Kenneth B. Farnsworth and Thomas E. Emerson, 92–120. Center for American Archaeology, Kampsville Seminars in Archaeology No. 2, Kampsville, Illinois.

Sassaman, Kenneth

1993 *Early Pottery in the Southeast: Tradition and Innovation in Cooking Technology.* Univ. of Alabama Press, Tuscaloosa.

Shane, Orin C., III

1975 The Leimbach Site: An Early Woodland Village in Lorain County, Ohio. In *Studies in Ohio Valley Archaeology,* edited by Olaf H. Prufer and Douglas H. McKenzie, 98–120. Kent State Univ. Press, Kent, Ohio.

Shane, Orin C., III, and James L. Murphy

1975 A Survey of the Hocking Valley, Ohio. In *Studies in Ohio Valley Archaeology,* edited by Olaf H. Prufer and Douglas H. McKenzie, 229–256. Kent State Univ. Press, Kent, Ohio.

Sherratt, Andrew

1991 Sacred and Profane Substances: The Ritual Use of Narcotics in Later Neolithic Europe. In *Sacred and Profane: Proceedings of a Conference on Archaeology, Ritual, and Religion, Oxford, 1989,* edited by Paul Garwood, David Jennings, Robin Skeates, and Judith Toms, 50–64. Oxford Univ. Committee for Archaeology.

Smith, Ira F., III

1978 Early Smoking Pipes in the Susquehanna River Valley. *Pennsylvania Archaeologist* 49(4):9–23.

Snow, Dean

1980 *The Archaeology of New England.* Academic Press, New York.

Spence, Michael W., and William A. Fox

1986 The Early Woodland Occupations of Southern Ontario. In *Early Woodland Archaeology,* edited by Kenneth B. Farnsworth and Thomas E. Emerson, 4–46.

Center for American Archaeology, Kampsville Seminars in Archaeology No. 2, Kampsville, Illinois.

Stafford, B. D., and M. B. Sant (editors)
1985 *Smiling Dan: Structure and Function at a Middle Woodland Settlement in the Illinois Valley.* Center for American Archaeology, Kampsville, Illinois.

Steinmetz, Paul B.
1984 The Sacred Pipe in American Indian Religions. *American Indian Culture and Research Journal* 8(3):27–80.

Stephens, B. W.
1957 Tube Pipes. *Central States Archaeological Journal* 4:30–33.

Stewart, R. Michael
1989 Trade and Exchange in Mid-Atlantic Prehistory. *Archaeology of Eastern North America* 17:47–78.

Theler, James L.
1986 The Early Woodland Component at the Mill Pond Site, Wisconsin. In *Early Woodland Archaeology,* edited by Kenneth B. Farnsworth and Thomas E. Emerson, 137–158. Center for American Archaeology, Kampsville Seminars in Archaeology No. 2, Kampsville, Illinois.

Thomas, Julian
1991 Reading the Body: Beaker Funerary Practices. In *Sacred and Profane: Proceedings of a Conference on Archaeology, Ritual and Religion, Oxford, 1989,* edited by Paul Garwood, David Jennings, Robin Skeates, and Judith Toms, 33–42. Oxford Univ. Committee for Archaeology.

Thomas, Ronald A.
1971 Adena Influences in the Middle Atlantic Coast. In *Adena: The Seeking of an Identity,* edited by B. K. Swartz, 56–87. Ball State Univ.

Thwaites, Reuben Gold (editor)
1959 *The Jesuit Relations and Allied Documents: Travels and Explorations of the Jesuit Missionaries in New France, 1610–1791.* Pageant Book Co., New York.

Tiffany, Joseph A.
1986 The Early Woodland Period in Iowa. In *Early Woodland Archaeology,* edited by Kenneth B. Farnsworth and Thomas E. Emerson, 159–170. Center for American Archaeology, Kampsville Seminars in Archaeology No. 2, Kampsville, Illinois.

Townsend, Thomas, and Delf Narona
1962 Grave Creek Mound. *West Virginia Archaeologist* 14:10–18.

Trubowitz, Neal
1992 Thanks, but We Prefer to Smoke Our Own: Pipes in the Great Lakes–Riverine Region during the Eighteenth Century. In *Proceedings of the 1988 Smoking Pipe Conference,* edited by Charles F. Hays III, 97–111. Research Records No. 2, Rochester Museum and Science Center, Rochester, N.Y.

Versaggi, Nina
1999 Regional Diversity within the Early Woodland of the Northeast. *Northeast Anthropology* 57:45–56.

Versaggi, Nina, and Timothy D. Knapp
2000 Steatite, Interaction, and Persistence: The Transitional Period of New York's

Upper Susquehanna. Paper presented at the 65th Annual Meeting of the Society for American Archaeology, Philadelphia, April 7, 2000.

von Gernet, Alexander

1992 Hallucinogens and the Origins of the Iroquoian Pipe/Tobacco/Smoking Complex. In *Proceedings of the 1988 Smoking Pipe Conference,* edited by Charles F. Hays III, 171–185. Rochester Museum and Science Service, Rochester, N.Y.

1995 Nicotian Dreams: The Prehistory and Early History of Tobacco in Eastern North America. In *Consuming Habits: Drugs in History and Anthropology,* edited by Jordan Goodman, Paul E. Lovejoy, and Andrew Sherrat, 67–87. Routledge, London and New York.

von Gernet, Alexander, and Peter Timmons

1985 The Symbolic Significance of an Unusual Early Iroquoian Assemblage. Unpublished manuscript.

1987 Pipes and Parakeets: Constructing Meaning in an Early Iroquoian Context. In *Archaeology as Long Term History,* edited by Ian Hodder, 31–42. Cambridge Univ. Press, Cambridge.

Wagner, Gail

1998 Tobacco. In *Archaeology of Prehistoric North America: An Encyclopedia,* edited by G. Gibbon, 840–841. Garland Publishing, New York.

Walthall, John A.

1980 *Prehistoric Indians of the Southeast: Archaeology of Alabama and the Middle South.* Univ. of Alabama Press, Tuscaloosa.

Webb, William S., and Raymond S. Baby

1957 *The Adena People, No. 2.* Ohio State Univ. Press, Athens.

Webb, William S., and William Funkhouser

1940 Ricketts Site Revisited. Site 3, Montgomery County, Kentucky. *Reports in Archaeology and Anthropology* 3(6). Univ. of Kentucky, Lexington.

Webb, William S., and Charles E. Snow

1974 *The Adena People.* Univ. of Tennessee Press, Knoxville.

West, George A.

1970 *Tobacco, Pipes, and Smoking Customs of the American Indians.* Greenwood Press, Westport, Conn. Originally published 1934.

Winter, Joseph C.

1991 Prehistoric and Historic Native American Tobacco Use: An Overview. Paper Presented at the 1991 Society for American Archaeology Annual Meetings, New Orleans, Louisiana.

2001 Traditional Uses of Tobacco by Native Americans. In *Tobacco: Sacred Smoke or Silent Killer,* edited by Joseph C. Winder, 9–58. Univ. of Oklahoma Press, Norman.

Yarnell, Richard A.

1964 *Aboriginal Relationships between Culture and Plant Life in the Upper Great Lakes Region.* Univ. of Michigan, Ann Arbor.

2. Stone Pipes of the Southern Coastal Region of North Carolina: Smoke, Ritual, and Contact

Jeffrey D. Irwin

In the Late Woodland period in the southern coastal region of North Carolina, stone pipes appear in association with a regional burial mound complex. Their appearance marks the first substantial evidence of prehistoric smoking in the region; yet, as relatively rare artifacts, these pipes, as well as those from neighboring regions, have received minimal archaeological attention. Beyond emerging consensus that prehistoric smoking in eastern North Carolina was more sacred than secular, more ritual than habitual, we know little regarding smoking as it developed among prehistoric groups. For the poorly known southern coastal region this is especially true. To begin to elicit meaning from these important and exotic artifacts, I summarize the variability of stone pipes from the southern coastal region and subsequently place these pipes into a regional and a panregional perspective. This kind of multiscalar approach reveals significant connections between stone pipes and broader trends of ritual intensification and intersocietal contact in the Late Woodland.

Stone pipes are not common artifacts in eastern North Carolina, and if one begins to look into privately held collections it appears that many more pipes exist there than in professional publications or government or academic institutions. For this study, stone pipes (n = 34) from regional universities and a local museum were physically examined, and several attributes, including stem and bowl form, raw material, incised decorations, and some metric dimensions were recorded. Additional stone pipes (n = 16) and other similarly decorated artifacts—for example, stone pendants and pottery—from eastern North Carolina and other states were documented through literature research and contact with informants.

The extent of information available on the latter pipes and other artifacts varies, ranging from a simple drawing or photo to a basic description with no illustration—for example, specimens unearthed in the early twentieth century and described in brief reports on mound excavation. Beyond those discussed here, additional stone pipes have been documented in an ongoing attempt to record specimens from the southern coastal region and neighboring areas. These pipes will ultimately be addressed under separate cover in a descriptive inventory. The goal here is to evoke patterns and ideas relating stone pipes to prehistoric culture in a relatively poorly known region.

Mounds and Chronology

The story of stone pipes in the southern coastal region of North Carolina begins with low sand accretional burial mounds. Most of these sand mounds have been destroyed and are known only through an extremely partial record consisting of descriptions by amateurs, avocational archaeologists, and early professionals. Three mounds have been at least partially excavated and reported upon over the past four decades: McLean (Cumberland County), Red Springs or Buie (Robeson County), and McFayden (Brunswick County). The McLean mound, near Fayetteville, North Carolina, was perhaps the largest mound and certainly witnessed the most extensive excavation. Howard MacCord's work in the early 1960s produced the largest artifact assemblage, including the most pipes, and the first radiocarbon date from any of the mounds (MacCord 1966a).

Mounds are generally recorded only in the portion of the coastal plain south of the Neuse River—that is, the southern coastal region (Map 2.1).[1] These mounds are often referred to as low sand mounds, reflecting their small size and the sandy soils of the region. Mounds were typically no more than three feet in height and were circular or oval in shape, ranging from fifteen to sixty feet in diameter or length. Estimates of the original height of two mounds reach six and fifteen feet (MacCord 1966a; MacCauley 1929). Types of inhumations include bundle burials, tightly flexed burials, and cremations. Several instances of either mass secondary interments or heavily mixed burials are noted in excavation descriptions. Grave offerings were present in several mounds but varied in quantity, ranging from none in some smaller mounds to marine shell beads, stone pipes, bone ornaments, and other artifacts in a few of the larger mounds. Mounds are not generally associated with habitation sites and appear to have been used by fairly mobile groups over many years, if not generations.

Although more radiocarbon dates and more research in general are needed, the burial mound complex appears to be a Late Woodland phenomenon (Irwin et al. 1999). An absolute date range is difficult to assess given the paucity of dates from mounds and the scarce association of domestic debris, including potentially

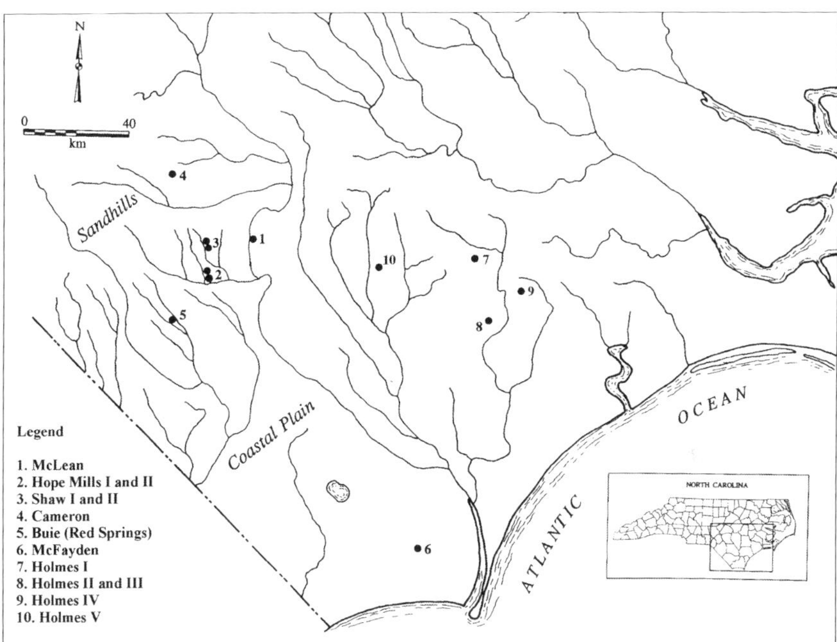

MAP 2.1. ▸ *Late Woodland burial mounds in the southern coastal region of North Carolina.*

diagnostic ceramics, with mound sites. McLean mound is, in fact, the only mound with radiocarbon dates. MacCord (1966a:17) secured a date of 970 ± 110 years B.P. (Cal A.D. 1028 with a 1 sigma range of A.D. 976–1212 [Eastman 1994:5; University of Michigan Laboratory M-1354]) on charcoal recovered adjacent to a bundle burial (SK78) located in the central (vertical) portion of the mound (twelve- to twenty-inch zone).[2] More recently, two dates have been attained from materials curated at the Research Laboratories of Archaeology at the University of North Carolina, Chapel Hill. A conventional radiocarbon date on charcoal adjacent to bundle burial SK205 in the upper portion of the mound (twenty inches to surface zone), produced a date of 760 ± 100 years BP (Cal A.D. 1270 with a 1-sigma range of 1190–1300 [Beta 145510]). The second recent date comes from soot removed from pottery. An AMS date on carbon from a sherd recovered in the lower portion of the mound produced a date of 1250 ± 40 years BP (Cal A.D. 770 with a 1-sigma range of 700–795 [Beta 143709]). Irwin et al. (1999) have argued previously that the ceramic assemblage from McLean is by and large homogenous enough to suggest most of the pottery is related to mound activity. The possibility that this sherd was incorporated as incidental fill seems to be enhanced by the slightly disparate date of A.D. 770. At the same time, the possibility that McLean was used for several centuries should not be easily dismissed. In her bioarchaeological analysis, Gold (1999) estimates that roughly contemporary accretional burial mounds in central Virginia were used for more than 350 years. Accepting the two dates in association with burials, the likely period of McLean's use may be considered as falling in the range of A.D. 900 to 1300 and, assuming ceramics are associated with mound use, perhaps as early as the eighth century A.D.

Other mounds in the southern coastal region have not been dated, though a general Late Woodland context seems likely (Irwin et al. 1999). Despite a history of smoking in the Eastern Woodlands extending back to the Late Archaic (Rafferty 1999), regional syntheses for eastern North Carolina do not mention pipes as elements of culture trait lists until the southeastern burial mound complex is described (Phelps 1983; Ward and Davis 1999). Indeed, the greatest frequency of stone pipes in eastern North Carolina appears to occur in the Late Woodland period, both in the southern coastal region and in neighboring areas—for example, the southern Piedmont and northern coastal plain (see below).

Southern Coastal Region Pipes

A total of thirty stone pipes from the southern coastal region were documented for this study (Table 2.1). Of these, twenty-five are from the interior coastal plain and twenty-seven are from burial mounds. Four of these burial mounds are in relative proximity in the interior coastal plain (Map 2.1). The McLean mound stands out with a *minimum* of nineteen stone pipes represented by complete specimens and numerous fragments. The Hope Mills mound, just ten miles south of McLean, produced at least two stone pipes. The most westerly mound, Cameron, roughly thirty miles west of McLean, produced three stone pipes. A fourth mound, known as the Buie or Red Springs mound, is located approximately twenty-five miles south of McLean, produced a single stone pipe bowl.

Elsewhere in the southern coastal region, at least two stone pipes were recovered from the McFayden burial mound near the coast, and a single stone pipe was collected from a probable burial context at Bogue Banks. A single pipe fragment was documented in the collections at the *Museum of the Cape Fear* in Fayetteville, North Carolina. Recently, a stone pipe was recovered near the coast in a nonmortuary context at the Long Point site (Shumate and Evans-Shumate 2000). Description of pipes from the southern coastal region begins with mound specimens and progresses to those from nonmound contexts.

Beyond implementation of the basic concept of a platform, there is considerable variation in pipe morphology. Five general forms are defined here for the McLean assemblage; the remains of several pipes are too fragmentary to assess overall shape. The first pipe form is represented by a single unique specimen, an impressive, large, *curved-base monitor* pipe (Figure 2.1). Heavily incised on the

TABLE 2.1 ▸ Southern Coastal Region Sites with Stone Pipes

Site	Number of Stone Pipes
31Bw67	2
31Cd3	3
31Cd7	19
31Cr29	1
31Htl	3
3IJn2	1
31Rb4	1
Unknown site, vie. Fayetteville	1

dorsal and ventral stem surfaces and bowl, this is one of a kind in the region (though similar ones have been documented elsewhere in the Eastern Woodlands [West 1934]). The second type is labeled *rounded stem* and is represented by three pipes with rounded stems and a large bowl set distally at a slightly obtuse or right angle. These pipes are similar to large elbow pipes and one has little more than a stub for a stem. A third type represents variations on the monitor form, with the bowls set distally, not centrally, and at a vertical or only slightly obtuse angle (Figure 2.2). On these pipes the stem expands gradually toward and may extend slightly beyond the bowl, and on each of these the stem is generally of uniform thickness—that is, lacking curvature or lateral thinning in cross section. These are referred to as *modified monitor,* as they resemble monitor pipes with one end of the stem removed or the bowl location shifted. At least five of these pipes are present in the McLean assemblage. Several pipes appear as amalgams combining elements of platform and tubular pipes. MacCord (1966a) referred to these as *bent-tube* pipes. Instead of appearing to be mounted on a platform, the bowl appears as more of a continuation of the stem. Four bent-tube pipes have distinct, weak shoulders at the bowl/stem juncture and a slightly biconvex or diamond-shaped stem (cross-section) and are referred to here as *weak-shouldered, bent-tube.* Two pipes are characterized as *alate bent-tube.* One of these is an especially large and elaborately decorated specimen (Figure 2.3). The latter bent-tube pipes are characterized by carefully thinned wings that expand in width towards the bowl.

Stone pipes from the Cameron and Hope Mills mounds were either never curated by a known institution or have been lost since their recovery. Limited descriptive terminology was used by MacCauley (1929) and Peabody (1910) however. MacCauley lists the stone pipes from Cameron as a "large platform pipe of steatite," a small "trumpet shaped pipe," and fragments of a platform pipe. From Hope Mills Mound I, Peabody recovered part of a "monitor pipe of the platform

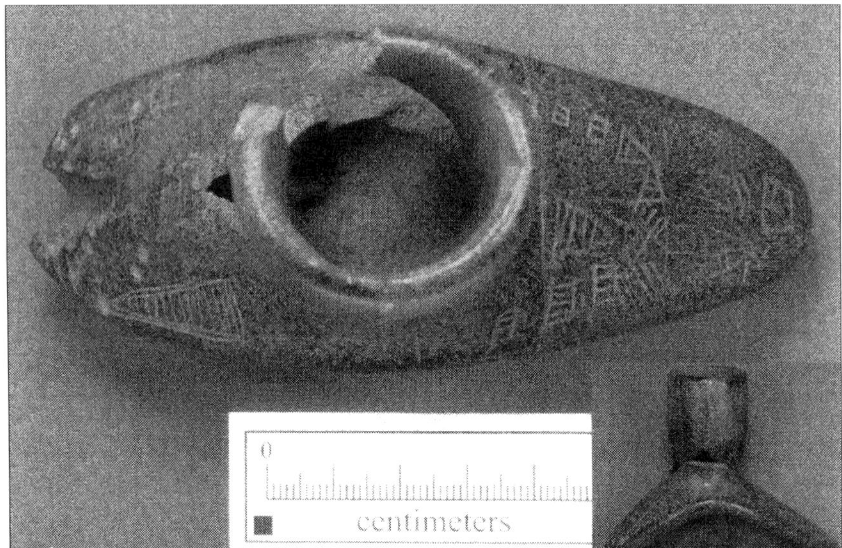

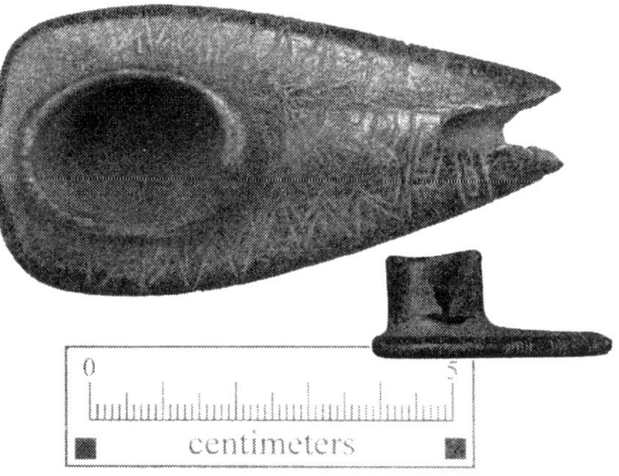

FIG. 2.1. ▸ *(Above) Curved-base monitor pipe (2102a129), McLean mound (31Cd7). Courtesy of the Research Laboratories of Archaeology, University of North Carolina, Chapel Hill.*

FIG. 2.2. ▸ *(Right) Modified monitor pipe (2102a63), McLean mound (31Cd7). Courtesy of the Research Laboratories of Archaeology, University of North Carolina, Chapel Hill.*

variety" and an "elongated monitor pipe." The latter site also produced a pipe fragment (raw material unspecified) and a biconical pipe of clay, which was incised with "a V-shaped motive design" (Peabody 1910:432). Given use of the terms *monitor* and *platform,* it is considered likely that there was some overlap if not great similarity between these pipes and those found in nearby McLean.

Of the two stone pipes from the McFayden mound, only one is available for inspection. This one is represented by a large biconvex stem section with an unusual pronounced lip around the bit (South 1962:20, Figure 5). The other pipe was recovered by an amateur and was shown to South. South describes it as "a

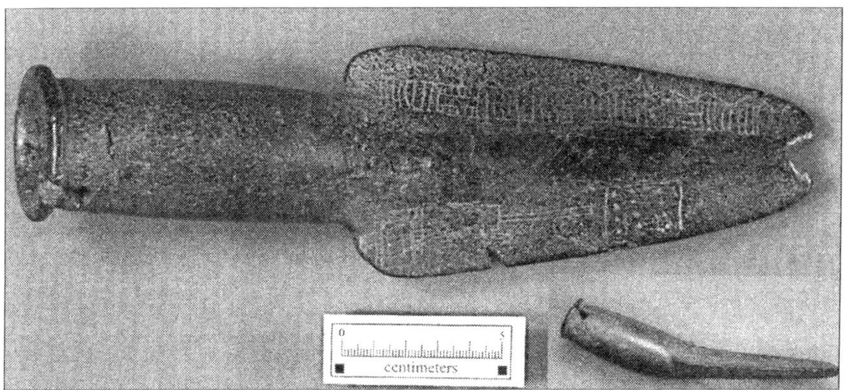

FIG. 2.3. ▸ *A late bent-tube pipe (2102a130), McLean mound (31Cd7). Courtesy of the Research Laboratories of Archaeology, University of North Carolina at Chapel Hill.*

complete pipe with a broken bowl . . . engraved with a series of squares and rectangles" and goes on to compare it in form and incising to an alate, obtuse angle pipe from the Lowder's Ferry site in Stanly County (South 1962:18, 20, see pipe in Figure 11).

The last pipe documented from a probable mortuary context is a single monitor stone pipe, recovered from a site located along the coast at Bogue Banks. Little is known about this site, as no professional excavations were conducted before its destruction in the late 1960s. A drawing of the pipe survives, however, and reveals it to be a monitor pipe with the stem extending at least partially beyond the bowl.

Pipes from nonmound sites in the southern coastal region include a flat-based monitor pipe from the Long Point site (31JN2). This pipe, recovered from a refuse pit dated to 1200 ± 50 B.P. (Cal A.D. 840 with a 1 sigma range A.D. 770–890), is made from marble and has unique, serrated margins (Shumate and Evans-Shumate 2000:5.59–64). Finally, a stone pipe stem was found by a local collector near the Cape Fear River in the general vicinity of Fayetteville. The proximal half of this stem is all that is present. It is biconvex in cross-section and expands in width toward the distal portion.

The majority of stone pipes from the southern coastal region are made from chlorite schist, which ranges in color from greenish gray to nearly black. The latter darker coloration may be attributed to a patina developing over time. At least one pipe is a brown schist material, and several are a typical gray steatite. Clay pipes constitute a minority at the above sites; a total of four clay pipes is represented across three mounds, McLean, Hope Mills I, and Buie. Many of the stone pipes may have had a bone stem inserted into the bit. There are two examples of

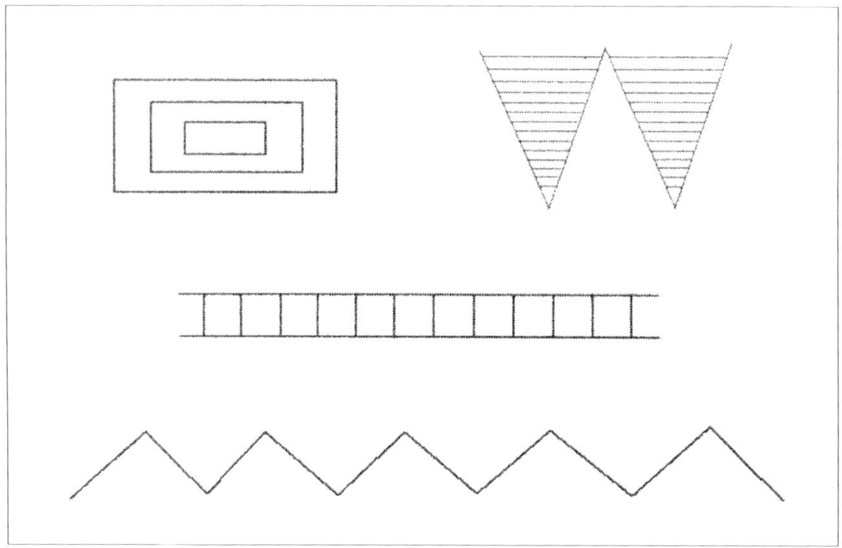

FIG. 2.4. ▸ *Incised designs from stone pipes in eastern North Carolina.*

bone stem fragments still lodged in the bit in Late Woodland stone pipes, one from North Carolina (Coe 1949) and one from Virginia (Pearce and Painter 1968).

While some degree of categorization is possible, particularly for the McLean mound pipes as indicated above, it is important to emphasize the inherent variability exhibited by stone pipes. Indeed, of the pipes from McLean alone, no two exhibit identical stems or bowls. Subtle to stark contrasts in bowl and lip forms exist as do disparities in stem thickness and shape, bit shape, and overall pipe size. Certainly common forms seem to have been recognized—for example, the tubular bowl and the monitor shape (albeit modified stem). Indeed, certain forms may have been imitated in manufacture. Yet overall, pipes were highly individualized objects.

Contributing to the uniqueness of pipes is decoration. At least twelve of the thirty pipes from the southern coastal region have some degree of incising on them.[3] Incising is generally somewhat rough and is not performed with a great degree of precision or refinement. The designs are simple geometric compositions, ranging from a few subtle parallel lines on a single pipe to extensive incising, nearly covering the stem and/or bowl. Four of the more common designs—that is, those found on more than one pipe and across multiple sites in and beyond the southern coastal region—include simple and concentric rectangles, ladders, barred triangles, and zigzags (Figure 2.4).[4] Again, no two pipes are alike in decoration. Though there are shared designs, the collection of symbols employed is unique to each pipe, adding another idiosyncratic dimension to these objects. Some pipes show evidence of incomplete designs that were not finished before the pipe was interred, suggesting the decorative process was a gradual one, with designs accruing over the use life of a pipe. Importantly, along this same line of thought, there is a significant discrepancy between the quality of craftsmanship in pipe manufacture and decorative incising. The careful polish, thin walls, and symmetry of these pipes reflect the energy-intensive work of an artisan. The rather crude, often irregular incising suggests the work of someone less skilled (Coe 1955:308), likely the pipe's owner.

Pipes, Smoking, and Ritual

The range of contexts in which tobacco was used historically, the roles tobacco played, and the symbolic power held is impressively diverse in historic accounts cast broadly over a few centuries and much of North America. Tobacco was offered to the spirits of game animals, to sacred stones, and to the forces of weather (Hariot 1946; West 1934). Tobacco served as a ritual fumigant for the dead and as an ingredient in Black Drink (Springer 1981). Perhaps most famously, tobacco acted through the Calumet ceremony as "the God of peace and war, the Arbiter of life and death" (Springer 1981:222). In short, tobacco and associated rituals were loaded with symbolic power (Hall 1983, 1987). Indeed, either as leaf or in smoke, tobacco constituted a primary element of ritual discourse in numerous ceremonies, facilitating communication with spirits as well as with allies and strangers. As Thomas Hariot remarked about coastal Carolina groups in the late sixteenth century, "This [tobacco] is so highly valued by them that they think their gods are delighted with it" (Hariot 1946:246).

Judging the likely context of pipe use and tobacco smoking among Late Woodland groups of the North Carolina southern coastal region to be ritual is relatively conservative. Several researchers in eastern North Carolina have concluded that indigenous smoking practices were more ritualized in late prehistory and more secular in the historic period (Coe 1995; Magoon 1999; Ward and Davis 1993). Isolating a more particular ritual context or function for the prehistoric pipes under consideration is a more venturous task, invoking ceremony and ideology and the more nebulous quarter of archaeological inquiry. We are not without some contextual clues, however. In particular, we may consider the general cultural context in which pipes appear and attempt to relate ritual smoking to broader trends. Additionally, the pipes themselves hold potential stylistic clues related to their use. If we want to understand how pipes were used, we must focus not on their status as artifacts interred with the dead, but on the life these objects held in a cultural setting over an extended use life.

The Late Woodland cultural context in which these pipes occur in the southern coastal region is characterized by the emergence of a burial mound complex, the delineation of broadly defined social territories, and the initiation of interregional exchange. These are undoubtedly interrelated trends. The establishment of communal burial mounds distinct from habitation sites reflects an intensification of mortuary ritual and the construction of a ritual landscape. Such a change in mortuary ritual most certainly reflects a dynamic social environment and possibly a changing subsistence economy. The closest analog may be in a contemporary, similar burial mound complex in central Virginia (Dunham 1994; Gold 1999; MacCord 1986). Dunham argues that the development of collective, accretional bone beds in Virginia marks an adaptive social response by incipient agricultural societies to a dynamic environment involving demographic pressure, adoption of agriculture, and increasing sedentism. The emphasis on corporate identity reflected in communal mounds is part of an attempt to mediate increasing social differentiation and inequality.

In the North Carolina southern coastal region, the emergence of collective mortuary facilities is undoubtedly a cultural response to a dynamic environment as well. Unfortunately, limited archaeological study of the region precludes reliable statements regarding subsistence or demography, factors that may have contributed to culture change and a cumulative effect on social tensions. While domesticated plants clearly become part of subsistence economies in eastern North Carolina during the Late Woodland, there is no direct correlation of mounds with agricultural villages. Indeed, in the Sandhills at least, late Middle and Late Woodland period sites exhibit a relatively high degree of residential mobility exercised by a small, dispersed population (Culpepper et al. 2000:24–37). Domesticated plant cultivation and population growth may have exerted new stress on the regional population; however, more data simply must be obtained on this issue. It seems quite clear that the mound complex that emerged in the Late Woodland was created by a small, mobile population that still maintained a fairly substantial hunting and gathering subsistence regime.

While further contextualization of demography and subsistence must await gradual accrual of data, one factor likely contributing to ritualization and emphasis on collective identities is the emergence of sociopolitical boundaries and interregional contact apparent in the Late Woodland. The intensification of mortuary ritual and the establishment of a ritual landscape occurs during a time of regionalization when historically known Algonquian, Iroquoian, and Siouan language groups are first detectable archaeologically (Phelps 1983; Ward and Davis 1999: 210–211), and when the only Mississippian chiefdom in eastern North Carolina emerges just west of the interior southern coastal plain (Coe 1995; Oliver 1992). Based on archaeological evidence and ethnohistoric records, a highly generalized social mosaic can be constructed for eastern North Carolina, circa A.D. 800–1400

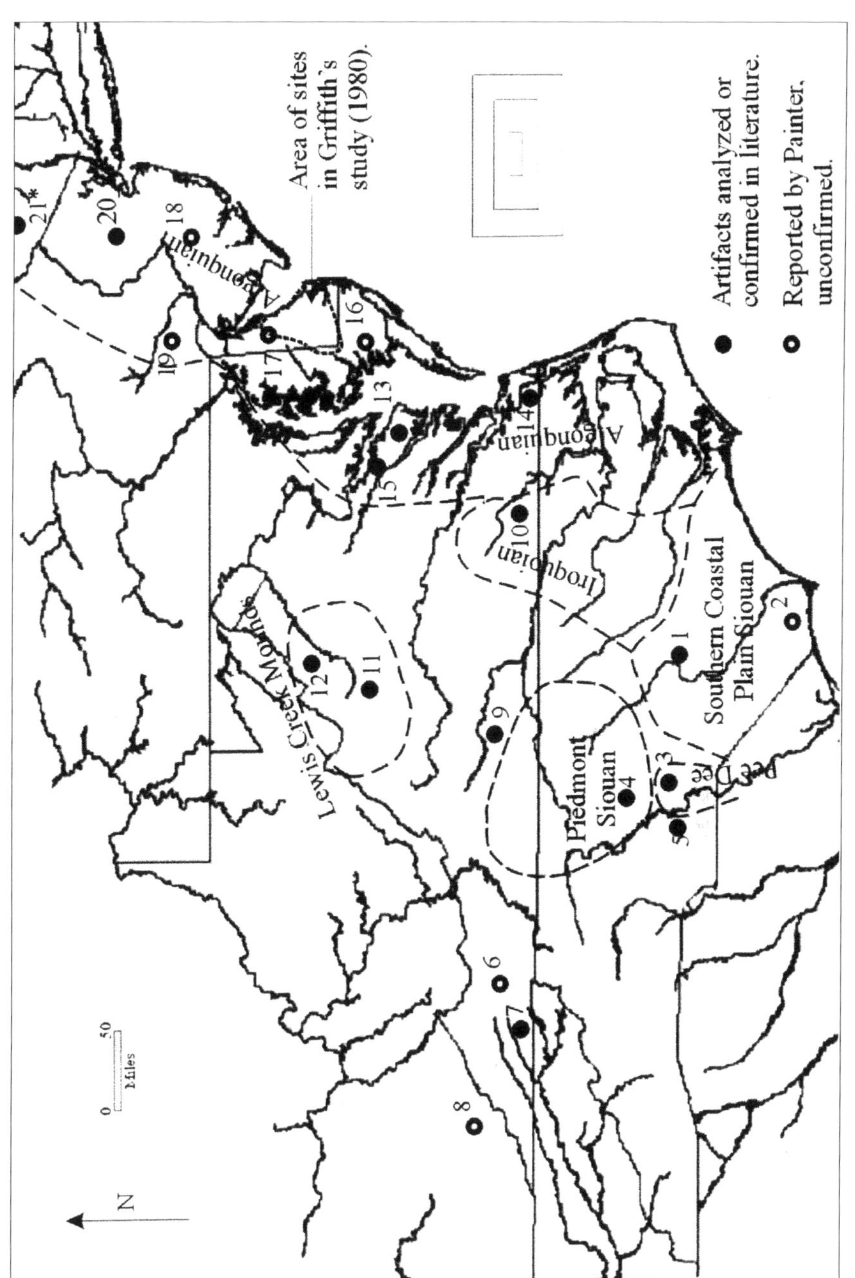

Map 2.2. ▸ *Distribution of concentric rectangle designs across social and linguistic regions.*

(Map 2.2). In the northern North Carolina Piedmont, extending into southwest Virginia, Siouan speaking groups of the Dan River focus are well known archaeologically and have been traced through the historic period (Ward and Davis 1993; Eastman 1999). In the southern North Carolina Piedmont, to the immediate west of the Sandhills, the Mississippian polity centered at Town Creek flourished during this time period (Oliver 1992). Meanwhile, in the southern coastal region, the scant evidence that exists suggests biological or linguistic affinities with Siouan groups (Coe et al. 1982; Swanton 1946). Furthermore, Late Woodland ceramic traditions and mortuary patterns of the southern coastal plain distinguish this area from contemporary traditions to the north and west.

In the same temporal frame that we see the formation of regional social boundaries, we see evidence of interaction across them. There is diffusion of ideas in ceramic technology and apparent trade involving pottery, particularly between Mississippian groups of the southern piedmont and Siouan groups of the northern Piedmont (Eastman 1999). In the northern coastal plain, Phelps (1982) suggests trade was extensive between Iroquoian and Algonquian groups and is evident in the common occurrence of Iroquoian ceramics on Algonquian sites. In terms of trade in ceramics and the diffusion of ceramic style or technology, the southern coastal region may be relatively isolated compared to these neighboring areas. Intensive surveying in the Sandhills has revealed virtually no evidence, for example, of trade or diffusion of Pee Dee complicated stamped ceramics eastward (Benson 1998; Clement et al. 1997; Idol and Becker 2001).

However, interregional exchange in exotic goods became pronounced during the Late Woodland period as well, and in this kind of interaction groups in the southern coastal region were active. Marine shell beads appear with some frequency in Late Woodland graves across the coastal plain and Piedmont of North Carolina (Mathis 1993; Phelps 1983; Ward and Davis 1999). Likewise, shell beads, primarily marginella, were relatively common in sand mounds, and other exotic grave goods from mounds include conch shells, a shell gorget, pottery, mica, copper, and stone pipes (Irwin et al. 1999; MacCord 1966a). In fact, stone pipes, or at least the material from which they were made, likely originated in the Piedmont or mountains (Eliot 1986) and had to be imported into the coastal plain. Trade of stone pipes over hundreds of miles should not be an unexpected pattern given the known distribution of traded catlinite pipes (Brown 1989) and the distance (three hundred to four hundred miles) covered by stone pipes acquired historically by the Narragansett (Williams 1973:45[1643]).

Tying the development of ritual smoking into this sweeping cultural context is a difficult task. Rafferty (1999) argues that in Early Woodland cultures pipes were integral elements in funerary ritual. The obvious association of pipes with mounds in the southern coastal region may relate smoking ceremony directly to mourning ritual and collective social incorporation into an ancestral bone bed. However, the terminal cultural position of pipes does not reflect the complexity of their actual roles outside of mortuary settings. Indeed, the fact that these pipes occur in a dynamic social climate of social boundary formation and interregional contact gives cause to consider a different role and context for Late Woodland smoking.

Pipes and Interaction

Evidence for a relationship between stone pipes and intersocietal contact can be seen in stylistic variation of pipes. Commonalties observed in pipe decoration over a broad geographic area, from New York to southeastern North Carolina, suggest some level of information exchange involving pipes and smoking. The distribution of some of the incised designs on pipes, most notably the concentric rectangle, reveals a theme connecting, in albeit an elusive manner, distant and diverse Late Woodland societies. In light of this, pipes may not have been simply traded goods nor the act of smoking exclusive to funerary events. Instead pipes and smoking may have been important ritual elements used to facilitate intersocietal interaction and/or to convey recognition of something ideological.

Addressing stylistic variation among pipes is a considerable challenge due to the significant variability exhibited by pipes and the small sample size available. Unlike Hopewell platform pipes (Seeman 1977), pipes from the southern coastal region and the broader geographic area in question are highly individualized objects. Morphologically, Late Woodland stone pipes from Mid-Atlantic states often exhibit a basic obtuse-angle or bent-tube platform shape. Alate or winged stems are somewhat common as well. However, the uniqueness of individual specimens eludes definition of a particular morphological style that may be linked to social behavior (see Carr 1995:165; Roe 1995:31). This is particularly true with respect to isochrestic variation (Sackett 1985, 1986). The unique form of individual pipes suggests skilled artisans made them infrequently, with common technological constraints, performance concerns, and perhaps some common preference for general form. Yet there appears to be little in the way of rote behavior that might be linked to patterns of social interaction.

A more symbolic or iconographic concept of style may be evoked, however, when we consider incising on pipes from the southern coastal region and place these designs into a panregional perspective. Pipes were likely traded into the southern coastal region from the west, however, as argued above, the incising on pipes appears to be a local embellishment. Accordingly, the systemic processes behind variation in pipe form and variation in pipe decoration are quite distinct, and the theoretical argument relating style to intended audience becomes key (Weissner 1983, 1985; Wobst 1977). Assuming these pipes were only used in a highly specialized context of ritual smoking, the visibility of incised designs would have been restricted. The absence of incising on pottery from the southern coastal region supports the interpretation of pipe designs as uncommon nonsecular symbols. If pipes were used in funerary ceremony, then the intended audience for these designs may have included local community members. However, there is a clear Mid-Atlantic or circum-Chesapeake Bay distribution to some of the incised designs that suggests a less provincial perspective.

The most conspicuous design suggestive of a Mid-Atlantic pattern is the concentric rectangle (also called nested squares).[5] Floyd Painter, an avocational archaeologist from Virginia, recognized this pattern decades ago (1971a, 1974).[6] In the southern coastal region, this particular design is seen on McLean mound pipes, where it is represented ten times on four pipes. Simple rectangles are more common, represented twenty-four times on six pipes. The concentric rectangle is anything but a local phenomenon however. In North Carolina, it is also seen on pipes from several sites in the southern Piedmont, including the Mississippian mound site Town Creek,[7] and the Siouan Keyauwee[8] and Lowder's Ferry[9] sites (Figure 2.5). Not only do the latter three pipes share concentric rectangles, but the alate pipe form is common as well. Though the pipe-bearing burials from these three sites have not produced radiocarbon dates, each site has a substantial Late Woodland or Mississippian component.

To the north, concentric rectangles are seen on pipes and other artifacts from several sites in Virginia and neighboring states (Table 2.2). An unusual stone alate pipe from an unknown cave site in southwest Virginia bears the concentric rectangle on the distal end of the stem's wing (West 1934), precisely like pipes from McLean, Town Creek, Keyauwee, and Lowder's Ferry. A stone pipe from the Late Woodland Leesville mound in south-central Virginia shows the

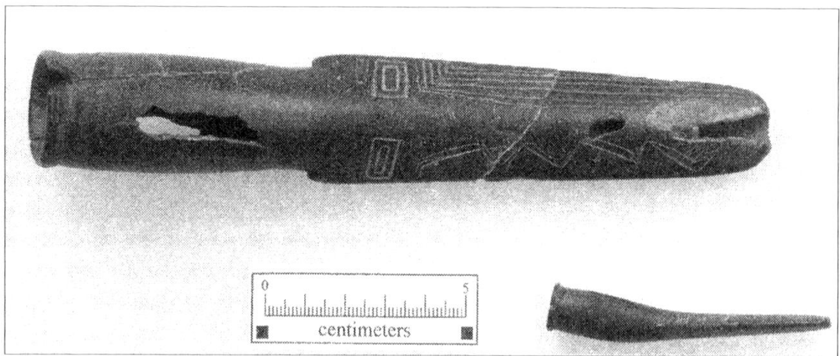

FIG. 2.5. ▸ *Alate Pipe (2101a259), Lowder's Ferry site (31St7). Courtesy of the Research Laboratories of Archaeology, University of North Carolina, Chapel Hill.*

Table 2.2 ▸ Sites with Concentric Triangle Design Occurrences

No.	Site Name	Artifact	Designs	Reference
1	McLean	Alate, modified monitor, curved-base monitor, bent-tube unidentified stone pipes	Concentric and Simple Rect.	MacCord 1966
2	McFayden	Alate stone pipe	"series of squares and rectangles"*	South 1962:22
3	Town Creek	Alate stone pipe	Concentric Reel.	Coe 1995
4	Keyauwee	Alate stone pipe	Concentric Reel.	Coo 1937; Ward and Davis 1999
5	Lowder's Ferry	Alate stone pipe	Concentric Reel.	Coe 1949; Ward and Davis 1999
6	Unnamed cave site	"Stone pipes"	Rectangles	Painter 1974
7	Unnamed cave site	Alate stone pipe	Concentric Rect.	West 1934
8	Unnamed cave site	"Stone platform pipe"	Rectangles	Painter 1974
9	Leesvillle Mound	Stone Alate pipe	Concentric Rect.	Davenport and Judge 1952
10	Hand site Stone	Alate pipe Infilled	Concentric Rect.	Smyth
11	Lewis Creek mound	Clay bent-tube pipes (2)	Rectangles	MacCord 1986
12	Senedo mound	"Soapstone monitor pipe", stone sisc	Concentric Rect.	McCary 1952, 1954; MacCord 1986
13	Lancaster County	Stone Alate pipe	Concentric Rect.	Barka 1968, Painter 1967, 1971a; Pearce 1968
14	Great Neck/Long Creek midden	Stone bent-tube pipe, clay pipe, stone pendant, pottery	Concentric Rect.	Pearce and Painter 1968
15	White Oak Point	Pottery	Concentric Rect.	Waselkov 1982
16	Unknown	Stone pipe	Concentric Rect.	Painter 1974
17	Unknown	Stone platform pipe	Concentric Rect.	Painter 1974
18	Unknown	Pottery	Concentric Reel.	Painter 1974
19	Overpeck site	Obtuse angle, clay pipe	Concentric Rect.	Painter 1974
20	Rowan site	Miniature human effigy stone pendant	Concentric Rect.	Bello and Kraft 1999
21	Unknown	Alate stone pipe	Concentric Rect.	West 1934:582, Plate 51

TABLE 2.3 ▸ SITES WITH BARRED TRIANGLE DESIGN OCCURRENCES

No.	Site Name	Artifact	Designs	Reference
1	McLean mound	Modified monitor, Alate, curved-base monitor, weak-shoulder bent-tube	Infilled triangle	MacCord 1966
2	McFayden mound	Unknown platform	Infilled triangle	South 1962:22
3	Kerney	Bent-tube	Infilled triangle	Phelps, personal communication 2001
4	Keyauwee	Alate	Infilled triangle	Coe 1937; Ward and Davis 1999
5	Town Creek	Modified monitor	Infilled triangle	Coe 1995
6	Gaston	Alate	Infilled triangle	Coe 1964
7	Hand	Alate	Infilled triangle	Smyth
8	Great Neck/Long Creek midden	Pottery	Infilled triangle	Painter 1967
9	Patawomeke	Clay Alate	Infilled triangle	Stewart 1992

same symbol in the same position, again on an alate pipe. In central Virginia at the Late Woodland Senedo Mound, the concentric rectangle is seen on a stone disc and a steatite monitor (alate?) pipe, the latter in an anthropomorphic figure.[10] The concentric rectangle is known from southeastern Virginia as well. A pipe from the Late Woodland Long Creek midden bears the symbol, and an alate pipe from the Late Woodland/Historic Hand site bears multiple concentric rectangles.[11] The northernmost example documented here is a bent-tube stone pipe from an unknown site in Oswego County, New York. This pipe bears the

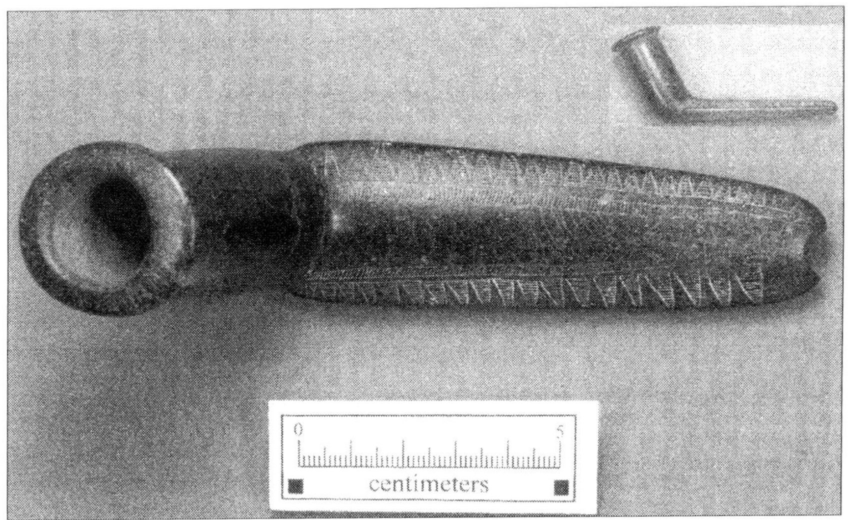

FIG. 2.6. ▸ *Bent-tube pipe (1539–158), Kerney site (31Gr84). Courtesy of East Carolina University.*

concentric rectangle again on the distal end, dorsal stem (West 1934). The concentric rectangle design is also found as an incised decoration on pottery, in particular on Late Woodland Townsend Ware in Virginia and Delaware (Griffith 1977; Painter 1967; Waselkov 1982).

A miniature stone effigy pendant from New Jersey provides a relatively unique but significant expression of the concentric rectangle (Bello and Veit 1999). Although they are rare artifacts, several miniature human effigies have been found in eastern and central Virginia (MacCord 1966b). One such miniature effigy was found in North Carolina at Town Creek in direct association with a stone pipe bearing the concentric rectangle. The latter pipe, mentioned above, was found in a single primary interment along with the effigy and a small stone smoking tube incised with rectangles incised around the rim (Coe 1995).

Another design that is relatively common in the southern coastal region and beyond is the barred triangle (Table 2.3). While less widespread than the concentric rectangle, the barred triangle does appear in several areas in North Carolina (Map 2.3). In the southern coastal region, this design occurs seven times on four pipes from the McLean mound and is prominent on a pipe from the McFayden mound. Elsewhere in the coastal plain this design is seen on a heavily decorated pipe from the Kerney site in Greene County. An obtuse angle tubular platform pipe, another kind of hybrid between a tube and platform, was

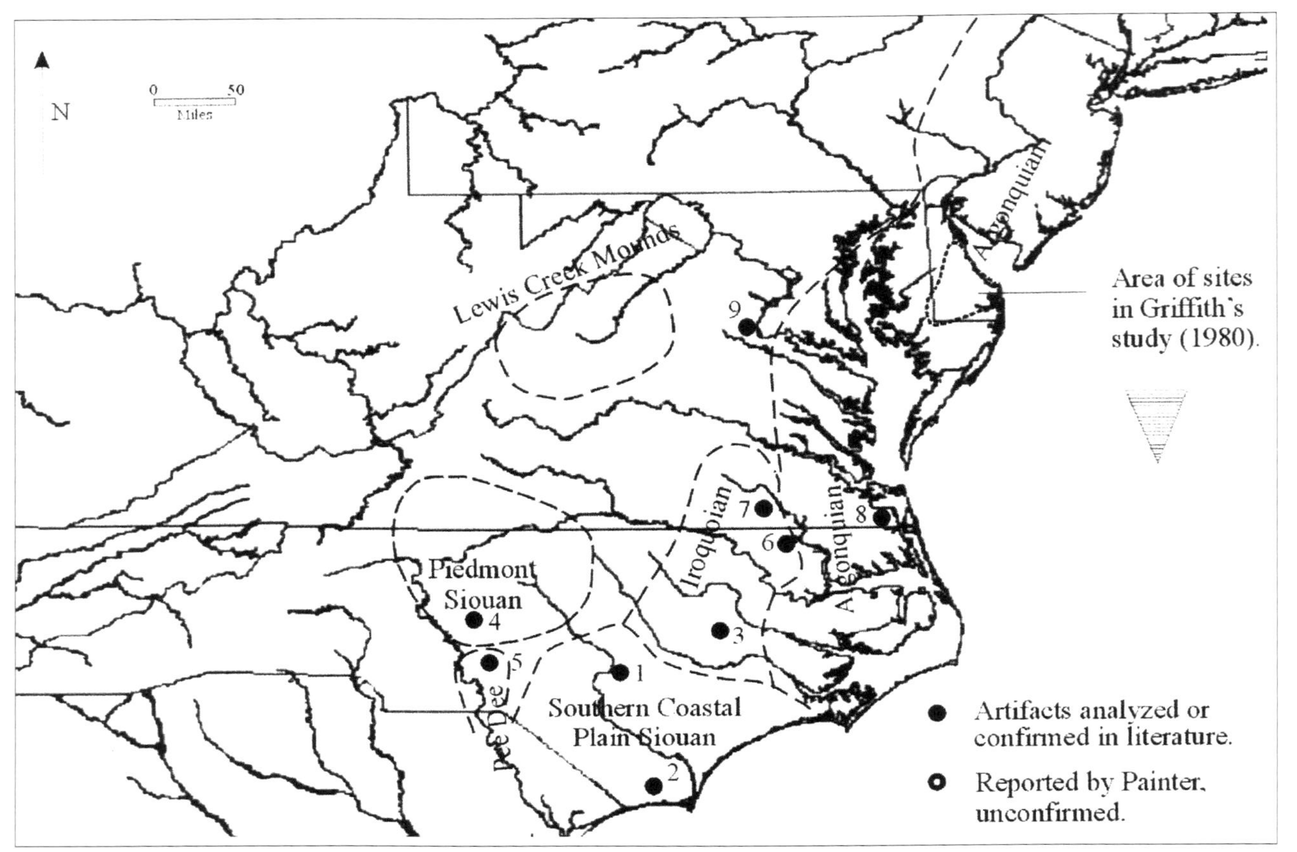

MAP 2.3. ▸ *Distribution of barred triangle designs across social and linguistic regions.*

recovered from a single inhumation at the Kerney site, another site with a strong Late Woodland component (David Phelps, personal communication 2001). The stem on this pipe lacks the distal expansion or marginal thinning characteristic of alate pipes. This is one of the most heavily incised specimens from the coastal region, with embellishments of rather crude quality on the ventral and dorsal stem surfaces and on the bowl (Figure 2.6). The barred triangle is known from the southern Piedmont as well, occurring on two stone pipes: one from the Lowder's Ferry site and one from Town Creek, where it is incorporated into a zoomorphic figure.[12] To the north, this design is elaborately expressed on a stone pipe from the Gaston site, a site with a substantial Late Woodland component as well. Though descriptions or frequencies are hard to come by, the barred triangle is apparently seen on Algonquian pottery from the coastal plain of Virginia and North Carolina and is likely a variant of the colloquial "hanging triangle." This design has apparently been found on Late Woodland Dan River ceramics from the northern piedmont of North Carolina as well (Ward and Davis 1999:108).

The widespread distribution of incised designs leads to an expansion of the relevant social mosaic created earlier for eastern North Carolina (Map 2.2, 2.3). To encompass the broad distribution of concentric rectangles in the Late Woodland period we can define a coastal and circum-Chesapeake Bay Algonquian culture area extending from North Carolina to New Jersey (Custer 1987; Snow 1978). In the interior of central Virginia, historically populated by Siouan speaking groups, we can draw an approximate line around the Lewis Creek burial mound complex mentioned earlier (MacCord 1986; Dunham 1994). Further north, in the vicinity of the Potomac River and south of the Susquehanna River, Custer (1987) suggests an Eastern Iroquoian/Siouan linguistic area. Even further north, extending from the Susquehanna River into New York, Iroquoian speakers dominate the landscape in the Late Woodland.

The distribution of the concentric rectangle encompasses at least portions of all of these broadly defined culture areas. With McLean mound and Town Creek as the southern terminus, concentric rectangles extend northward through the eastern Woodlands to New York (Map 2.2). Barred triangles show a more limited southerly and easterly distribution (Map 2.3). Both symbols effectively connect the mounds of the southern coastal region to distant and diverse cultures spread over a vast area. In the case of McLean mound, the connection is more than subtle. Indeed, in his consideration of this same panregional pattern, Painter (1974) declared the heavily decorated, alate pipe in Figure 2.3 to be a Rosetta stone of sorts, integrally linked to what he conceived of as a "Chesapeake Cult." Rosetta stones and cults aside, the use of symbols across multiple social and linguistic boundaries, by groups hundreds of miles distant, suggests that these designs were in fact recognized cross-culturally. The specific nature of how these symbols were shared and how they became so widely distributed is difficult to model, though their general origin may be discernible and some scenarios relating pipe decoration to broad-scale interaction and ritual smoking proposed.

Algonquian Connection

Most of the more prominent designs on stone pipes, including concentric and simple rectangles, barred triangles, zigzags, and ladders, appear to have some relationship to Algonquian cultures in the Mid-Atlantic region. Incising as a decorative treatment is a distinct characteristic of Late Woodland Townsend Ware pottery found from southern New Jersey to the coastal region of North Carolina (Egloff 1985; Griffith 1977; Phelps 1983; Potter 1993; Turner 1992). The coastal, circum-Chesapeake distribution of Townsend Ware, as well as its precursor Mockley Ware, corresponds with the historic coastal distribution of Algonquian-speaking groups (Custer 1987; Snow 1978). The discernible coastal pattern of similar ceramic traditions is likely the product of diffusion through interaction among Algonquian groups along the Atlantic coastal plain. Snow (1978) suggests this broadly defined Algonquian culture was facilitated by trade and intermarriage between Algonquian societies and reinforced by contrasts with piedmont Siouan and Iroquoian groups. Custer attributes the coastal spread of Mockley Ware to "open and fluid exchange networks throughout the Delmarva Peninsula" (1985:147).

The designs noted above from stone pipes definitely occur on Townsend Ware pottery from Delaware (Griffith 1977) and eastern Virginia (Painter 1967; Waselkov 1982). However, while incising as a decorative treatment appears to have spread south along the coast into North Carolina, manifest as a minority surface treatment in Colington Series pottery (Phelps 1983), it is generally not found on pottery in the southern coastal region of North Carolina. Indeed, outside of the Chesapeake Bay region, the designs occur largely on pipes or other stone artifacts divorced from a ceramic incising tradition such as Townsend. Given the temporal depth and strong cultural tradition of incising geometric designs in Algonquian culture, it seems logical to associate an origin for designs such as the concentric rectangle with coastal Algonquian societies somewhere in the circum-Chesapeake area. An important temporal linkage in this regard is apparent with respect to the North Carolina southern coastal region. Complex geometric designs on Townsend Ware in Delaware appear to date to the early Late Woodland, circa A.D. 900–1300 (Griffith 1977, 1980), and a Rappahannock Incised rim with nested squares and with triangles was directly associated with a provenience dated to A.D. 1005 (uncorrected radiocarbon date [Waselkov 1982:241, 258]). Both Griffith's Delaware and Waselkov's Virginia data relate to a time frame generally consistent with the estimated date range for McLean mound.

Discussion

Symbols like the concentric rectangle or barred triangle may appear simple and meaningless today, but we should consider the potential meaning of simple designs in late prehistory. In the late sixteenth century, John White depicted some of the tattoos worn by Algonquian groups living in coastal North Carolina. These simple designs, consisting largely of arrows and lines in different arrangements, functioned in the way of Weissner's (1985) emblemic style, declaring social affinity and political allegiance of individuals. These tattoos, worn on the back of "all the inhabitants of this country . . . show whose subjects they are and where they come from" (Lorant 1946:271). The simple designs on stone pipes may likewise have conveyed significant information, though emblemic style seems unlikely.

If we accept an Algonquian origin for the designs on pipes, then it seems obvious, as noted above, that the symbolic codes on pipes are not emblemic expressions. The distance between sites and the great diversity of cultures in which these pipes and designs appear preclude a common statement of social identity or political allegiance. The relatively common occurrence of incised designs on Algonquian pottery, compared to the rare occurrence of designs on pipes outside the range of Townsend Ware, suggests a difference in the meaning of shared symbols. Within Algonquian societies, individual designs such as the concentric rectangle were likely more public symbols, intertwined in cultural systems. In contrast, outside of the circum-Chesapeake Bay region, these symbols were rare, more exotic, and were likely associated with a separate culture or perhaps a widely known deity or spirit.

Instead of widespread emblemic expression, the Algonquian connection may reflect a primary role for Algonquian cultures in interregional interaction in the Mid-Atlantic area. Such a primary role may have included originating trade, actively facilitating interaction, or developing an ideology or ritual ultimately shared or emulated by others. Painter's (1974) attempt to leverage religious ideology is understandable, particularly if we accept that smoking was a ritual act involving religious reference. We can obviously not be certain that smoking ritual involved reference to a common myth, mythical figure, or spirit, especially considering the broadly cast net of cultures—from North Carolina to New York. Nonetheless, the consistency of message is not necessarily as important as the act of ritual and the symbolic reference itself. In remote areas like the southern coastal region, the use of an Algonquian symbol in the context of ritual smoking may have been deemed an important and elaborate statement. Embellishing a stone pipe with an Algonquian design may have been an assertion of power as a local ritual leader sought to legitimize his authority by reference to either a powerful ideological concept or simply his participation in extralocal social relations.[13]

Although there is obviously no connection between the historically documented Calumet ceremony and the late prehistoric Southeast (Brown 1989), it is also quite possible that ritual smoking in the panregional context discussed here functioned in ways not unlike those observed by French explorers in the Mississippi Valley in the seventeenth century or even Bartram in the eighteenth century Southeast (Springer 1981; Waselkov and Braund 1995). In both cases ritual smoking served a primary symbolic role in ceremonies sealing social alliances and facilitating trade relations. Given the widespread distribution of pipes across a culturally diverse landscape, the common use of symbols on pipes, and the general correlation, at least in the southern coastal region, between pipes and the occurrence of exchange, it is possible that ritual smoking helped facilitate and/or mediate intrasocietal and intersocietal relations. In this scenario ritual smoking was not part of the more regular interaction between neighboring areas, manifest in the diffusion of ceramic traits (Eastman 1999), but was likely an uncommon event, restricted to ceremonies and meetings involving representatives of distant societies. The employ of widely recognized Algonquian symbols would add context to the ritual discourse between groups, signifying the knowledge and intent of interested parties.

Conclusion

Not unlike William Bartram examining a prehistoric stone pipe unearthed from an Indian grave, stone pipes from burial mounds present to us a "strange curiosity" (Waselkov and Braund 1995:289). Rare and somewhat exotic artifacts, pipes from the southern coastal region reflect variations on a platform design. Bent-tubes, obtuse angle bowls, modified monitor, and alate stems are all form attributes found in southern coastal region specimens. Individualized and highly crafted objects, these pipes were made from chlorite schist or steatite and were traded into eastern North Carolina, where they ultimately found their way into burial mounds. It is assumed that these unique artifacts served in a ritual capacity. Isolating the meaning or social function of such ritual is a challenge, but it is also an opportunity to learn something about the Late Woodland period.

The extant evidence, however limited, suggests these unique artifacts are linked to cultural trends at the local and macro levels. The emergence of smoking ritual occurs concurrent with intensification of mortuary ritual, participation in exchange, and, possibly, change in the subsistence economy. The development of smoking ritual may be part of a complex cultural response to increasing social tensions brought on by any or all of these factors. Smoking may have been employed in mound interments as a tool of discourse between the living and the dead or between humans and spirits. As highlighted in the above discussion, pipes and, by association, tobacco and smoking seem to be powerful symbolic elements related to intersocietal contact. The widespread distribution of incised designs found on some pipes reveals a common symbolic element to smoking across a broad geographic area and many different cultures.

Recognizing the close link between smoking and regional culture change as well as intersocietal contact in the southern coastal region is but one premise with which we can begin to investigate both the interaction sphere in which pipes and smoking were involved and the culture change that seems to characterize the Late Woodland. The ideas presented here will hopefully inspire future consideration of the complex ways in which simple Woodland societies engaged widespread ideologies through culture contact and how ritual behavior relates to regional culture change. There is much to learn within the broad territory defined by concentric rectangles, barred triangles, stone pipes, and burial mounds. A multiscalar approach (Nassaney and Sassaman 1995) is obviously essential to understanding broad cultural connections that likely impacted local societies. Future archaeological research in individual regions, such as the southern coastal region of North Carolina, will hopefully elucidate cultures and political systems that adopted ritual smoking. For now, pipes should be seen not as simply curious grave goods but as potential indicators of ritual and ideology amidst intersocietal contact and culture change.

Notes

1. This proposed consensus is largely based on studies of northern Piedmont and northern coastal plain cultures (Coe 1995; Magoon 1999; Ward and Davis 1993).

2. There are two or three possible exceptions to the Neuse River boundary, with two purported mounds lying on the north side of the river (Holmes 1883; Phelps 1983). Measurements are above the observed old sod line, or pre-mound ground surface (MacCord 1966).

3. This number should be considered a minimum since several pipes are either represented by fragments only or have been lost since recovery and are unavailable for inspection.

4. Given the small number of occurrences dealt with here, no attempt is made to analyze design grammar or categorize motifs for these designs. Note, however, that for Custer (1987) squares, triangles, and zig-zags are forms that constitute design elements in ceramic design motifs.

5. Variations in the concentric rectangle design include two or more rectangle s/squares (two or three are most common), incised lines within and perpendicular to rectangle/square edges, and incorporation into an anthropomorphic figure.

6. Information from Painter's map is incorporated into Map 2.2 here. An attempt was made to confirm as many of Painter's mapped occurrences as possible.

7. This pipe from Town Creek was recovered from Burial 135, which Coe (1995:223) labels as a semiflexed adult Siouan, though he does not specify why. Two other artifacts were found with this burial, including an unusual smoking tube (1995:224), and a miniature stone-carved human face with several holes drilled though it and the back side hollowed out. The stone tube is decorated with incised rectangles encircling the rim. The miniature stone human face, which Coe interprets as a "clasp to hold a fan of feathers as a clothing ornament or as a decoration on a calumet-type pipe stem," closely resembles several miniature human faces from Virginia (MacCord 1966b).

8. There are no radiocarbon dates and only preliminary reports from the Keyauwee site (Coe 1937). Based on similarities in grave goods with other Piedmont sites, Ward and Davis (1999:137) suggest the primary Keyauwee occupation occurred in the Late Woodland period (Ward and Davis 1993).

9. There is no site report nor are there radiocarbon dates for the Lowder's Ferry site. Coe (1949) notes "two major occupations" at the site, Late Archaic and Uwharrie (ca. a.d. 1200), with other occupations including Guilford, PeeDee, and Caraway.

10. Neither the Leesville nor Senedo mounds have been radiocarbon dated; however, MacCord (1966b) places these mounds in the Late Woodland burial mound complex he terms Lewis Creek.

11. The Hand site is interpreted by Smith (1984) as a protohistoric and historic Nottoway village; however, he does not report any radiocarbon dates. Stephen Potter (personal communication, 2000) has dated a burial at the Hand site to a.d. 690–790. Potter's interpretation of the sequence of occupations include a late Middle Woodland occupation followed by an early Late Woodland Algonquian, Colington Phase occupation, ultimately followed by the protohistoric/historic Nottoway.

12. This pipe was recovered from a pit feature in square 70L50, located within a circular structure at Town Creek (Steve Davis, personal communication 2001).

13. Use of male gender is based on ethnohistorical and archaeological evidence linking males to tobacco cultivation and smoking as well as pipe manufacture (Eastman 1999; Rafferty 1999; Springer 1981:218; Waselkov and Braund 1995:127; Williams 1973).

References Cited

Barka, N. F.

1968 A Polished Stone Pipe from Lancaster County, Virginia 50–1. *Quarterly Bulletin, Archaeological Society of Virginia* 23(1):50–51.

Bello, C. A., and R. Veit

1999 An "Upside-Down" Pendant from South Trenton. *Bulletin of the Archaeological Society of New Jersey* 54:137.

Benson, R.

1998 *Living on the Edge: Cultural Resources Survey of the Overhills Tract, 10,546 Acres in Harnett and Cumberland Counties, North Carolina.* Report prepared for the U.S. Army Corps of Engineers, Savannah, Ga.

Brown, I.
1989 The Calumet Ceremony in the Southeast and Its Archaeological Manifestations. *American Antiquity* 54(2):311–331.

Carr, C.
1995 Building a Unified Middle-Range Theory of Artifact Design. In *Style, Society, and Person: Archaeological and Ethnological Perspectives,* edited by C. Carr and J. E. Neitzel, 151–170. Plenum Press, New York.

Coe, J.
1937 Keyauwee—A Preliminary Statement. *Bulletin of the Archaeological Society of North Carolina* 4(1):8–16.
1949 Excavating in a Parking Lot at Morrow Mountain State Park. *Southern Indian Studies* 1(1):20–21.
1952 The Cultural Sequence of the Carolina Piedmont. In *Archeology of Eastern United States,* edited by James B. Griffin. Univ. of Chicago Press, Chicago.
1964 *The Formative Cultures of the Carolina Piedmont.* Transactions of the American Philosophical Society, n.s., 54, pt. 5. American Philosophical Society, Philadelphia.
1995 *Town Creek Indian Mound: A Native American Legacy.* Univ. of North Carolina Press, Chapel Hill.

Coe, J., H. T. Ward, M. Graham, L. Navey, H. Hogue, and J. H. Wilson Jr.
1982 *Archaeological and Paleo-osteological Investigations at the Cold Morning Site, New Hanover County, North Carolina.* Report prepared for the Interagency Archeological Services (Atlanta) by the Research Laboratories of Anthropology, Univ. of North Carolina, Chapel Hill.

Culpepper, W. S., C. L. Heath, J. D. Irwin, and J. M. Herbert
2000 *From Drowning Creek to Sicily: Archaeological Investigations at Fort Bragg, North Carolina.* Fort Bragg Cultural Resources Program, Research Report No. 2. Submitted to the North Carolina State Historic Preservation Office.

Custer, J. F.
1985 Woodland Ceramic Sequences of the Lower Delmarva Peninsula. *Quarterly Bulletin, Archeological Society of Virginia* 40(4):145–166.
1987 Late Woodland Ceramics and Social Boundaries in Southeastern Pennsylvania and the Northern Delmarva Peninsula. *Archaeology of Eastern North America* 15:13–27.

Davenport, S. L., and J. R. Judge
1952 The Leesville Mound. *Quarterly Bulletin, Archeological Society of Virginia* 7(2).

Dunham, G. H.
1994 Common Ground, Contesting Visions: The Emergence of Burial Mound Ritual in Late Prehistoric Central Virginia. Unpublished Ph.D. dissertation, Dept. of Anthropology, Univ. of Virginia, Charlottesville.

Eastman, J. M.
1994 The North Carolina Radiocarbon Date Study (Part 2). *Southern Indian Studies* 43:5.
1999 The Sara and Dan River Peoples: Siouan Communities in North Carolina's Interior Piedmont from A.D. 1000 to A.D. 1700. Unpublished Ph.D. dissertation, Dept. of Anthropology, Univ. of North Carolina, Chapel Hill.

Egloff, K.
1985 Spheres of Cultural Interaction across the Coastal Plain of Virginia in the Woodland Period. In *Structure and Process in Southeastern Archaeology,* edited by Roy S. Dickens Jr. and H. Trawick Ward, 229–242. Univ. of Alabama Press, Tuscaloosa.

Eliot, D. T.
1986 *The Live Oak Soapstone Quarry, Dekalb County, Georgia.* Submitted by Garrow and Associates to Georgia Waste, a Division of Waste Management of North America.

Gold, D.
1999 Subsistence, Health, and Emergent Inequality in Late Prehistoric Interior Virginia. Unpublished Ph.D. dissertation, Dept. of Anthropology, Univ. of Michigan, Ann Arbor.

Griffith, D. R.
1977 Townsend Ceramics and the Late Woodland of Southern Delaware. Unpublished master's thesis. American Univ., Washington, D.C.
1980 Townsend Ceramics and the Late Woodland and Southern Delaware. *Maryland Historical Magazine* 75(1):23–41.

Hall, R. L.
1983 The Evolution of the Calumet-Pipe. In *Prairie Archaeology: Papers in Honor of David A. Barreis,* edited by G. E. Gibbon, 37–52. Publications in Anthropology No. 3. Univ. of Minnesota, Minneapolis.
1987 Calumet Ceremonialism, Mourning Ritual, and Mechanisms of Inter-tribal Trade. In *Mirror and Metaphor: Material and Social Constructions of Reality,* edited by D. W. Ingersoll Jr. and G. Bronitsky, 29–43. Univ. Press of America, Lanham, Md.

Hariot, T.
1946 A Brief and True Report of the New Found Land of Virginia. In *The New World: The First Pictures of America,* edited by S. Lorant. Duell, Sloan, and Pearce, New York.

Herbert, J. M., J. K. Feathers, and A. S. Cordell
2002 Building Ceramic Chronologies with Thermoluminescence Dating: A Case Study from the Carolina Sandhills. *Southeastern Archaeology* 21(1):92–108.

Holmes, J. A.
1883 Indian Mounds of the Cape Fear. *(Wilmington, N.C.) Weekly Star.* Reprinted in *Southern Indian Studies* 18 (1966):48–54.

Irwin, J. D., W. C. J. Boyko, J. M. Herbert, C. Braley
1999 Woodland Burial Mounds in the North Carolina Sandhills and Southern Coastal Plain. *North Carolina Archaeology* 48:59–86.

Knick, S.
1988 *Robeson Trails Archaeological Survey: Reconnaissance in Robeson County.* Native American Resource Center, Pembroke State Univ., Pembroke, N.C.
1993 *Robeson Crossroads Archaeological Survey: Phase II Testing in Robeson County.* Native American Resource Center, Pembroke State Univ., Pembroke, N.C.

Lorant, S. (editor)
1946 *The New World: The First Pictures of America.* Duell, Sloan, and Pearce, New York.

MacCauley, C.
1929 Notes on the Cameron Mound, Harnett County. Reprinted in *Southern Indian Studies* 18(1966):46–47.

MacCord, H. A., Sr.
1966a The McLean Mound, Cumberland County, North Carolina. *Southern Indian Studies* 18:3–45.
1966b Miniature Human-Effigy Heads in Virginia. *Quarterly Bulletin, Archeological Society of Virginia* 3(1):66–76.
1986 *The Lewis Creek Mound Culture in Virginia.* Privately printed, Archaeological Society of Virginia, Richmond.

Magoon, D. T.
1999 "Chesapeake" Pipes and Uncritical Assumptions: A View from Northeastern North Carolina. *North Carolina Archaeology* 48:107–126.

Mathis, M.
1993 Broad Reach: The Truth About What We've Missed. In *Site Destruction in Georgia and the Carolinas,* edited by David G. Anderson and Virginia Horak, 39–48. Interagency Archeological Services Division, National Park Service, Atlanta.

McCary, B. C.
1952 Artistic Efforts of the Virginia Indians. *Quarterly Bulletin, Archeological Society of Virginia* 7(1).
1954 A Decorated Stone from Smith Creek Mound, Virginia. *Quarterly Bulletin, Archeological Society of Virginia* 9(2).

McGuire, Joseph D.
1899 Pipes and Smoking Customs of the American Aborigines, 351–645. Annual Reportof the United States National Museum for 1896–97.

Nassaney, M. S., and K. E. Sassaman
1995 Introduction: Understanding Native American Interactions. In *Native American Interactions: Multiscalar Analyses and Interpretations in the Eastern Woodland,* edited by M. S. Nassaney and K. E. Sassaman, xix–xxxviii. Univ. of Tennessee Press, Knoxville.

Oliver, B. L.
1992 Settlements of the Pee Dee Culture. Unpublished Ph.D. dissertation, Dept. of Anthropology, Univ. of North Carolina, Chapel Hill.

Painter, F.
1967 Geometrically Incised Decorations on Great Neck Ceramics: The Long Creek Midden, Part 3. *Chesopiean* 5(4):94–110.
1971a Concentric Rectangles: A Recurring Decorative Motif Having Possible Magico-Religious Significance. *Chesopiean* 9(5&6):84–94.
1971b An Engraved Hematite Pendant from Long Creek Midden. *Chesopiean* 9(4):63–64.
1974 Concentric Rectangles: The Chesapeake Cult Symbol. *Chesopiean* 12(4&5):126–145.

Peabody, C.

1910 The Exploration of Mounds in North Carolina. *American Anthropologist* 12(3):425–433.

Pearce, G.

1968 Long Creek Midden, Part 4: Clay Tobacco Pipes. *Chesopiean* 6(2):44–47.

Pearce, G. B., and F. Painter

1968 A Decorated Stone Pipe with a Bone Stem: Long Creek Midden, Part 6. *Chesopiean* 6(6):144–145.

Phelps, D. S.

1982 *Archaeology of the Chowan River Basin: A Preliminary Study.* Archaeological Research Report No. 4, Dept. of Sociology and Anthropology, East Carolina Univ., Greenville, N.C.

1983 Archaeology of the North Carolina Coast and Coastal Plain: Problems and Hypotheses. In *The Prehistory of North Carolina: An Archaeological Symposium,* edited by Mark A. Mathis and Jeffrey J. Crow, 1–52. North Carolina Division of Archives and History, Raleigh.

Plog, F.

1977 Modeling Economic Exchange. In *Exchange Systems in Prehistory,* edited by T. K. Earle and J. E. Ericson, 127–140. Academic Press, New York.

Potter, S. R.

1993 *Commoners, Tribute, and Chiefs: The Development of Algonquian Culture in the Potomac Valley.* Univ. Press of Virginia, Charlottesville.

Rafferty, S.

1999 *Regional Patterns in Early Woodland and Adena Smoking Pipes.* Paper presented at the 1999 Annual Meeting of the Society for American Archaeology, Chicago.

Roe, P. G.

1995 Style, Society, Myth, and Structure. In *Style, Society, and Person: Archaeological and Ethnological Perspectives,* edited by C. Carr and J. E. Neitzel, 27–76. Plenum Press, New York.

Sackett, J. R.

1985 Style and Ethnicity in the Kalahari: A Reply to Weissner. *American Antiquity* 50(1):154–159.

1986 Isochrestism and Style: A Clarification. *Journal of Anthropological Archaeology* 5:266–277.

Seeman, M.

1977 Stylistic Variation in Middle Woodland Pipe Styles: The Chronological Implications. *Midcontinental Journal of Archaeology* 2(1):47–66.

Shumate, M. S., and P. Evans-Shumate

1999 Archaeological Investigations at Long Point (31JN2) and Haywood Landing (31JN3) on the Croatan National Forest, Jones County, North Carolina. Appalachian State Univ. Laboratories of Archaeological Science and Blue Ridge Cultural Resources, Asheville. Report submitted to National Forest Service, Asheville.

Smith, G. P.

1984 *The Hand Site, Southampton County, Virginia.* Archeological Society of Virginia, Special Publication 11.

Snow, D. R.

1978 Late Prehistory of the East Coast. In *Handbook of North American Indians, Volume 15,* edited by B. G. Trigger, 58–69. Smithsonian Institution Press, Washington, D.C.

South, S.

1962 Exploratory Excavation of the McFayden Mound, Bwo 67, Brunswick County, North Carolina, by the Lower Cape Fear Chapter of the Archaeological Society of North Carolina. Ms. on file, Research Laboratory of Archaeology, Univ. of North Carolina, Chapel Hill.

Springer, J. W.

1981 An Ethnohistoric Study of the Smoking Complex in Eastern North America. *Ethnohistory* 28(3):217–235.

Stewart, T. D.

1992 *Archeological Exploration of Patawomeke: The Indian Town Site (22St2) Ancestral to the One (44St1) Visited in 1608 by Captain John Smith.* Smithsonian Contributions to Anthropology, No. 36. Smithsonian Institution Press, Washington, D.C.

Swanton, J. R.

1946 *The Indians of the Southeastern United States.* Bureau of American Ethnology Bulletin 137. Smithsonian Institution Press, Washington, D.C.

Turner, E. R., III.

1992 The Virginia Coastal Plain during the Late Woodland Period. In *Middle and Late Woodland Research in Virginia: A Synthesis,* edited by Theodore R. Reinhart and Mary Ellen N. Hodges, 97–136. Special Publication No. 29 of the Archeological Society of Virginia.

Ward, H. T., and R. P. S. Davis Jr.

1993 *Indian Communities on the North Carolina Piedmont, A.D. 1000–1700.* Monograph No. 2, Research Laboratories of Anthropology, Univ. of North Carolina, Chapel Hill.

1999 *Time before History: The Archaeology of North Carolina.* Univ. of North Carolina Press, Chapel Hill.

Waselkov, G. A.

1982 Shellfish Gathering and Shell Midden Archaeology. Unpublished Ph.D. dissertation, Dept. of Anthropology, Univ. of North Carolina, Chapel Hill.

Waselkov, G. A., and K. E. H. Braund (editors)

1995 *William Bartram on the Southeastern Indians.* Univ. of Nebraska Press, Lincoln.

Weissner, P.

1983 Style and Social Information in Kalahari San Projectile Points. *American Antiquity* 48(2):253–276.

1985 Style or Isochrestic Variation? A Reply to Sackett. *American Antiquity* 50(1):160–166.

West, G. A.

1934 *Tobacco, Pipes, and Smoking Customs of the American Indians.* Bulletin of the Public Museum of the City of Milwaukee 17:1–994. Milwaukee Public Museum.

Wetmore, R. Y.

1978 Report on the Excavations at the Buie Mound, Robeson County, North Carolina. *Institute of Archeology and Anthropology, Notebook* 10:30–71.

Williams, R.

1973 *A Key in the Language of America.* Wayne State Univ., Detroit.

Wobst, H. M.

1977 Stylistic Behavior and Information Exchange. In *For the Director: Research Essays in Honor of James B. Griffin,* edited by C. E. Cleland, 317–342. Univ. of Michigan, Museum of Anthropology, Ann Arbor.

3. Pipes, Leadership, and Interregional Interaction in Protohistoric Midwestern and Northeastern North America

Penelope B. Drooker

Smoking pipes are a particularly useful archaeological marker for interregional interaction among late prehistoric and protohistoric communities in many parts of eastern North America.[1] In most areas, small, portable pipes became common during this time period, in contrast with massive stone ceremonial pipes of earlier centuries, such as the famous human and animal effigies from Mississippian mound centers (for example, Brown 1996:513–526; Emerson 1982, 1983, 1989:54–58; Farnsworth and Emerson 1989; Fundabark and Foreman 1957:Plates 95, 99, 100, 102, 103).

In addition to other functions that pipes served during this later period, they were, among a number of groups, part of greeting ceremonies during which pipe bowls might be exchanged or given as gifts. Under less formal circumstances, travelers' personal pipes might be lost or broken and discarded in foreign communities. The considerable variation in pipe forms and locally available materials among regions affords the opportunity to determine whether a pipe excavated at a particular site was of local or nonlocal origin. A pipe's condition and context of disposition can provide evidence for the nature of its use, the status of its user(s), and political and economic relationships between groups living in widely separated regions.

This chapter uses a case study from a protohistoric site in the central Ohio River Valley plus selected examples from the upper Mississippi Valley and the Northeast to illustrate the usefulness of pipes and pipe bowls in tracing interpersonal and intergroup interaction patterns.

Greeting Ceremonies and Pipe Smoking

Most North American peoples had formal ceremonies for greeting strangers and incorporating them into the group so that interaction could take place. Much of this ritual involved nonmaterial or perishable components, such as singing, speechmaking, feasting, or the presentation of clothing, but nonperishable gifts also were included (for example, see Clayton, Knight, and Moore 1993:1:278; Lankford 1984, 1988; Smith and Hally 1992:100–102). Pipe smoking often was part of these ceremonies.

Early historical accounts document a variety of protocols for intergroup interaction in eastern North America. In groups organized as simple or complex chiefdoms, chiefly duties typically included ambassadorial functions, control of trade, and/or hosting visitors (Feinman and Neitzel 1984:50). Among groups with less hierarchical organization, such duties might fall to lineage heads. Thus, incoming strangers, including members of the earliest European expeditions, typically were greeted initially by a political leader or his or her representative. Some sort of ceremony, usually accompanied by gift exchange, was almost universal on such occasions. Ceremonies with similar material correlates also accompanied the arbitration of interpolity disputes and the cementing of alliances; additionally, in such cases hostages might be exchanged (for example, see Dye 1995:296; Heidenreich 1978:383). Greeting rituals for known outsiders, such as regular trading partners, also invariably included the exchange of gifts (for example, see McClellan 1975:501–507; Spielmann 1983), and frequently included smoking.

Members of the Hernando de Soto entrada and other Spanish expeditions to the interior Southeast in the mid-sixteenth century recorded the elements of elite greeting ceremonies enacted as they entered each new polity. These included greetings at the town outskirts by high-level emissaries in ceremonial dress who were carried in litters and accompanied by singing, flute-playing attendants; formal speeches; and presentation of gifts, including food, clothing, and pearl or shell beads (Brown 1989:315; Clayton, Knight, and Moore 1993:1:278–279; Smith and Hally 1992). Intra- and interpolity political negotiations were accompanied by "feasting, ceremonial smoking, and gift exchange" (Dye 1995:296).

Somewhat later, English settlers noted similar customs around Chesapeake Bay. Among Powhatans and surrounding groups in eastern Virginia, greeting ceremonies included entry to the town through two lines of residents, stroking, oratory, feasting, dancing, and smoking (Rountree 1993:39–41). All trade and prestige goods were controlled by the chief (Potter 1989).

When the French penetrated the western Great Lakes and upper Mississippi Valley in the seventeenth century, they learned that calumet ceremonialism was an important validation of intertribal alliance and exchange. The calumet (wand or pipe stem) was "very sacred and could be used as a safe-conduct pass when travelling through potentially hostile territory," but it also figured importantly in greeting rituals that served as adoption ceremonies "used to establish fictions of kinship between prominent Indians in different villages or different tribes and . . . between welcome Europeans and the bands or villages they visited" (Hall 1987:30, 31). The entire ritual as experienced by Europeans, with details differing in different areas, incorporated ceremonial smoking, ritualized weeping, stroking, presentation of clothing, dancing, speechmaking, and feasting (Blakeslee 1981; Brown 1989; Hall 1987:32). It could include presentation or exchange of pipe bowls or of the calumet alone.

Among Iroquoian groups in what is now southern Ontario and New York, village external affairs were the domain of councils of ranking clan chiefs and elders; trade routes were in the hands of individuals who usually had considerable social and political status (for example, see Fenton 1978:314–315; Heidenreich 1978:283–285). Heidenreich (1978:283) notes that "the Huron did not trade with . . . strangers with whom they had no formal peace treaties. . . . Such alliances were initiated and renewed through reciprocal gift giving, feasts, long speeches, and eventually a limited exchange of people." Early European accounts state that that pipe smoking was an important component of political councils (for example, see Kuhn and Sempowski 2001:304). Interaction with visitors involved group smoking but not necessarily pipe presentation (Fenton 1953; Paper 1992:163–165). Among the Huron, for instance, lighted smoking pipes were shared with visitors but not given to them (Smith 1992:17–18; Tooker 1964:57). The Iroquois, however, were known to have "presented pipes as gifts to other tribes as a symbol of friendship and alliance" during the colonial period (Kuhn and Sempowski 2001:304, citing Jacobs 1966:24). Among groups such as Neutrals and St. Lawrence Iroquoians, French explorers and missionaries recorded that pipes and tobacco were used only by men (Noble 1992:41; Pendergast 1992:51).

Pipes as Archaeological Correlates of Intergroup Interaction

In areas where greeting ceremonies included the presentation or exchange of pipe bowls, communities with regular outside contacts would show evidence of this in their pipes. Statistical frequencies of particular exotic pipe styles and/or materials would be one indicator of the frequency and intensity of contact with particular groups, particularly male interactions. The condition and provenience of nonlocal pipes can provide evidence about the types of relationships that resulted in their presence.

Pipes received as honored gifts from allies would be carefully curated rather than casually discarded. Among other possibilities, individuals strongly associated with greeting ceremonies, such as leaders who habitually enacted such rituals, might retain and be buried with important gift pipes. Such people typically would be buried with other distinctive objects indicative of their special status.

Deliberately "killed" pipes might have been so treated either because of their own perceived attributes, such as power connected with spiritual aspects of smoking that would be dangerous in the hands of the noninitiated, or because of their connection with a spiritually or politically powerful individual or group.

Discarded nonlocal pipes or broken fragments might come from the hands of visitors, captives, or locals returned from long-distance trips. Foreign pipes of a particular style clustered within a site would be a good indicator of the presence of a group of longer-term male visitors, voluntary or involuntary. For example, concentrations of distinctive Huron Coronet Trumpet pipes within Iroquois Confederacy territory that postdate the 1649 Huron dispersal by the Five Nations Iroquois may well be associated with villages of captive Hurons (Pendergast 1992:60).

Exotic materials for pipe making might be imported from great distances, obtained through down-the-line or long-distance exchange, or through travel to

MAP 3.1. ▸ *Late prehistoric and protohistoric archaeological traditions, archaeological sites, and historically known groups.*

quarries or other source locations. Visitors or local craftspeople might manufacture pipes in admired nonlocal styles using local materials. Poorly made pipes (for example, asymmetrical or poorly finished) in foreign styles might be due to inept craftsmanship, the use of less than optimal materials, imitation of a form seen and described by someone other than the maker, or culturally related aesthetic differences, among other possibilities.

Pipe material, form, decoration (technique and motif), and utilitarian details such as attachment holes used to tie pipe bowls to separate stems all can be useful in determining the origin of a particular artifact. (These attributes, of course, can be temporal indicators as well.) Sources of materials are most accurately identified by analysis of trace element and mineral compositions. Distinctive stones and minerals sometimes can be confidently identified visually, but petrographic and chemical analyses comparing artifact materials to their potential sources are far more reliable (for example, Emerson and Hughes 2001; Gundersen 1982a, 1982b, 1993; Hughes et al. 1998; Penman and Gundersen 1999). Clays used for ceramics ordinarily can only be distinguished by such methods (for example, Kuhn 1985, 1986, 1987), although macroscopically evident tempering materials, such as shell versus grit, can provide some information.

Distinctive Fifteenth–Seventeenth Century Pipe Styles and Materials in the Great Lakes–Ohio Valley–Upper Mississippi Valley Region

During the late prehistoric and protohistoric periods, the broad region from the upper Mississippi Valley through the Great Lakes and Ohio River Valley to southern Ontario and New York was anchored by distinctive pipe styles and materials at either end, associated with Oneota groups in the west and Iroquoian groups in the east (Map 3.1).

Upper Mississippi Valley Redstone Disk Pipes

Disk pipes (for example, Figure 3.1, top) made of red pipestone and typically smoked through a stem inserted into one end constitute a diagnostic Oneota style (for example, see Brown 1989; Hamilton 1967; Salter 1977; West 1934:Plates 140, 141, 143, 145, 147, 150, 151, 257; line drawings in Figure 3.1 by Penelope Drooker, after Ahlstrom 1979:Pls. XII, XVIII; Brown 1989:Fig. 3; Low 1880:Figs. 6, 14, 26; Noble 1992:Fig. 2; Pendergast 1992:53, 55, 57, 58; Shetrone 1926:Fig. 27; and personal observation of museum specimens). This style of pipe also was made of black argillites, gray limestone, and other materials, particularly in later years.[2] A minority incorporated carved effigies into the base of the pipe, below the disk, which invariably faced away from the smoker.

Although redstones used to make pipes are often referred to generically as catlinite, this term should be reserved for a particular metamorphosed claystone quarried in southwestern Minnesota, near the present Pipestone National Monument. Visually similar red pipestones (a general term used for fine-grained claystones and related metamorphic rocks) are known from other nearby localities in Minnesota, Wisconsin, and South Dakota, as well as Kansas, Arizona, and southeastern Ohio (Emerson and Hughes 2001:151–152; Penman and Gundersen 2000: 47–48; Sigstad 1973:Map 1). Catlinite use was rare before 1300 and most common from the fifteenth century onward.

Redstone disk pipes occur after circa 1400 at Oneota sites in southern Wisconsin, the region where they are most common (Gibbon 1986:328). They have been excavated from at least a few sites with European goods (for example, see Drooker 1997:Figures 6–20, 8–26; Fox 2002:137; Hamilton 1967; Hanson 1975:89; O'Brien 1994:239). Although some have survived in historically utilized war bundles, Ian Brown places their production mainly within prehistoric-protohistoric times; they do not appear to have been fashioned with metal tools (Brown 1989:317–322; West 1934:207). According to William Green (1993:300), most "prototypical" late Oneota redstone disk pipes date to circa 1450–1650.

Disk pipes may have become smaller over time. For example, more-compact shapes (short "handle" or "prow," relatively small disk), often rendered in limestone rather than red pipestone, are known to be associated with very late prehistoric to protohistoric Orr Phase (Ioway) sites in northeastern Iowa and form a significant portion of the large pipe assemblage from the historically occupied Utz site in Missouri (Hamilton 1967:Figures 11, 12, 13; Wedel 1959:Figure 11; West 1934:Plate 259). However, their total time frame is unknown. Production of large-disk, long-handled catlinite disk pipes (for example, Figure 3.1, top left) may perhaps have been confined almost entirely to prehistoric times (Brown 1989:322). These finely made artifacts may have a particular history as diplomatic gifts; at any rate, a significant number have been excavated far from their region of origin (for example, see Brown 1989; Witthoft, Schoff, and Wray 1953:Plate 2.2). Map 3.2 illustrates the distribution of redstone pipes, with no distinction between large-disk and small-disk types (Map 3.2 after Drooker 1997:Figure 8-29; data from Brown 1989; Fox 2002:131–138; Hamilton 1967; Moorehead 1906; Pollack et al. 1996; Salter 1977:Figure 5; Skinner 1926; Wedel 1959; West 1934; personal examination of museum collections; drawing after Hamilton 1967:cover).

Redstone elbow pipes (both L-shapes and T-shapes), strongly associated with calumet ceremonialism, are a later form that probably dates from the mid-seventeenth century onward (Brown 1989:311, 322–326, Figure 7; Witthoft, Schoff,

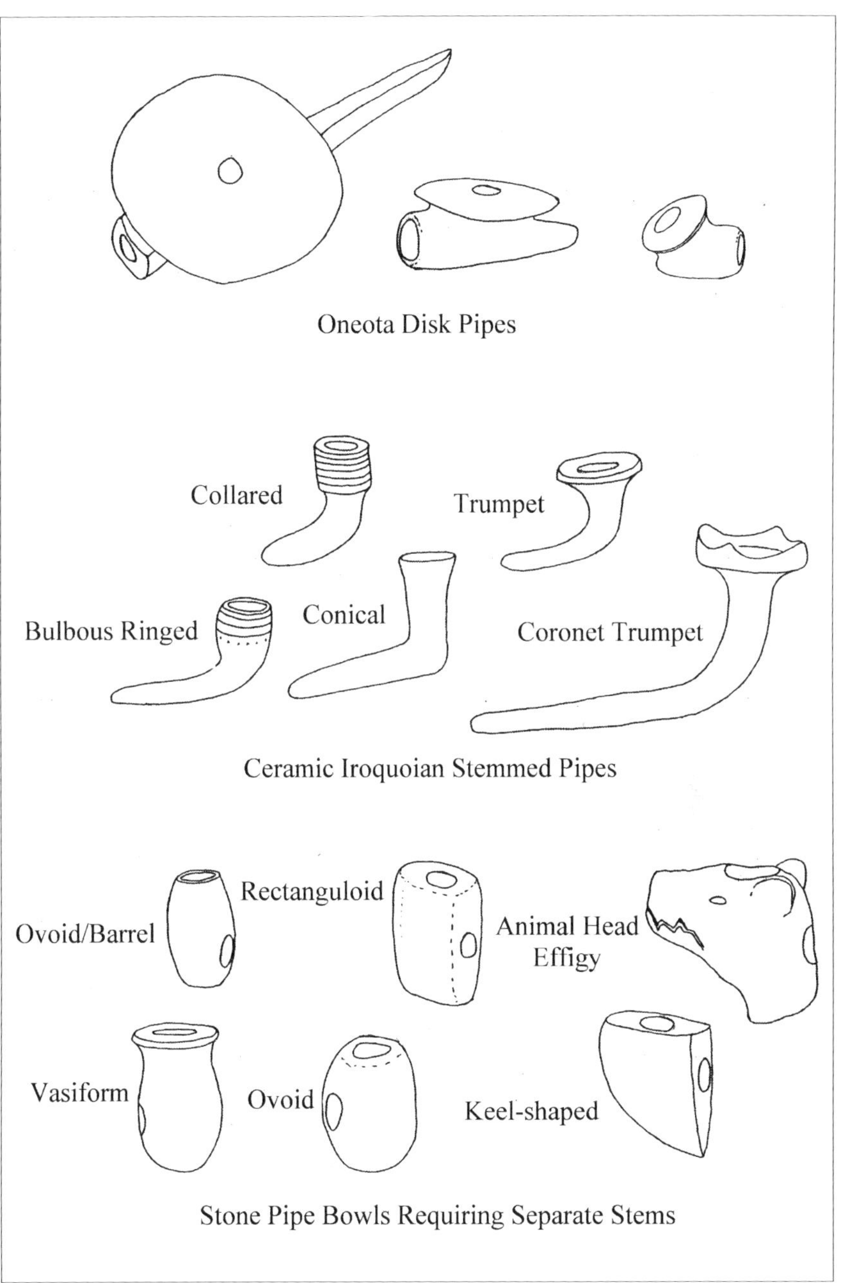

FIG. 3.1. ▸ *Typical pipe forms discussed in the text.*

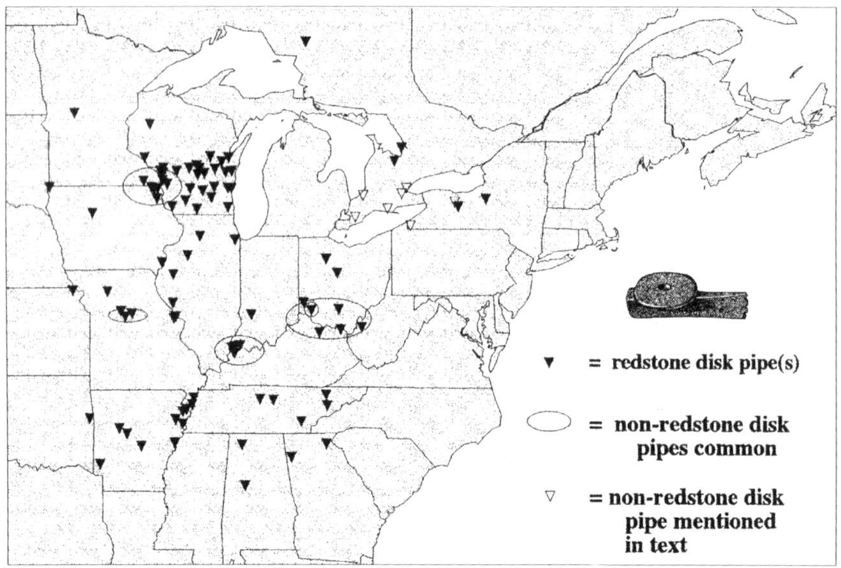

MAP 3.2. ▸ *Geographical distribution of excavated disk pipes.*

and Wray 1953:Plate 2). Likewise, redstone Micmac-style pipes (taller than they are wide or deep, with bowl and base separated by a constricted central portion [for example, West 1934: Plates 121.2, 121.3; Witthoft, Schoff, and Wray 1953: Plates 2, 3]) apparently date to the late seventeenth and early eighteenth centuries and after (Brown 1989:317; Witthoft, Schoff, and Wray 1953). The archaeological (and ethnographic) distribution of these styles differs from the disk pipe.

Iroquoian Stemmed Pipes

The most common and best-known Iroquoian pipe styles are ceramic, with self-stems at a 90–135 degree angle to the bowl. The range of pipe bowl forms and decorative elements has been described in typologies and attribute analyses for pipes from particular geographic regions and time periods (for example, Emerson 1954; Lenig 1965; Noble 1992; Pendergast 1992; Weber 1970, 1971; West 1934:Plates 132, 212, 214, 216). Some common bowl shapes include bulbous ("acorn ring," "apple bowl," "bulbar," "ring-bowl," and "round-topped"), barrel, cylindrical ("collared"), conical, and excurvate round and square trumpet forms (for example, Figure 3.1, middle; left to right: bulbous ringed, collared, conical, trumpet, coronet trumpet). Many types of effigy bowls were produced, which typically face the smoker (for example, Mathews 1979, 1980, 1981; Noble 1979; see also Brasser

1980). Since Iroquoian ceramic pipes differ in form, material, and effigy orientation from upper Mississippi Valley and Ohio Valley pipes, they stand out as "foreign" in any assemblage outside their home area (mapped in West 1934:Map 16).

Stemmed limestone pipes, often with lizard effigies clinging to the outside of the bowl, their tails along the bottom of the stem, appear in small numbers among Ontario Iroquoian groups (notably Neutrals) during the early seventeenth century (Laidlaw 1914, 1916; Noble 1992:42).

Stemmed steatite or pipestone pipes, along with more common stemmed ceramic pipes, are associated with late prehistoric and protohistoric Monongahela sites in southwestern Pennsylvania (for example, Mayer-Oakes 1955: Figure 26I), the residents of which might perhaps have been Iroquoian (Johnson 2002). Monongahela ceramic stemmed pipes are most commonly cordmarked (Mayer-Oakes 1955:107–109, Plates 53–55, Figure 26N-R).

Ohio Valley–Great Lakes Separate-Stemmed Stone Pipes

Between the Oneota and Iroquoian homelands, a variety of pipe styles was in use during late prehistoric-protohistoric times. Compact stone pipes that would require a separate stem made of wood or cane are typical. Common shapes include ovoid, globular, rectanguloid, trianguloid, and trapezoidal; barrel and cylindrical; semi-elbow (often ovoid, with very short perpendicular extension at the stem hole); vasiform (with globular bottom and constricted neck, often excurvate rim); and keel (larger front-to-back than side-to-side dimension, with tapered front end) (for example, Figure 3.1, bottom; for photographs of many examples, see Ahlstrom 1979; Drooker 1998; West 1934). Distributions of different forms vary, but all types occur in significant numbers in and around Ohio. Many different materials were utilized, including limestone, fine sandstone, quartzite, chalcedonies, and pipestones of various colors. Decoration included engraved designs and images carved in relief. In contrast to Iroquoian pipes, effigies typically face away from the smoker.

Ovoid pipes and related shapes (for example, rectanguloid, barrel) range from finely made, polished objects in showy, colorful materials to examples that appear to be simply drilled natural stones ("pebble pipes") (see Figure 3.1, bottom, second, third, and fourth from the left). They are found from the eastern edges of trans–Mississippi River states to New York and southern Ontario (Noble 1992:Tables 1, 2; Parker 1918:33; Rutsch 1973:80–85; West 1934:Map 8). For a variety of examples of ovoid and related shapes, see Ahlstrom 1979:Plates 11, 17; Drooker 1997:Figures 7-5a, 7-5d, 8-26, 1998:Photo 655; West 1934:Plates 156.4, 156.5, 164; Witthoft, Schoff, and Wray 1953:Plate 1).

Vasiform pipes (for example, Ahlstrom 1979:Plates 5, 8; Drooker 1997:Figures 7-5a, 7-5b, 1998:Photo 656; West 1934:Plate 100; see Figure 3.1, bottom left) also are found across the same region (West 1934:Map 9, to which southwestern Indiana should be added), but some local variations can be noted. Redstone vasiform pipes are concentrated west of Lake Michigan, in Oneota territory (Salter 1977:Figure 19). Although all vasiform pipes that I have examined from Fort Ancient, Oneota, and Caborn-Welborn territory are more or less round in horizontal cross section, quite a few of those I have seen from Seneca Iroquois sites are much narrower side to side than back to front (for example, Parker 1922:Plate 49.6; Sempowski and Saunders 2001:257; Witthoft, Schoff, and Wray 1953:Plate 1). Examples from Iroquoian sites also often have high "collars," echoing the shapes of local pottery; likewise, Fort Ancient examples show rim and body shapes evocative of both Early–Middle and Late period local pots (for example, Drooker 1997:Figure 7-5b, bottom).

I have seen attachment holes on the bottoms only of examples from northeastern sites, none from Fort Ancient territory. This is true of stone pipes in other forms as well.

Keel-shaped pipes (for example, Ahlstrom 1979:Plate 18; Drooker 1997:Figures 7-5a, top right, 8-25, third row center and right, 1998:Photos 369–372, 409–410, 455–456, 473–475, 489–491, 512–514, 567, 578–581, 650–654, 657; West 1934:Plate 162; see Figure 3.1, bottom, second from right) are found primarily in Wisconsin and Ohio (Map 3.3; data from Ahlstrom 1979:Plate 18; Drooker 1997:Tables 4-3, 6-5; Vietzen 1974:111; West 1934:Plates 134.2, 162; drawing from Hooton and

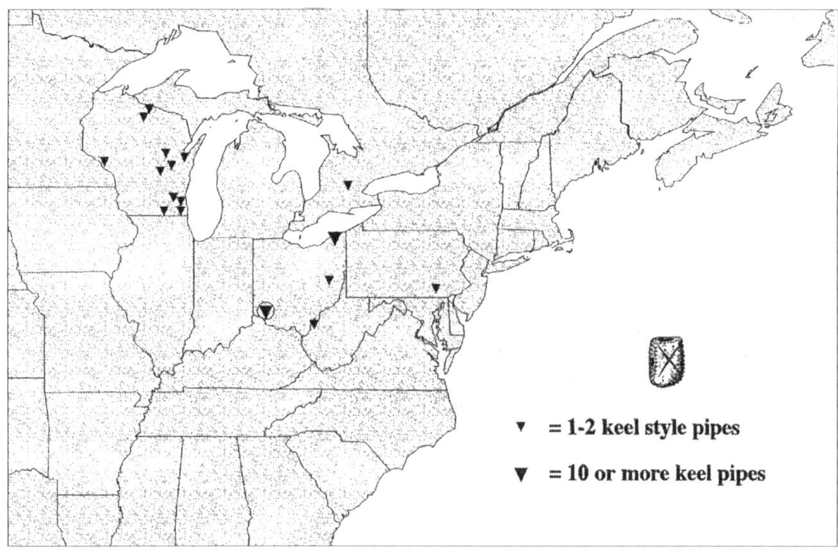

MAP 3.3. ▸ *Geographical distribution of excavated keel-shaped pipes.*

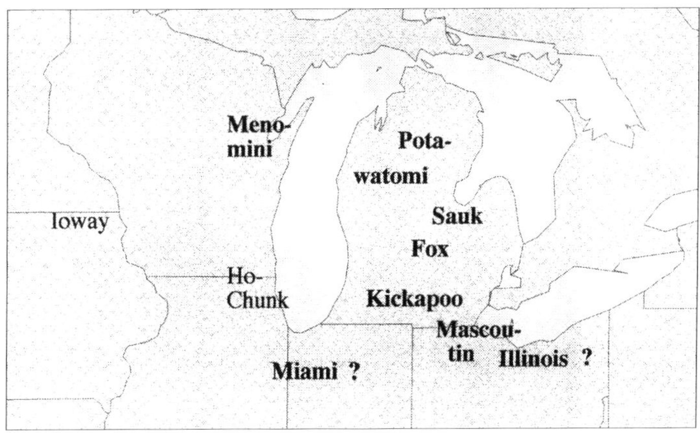

MAP 3.4A. ▸ *Locations of selected Upper Mississippi–Great Lakes groups circa 1600.*

Willoughby 1920:Plate 19a). They may be a late form. The distribution of Wisconsin examples published by West (the locations of which are given only by county, not by site) shows a clustering southwest of Green Bay that is congruent with late-seventeenth-century settlement patterns for Central Algonquian groups displaced to that area under pressure from Iroquois raiding (Map 3.4a,b)

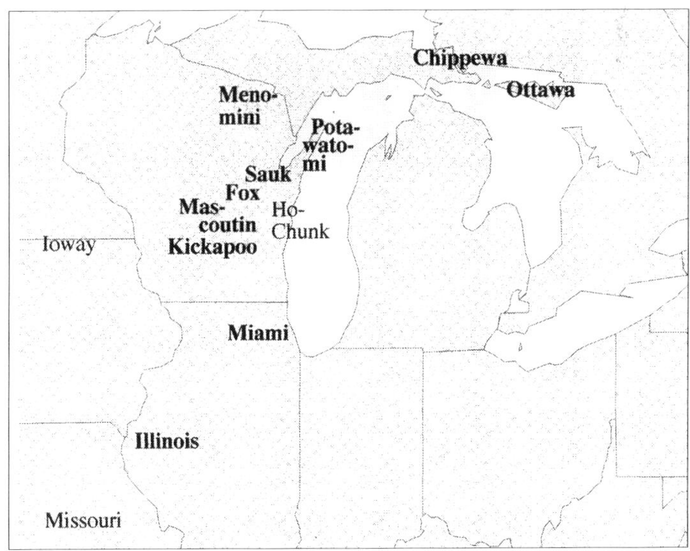

MAP 3.4B. ▸ *Locations of selected Upper Mississippi–Great Lakes groups circa 1670.*

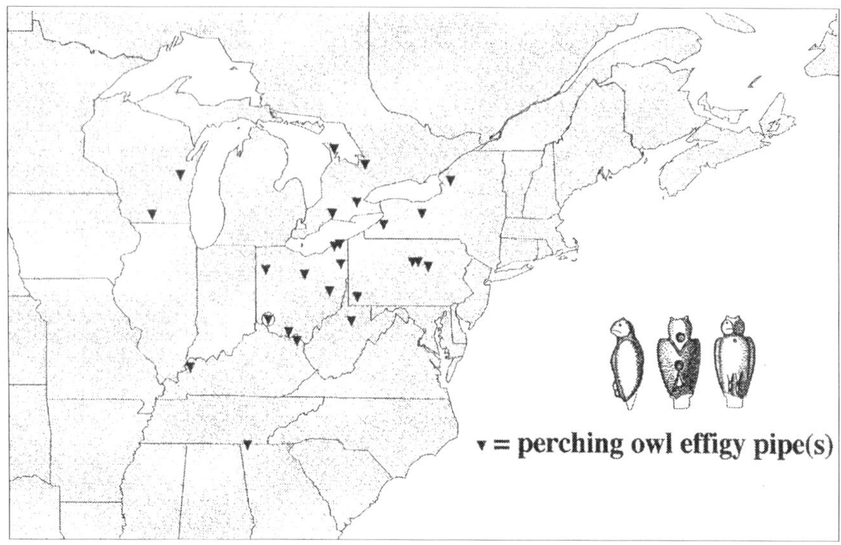

MAP 3.5. ▸ *Geographical distribution of perched owl stone effigy pipes.*

(Drooker 1997:56, 2002; Drooker and Cowan 2001:Figure 8-12; see also below). (References for Map 3.4 include Brose 2000:110; Callender 1962:Figure 1; Drooker 1997:56, 103–105, 1999:76–77, 2001:123–124, 2002; Esarey 2003; Hall 2003:250; Stothers 2000:72–74).[3]

Some stone pipes of all shapes have *engraved designs,* a few with region-specific iconography. For instance, "weeping eye" designs found on ovoid and keel-shaped pipes (for example, see Drooker 1997:Figures 6-20, 8-25, 8-26, 8-42, 1998: Photos 355–59, 393–394, 512, 578–580, 650–654) are related to symbols on southeastern engraved marine shell cups and mask gorgets (Brain and Phillips 1996; Phillips and Brown 1978, 1984; Smith and Smith 1989), among other media. Thunderbirds (for example, see Drooker 1997:Figures 8-25, 8-26; Photos 369–372; 650–654) and animals with zigzag "heartlines" are linked to Oneota imagery. A number of pipes from the Fort Ancient Madisonville site (keel, vasiform, ovoid, and disk) have a "+" engraved at one end (for example, see Drooker 1998:Photos 662, 663), a symbol that also occurs on 20 percent of the grooved stone club heads from the site (Drooker 1997:316, Figure 6-17b); two vasiform mortuary pipes from the eastern Fort Ancient Neale's Landing site also were marked in this way (Hemmings 1976:58).

Carved stone effigy pipes from this broad region almost always face away from the smoker (see Figure 3.1, bottom right). Exceptions have come primarily from

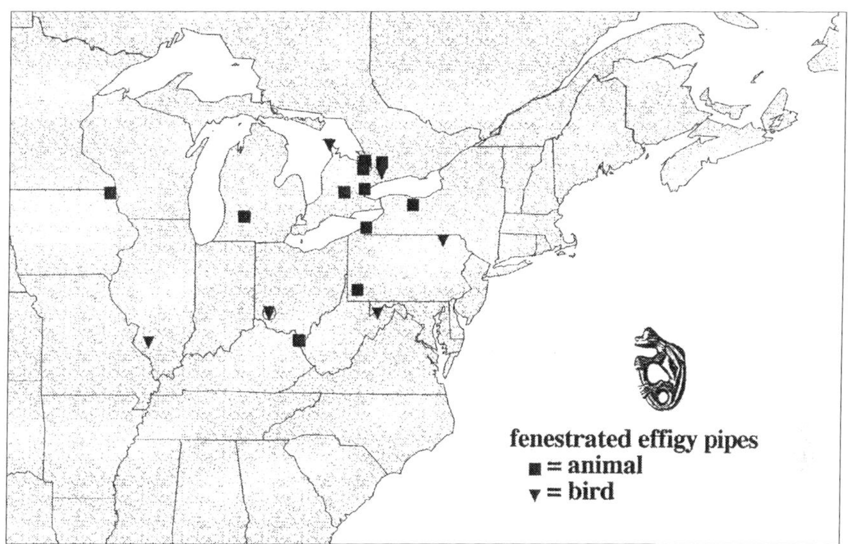

MAP 3.6. ▸ *Geographical distribution of fenestrated stone animal effigy pipes.*

Iroquoian territory, most notably *stemmed* and *nonstemmed pipes with a lizard or other animal clinging to the front,* nose up or toward the smoker (for example, Laidlaw 1914:49–73). It must be noted that in the case of lizards, with eyes at tops of heads, it often is difficult to tell whether they are looking toward or away from the smoker. Although most stone human head effigies face outward, collections from the late prehistoric Seneca or Cayuga Richmond Mills (Reed Fort) site, curated at the Rochester Museum and Science Center (RMSC), include at least six ovoids with crudely engraved human features on the side toward the smoker, with the stem hole serving as a mouth.[4]

Common outward-facing stone effigy types for this time period include the following: *Perched birds* (for example, Ahlstrom 1979:Plates 7, 14, 15, 22, 23; Drooker 1997:Figure 7-5c; Hanson 1975:70; Laidlaw 1903:44–51, 1913, 1914:46, 48; 1916:66, 67, 73, 75, 77–78, 80; West 1934:Plates 128.2, 135.1; Witthoft, Schoff, and Wray 1953: Plate 1) have been found primarily in Ohio, Pennsylvania, New York, and Ontario (see Map 3.5, after Drooker 1997:Figure 8-30; drawing from Hooton and Willoughby 1920:Figure 5), with a particularly large number of both pipes and blanks coming from the Reeve site in northeastern Ohio (Map 3.1). They are the “favorite form” of stone effigy pipe at Monongahela sites (Mayer-Oakes 1955:109). Their distribution echoes the distribution of perched bird effigy pipes in general. *Human and animal heads* (for example, Drooker 1997:Figures 7-5b, 7-6, 1998:Photos 352, 394, 467–469,

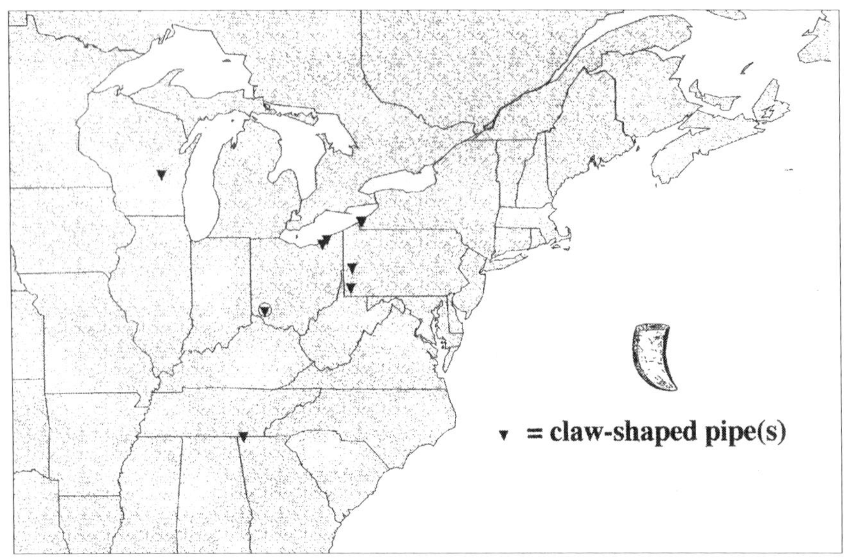

MAP 3.7. ▸ *Geographical distribution of stone claw effigy pipes.*

507–508, 519–522, 583–587, 598–601, 622–623; Hanson 1975:70; West 1934:Plates 122.3, 134.4; Witthoft, Schoff, and Wray 1953:Plate 1; see Figure 3.1, bottom right) are most common in Fort Ancient territory. *Fenestrated birds and animals* (for example, Drooker 1997:Figure 7-5a; 312–314; Laidlaw 1903:40–45, 1913:37–42, 46–47, 59, 61, 1914:47, 1915:60; West 1934:Plate 122.6; Witthoft, Schoff, and Wray 1953: Plate 1) are most common east of the Ohio River (Map 3.6; data from Drooker 1997: 312–314, Figure 8-32; Laidlaw 1903:Figures 19–23, 25, 1913:37–41, 46–47, 59, 61, 1914:47–48, 77–78, 1915:60; Mallam 1983; West 1934:Plate 122.6; Rochester Museum and Science Center cat. no. 5042/99; New York State Museum cat. no. 3572; drawing from Laidlaw 1914:47), and probably date entirely to the post-Contact period. These pipes are penetrated by one or more side-to-side holes. The most common forms are animals clutching their tails and long-beaked birds with beak tips touching feet. *Claw* effigies (for example, Ahlstrom 1979:Plate 16; Drooker 1997:309, Figure 7.5d) are represented at a few sites, most of them close to the Ohio-Pennsylvania line (Map 3.7, after Drooker 1997:Figure 8-31; drawing from Hooton and Willoughby 1920:Plate 19q; the Madisonville and Reeve sites each produced three examples).

Limestones, sandstones, and pipestones are the most common materials for these separate-stemmed pipes. Also seen are chalcedony (cryptocrystalline quartz), at least some golden-hued specimens probably from cave deposits in West

Virginia (Drooker 1997:309), black to dark green steatite, well-known sources of which are located on the eastern slope of the Virginia Appalachians, and crystalline anorthosite, particularly well represented in both pipes and pipe blanks at the Reeve site in northeastern Ohio (Map 3.1) (Ahlstrom 1979; Drooker 1997:312). Occasionally, fossils such as horn corals or brachiopods were utilized (for example, Ahlstrom 1979:57; Drooker 1998:Photos 434–435, 457–458, 588–589), as were antler, wood, and less easily shaped stones and minerals such as slates and crystalline quartzes.

Ohio pipestone, a fine-grained, soft stone that takes a handsome polish, is among the most distinctive of pipe-making materials. However, identification can be tricky. Ohio pipestone, quarried at a number of localities in southeastern Ohio, is known by a variety of names (for example, Portsmouth fireclay and Sciotoville flint clay) and occurs in a range of colors, including red, tan, and gray (Converse 1995; Drooker 1997:310, 312; Holzapfel 1995; Hughes et al. 1998:715, 717; Murphy 1996). Red varieties have been mistaken for midwestern pipestones such as catlinite. Gray varieties often are seen in late period pipes. Similar pipestones are known from central Pennsylvania (harder and darker than the Ohio materials [Witthoft, Schoff, and Wray 1953:93]) and northern Illinois. The latter are very close in appearance to pipestones used for Ohio Hopewell platform pipes and until recently were consistently misidentified as being from Ohio sources, but they can be distinguished by mineralogical analysis (Hughes et al. 1998).

Madisonville and Related Fort Ancient Sites

The protohistoric Fort Ancient Madisonville site, located in what is now suburban Cincinnati, provides an excellent case history of pipes as archaeological correlates of interregional interaction. Particularly in conjunction with interaction patterns traced by European metal artifacts, pipes provide evidence for both interpersonal and intergroup relationships during this turbulent period.

Between the eleventh and seventeenth centuries, the central Ohio River Valley, from extreme southeastern Indiana through southern Ohio and northern Kentucky to western West Virginia, was home to the Fort Ancient archaeological tradition (Griffin 1943; Drooker 1997:47–48, 63–105, 2000).[5] Villages of Fort Ancient floodplain horticulturists were found along the Ohio and far up its major tributaries in this area. Before the mid-fifteenth century, settlements were relatively small and subregions were distinguished by variations in pottery styles and tempering materials. During the Late Fort Ancient period, from the mid-fifteenth to seventeenth centuries, villages became larger and most settlements were located within twenty kilometers of the Ohio River (Map 3.8). Pottery

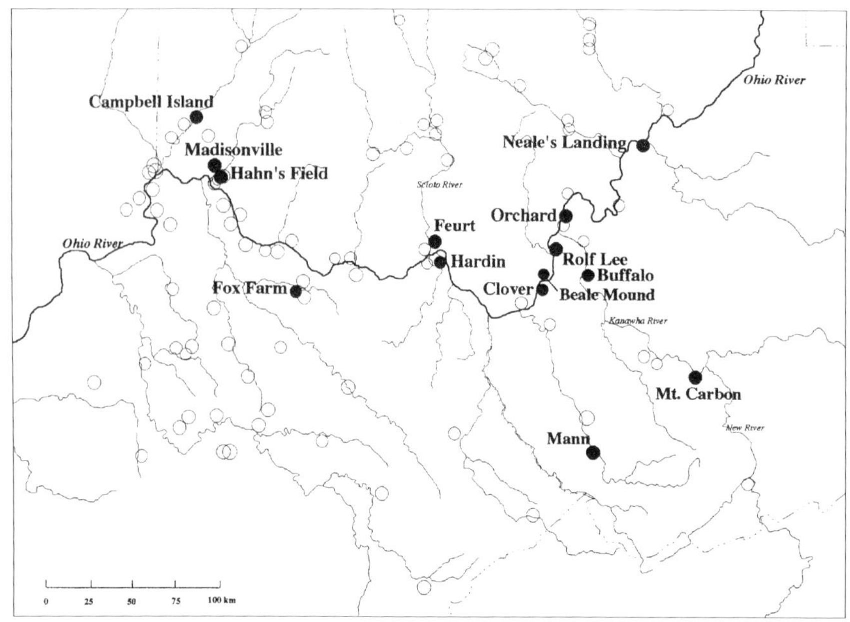

MAP 3.8. ▸ *Late Fort Ancient sites mentioned in the text. Unnamed sites indicate prehistoric extent of Fort Ancient settlements.*

became more similar throughout the region, and the prevailing style gave its name to the period: the Madisonville Horizon. Small items of European origin arrived in the region perhaps as early as 1540; the vast majority of these objects were available before 1640 (Drooker 1996, 1997:Table 4-9). Mortuary analyses of individual sites have provided no evidence for ascribed ranking, but a two-tiered system of achieved leadership appears to have been in operation (Drooker 1995: 6, 9–10, 1997:279–282).

Because of discontinuities between the archaeological and the historical records, the historical identity of Fort Ancient people is unknown. Historians, linguists, and archaeologists have most frequently postulated a connection with Central Algonquian groups, particularly the Shawnee, but eastern Siouan groups also have been proposed (Drooker 1997:103–105, 227, 2002:123–124).

Madisonville was the westernmost protohistoric Fort Ancient settlement, the only one in southwestern Ohio from which European artifacts have been formally excavated. Some 1450 burials and 1280 refuse pits were excavated at this densely inhabited two-hectare village and cemetery. Madisonville is among the most completely explored Fort Ancient sites, although most fieldwork was carried out before modern methods had been wholly developed, between 1879 and 1911 (Hooton and

Willoughby 1920; Drooker 1997:Table 5-4). I utilized materials from that work and from more recent small-scale salvage excavations by the Cincinnati Museum of Natural History to study western Fort Ancient social organization and interregional interaction patterns (Drooker 1995, 1996, 1997, 1998, 1999, 2000; Drooker and Cowan 2001). Pipes figured importantly in my analyses.

Pipes as Status Indicators at Madisonville

Smoking pipes were among the primary status indicators at Madisonville. Over 180, in a great variety of forms and materials, were excavated, the largest well-provenienced assemblage of pipes from any Fort Ancient settlement.[6] As grave goods (n = 30), they were strongly correlated with adult males, one of the very few types of artifacts identified as statistically significant indicators of age or sex (Drooker 1997:230–234, Tables 7-16, 7-17, 7-18). Madisonville mortuary pipes were significantly larger in size, lighter in color, and less likely to be damaged than nonmortuary pipes. The three individuals with the most diverse grave-good assemblages (two adult males over the age of twenty-five and one adult of unknown age and sex) all were buried with distinctive pipes, as were the two adult men with large double-barred copper pendants, thought to be important supralocal status indicators (Drooker 1997:274–275, 292).

In general, burials with pipes correlated significantly with two other artifact functional categories, projectile points and bone/antler ornaments, and also with three or more subsidiary burials, decorated artifacts, large/unique artifacts, and highly diverse grave-good assemblages. These associations are appropriate for people whose recognized status was associated with multiple, important social identities. Male-associated grave-good categories at Madisonville, including pipes, projectile points, large copper ornaments, and bone ornaments, underline the importance of men as hunters, warriors, and diplomats. Pipes probably signaled a particular adult male social identity or leadership role, very likely including ritual greeting and external interaction (Drooker 1997:246–247, 279–280). As discussed below, a significant proportion of mortuary pipes at Madisonville were of nonlocal styles or materials. This fits well with the idea of pipes as symbols of external interaction.

Pipes were negatively correlated with another important type of male-associated artifact. Small animal and bird skulls, thought to be the remains of medicine bags, were not found with known females. Only one of eleven burials accompanied by such remains also had a pipe. In the best-mapped portion of the Madisonville site, burials with medicine bags tended to be located on the north side of a small plaza, while burials with pipes were more common to its south. This was interpreted as possible evidence of functional dual division within the village (Drooker 1997:280–281).

Fort Ancient Interaction Patterns: Non-Pipe Evidence

Not surprisingly, since Fort Ancient territory was located at a nexus of important trails and water transportation routes, there is archaeological evidence for interregional interaction throughout the existence of this cultural tradition.

In addition to participating in relatively far-flung interaction networks, discussed below, both eastern and western Fort Ancient settlements had long-term ties to northern Ohio, manifest in utilitarian objects such as pottery and bone and stone tools (Drooker 1997:315–325, 329, 331). Middle Fort Ancient people also appear to have had strong relationships with Oliver phase people in central Indiana (Drooker 1997:47; McCullough 2000:253–256; Redmond and McCullough 2000:663–667, 672, 675–676).

During Early-Middle Fort Ancient (circa A.D. 1000–1450), the strongest long-distance ties were westward, to the upper Mississippi Valley, perhaps continuing a relationship in place since Hopewell times. Materials and artifacts at Early-Middle Fort Ancient sites from the upper Mississippi Valley or influenced by its material culture include particular styles of marine shell gorgets, native copper (presumably from the upper Great Lakes but never sourced using trace element analysis), ceramics, and large stone effigy pipes (Drooker 1994, 1997:89–95).

These upper Mississippi Valley ties were maintained during the Late Fort Ancient Madisonville Horizon (circa A.D. 1450–1700), particularly with western Fort Ancient sites (Drooker 1997:283–337). Oneota disk pipes (discussed below) are among the strongest indicators, but ceramics, protohistoric metal ornaments, and grave-good assemblages interpreted as medicine bags, among other evidence, also mark interaction between the two regions (Drooker 1996, 1997:331–332, 1999). Protohistoric sites in the two regions shared several types of copper and brass artifacts, the most distinctive of which were serpent-shaped pendants made from thin metal tubes and flat "cross-shaped" pendants (Drooker 1996, 1997:284–285, 292–293, Table 8-1, Figures 6-21f, 7-30b, 8-7, 8-9).

Small numbers of marine shell and ceramic items with connections to Armorel phase chiefdoms in the central Mississippi Valley also were present at the western Fort Ancient Madisonville site (Drooker 1997:332). Eastern Fort Ancient sites in West Virginia and nearby Kentucky show evidence for interaction with Dallas Mississippian communities to their south, including ceramic stylistic similarities and the presence of engraved marine shell gorgets in styles typical of eastern Tennessee (Brashler and Moxley 1990; Drooker 1997:294–305, 332; Hoffman 1998, 1999).

During the sixteenth and seventeenth centuries, some European artifacts reached Fort Ancient territory via these Mississippian connections. For example, a brass bell from the Madisonville site is of a type associated with the de Soto entrada (1539–1543); this site is the northernmost location from which such a

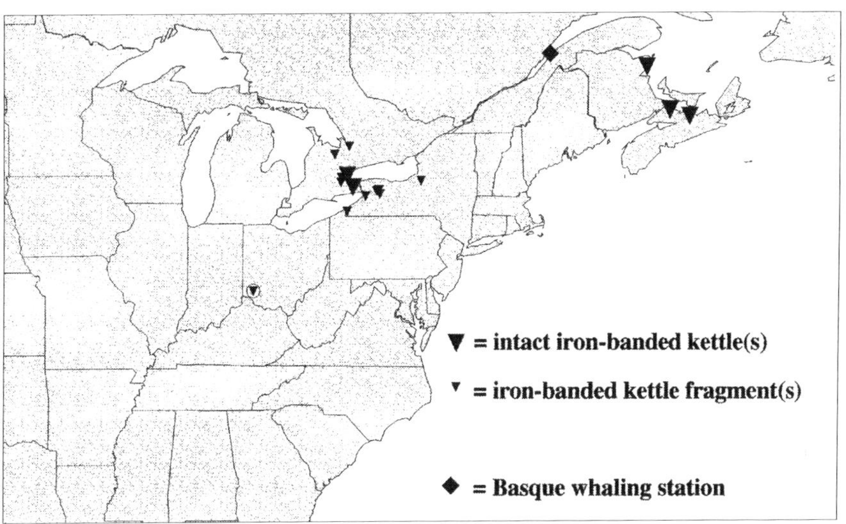

MAP 3.9. ▸ *Geographic distribution of large iron-fitted copper "Basque kettles" and parts.*

bell has come (Drooker 1997:162, Figure 8-1, 1998:Report 6). Brass side-view fish and animal effigy cutouts from the Clover and Beale Mound sites and large brass armbands from the Rolf Lee site represent artifact types primarily distributed in the seventeenth century Southeast from Spanish sources (Drooker 1997:172, 293, Table 4-9, Figures 8-12, 8-14; Waselkov 1989:126–127).

There is no archaeological evidence for pre–sixteenth century interaction between Fort Ancient and Iroquoian peoples (Drooker 1996:177; see also comments by Griffin [1993] on Dincauze and Hasenstab 1989). Surprisingly, interaction between the two regions suddenly becomes apparent in the late sixteenth century, flourishing briefly into the early 1600s. Evidence is particularly strong at the Madisonville site, where friable "Early Blue" glass beads, pieces of distinctive large copper kettles with iron fittings, an iron dagger guard, and a "Basque earring" spiral made from a thin tube of brass all are tied to Iroquoian territory and to the late sixteenth to early seventeenth century time period (Drooker 1996, 1997:89–97, 283–292, 333–335).

The kettle pieces and spiral ornament excavated at Madisonville are the westernmost examples of artifacts with very strong Iroquoian associations (Map 3.9; for site names, see Drooker 1997:Figure 8-2, to which add Ripley and Smokes Creek, New York; Gramly 1996:Figure 9d; New York State Museum cat. no. A88.32.39.06). The kettles (often called "Basque kettles"), excavated from both Northern Algonquian sites in the Maritime Provinces and Iroquoian sites in Ontario and New York, were obtained from Basque fishermen in the lower

St. Lawrence estuary starting around 1580 (Fitzgerald et al. 1993; Turgeon 1990, 1997). The spirals, manufactured indigenously from European metals, have been found almost exclusively at Iroquoian sites in Ontario, New York, Pennsylvania, and West Virginia (Bradley and Childs 1991; Drooker 1997:Figure 8-5).

It seems likely that much of the considerable quantity of European copper and brass at Madisonville was obtained via this northeastern avenue. The site produced more metal than any other protohistoric Fort Ancient site (Drooker 1997:Table 8-3). Since the metal assemblage included scrap, blanks for the production of small ornaments (Drooker 1997:Figures 6-21d, 6-21e), and discarded broken ornaments, such items probably were being made on site. Besides the spiral, Madisonville also produced many examples of small ring shapes and coil shapes made from thin metal tubes, plus distinctive finely wrought serpent shapes, more than at any other known site (Drooker 1997:Figures 6-21c, 6-21e, 6-21f, 7-30b). The distribution patterns for the coils and serpents strongly hint that Madisonville people were making these ornaments for exchange toward the west, using metal they obtained through Iroquoian peoples (Drooker 1997:Figures 8-5–8-8). Excavations at both an Ontario Neutral site and a New York Seneca site have produced bundles of metal pieces of the type that William Fitzgerald suggests might have been "gift packs" for external exchange (Fitzgerald 1990:546; RMSC catalog no. 12055/99).

If metal indeed was reaching Madisonville through Ontario and western New York, how was it being transported? Were Madisonville people, such as the young adult (I-60) buried in a belt decorated with large pieces of copper probably from a Basque kettle (Drooker 1997:262, 270, Figure 6-21b), trekking to southwestern Iroquoia, or might Iroquoian people have been traveling to the Ohio Valley? It is quite possible that both things were happening during a short period right around 1600. As will be discussed below, smoking pipes have been helpful in attempting to answer this question.

The Mid-Atlantic region probably was the source of some European goods excavated at other Late Fort Ancient sites. Glass beads from Rolf Lee are congruent with early seventeenth-century types present at Susquehannock sites (Drooker 1997:328, 333, Table 4-9; Graybill 1981:126–127). At least some metal at the Hardin site in Kentucky also might have come via the Chesapeake Bay region (Drooker 1997:294).

All European materials from the Madisonville site would have been available on this continent by around 1600. A few other Fort Ancient sites had somewhat later assemblages, but virtually all artifacts could have been obtained prior to midcentury (Drooker 1996, 1997:Fig. 3-8, Table 4-9).[7]

Nonlocal pipe types and pipe-making materials at protohistoric Fort Ancient sites and at selected protohistoric northeastern sites can provide further information on the nature and timing of these exchange relationships.

Fort Ancient Interaction Patterns: Evidence from Pipes

The most common pipes at Late Fort Ancient sites are ovoid and related forms like rectanguloid, made of local sandstone and limestone (Drooker 1997:Tables 4-3, 6-5). These and vasiforms constitute the core Late Fort Ancient types. None, however, is exclusive to Fort Ancient territory.

Pipes from the large Madisonville site assemblage objectify the interactions its residents enjoyed with peoples from an extremely broad surrounding area. Besides numerous nonlocal pipes excavated from middens and refuse pits (for example, Drooker 1997:8-25, 8-26), at least 33 percent of the thirty known mortuary pipes were of exotic material, nonlocal style, or both. Nonlocal materials in mortuary pipes included gray and red pipestone probably from both southeastern Ohio and the southern Minnesota–southern Wisconsin area, golden chalcedony probably from West Virginia, a crystalline anorthosite associated with northeastern Ohio, and a pisolithic rock from Arkansas (Drooker 1997:304–305, 309–310, 312). Mortuary pipes in styles with important interregional connections included at least four disk pipes, two keel-shaped pipes, a large perched bird effigy, two claw effigies, and a fenestrated bird effigy (Drooker 1997:302–315, Table 7-18, Figures 7-5, 7-6, 7-30a, 1998:Photos 335–340, 355–359, 419–422, 452–454, 485–491). The first type has upper Mississippi valley (Oneota) connections (and also constitutes an important Caborn-Welborn type), the second has both upper Mississippi Valley and northeastern Ohio connections, and the latter three have connections to the Northeast. The two largest Madisonville mortuary pipes—a perched owl made from Arkansas pisolithic rock and a bird effigy disk pipe made from West Virginia(?) chalcedony—combined exotic materials and forms from "opposite" directions and so might have been locally made hybrids.

Pipes with Oneota connections are not unexpectedly common, underlining the long-term interaction relationship between Ohio Valley and upper Mississippi Valley peoples. The disk pipe is the most common Fort Ancient pipe form with nonlocal connections (Drooker 1997:303–305, 309). Many disk pipes also have come from Caborn-Welborn territory farther west along the Ohio, often rendered in limestone (McGuire 1899:Figure 100; Moorehead 1906; Pollack, Munson, and Henderson 1996:21). For instance, the majority of mortuary pipes at the Murphy site in southwestern Indiana were of this form; at least one vasiform also was present (Moorehead 1906:Figure 23).

Madisonville has produced more disk pipes than any other Fort Ancient site: at least fourteen, almost 8 percent of the pipe assemblage at the site (Drooker 1997:Figures 7-5a, 7-6, 7-30, 8-25, 8-26, 1998:Photo 658). Disk pipes are statistically more common than expected in burials, constituting more than 13 percent of mortuary pipes. More than 30 percent of disk pipes at the site were grave goods.

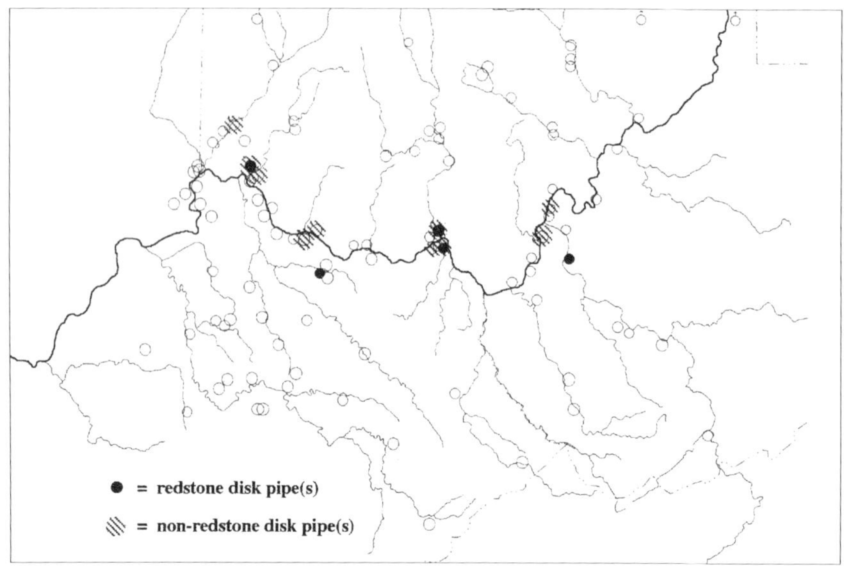

MAP 3.10. ▸ *Fort Ancient sites from which disk pipes have been excavated.*

These statistics corroborate other evidence (summarized in Drooker 1997:331–332) that the relationship between Madisonville residents and Oneota peoples was long term, positive, and important.

The most common disk pipe style present at the site is compact with a small disk (for example, Figure 3.1, top right), similar to pipes from protohistoric Orr Focus sites in northeastern Iowa (Wedel 1959:Figure 11; West 1934:Plate 257). Only three of the thirteen Madisonville disk pipes were made from red stone; one of these, from a burial, was engraved with the "forked eye" symbol (Drooker 1997:Figures 6-20, 7-6). One large, fine bird effigy disk pipe from a rich burial was carved of a golden chalcedony, probably from West Virginia (Drooker 1997:305, 309, Figure 7-30a). Many Madisonville disk pipes were fashioned from local materials, very likely locally made.

In addition to disk pipes proper, Madisonville also has produced forms that often are called "disk" in the literature (they are found associated with disk pipes in the upper Mississippi Valley), but in which the disk itself has shrunk to miniscule proportions (for example, Drooker 1997:Figure 8-26, bottom right, Figure 8-42, below; see also Hooton and Willoughby 1920:Plate 19l; compare with Hamilton 1967:Figures 3A, 3E, 4A, 4B, 4F; Wedel 1959:Figures 11h, 11i). Some of them may be transitional to later elbow ("calumet") forms.

Many other late prehistoric and protohistoric Fort Ancient sites have produced one or two disk pipes (Map 3.10; Drooker 1997:Figure 8-28; for descriptions and references, see Drooker 1997:90–91, 304; again note that the largest number has come from the Madisonville site). Disk pipes were found as grave goods at three of these sites at least. Although four finely made redstone large-disk "war bundle"–style pipes have been reported from Fort Ancient territory, none is firmly provenienced (Drooker 1997:304).

Not only disk pipes but also a variety of other pipe forms from Fort Ancient settlements were fashioned from red pipestone. At least some of them very likely were made from Minnesota catlinite or related upper Mississippi Valley redstones, as apparently confirmed by an early trace element analysis project that also detected Ohio pipestone at Utz, an early historical Oneota site in Missouri (Sigstad 1973). Unfortunately, analytical methods from that sourcing study were not adequate by today's standards (compare with Gundersen 1993). Analyses have been initiated on additional samples from Kentucky Fort Ancient sites (David Pollack, personal communication 2000). Madisonville site redstone has not been chemically sourced, but from visual characteristics, streak color, and hardness, at least three different types of redstone are present (Drooker 1997: 304–305, 1998:Photos 355–359, 542–544, 592–596, 1006–1011).

Keel-shaped pipes were very common at the Madisonville site (5 percent of the total pipe assemblage), so much so that I originally thought of them as a Fort Ancient style. However, they have been excavated at only one other Fort Ancient site, Orchard. The greatest known concentration of keel-shaped pipes was unearthed at the northeastern Ohio Reeve Village site (Ahlstrom 1979:Plate 18 and associated photographs). Examples of keel-shaped pipes also have come from a number of locations in Wisconsin (Map 3.3). Engraved motifs such as forked eyes and thunderbirds on some of the Madisonville examples, including one mortuary pipe, indicate a Mississippi Valley connection (Drooker 1997:Figures 7-6, 8-25, 8-26, 1998:Photos 369–372, 578–581, 650–654, 657); one specimen has both of those motifs, plus the Fort Ancient "+" motif (Drooker 1998:Photos 650–654). If, as noted above, the Wisconsin examples are connected with late-seventeenth-century Central Algonquian groups (see Map 3.4b), this provides additional evidence for the theory that Fort Ancient people were Central Algonquian speakers (Drooker 1997:227).

Iroquoian-style pipes were unexpectedly common at Madisonville, second only to disk pipes in their numbers (see Drooker 1997:308–309, 314 for detailed descriptions). Almost 7 percent of pipes, fragments, and blanks excavated at the site were stemmed Iroquoian types (both ceramic and stone). However, unlike Oneota disk pipes and northeastern forms with distributions concentrated outside Iroquoian territory such as bird and claw effigies, none were deposited as grave goods.

Iroquoian stemmed ceramic pipe fragments at Madisonville included trumpet, conical, acorn, and effigy forms in a variety of pastes (Drooker 1997:Figures 8-27a, 8-27b, 1998:Photos 368, 374–375, 382–384, 461, 462, 536, 537, 568–570). Three out of four extant ceramic stem fragments exhibit the bulbous ends found

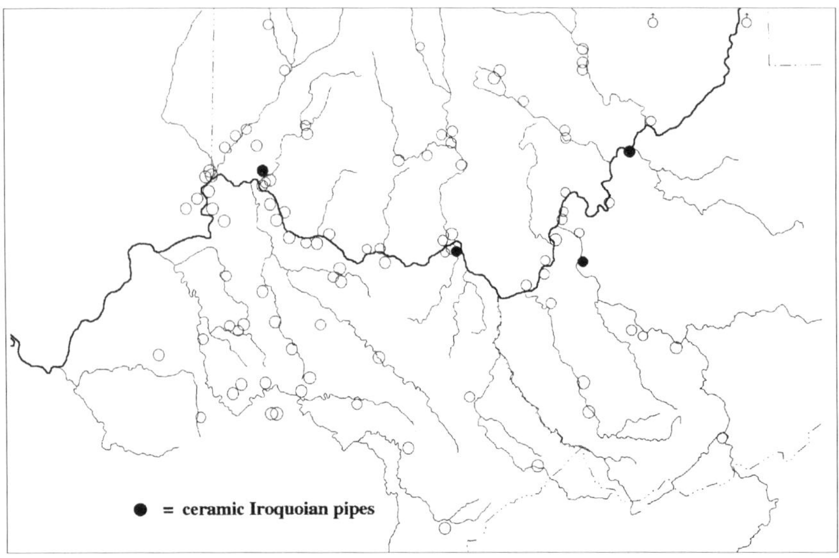

MAP 3.11. ▸ *Fort Ancient sites from which Iroquoian ceramic stemmed pipes or fragments have been excavated.*

on pipes from late-sixteenth- to early-seventeenth-century Erie and Neutral sites in western New York and southeastern Ontario, some of which also produced Basque kettle parts (Fitzgerald 1982:153–154; Lennox 1981:Figures 18, 42; White 1978:Figure 4; compare with Fitzgerald et al. 1993:Tables 1 and 4). Most other ceramic pipe fragments had similarities to examples from the western New York-southeastern Ontario region. Both of the ceramic effigy pipe fragments (owl and sitting human) correspond to Ontario effigy types defined by Noble (1979:Figures 1, 6), although owl effigies are fairly widely dispersed. For instance, some examples from Susquehannock sites (for example, Kent 1984:Figure 26) also are similar to the Madisonville fragment.

Several stone pipes from the Madisonville site have Iroquoian connections. Stems from two limestone lizard effigy pipes (Drooker 1997:Figure 8-27a, 1998: Photos 348, 626, 627) are similar but not identical in form to examples from a number of Ontario Iroquoian sites, and to one found under a copper kettle in Nova Scotia (Laidlaw 1914:56, 62–67). A gray stone pipe bowl, missing its stem, has a square collar encircled by horizontal lines (Drooker 1997:Figure 8-27a, 1998: Photos 616, 617), not unlike a cross between a round collared type and a coronet trumpet type (Figure 3.1, middle, second left, and rightmost examples). A carved sandstone ovoid human head effigy pipe bowl, unlike all other effigies from the site, has features that face the user (Drooker 1998:Photos 519–522). However, it is more finished than the most similar specimens that I have found: engraved stone ovoid examples from the late prehistoric Richmond Mills site in western New York (RMSC catalog nos. 70/101, 6015/101, 6459/101, 6460/101, 6463/101).

Only one of the Madisonville ceramic Iroquoian-style pipes was whole (a plain, narrowly flared trumpet or conical type [Drooker 1998:Photos 374–375]), and all of the specimens came from refuse pits or middens widely scattered around the site, not from mortuary contexts. Although smoking was important in Iroquoian ritual and everyday life, pipe bowls were not typically exchanged by individuals, in contrast to upper Mississippi Valley/Great Lakes customs. Thus, the presence of Iroquoian pipes implies the presence of Iroquoian people rather than transport of gift pipes by Fort Ancient people. The variety of pipe styles and pastes, and of intrasite proveniences, imply multiple visits by individuals from a variety of home locations. Among Fort Ancient sites, Madisonville has produced the largest number and the greatest variety of Iroquoian-style pipe fragments, both ceramic and stone (See Map 3.11 for the distribution of Iroquoian ceramic pipes and fragments within Ft. Ancient territory.) The largest number (nine) has come from the Madisonville site, which also has produced several stone pipes related to Iroquoian forms.

At least three other protohistoric Fort Ancient sites have produced ceramic Iroquoian pipes or fragments. A complete stemmed ceramic bulbous ringed pipe, obtained from the Hardin site by a private collector (Figure 3.2; Henderson et al. 1986:Figure 33A), is almost identical in form to examples from late-sixteenth to early-seventeenth-century Neutral, Erie, and Seneca sites (for example, Gramly 1996:25, Figure 5a; Lennox and Fitzgerald 1990:Figure 13.9; White 1978:Figure 4; RMSC catalog no. 5138/102). According to Pendergast, the bulbous ringed form "is widely acclaimed to be the 'normal' and 'usual' ceramic pipe used by the Iroquois over a large area and long time-span" (1992:52). The Hardin specimen was decorated with not only typical horizontal lines encircling the bowl but also an engraved lizard clinging to the bottom.

Additional ceramic pipe remains from protohistoric Fort Ancient sites include both fragments of Iroquoian pipes and probably non-Iroquoian shell-tempered specimens as follows: fragments from the upper three levels of controlled excavations at Hardin (Hanson 1966:115, Figure 46i); a shell-tempered ceramic pipe stem from the Clover site (Huntington Art Museum catalog number 80.206.823); three pipe bowl fragments from Blennerhasset Island, including one plain, narrowly flared trumpet or conical style (Hemmings 1976:57, Figure 1); and two ceramic stems from the Buffalo site, one of them shell tempered (Hanson 1975:87; West Virginia Division of Culture and History Collections Management Facility catalog nos. 206/453, 206/10301). Mayer-Oakes lists two ceramic pipe bowls, temper unknown, from his eastern Fort Ancient "Clover complex" sites, but neither their exact form nor the site name(s) are provided (1955:173).

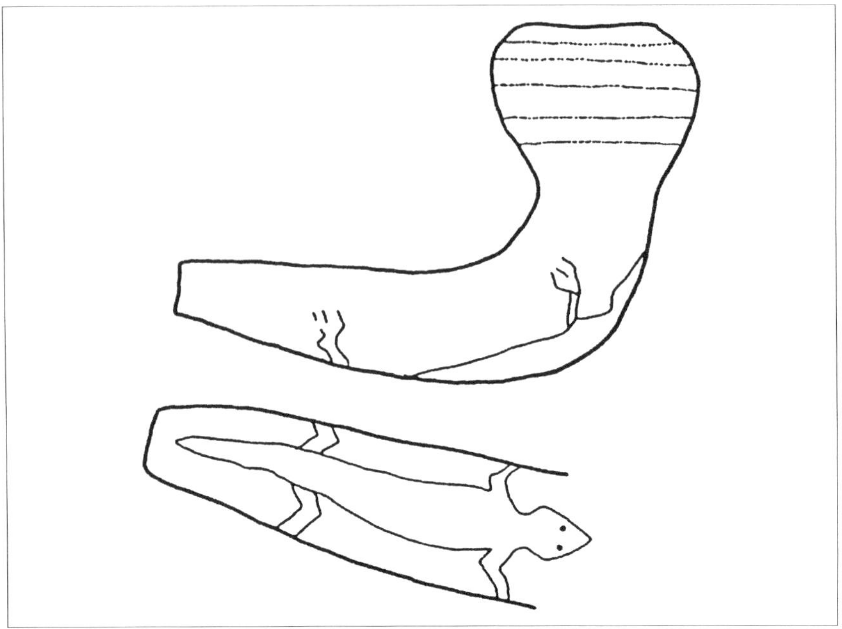

FIG. 3.2. ▸ *Drawing of engraved bulbous ring ceramic pipe from the Fort Ancient Hardin site.*

Relative strength and time depth of Iroquoian versus Oneota interactions with Fort Ancient people are apparent in the distributions of their pipes in the central Ohio River Valley. As perhaps might be expected, the disk pipe distribution in Fort Ancient territory extends farther westward than that of Iroquoian ceramic pipes (Map 3.10), while Iroquoian ceramic pipes are found farther to the east (Map 3.11). Madisonville has produced significantly more of both types than any other central Ohio Valley site. Disk pipes were present in greater numbers and at more Fort Ancient sites than Iroquoian pipes, and they were excavated at both prehistoric and protohistoric settlements. In contrast, Iroquoian pipes have been found exclusively at late-sixteenth- to early-seventeenth-century sites. I know of no Iroquoian pipes from Fort Ancient sites that have produced post-1630 artifacts (for example, Clover, Rolf Lee, Orchard, and Marmet).[8]

Some eastern Fort Ancient sites, including Orchard and Man, have produced Monongahela-style stemmed stone pipes, including one with a brass insert (Moxley 1985a:46, 1988:Figure 13). A steatite turkey effigy elbow pipe from Madison ville and a similar limestone bird effigy pipe from a burial at the Mt. Carbon site have the basic Monongahela stone pipe form (McMichael 1962:Plate 8; Drooker 1997:314–315, Figure 8-25). I do not know of any Monongahela Monyock Cord-impressed ceramic pipes from Fort Ancient sites.

Several other pipes from Fort Ancient sites, the majority of them from male burials at Madisonville, point toward interaction with *northeastern Ohio, Pennsylvania, and perhaps farther north.* Two fenestrated bird effigies were excavated at Madisonville, the only fenestrated pipes of known provenience from Fort Ancient territory (Map 3.6). One, a two-headed swan, was a mortuary offering for a young adult male (Drooker 1997:Figure 7-5a, 1998:Photos 548–552). Only one perching bird effigy was excavated at Madisonville, but it was spectacular: a very large owl buried with a young adult male (Drooker 1997:Figure 7-5c). Although distribution of the perching owl form is primarily to the northeast of Madisonville (Map 3.5), this particular pipe was made of a distinctive speckled stone from Arkansas (Drooker 1997:309–310). Perching bird pipes from eastern Fort Ancient sites include a vulture effigy buried with a young child at Neale's Landing and an eagle or other predator with a human head in its talons buried with an adult male at Buffalo (Hanson 1975:Figure 70; Hemmings 1976:Figure 1d). Of the three claw effigies excavated at Madisonville (see Map 3.7 for geographical distribution of this form), two were mortuary offerings with adults, one of whom was an older male who was among the two or three highest status people interred at the site (Drooker 1997:258–282).

Various unique stone pipes from nonmortuary contexts at the Madisonville site point toward *additional areas of contact.* A scratched and battered long-beaked bird head fragment (Drooker 1997:Figure 8-25, third row, 1998:Photos 605–609) is stylistically close to "woodpecker or kingfisher" and turtle effigy pipes from Dumaw Creek in west central Michigan (Quimby 1966:52–53); stylistically similar examples from Wisconsin and Oneida River, New York, have been published by Laidlaw (1913:64, 66; see also Beauchamp 1897:Figure 103). A finely made fish effigy pipe and a ridged-shell turtle effigy pipe (Cowan 1987:Figure 30; Drooker 1997: Figures 8-25, 8-26, 1998:Photos 365–367, 571–574) are amazingly similar to ceramic effigy vessels from protohistoric central Mississippi Valley sites (for example, Brown 1926:Figures 286, 287; Hathcock 1976:130–133, 138; Thruston 1897:Plate 7).

At least eleven finely made highly varied foreign-style stone pipes at Madisonville were fashioned from visually similar materials, gray limestone(s) with white inclusions (Drooker 1997:Figures 8-27a bottom, 8-42, 1998:Photos 331, 348, 448, 451–454, 509–511, 512–514, 518, 558, 567, 571–574, 660). These pipes included disks and related forms, keel shapes, Iroquoian-style stemmed lizard effigy pipes, a claw effigy, and the fish effigy mentioned above. None were deposited with burials. I have proposed that they perhaps represent pipes made at this settlement for presentation to interaction partners from a variety of different regions (Drooker 1997:336).

All in all, the Madisonville site is a superb example of how pipes can indicate not only the locations of foreign interaction partners but also the nature of the interactions. For example, the high representation of disk pipes among grave goods of important adult men at Madisonville, together with several instances of locally made disk pipes, underline a positive and intimate long-term relationship with upper Mississippi Valley Oneota people. In contrast, Iroquoian ceramic pipe fragments, all from nonmortuary contexts, in conjunction with a sudden influx of small European items funneled from the St. Lawrence region, marked the presence of short-term visitors connected with a trade network active for only a few decades around A.D. 1600. Finally, although there were relatively few bird and claw effigy pipes at Madisonville, most were placed as mortuary offerings with adult males. The closest site from which a significant number of such pipes has been recovered is Reeve Village in northeastern Ohio, lending support to the hypothesis that men from southwestern and northeastern Ohio had direct and positive interaction relationships (Drooker 1997:329, 331).

Studying the Madisonville pipe assemblage in depth has made me particularly aware of the information potential of pipes at other archaeological sites. A brief look at a few other contemporaneous sites will show some additional relationships.

The Reeve Site

The Whittlesey archaeological tradition was present in northeastern Ohio until the early seventeenth century (Brose 2000:106–108; Drooker 1997:46–47). Brose places the Algonquian/Iroquoian interface immediately to its east, around Ashtabula, where he recognizes an Iroquoian-affiliated Eastwall complex (Brose 2000: 111). Exotic ceramics and other diagnostic artifacts at Whittlesey sites provide evidence for interaction with Oneota, Indian Hills, Fort Ancient, Riker-Wellsburg, and Iroquoian peoples (Brose 2000:107–108).

The Reeve Village (Willoughby) site, on the Chagrin River a mile from Lake Erie, was among the first Whittlesey settlements to be excavated by professional archaeologists, but only after some fifty years of amateur depredations, which continued at least until 1973–1974, when a condominium complex was built there (Ahlstrom 1979:9–14; Greenman 1935:5–7). Even during the 1929 excavations by the Ohio State Archaeological and Historical Society, “few measurements were taken, either vertically or horizontally” (Greenman 1935:5), so provenience and context are lacking for most of the artifacts collected.

Nevertheless, the large pipe assemblage from the site, documented primarily through a concerted effort by the Lake County Chapter of the Archaeological Society of Ohio, contains much useful data. One hundred eighty pipes were recorded as definitely from the site. At least some post-Contact site use is indicated by the presence of nine European white ball clay pipe fragments, although most were from disturbed contexts (Ahlstrom 1979:Plate 21; see Stothers 2000:76 for a summary of [uncalibrated] seventeenth-century radiocarbon dates from related Whittlesey sites). No pipes were recorded as coming from burials; indeed, only one burial was reported, of a woman and child (Greenman 1935:10–11). Pipe blanks were not uncommon, indicating the possible manufacture of pipes at the site. A wide variety of forms and materials were present, implying significant interregional interaction. Quite a few pipes and blanks were made from a white crystalline anorthosite or quartzite (for example, AMNH catalog nos. 9/68, 9/87, 9/89 from the Williams Collection). Two mortuary pipes and a pipe blank of this material that were excavated at Madisonville are interpreted as originating at or near the Reeve site (Drooker 1997:2–7, 209). At least eighteen pipes were of pipestone, including reddish, reddish brown, brown, tan, and gray colorations (Ahlstrom 1979:Plates 1, 11, 26, 27, 74, 75, 79, 81, 82, 85, 92, 93, 115, 120, 121, 126, 133, 150); it is likely that much of this material came from southeastern Ohio. Recognizable forms made from pipestone included ovoid, trapezoidal (3), vasiform (6), keel, elbow, semi-elbow, bird effigy (2), animal head effigy, and a small disk pipe of reddish pipestone.

At 21 percent each, vasiforms and ovoids/rectanguloids/trapezoidals—typical of Fort Ancient pipe assemblages—were the most common forms (Ahlstrom 1979:Plates 11, 17, 18). The keel shape, present as 5 percent of the Madisonville pipe assemblage, represented 11 percent of the assemblage at Reeve, both a larger proportion and a larger number than at any other known site (Ahlstrom 1979:Plate 18). The geographical distribution of keel-shaped pipes (Map 3.3) implies a relationship with later seventeenth-century Central Algonquian groups in Wisconsin (Map 3.4b). Perched bird effigies and blanks, at 14 percent, constitute the largest group of this pipe form that I know of from any site; its production may well be centered in this region (Ahlstrom 1979:Plates 7, 14, 15, 22, 23). Birds with short, blunt beaks, like those of Carolina parakeets, and owl forms predominated among this effigy type. There were three claw effigies (more than from any other known site except for Madisonville), and at least one each human head and animal head effigies (Ahlstrom 1979:Plate 16), comparatively common at Fort Ancient sites. Iroquoian stemmed ceramic pipes and fragments (Ahlstrom 1979:Plates 9, 10) make up 12 percent of the assemblage, indicating an intensity of interaction second only to that with Fort Ancient people. Forms include an undecorated trumpet, a bulbous ring pipe, a bulbous form without engraved horizontal lines, a collared specimen, and less-bulbous styles classifiable as conical, elongated, or barrel (Noble 1992:Figures 1, 2; Pendergast 1992:57). There were no ceramic effigy pipes. Only two disk type pipes, with very small disks, were recorded (Ahlstrom 1979: Plates 74, 142). One, of reddish pipestone, might be an Oneota import; the other, of quartzite, might be made from local stone.

Clearly, Reeve Village residents participated in an interaction network that included all of their immediate neighbors and Fort Ancient people as far as three hundred miles away, and that may have extended ultimately from the upper

Mississippi Valley to the St. Lawrence estuary. Because of sparse contextual information and lack of mortuary pipes, no detailed interpretation of the sociopolitical relationships behind these interactions is possible. However, this settlement appears to have been, at the very least, a significant node in the network.

The Ripley Site

The late prehistoric-protohistoric Ripley site is located on a bluff above Lake Erie near the Pennsylvania line in southwestern New York. Major excavations were carried out by institutional teams in 1904, 1906, and 1988 and by amateurs in 1957–1959 and 1962–1965 (Conklin 1989; Parker 1907; Sullivan et al. 1996:28–52). Important features included an earth ring, more than two hundred burials, and numerous storage and refuse pits. Relatively few house features were reported, none of them longhouses. From radiocarbon dates, artifact assemblages, and European objects present, Ripley appears to have been utilized over a period of several centuries, perhaps as late as the early 1600s (Sullivan 1996:122). Sullivan suggests that this might have been a special-purpose site, oriented toward mortuary ritual (1996:123–127).

Although early investigators suggested an Erie affiliation (Parker 1907), current researchers find no clear correlations between site occupants and any historically named group (Sullivan 1996:122–123). According to Engelbrecht and Sullivan, "At the present time, the culture history of late prehistoric and early historic times in the southeastern Lake Erie Basin is just a bare outline into which the Ripley site can only crudely be fitted (1996:27)." Their research, however, has made progress toward fleshing out that outline. For example, an attribute analysis of Ripley ceramics from curated collections and comparison with assemblages from eleven other western New York sites found the highest coefficient of agreement between Ripley pottery and the assemblage from Newton-Hopper, a Niagara frontier site just west of Buffalo, about seventy miles to the northeast of Ripley (Engelbrecht 1996:66–68). A comparison of mortuary treatments at Ripley with those at four mid- to late-sixteenth-century Seneca sites found differences significant enough to suggest ethnically separate groups (Sullivan and Coffin 1996:115–118).

Engelbrecht and Sullivan note (1996:27) that the southeastern Lake Erie basin region appears to be "a natural laboratory for examining questions related to interaction spheres between the resident populations, neighboring Iroquoian groups, and the late cultures of the Upper Midwest. Both environmental and cultural characteristics strongly suggest this area played a key role in relationships between the better known 'culture areas' to the east and west. . . . The nature of these interactions is unknown, and this important question cannot be explored effectively until more basic questions regarding settlement patterns and temporal relationships are better delineated."

Smoking pipes and European-related artifacts from the Ripley site can be very helpful in elucidating some of these interregional relationships.

From its assemblage of European metal and glass items, Ripley appears to have been closely contemporaneous with Madisonville. Both have produced examples of the earliest types of European objects traded in via the St. Lawrence estuary (Drooker 1996). Ripley is the closest site to Madisonville (and the southwesternmost Iroquoian site) at which Basque kettle fragments are known to have been excavated (Map 3.9). Both sites have produced examples of the "Early Blue" glass bead type common in the years around 1600 (Drooker 1996, 1997:163, Figure 8-4, 1998:Photos 39, 150–155; Parker 1907:494; Harvard University Peabody Museum Ripley site collection). Other artifact types shared with Madisonville include spirals made of thin metal tubes, iron dagger parts, and crude finger rings made from rectangular pieces of brass (Drooker 1997:Table 8-1, Figures 6-21b, 6.21f; Parker 1907:546, Plates 37.5, 37.10; Sullivan and Coffin 1996:Figure 9.9; New York State Museum cat. nos. 36904, 75688). Fitzgerald, in his summary of European objects at Ontario sites circa 1500–1650, lists this type of finger ring as coming only from late-sixteenth-century sites: one Huron-Petun, one Neutral, and one Niagara Frontier, near Buffalo (1990:Table 33); another has come from the late-sixteenth-century Indian Hills Muddy Creek site (Stothers 2000:65, 67), plus several examples from Seneca sites (see below).

The Ripley metal assemblage contains more iron than that of Madisonville, as well as objects such as spoons that are not present at the latter site. The Ripley glass bead assemblage may be larger than Madisonville's. In addition to the "Early Blue" beads found as grave goods with two burials, in the New York State Museum (NYSM) Ripley collection there are white, blue, and red tubular "Ontario" types that date to the first half of the seventeenth century; unfortunately, their intrasite provenience is unknown (Kenyon and Kenyon 1983; NYSM cat. no. 70156). Percentages of burials with European goods are about twice as high at Ripley as at Madisonville (Drooker 1997:Table 7-6; Sullivan and Coffin 1996:Figure 9.11). This reflects the New York site's location closer to the source of supply, and perhaps a somewhat longer occupation period. Because of the lack of striped polychrome glass bead types, it seems unlikely that Ripley residents participated in the interaction network receiving Dutch trade goods from Albany after around 1610 (Fitzgerald 1990; Kenyon and Fitzgerald 1986).

Smoking pipes at Ripley were notably eclectic, reflecting just the sorts of interregional interactions in which Engelbrecht and Sullivan were interested. Mortuary pipes, in particular, contain a disproportionate number of specimens with nonlocal connections. At least sixty-seven pipes and pipe fragments have come from Ripley, most of them ceramic stemmed Iroquoian styles. Of the eleven stone pipes, all but one require separate stems.

Seven percent of the burials were interred with pipes (a much higher proportion than Madisonville's 2 percent). Mortuary pipes are strongly but not exclusively associated with adults and with males at Ripley. One subadult and perhaps one adult female were buried with pipes, as were nine known men, an adult, and two unidentified individuals; age was known for four of the men, who all were over thirty.

Nonlocal pipes are significantly more common as grave goods than expected from their frequency in the assemblage as a whole, some 43–50 percent of all mortuary pipes. Whereas only 16 percent of all the pipes were stone, at least 36 percent of the mortuary pipes were stone (one is of unknown material), including styles associated with Fort Ancient, Whittlesey, and Monongahela sites. Some ceramic mortuary pipes also had nonlocal associations.

An outstanding ceramic two-faced Janus human effigy pipe was interred with a mature adult man (age thirty-one to forty) who also was one of seven adults with a cut bear maxilla headdress, one of the few authority or status markers identified at the site (Parker 1907:Plates 8.1, 31.3, 31.4, Figure 9; Sullivan and Coffin 1996:110, 112). No other pipe of this style is known from the southeastern Lake Erie basin. Nine examples are recorded from Huron territory, 35 percent of the known specimens of this type (Pendergast 1980:Table 2). The style of the face appears very similar to that of the non-Janus Roebuck human effigy pipe, from a St. Lawrence Iroquoian site (Pendergast 1992:54).

Another ceramic mortuary pipe with Ontario Iroquoian affiliations is the only coronet trumpet pipe from the site, buried with an older man (over forty) (Parker 1907:Plates 8.2, 31.2). According to Noble, this style "appears on all historic Neutral sites often in burial association with adult males of distinction" (1992:44). Pendergast, however, says that it "has long been diagnostically associated with the Huron and Petun" (1992:58). (These are not, of course, mutually exclusive statements.) Its presence on St. Lawrence Iroquoian sites near the confluence of the Ottawa and St. Lawrence Rivers, far from Huron territory, has been interpreted as marking interaction associated with exchange of European goods during the very early Contact period (Pendergast 1992:58; see also Trigger 1986:150).

Another "one-of-a-kind" pipe at the site, a stone fenestrated animal effigy buried with an older man (Parker 1907:Plate 22.5, Figure 14), also is a type that has its greatest concentration in Huron and Neutral territory (Map 3.6). Its material is a light gray pipestone, perhaps of Ohio origin.

Other stone pipes found with burials include an ovoid (either with a female burial or from a pit above [Parker 1907:Plate 22.3; Sullivan and Coffin 1996:117] and a claw effigy (Parker 1907:Plate 22.4)—types associated with Ohio sites—a Monongahela style stemmed pipe made of what appears to be Ohio pipestone (Parker 1907:Plate 22.6), and a rectanguloid elbow pipe with similarities to pipes from the late prehistoric Algonquian Dumaw Creek site in western Michigan (Parker 1907:Plate 22.7; Quimby 1966:Figure 20).

Nonmortuary stone pipes at the site included a second claw effigy (Parker 1907:Plate 22.1), a vasiform (Parker 1907:Plate 22.2), and a rectanguloid. A frag-

TABLE 3.1 ▸ Results of Trace Element Analysis of Ceramic Pipe Fragments from Seneca Sites

Sites	Approx. Dates	Specimens Analyzed	Specimens Classified as Mohawk
Richmond Mills	ca. 1550	17	
Belcher	ca. 1550	9	
Adams	1565–1575	3	
Tram	1575–1590	4	
Cameron	1590–1605	14	1
Fugle	1605–1625	6	
Dutch Hollow	1605–1620	22	1
Factory Hollow	1610–1625	21	3

ment of a disk pipe decorated with a crudely engraved underwater panther figure was excavated at Ripley (Harvard University Peabody Museum cat. no. 04-3-10/65225). However, it was treated rather differently than the other nonlocal pipes—the surviving fragment appears to have been hacked to pieces.[9]

Whether or not the Ripley site functioned primarily as a ceremonial center associated with mortuary ritual, it also has the earmarks of an interaction network node. The variety of foreign-style mortuary pipes implies positive relationships with a number of different groups, both Iroquoian and non-Iroquoian but excluding Oneota. It is quite possible that these relationships involved the exchange of European metal and glass obtained via down-the-line exchange from Basque and French traders in the St. Lawrence estuary.

Early Seneca Sites

One more brief case history will further illustrate the usefulness of smoking pipes as markers of interaction.

Robert Kuhn and Martha Sempowski have investigated the initiation of interaction between the easternmost (Mohawk) and westernmost (Seneca) members of the Iroquois League through trace element analysis of ceramic pipes excavated at Seneca sites (Kuhn and Sempowski 2001). Their sample included ninety-six pipes from eight Seneca sites dating between 1550 and 1625. Pipe fragments made from Mohawk Valley clays were not detected at the four earliest sites tested but were identified at three of the four most recent sites: Cameron, Dutch Hollow, and Factory Hollow (Table 3.1).

It is noteworthy that the earlier sites in this sequence evidence a significant number of westward connections in their pipes and metals, compared with the later sites. Before returning to the trace element study, I include a brief summary of pipe types and proveniences from these sites.

The prehistoric mid-sixteenth century site, Richmond Mills (Reed Fort), appears to be where East meets, and even merges with, West in the pipe assemblage. Of more than 80 pipes from the site in the collections of the Rochester Museum and Science Center (RMSC) and the New York State Museum (NYSM), approximately half are stone and half ceramic. (Parker, who excavated at the site, recorded a total of 124 pipes from it [1918:32; see also Parker 1922:182–207], but many must have remained in private hands. The RMSC and NYSM collections include pipes excavated both before and after Parker's count.)

The twenty-one stone ovoid forms from the site include six very rough human effigy heads, all of which—unlike examples from the Ohio Valley—face the smoker (RMSC cat. nos. 70/101, 6015/101, 6016/101, 6459/101, 6460/101, 6463/101). This is the only site of which I know that has more than one such effigy. Many of the other stone pipes from the site—at least nine—are rectanguloid or trianguloid. None of these shapes, although perhaps rougher than the norm, would appear out of place on a Fort Ancient site.

At least one and perhaps two portions of perched bird effigy pipes came from the site (RMSC 6017/101, 18235/101). Two sandstone pipes are similar in form to keel-shaped pipes but have stem holes in the wide side rather than the narrow side (RMSC 5002/101, 6462/101). One small fragment of gray pipestone appears to be a piece of a conical bowl from a stemmed pipe—that is, an Iroquoian form in an Ohio Valley material (RMSC AR39029). Likewise, an ovoid with a lizard grasping the bowl and peering over it toward the smoker (NYSM 28813)—a nonfenestrated form most similar to fenestrated examples from southern Ontario and Jefferson County, New York (for example, Laidlaw 1914:49–52)—is of mottled gray pipestone. Nonfenestrated examples with short stems are known from Pennsylvania, Maine, and Blennerhassett Island, West Virginia, where the Fort Ancient Neale's Landing site is located (Hemmings 1976:Figure 3a; Laidlaw 1915:Figures 1, 2).

Among the ceramic pipes and fragments is a coronet trumpet bowl (NYSM 36050), a style associated with Huronia. Stemmed ceramic human effigy pipes (similar to examples in Parker 1922:Plates 67.2, 67.3, 67.6) were relatively common at the site. According to Wray et al. (1987:133), they are distinctive and consistent in both style and paste. Examples are known from two other early Seneca sites, including several from Belcher (Table 3.1), but the style abruptly disappears from the Seneca sequence after that, for reasons unknown.

Only two pipes were found with burials at Richmond Mills. Like the pipe assemblage as a whole, they symbolize interaction in two opposite directions. One is an outstanding ceramic human effigy (RMSC 5003/101). The other, a finely made redstone large-disk pipe almost certainly of Oneota origin (RMSC 5028/101), was buried in front of the face of an adult male (Hamilton 1967:24, Figure 15A; Witthoft, Schoff, and Wray 1953:92, Plate 2.2). According to Witthoft, Schoff, and Wray, "The pipe is almost certain evidence of Iroquoian familiarity with the prairie forms of pipe ceremonialism in political life at this early period" (1953:92). Both mortuary pipes were broken ("killed") at the time of interment (all pieces were present), perhaps underscoring their perceived power (Witthoft, Schoff, and Wray 1953:92; conservator's report for 5003/101 on file at RMSC).

No European goods have been reported from Richmond Mills, so whatever interaction patterns are objectified in its pipes apparently were not impelled by European-era trade.

The sequentially occupied Adams, Tram, and Cameron sites (Table 3.1) are among the earliest in the Seneca sequence from which have come European goods (only one, Culbertson, has earlier dates). These include objects very similar to those from the roughly contemporaneous Madisonville and Ripley sites, but generally in larger numbers and more variety (Wray et al. 1987:48–61,114–122, 128, 132, 1991:70–83, 119–126, 134–140, 244–257, 317–328). Glass beads of several types have come from all three of these sites, including "Early Blue" specimens from Adams and Cameron. Cylindrical finger rings were found at Adams and Tram. All three sites produced spirals made from thin metal tubes, with rings and a coil made from thin metal tubes additionally coming from Adams. Some of the iron from these sites might perhaps be from Basque kettle fittings, but they have not been identified as such. A piece of an iron sword blade came from Adams (Wray et al. 1987:Figure 3-64b), and iron dagger or sword guards were excavated at Cameron and at the later Fugle (or Feugle) site (Sempowski and Saunders 2001:639–640; Wray et al. 1991:325, Figure 7-106), similar to one excavated from a burial at the Madisonville site (Drooker 1997:Figure 6-21f).

The Adams site collection was excavated primarily from burials (Wray et al. 1987:11). It includes only eleven pipes and fragments: four each ceramic and stone, and (likely) three of wood, deduced from the patterns of shell inlay that were their only remains (Wray et al. 1987:132–134, 145, Figures 3-90, 3-91, 3-92). Seven of the eleven were deposited as grave goods, all with adult males, the majority of whom also had European-derived objects. Three mortuary pipes were wooden. Only one was ceramic, a crudely made trumpet. The three separate-stemmed stone mortuary pipes include a large polished red slate vasiform, an engraved sandstone ovoid, and a unique carved limestone two-headed human effigy pipe with the heads protruding to the two sides. In addition, a fragment of a conical pipe bowl of gray Ohio fireclay came from a nonmortuary context.

The collection from Tram likewise was obtained mainly from excavation of burials (Wray et al. 1991:14). Of eight pipes and fragments from the site, there were three mortuary pipes: one out of six ceramic specimens (known only from excavation notes), a separate-stemmed sandstone trapezoidal pipe bowl (the only stone pipe from the site), and an unusual antler bird effigy pipe (Wray et al.

1991:47–48, 142–144). Age and sex of the burial with the stone pipe are unknown, but the others were adult males, neither of which had European goods.

The Cameron assemblage came from both excavation of burials and surface survey (Wray et al. 1991:179, 335–338). Only one pipe of thirty-seven whole or partial specimens in the collection was with a burial. It is a unique wooden ovoid, interred with an adolescent whose many other grave goods included brass/copper ornaments. The remainder of the specimens include thirty-two ceramic fragments and four stone examples. Among the ceramics, there is at least one coronet trumpet fragment. Stone specimens include a limestone ovoid, a sandstone trianguloid, and two pipestone stem fragments.

All of the complete stone pipes from these three sites are consistent with forms from Richmond Mills and would not be unusual finds at a Fort Ancient site.

Smoking pipes increased in numbers, variety, and presence as grave goods at the three early-seventeenth-century sites included in the Kuhn and Sempowski analysis: Fugle, Dutch Hollow, and Factory Hollow (Kuhn and Sempowski 2001:311–312; Sempowski and Saunders 2003:239). Ringbowl and effigy pipes are the most common ceramic types. Stone pipes were present only in very small numbers, but a relatively high proportion of them were deposited as grave goods.

Fugle, the smallest of these sites, yielded twenty-six pipes, all of them ceramic except for one unique brass pipe. Four of these (three ceramic, one brass) were deposited as grave goods (Sempowski and Saunders 2001:646–651).

Factory Hollow, a large village with outlying cemetery areas, is the latest-occupied Seneca site that has produced a stone pipe (Sempowski and Saunders 2001:516–533). Of 217 pipes and fragments from the site, just 1 was stone, a flattened vasiform with a castellated rim and an attachment hole at its base (Sempowski and Saunders 2001:Figure 7-206). This pipe was a burial offering with an adult probable male who also had a number of iron European objects. Of 3 coronet trumpet pipes at the site (a type with Ontario Iroquoian affiliations), none were grave goods; 1 of the 3 that was among the 21 pipes from the site tested by Kuhn was found to be of local clay (Sempowski and Saunders 2001:528). Fifteen (7 percent) of the 217 pipes at the site were mortuary; 1 each were stone and wood, the rest were ceramic.

Dutch Hollow, a large village site with several surrounding cemetery areas that was occupied concurrently with Factory Hollow, but beginning and ending slightly earlier, produced at least 232 aboriginal smoking pipes: 224 ceramic, 6 stone, and 2 wood with metal pipe liners (Sempowski and Saunders 2001:239–259). Twenty-one (9 percent) of the pipes were mortuary, including 3 stone, 16 ceramic, and 2 wood. Among the ceramic pipes were 2 coronet trumpet pipes, one of which (Sempowski and Saunders 2001:Figure 3-195) was buried with a young adult male whose grave goods included another ceramic pipe, a dog tooth and shell bead necklace, a bear jaw and humerus, red ochre, and an iron knife. The stone pipes included 2 white limestone stem fragments, 2 vasiform pipes,

1 ovoid with a slight elbow (described as vasiform by Sempowski and Saunders), and 2 fragments from a polished gray pipestone disk pipe (Sempowski and Saunders 2001:Figures 3-197, 3-198, 3-199, 3-200). The ovoid and vasiforms all are flattened in form and have attachment holes at their bottoms, and all three were interred with burials. A fourth stone pipe, no longer in the RMSC collection, also was said to have been mortuary. These four burials were adults, three known to be male or probably male. Three of the four had elaborate grave-good assemblages that included two or more types of European goods; the fourth had a turtle shell rattle, a cut section of bear skull, and bird bones.

It is of interest that all four of the extant stone mortuary pipes from Factory Hollow and Dutch Hollow were fashioned of a yellowish-tan chalcedony or similar banded siliceous stone very much like specimens from Madisonville (personal observation), which probably comes from a West Virginia source (Drooker 1997:305, 309). These pipes were finely polished, some with engraved decoration. Unlike the vasiforms and ovoids from earlier Seneca sites, however, these differ from typical Ohio pipe forms in their castellated rims, flattened cross sections, and attachment holes.

In contrast to the ovoid and vasiform pipes deposited as grave goods, the fragmentary disk pipe from Dutch Hollow (Saunders and Sempowski 2001:Figure 3-200) may well have been deliberately smashed.

Thus, until the end of the sixteenth century, stone mortuary pipes in styles congruent with Ohio Valley forms were frequently buried with men whose other grave goods included European items and other significant artifacts. Ceramic mortuary pipes were less common than pipes made from other materials. After the turn of the century, stemmed ceramic pipes come to the fore. Kuhn and Sempowski note that numbers of ceramic pipes increase dramatically in the Dutch Hollow and Factory Hollow assemblages compared with earlier sites (2001:311–312). They tie this, along with the appearance of Mohawk pipes at Seneca sites, to "Seneca inclusion in an expanding confederacy" (2001:312).

Two other relevant phenomena are associated with Seneca sites of the early seventeenth century: "a significant elaboration of mortuary practices . . . which may reflect a heightened interest in condolence associated with League ceremonialism," and a significant increase in trade goods of types connected with Dutch traders operating near Albany, goods that would have had to have been obtained through the Mohawks, the easternmost members of the League (Kuhn and Sempowski 2001:312; Sempowski 1994:60). From this and other evidence, including oral tradition, Kuhn and Sempowski propose that the Seneca, the last of the original Five Nations to join the Iroquois confederacy, were brought into it during this period (2001:311).

In an earlier publication, Sempowski (1994) presented evidence that the Seneca seemed to break off relations with former non-League Iroquoian trading partners at about this same time (see also Sempowski and Saunders 2001:

687–690). Until the early 1600s, the Seneca had been middlemen in the exchange of marine shell from Iroquoian Susquehannock people at the head of Chesapeake Bay, northwest through the Niagara Falls area to Neutral, Huron, and other groups in Ontario. After that time, the Seneca marine shell supply plummeted, while Dutch-style polychrome glass beads became common relative to the types of glass beads being supplied to Ontario Iroquoians by the French in Quebec. Amounts of other European goods, acquired from Dutch traders through the Mohawk at the eastern door of the Iroquois confederacy, increased significantly. Within a decade or two, the so-called Beaver Wars between the Iroquois League and their western neighbors were in full swing.

Conclusion

It is those mid-seventeenth-century wars that until recently have dominated the historical record of Iroquois interactions with their neighbors (for example, Hunt 1940; Jennings 1984:84–112; White 1991). Without input from archaeology, it is doubtful whether we would have had any idea that there was at least a short period when the Seneca apparently were on good terms with groups to their south and west, or that a late sixteenth-century exchange network reached all the way from the St. Lawrence estuary to southwestern Ohio and beyond. The variety of information that can be obtained from smoking pipes in use across this wide region is essential to deciphering both intra- and interregional political and economic relationships during the protohistoric period.

Notes

1. Protohistoric refers to the time period between "the first appearance of European goods and the earliest substantial [written] historical records" (Trigger 1986:116).

2. See Hughes et al. (1998:711) for nomenclature related to the soft, easily carved pipestones favored by midwestern artists. The definitions in that publication are "generally accepted by geologists." Usage of some terms differs from other current literature. For example, the definition of argillite (metamorphic rock, originally a claystone) differs from the usage by Emerson and Hughes, who define it as a sedimentary rock (2001:151).

3. From pottery styles and other evidence, it is thought that Central Algonquian speakers resided prehistorically across most of northern Ohio (Drooker 1999:76–77); recent research is refining this picture (e.g., Esarey 2003; Hall 2003). Callender places the Central Algonquian Shawnee in the central Ohio Valley, but other locations also have been hypothesized for this group (Drooker 1997:103–105, 2001:123–124).

4. Stone effigy pipes that face away from the user are known from Iroquoian territory (for instance, see Laidlaw 1903, 1913, 1914, 1915, 1916, 1924 for many examples of perching

and fenestrated birds and animals from Ontario and western New York). Jordan Paper has proposed that among Iroquoian speaking peoples, stemmed pipes were for individual use, while separate-stemmed pipes probably were "reserved for inter-tribal rituals and the welcoming of alien visitors" (1992:163; see also 1988). He implies, but does not state, that both types of pipes were locally made. It seems possible that many such pipes, particularly those with outward-facing effigies, were produced by non-Iroquoians. Some researchers have interpreted the presence of stone pipes made from nonlocal materials at Iroquois sites as indicative of intergroup trade (Kuhn and Sempowski 2001:304, citing Bradley 1979:166 and Wray et al. 1987, 1991).

5. Unlike surrounding regions, the Ohio River Valley seldom was visited by Europeans until the mid-1700s (Drooker 1997:63–64, Figures 3-4, 3-5, 3-6, 2002:124–128). No firsthand historical accounts exist from before the second quarter of the eighteenth century. Since the area was depopulated during the late seventeenth century, the identity of Fort Ancient people with a historically known group(s) never has been definitively established. A number of researchers equate them with the Shawnee or related Central Algonquian speakers, but evidence for eastern Siouan affiliations also has been mustered (Drooker 1997:103–105).

6. Many additional pipes reported to have been excavated at Madisonville are in private hands. The collection of the Cincinnati Museum Center includes a large number of unprovenienced pipes donated by local collectors that probably came from this site. Many (perhaps most) other Fort Ancient sites have incompletely recorded pipe assemblages (e.g., Drooker 1997:Table 4-3). Mills excavated "perhaps fifty" pipes from the Middle-Early Late Fort Ancient Feurt site at Portsmouth, Ohio, but noted more than seventy-five additional specimens from three private collections, illustrating some of them in his site report (1917:388–402). More than fifty pipes were excavated under incompletely controlled conditions at the Late Fort Ancient Orchard site near Point Pleasant, West Virginia, many of them from burials (Hoffman 2001:2, Figures 27–29; Moxley 1988a, 1988b). Only seven, eight, and twenty-two pipes (and pipe fragments) respectively were published from Buffalo, Neale's Landing, and Hardin, the three other protohistoric Fort Ancient sites at which large-scale, controlled excavations have taken place (Hanson 1966, 1975; Hemmings 1976, 1977), but additional poorly provenienced examples are known from private collections.

7. Early-mid-eighteenth century artifacts were excavated at Kentucky sites associated with Shawneetown, a historically known trading settlement near the mouth of the Scioto River (Henderson et al. 1986; Pollack and Henderson 1984). A few other sites in eastern Fort Ancient territory have yielded scattered finds of late-seventeenth-century style glass beads (Drooker 1997:Table 4-9).

8. The shell-tempered pipe stem from the Clover site might be an exception: it has a form not unlike some Iroquoian pipe stems. However, Iroquoian ceramic pipes typically are not shell-tempered.

9. A similar, but whole, disk pipe of "indurated fireclay" with a finely engraved underwater panther figure was recovered from a southern Ontario location in Neutral territory (Fox 2002:134–135; Skinner 1926; West 1934:Plates 149.3, 149.4). According to Fox (2002:134), its light brown, polished stone might perhaps be Ohio pipestone. Unfortunately, its context is not described, although the location from which it came is not far from documented 1580–1640 Neutral villages and cemeteries (Fox 2002:135). Fox notes that

none of the five known disk pipes from Neutral territory are redstone. Most of them could be of central Ohio Valley materials, which is congruent with other evidence of interaction between the two regions (Drooker 1997:333–335; Fox 2002:145). In contrast, the three redstone disk pipes known from farther north in Ontario would have been associated with Huron/Petun/Odawa interaction networks (Fox 2002:145–146).

References Cited

Ahlstrom, Richard M.
1979 *Prehistoric Pipes: A Study of the Reeve Village Site, Lake County, Ohio.* Lake County Chapter, Archaeological Society of Ohio.

Beauchamp, William M.
1897 *Polished Stone Articles Used by the New York Aborigines before and during European Occupation.* Bulletin 18. Univ. of the State of New York, New York State Museum, Albany.

Blakeslee, Donald J.
1981 The Origin and Spread of the Calumet Ceremony. *American Antiquity* 46:759–768.

Bradley, James W.
1979 *The Onondaga Iroquois: 1500–1655, A Study in Acculturative Chage and Its Consequences.* Ph.D. Dissertation, Syracuse University. University Microfilms, Ann Arbor, Michigan.

Bradley, James W., and S. Terry Childs
1991 Basque Earrings and Panther's Tails: The Form of Cross-Cultural Contact in Sixteenth Century Iroquoia. In *Metals in Society: Theory Beyond Analysis,* edited by Robert M. Ehrenreich, 7–17. MASCA Research Papers in Science and Archaeology, vol. 8, pt. 2. MASCA, Univ. Museum of Archaeology and Anthropology, Univ. of Pennsylvania, Philadelphia.

Brain, Jeffrey P., and Philip Phillips
1996 *Shell Gorgets: Styles of the Late Prehistoric and Protohistoric Southeast.* Peabody Museum of Archaeology and Ethnology, Harvard Univ., Cambridge, Mass.

Brashler, Janet G., and Ronald W. Moxley
1990 Late Prehistoric Engraved Shell Gorgets of West Virginia. *West Virginia Archaeologist* 42(1):1–10.

Brasser, Ted J.
1980 Self-Directed Pipe Effigies. *Man in the Northeast* 19:95–105.

Brose, David S.
2000 Late Prehistoric Societies of Northeastern Ohio and Adjacent Portions of the South Shore of Lake Erie: A Review. In *Cultures Before Contact: The Late Prehistory of Ohio and Surrounding Regions,* edited by Robert Genheimer, 96–122. Ohio Archaeological Council, Cincinnati.

Brown, Calvin S.
1926 *Archeology of Mississippi.* Mississippi Geological Survey, University, Mississippi.

Brown, Ian W.

1989 The Calumet Ceremony in the Southeast and Its Archaeological Manifestations. *American Antiquity* 54(2):311–331.

Brown, James A.

1996 *The Spiro Ceremonial Center: The Archaeology of Arkansas Valley Caddoan Culture in Eastern Oklahoma.* Memoir No 29. University of Michigan Museum of Anthropology, Ann Arbor.

Callender, Charles

1962 *Social Organization of the Central Algonkian Indians.* Publications in Anthropology, Milwaukee Public Museum, Milwaukee.

Chapdelaine, Claude

1992 The Mandeville Site: A Small Iroquoian Village and a Large Smoking-Pipe Collection—An Interpretation. In *Proceedings of the 1989 Smoking Pipe Conference,* edited by Charles F. Hayes III, Connie C. Bodner, and Martha L. Sempowski, 31–40. Research Records No. 22, Rochester Museum and Science Center, Rochester, N.Y.

Clayton, Lawrence A., Vernon J. Knight Jr., and Edward C. Moore (editors)

1993 *The de Soto Chronicles: The Expedition of Hernando de Soto to North America in 1539–1543.* Univ. of Alabama Press, Tuscaloosa.

Conklin, Carlton S.

1989 The Dewey Knoll Site at Ripley, New York. *Iroquoian* 16:3–29.

Converse, Robert N.

1995 A Turtle Effigy Pipe. *Ohio Archaeologist* 45(4):25.

Cowan, C. Wesley

1987 *First Farmers of the Middle Ohio Valley: Fort Ancient Societies, A.D. 1000–1670.* Cincinnati Museum of Natural History, Cincinnati.

Dincauze, Dena F., and Robert J. Hasenstab

1989 Explaining the Iroquois: Tribalization on a Prehistoric Periphery. In *Centre and Periphery,* edited by Timothy C. Champion, 67–87. Unwin Hyman, London.

Drooker, Penelope B.

1994 Representations of Gender in Fort Ancient versus Mississippian Culture Areas. Paper presented at the Third Archaeology and Gender Conference, Boone, N.C.

1995 Asking Old Museum Collections New Questions: Protohistoric Fort Ancient Social Organization and Interregional Interaction. *Museum Anthropology* 19(3):1–16.

1996 Madisonville Metal and Glass Artifacts: Implications for Western Fort Ancient Chronology and Interaction Networks. *Midcontinental Journal of Archaeology* 21(2):1–46.

1997 The View from Madisonville: Protohistoric Western Fort Ancient Interaction Patterns. Memoir 31. Museum of Anthropology, Univ. of Michigan, Ann Arbor.

1998 Zoom-In to Madisonville. CD-ROM to accompany The View from Madisonville: Protohistoric Western Fort Ancient Interaction Patterns. Memoir 31. Museum of Anthropology, Univ. of Michigan, Ann Arbor.

1999 Exotic Ceramics at Madisonville: Implications for Interaction. In *Taming the Taxonomy: Toward a New Understanding of Great Lakes Prehistory,* edited by Ron Williamson, 71–81. Ontario Archaeological Society, Toronto.

2000 Madisonville Focus Revisited: Reexcavating Southwestern Fort Ancient from Museum Collections. In *Cultures before Contact: The Late Prehistory of Ohio and Surrounding Regions,* edited by Robert Genheimer, 228–270. Ohio Archaeological Council, Cincinnati.

2002 The Ohio Valley, 1550–1750: Patterns of Sociopolitical Coalescence and Dispersal. In *Transformation of the Southeastern Indians, 1540–1760,* edited by Robbie Ethridge and Charles Hudson, 115–133. Univ. Press of Mississippi, Jackson.

Drooker, Penelope B., and C. Wesley Cowan

2001 The Dawn of History and the Transformation of the Fort Ancient Cultures of the Central Ohio Valley. In *Societies in Eclipse,* edited by David S. Brose, Robert C. Mainfort Jr., and C. Wesley Cowan, 83–106. Smithsonian Institution Press, Washington, D.C.

Dye, David H.

1995 Feasting with the Enemy: Mississippian Warfare and Prestige-Goods Circulation. In *Native American Interactions: Multiscalar Analyses and Interpretations in the Eastern Woodlands,* edited by Michael S. Nassaney and Kenneth E. Sassaman, 289–316. Univ. of Tennessee Press, Knoxville.

Emerson, J. Norman

1954 The Archaeology of the Ontario Iroquois. Unpublished Ph.D. dissertation, Dept. of Anthropology, Univ. of Chicago.

Emerson, Thomas E.

1982 Mississippian Stone Images in Illinois. Circular 6. Illinois Archaeological Survey, Urbana.

1983 The Bostrom Figure Pipe and the Cahokian Effigy Style in the American Bottom. *Midcontinental Journal of Archaeology* 8:257–267.

1989 Water, Serpents, and the Underworld: An Exploration into Cahokian Symbolism. In *The Southeastern Ceremonial Complex: Artifacts and Analysis (The Cottonlandia Conference),* edited by Patricia Galloway, 45–92. Univ. of Nebraska Press, Lincoln.

Emerson, Thomas E., and Randall E. Hughes

2001 De-Mything the Cahokia Catlinite Trade. *Plains Anthropologist* 46(175):149–161.

Emerson, Thomas E., and Douglas K. Jackson (editors)

1982 *The BBB Motor Site: An Early Mississippi Occupation.* FAI-270 Archaeological Mitigation Project Report 38. Dept. of Anthropology, Univ. of Illinois, Urbana.

Engelbrecht, William

1996 Ceramics. In *Reanalyzing the Ripley Site: Earthworks and Late Prehistory on the Lake Erie Plain,* edited by Lynne P. Sullivan, 53–68. Bulletin No. 489. New York State Museum, Univ. of the State of New York, State Education Dept., Albany.

Engelbrecht, William, and Lynne P. Sullivan

1996 Cultural Context. In *Reanalyzing the Ripley Site: Earthworks and Late Prehistory on the Lake Erie Plain,* edited by Lynne P. Sullivan, 14–27. Bulletin No. 489. New York State Museum, Univ. of the State of New York, State Education Dept., Albany.

Esarey, Duane

2003 The Illinois Indians before 1673. Paper presented at "The Illinois at the Dawn of History: Views from the Iliniwek Village," 68th Annual Meeting of the Society for American Archaeology, Milwaukee.

Farnsworth, Kenneth B., and Thomas A. Emerson

1989 The Macoupin Creek Figure Pipe and Its Archaeological Context: Evidence for Late Woodland–Mississippian Interaction beyond the Northern Border of Cahokian Settlement. *Midcontinental Journal of Archaeology* 14(1):18–37.

Feinman, Gary, and Jill E. Neitzel

1984 Too Many Types: An Overview of Sedentary Prestate Societies in the Americas. In *Advances in Archaeological Method and Theory,* vol. 7, edited by Michael B. Schiffer, 39–102. Academic Press, New York.

Fenton, William N.

1953 The Iroquois Eagle Dance: An Offshoot of the Calumet Dance. Bulletin No. 156. Bureau of American Ethnology, Washington, D.C.

1978 Northern Iroquoian Culture Patterns. In *Northeast,* edited by Bruce G. Trigger, 296–321. Handbook of North American Indians, Vol. 15. Smithsonian Institution Press, Washington, D.C.

Fitzgerald, William R.

1982 *Lest the Beaver Run Loose: The Early Seventeenth Century Christianson Site and Trends in Historic Neutral Archaeology.* Archaeological Survey of Canada, Mercury Series Paper No. 111. National Museum of Man, Ottawa.

1990 Chronology to Cultural Process: Lower Great Lakes Archaeology, 1500 to 1650. Unpublished Ph.D. dissertation, Dept. of Anthropology, McGill Univ., Montreal.

Fitzgerald, William R., Laurier Turgeon, Ruth Holmes Whitehead, and James W. Bradley

1993 Late-Sixteenth-Century Basque Banded Copper Kettles. *Historical Archaeology* 27(1):44–57.

Fox, William A.

2002 *Thaniba Wakondagi* among the Ontario Iroquois. *Canadian Journal of Archaeology* 26(2):130–151.

Fundabark, Emma L., and Mary D. F. Foreman

1957 *Sun Circles and Human Hands: The Southeastern Indians, Art, and Industries.* Emma Lila Fundabark, Luverne, Ala.

Gibbon, Guy

1986 The Mississippian Tradition: Oneota Culture. *Wisconsin Archaeologist* 67(3–4):315–337.

Gramly, Richard Michael

1996 *Two Early Historic Iroquoian Sites in Western New York.* Persimmon Press, Buffalo, N.Y.

Graybill, Jeffrey R.

1981 The Eastern Periphery of Fort Ancient (A.D. 1050–1650): A Diachronic Approach to Settlement Variability. Ph.D. dissertation, Dept. of Anthropology, Univ. of Washington. University Microfilms, Ann Arbor.

Green, William
1993 Examining Protohistoric Depopulation in the Upper Midwest. *Wisconsin Archeologist* 74(1–4):290–323.

Greenman, Emerson F.
1935 Excavation of the Reeve Village Site, Lake County, Ohio. *Ohio Archaeological and Historical Quarterly* 44(1):2–64.

Griffin, James B.
1943 *The Fort Ancient Aspect: Its Cultural and Chronological Position in Mississippi Valley Archaeology.* Univ. of Michigan Press, Ann Arbor.
1993 Cahokia Interaction with Contemporary Southeastern and Eastern Societies. *Midcontinental Journal of Archaeology* 18(1):3–17.

Gundersen, James N.
1982a Comments on the Distribution of Pipestone and Pipestone-Bearing Clastics in Kansan Drift, Southeastern Nebraska. *Proceedings of the Nebraska Academy of Science* 92:2.
1982b The Mineralogy of Pipestone Artifacts of the Linwood Site (Historic Pawnee) of East Central Nebraska. *Proceedings of the Nebraska Academy of Science* 92:3.
1993 "Catlinite" and the Spread of the Calumet Ceremony. *American Antiquity* 58(3):560–562.

Hall, Robert L.
1987 Calumet Ceremonialism, Mourning Ritual, and Mechanisms of Inter-Tribal Trade. In *Mirror and Metaphor: Material and Social Construction of Reality,* edited by Daniel W. Ingersoll Jr. and G. Bronitsky, 29–43. Univ. Press of America, Lanham, Md.
1997 *An Archaeology of the Soul: North American Indian Belief and Ritual.* Univ. of Illinois Press, Urbana.
2003 Rethinking Jean Nicolet's Route to the Ho-Chunks in 1634. In *Theory, Method, and Practice in Modern Archaeology,* edited by Robert J. Jeske and Douglas K. Charles, 238–251. Praeger, Westport, Conn.

Hamilton, Henry W.
1967 *Tobacco Pipes of the Missouri Indians.* Memoir No. 5. Missouri Archaeological Society, Columbia.

Hanson, Lee H., Jr.
1966 *The Hardin Village Site.* Studies in Anthropology 4. Univ. of Kentucky Press, Lexington.
1975 *The Buffalo Site: A Late Seventeenth Century Indian Village Site (46 Pu 31) in Putnam County, West Virginia.* Report of Archaeological Investigations 5. West Virginia Geological Survey, Morgantown.

Hathcock, Roy
1976 *Ancient Indian Pottery of the Mississippi River Valley.* Hurley Press, Camden, Ark.

Heidenreich, Conrad E.
1978 Huron. In *Northeast,* edited by Bruce Trigger, 368–388. *Handbook of North American Indians, Vol. 15.* Smithsonian Institution Press, Washington, D.C.

Hemmings, E. Thomas
1976 Fort Ancient Pipes from the Blennerhassett Island Area. *West Virginia Archaeologist* 25:56–66.

1977 Neale's Landing: An Archaeological Study of a Fort Ancient Settlement on Blennerhassett Island, West Virginia. Draft ms. on file, West Virginia Geological and Economic Survey, Morgantown, W.Va.

Henderson, A. Gwynn, Cynthia E. Jobe, and Christopher A. Turnbow

1986 *Indian Occupation and Use in Northern and Eastern Kentucky during the Contact Period (1540–1795): An Initial Investigation.* Ms. on file, Kentucky Heritage Council, Frankfort.

Hoffman, Darla S.

1998 From the Southeast to Fort Ancient: A Survey of Shell Gorgets in West Virginia. Unpublished master's thesis, Dept. of Sociology, Marshall Univ., Huntington, W.Va.

1999 From the Southeast to Fort Ancient: A Survey of Shell Gorgets in West Virginia. *West Virginia Archeologist* 49(1–2):1–40.

2001 A Preliminary Analysis of Data from the Late Prehistoric Orchard Site (46Ms61) to Locate the Site in the Cultural Temporal Sequence in Upper Ohio Valley Fort Ancient. Paper presented at the Society for American Archaeology Annual Meeting, New Orleans.

Holzapfel, Elaine

1995 Ohio Pipestone. *Ohio Archaeologist* 45(3):4–6.

Hooton, Earnest A., and Charles C. Willoughby

1920 Indian Village Site and Cemetery near Madisonville Ohio. Papers of the Peabody Museum of American Archaeology and Ethnology, Harvard Univ., vol. 8, no. 17. Peabody Museum, Cambridge, Mass.

Hughes, Randall E., Thomas E. Berres, D. M. Moore, and Kenneth B. Farnsworth

1998 Revision of Hopewellian Trading Patterns in Midwestern North America Based on Mineralogical Sourcing. *Geoarchaeology* 13(7):709–729.

Hunt, George T.

1940 *The Wars of the Iroquois: A Study in Intertribal Trade Relations.* Univ. of Wisconsin Press, Madison.

Jacobs, W. R.

1966 *Wilderness Politics and Indian Gifts: The Northern Colonial Frontier, 1748–1763.* Univ. of Nebraska Press, Lincoln.

Jennings, Francis

1984 *The Ambiguous Iroquois Empire: The Covenant Chain Confederation of Indian Tribes with English Colonies from Its Beginnings to the Lancaster Treaty of 1744.* W. W. Norton, New York.

Johnson, William C.

2002 The Protohistoric Monongahela and the Case for an Iroquois Connection. In *Societies in Eclipse,* edited by David S. Brose, Robert C. Mainfort, and C. Wesley Cowan. Smithsonian Institution Press, Washington, D.C.

Kapches, Mima

1992 "Rude but Perfect" (Beauchamp 1899): A Study of Miniature Smoking Pipes in Iroquoia. In *Proceedings of the 1989 Smoking Pipe Conference,* edited by Charles F. Hayes III, Connie C. Bodner, and Martha L. Sempowski, 71–81. Research Records No. 22. Rochester Museum and Science Center, Rochester, N.Y.

Kent, Barry C.

1984 *Susquehanna's Indians*. Anthropological Series, No. 6. Pennsylvania Historical and Museum Commission, Harrisburg.

Kenyon, Ian T., and Thomas Kenyon

1983 Comments on Seventeenth Century Glass Trade Beads from Ontario. In Proceedings of the 1982 Glass Trade Bead Conference, edited by Charles F. Hayes III, Nancy Bolger, Karlis Karklins, and Charles F. Wray, 59–74. Research Records No. 16. Rochester Museum and Science Center, Rochester, New York.

Kenyon, Ian T., and William Fitzgerald

1986 Dutch Glass Beads in the Northeast: An Ontario Perspective. *Man in the Northeast* 32:1–34.

Kuhn, Robert D.

1985 Trade and Exchange among the Mohawk-Iroquois: A Trace Element Analysis of Ceramic Smoking Pipes. Ph.D. dissertation, State Univ. of New York at Albany.

1986 Interaction Patterns in Eastern New York: A Trace Element Analysis of Iroquoian and Algonkian Ceramics. *Bulletin: Journal of the New York State Archaeological Association* (92):9–21.

1987 Trade and Exchange among the Mohawk-Iroquois: A Trace-Element Analysis. *North American Archaeologist* 8(4):305–316.

Kuhn, Robert D., and Martha L. Sempowski

2001 A New Approach to Dating the League of the Iroquois. *American Antiquity* 66(2):301–314.

Laidlaw, George E.

1903 Effigy Pipes in Stone. *14th Annual Archaeological Report for Ontario for 1902:* 37–57. Toronto.

1913 Ontario Effigy Pipes in Stone. *25th Annual Archaeological Report for Ontario for 1913:* 37–67. Toronto.

1914 Ontario Effigy Pipes in Stone, Third Paper. *26th Annual Archaeological Report for Ontario for 1914:* 44–76. Toronto.

1915 Ontario Effigy Pipes in Stone, Fourth Paper. *27th Annual Archaeological Report for Ontario for 1915:* 58–62. Toronto.

1916 Ontario Effigy Pipes in Stone, Fifth Paper. *28th Annual Archaeological Report for Ontario for 1916:* 63–82. Toronto.

1924 Effigy Pipes in Stone, Sixth Paper. *34th Annual Archaeological Report for Ontario for 1924:* 57–80. Toronto.

Lankford, George

1984 Saying Hello to the Timucua. *Mid-America Folklore* 12:7–23.

1988 Saying Hello in the Mississippi Valley. *Mid-America Folklore* 16:24–39.

Lenig, Donald

1965 The Oak Hill Horizon and Its Relation to the Development of Five Nations Iroquois Culture. *Researches and Transactions of the New York State Archaeological Association* 15(1):1–114.

Lennox, Paul A.

1981 The Hamilton Site: A Late Historic Neutral Town. *National Museum of Man, Archaeological Survey of Canada Mercury Series Paper* 103:211–403.

Lennox, Paul A., and William R. Fitzgerald

1990 The Culture History and Archaeology of the Neutral Iroquoians. In *The Archaeology of Southern Ontario to A.D. 1650,* edited by Chris J. Ellis and Neal Ferris, 405–456. Occasional Publication of the London Chapter, OAS, No. 5. Ontario Archaeological Society, London, Ontario.

Low, Charles F.

1880 Archaeological Explorations new Madisonville, Ohio. *Journal of the Cincinnati Society of Natural History* 3:40–68, 128–139, 203–220.

Mallam, R. Clark

1983 Ratcliff Dragon Pipe. *Iowa Archeological Society Newsletter* (105):2–3, cover.

Mathews, Zena P.

1979 Pipes with Human Figures from Ontario and Western New York. *American Indian Art* 4:43–47.

1980 Of Man and Beast: The Chronology of Effigy Pipes among Ontario Iroquoians. *Ethnohistory* 27(4):295–307.

1981 Janus and Other Multiple-Image Iroquoian Pipes. *Ontario Archaeology* 35:3–22.

Mayer-Oakes, William J.

1955 *Prehistory of the Upper Ohio Valley; An Introductory Archeological Study.* Annals of the Carnegie Museum, Vol. 34, Anthropological Series, No. 2. Carnegie Museum, Pittsburgh.

McClellan, Catharine

1975 *My Old People Say: An Ethnographic Survey of the Southern Yukon Territory.* National Museum of Canada, Ottawa.

McCullough, Robert G.

2000 The Oliver Phase of Central Indiana: A Study of Settlement Variability as a Response to Social Risk. Unpublished Ph.D. dissertation, Dept. of Anthropology, Southern Illinois Univ., Carbondale.

McGuire, Joseph D.

1899 Pipes and Smoking Customs of the American Aborigines, Based on Material in the United States National Museum. *United States National Museum Annual Report for 1897,* pp. 351–654.

McMichael, Edward V.

1962 Preliminary Report on Mount Carbon Village Excavations, 46Fa7. *West Virginia Archeologist* 14:36–51.

Mills, William C.

1917 Exploration of the Feurt Mounds and Village Site. *Ohio Archaeological and Historical Quarterly* 26(3):305–449.

Moorehead, Warren K.

1906 A Narrative of Explorations in New Mexico, Arizona, Indiana, etc. *Phillips Academy Department of Archaeology Bulletin* 3.

Moxley, Ronald W.

1985 Recent Excavations at the Man Site (46LG5). *West Virginia Archaeologist* 37(1):44–46.

1988a The Orchard Site: A Proto-Historic Fort Ancient Village Site in Mason County, West Virginia. *Ohio Archaeologist* 38(3):4–11.

1988 The Orchard Site: A Proto-Historic Fort Ancient Village Site in Mason County, West Virginia. *West Virginia Archaeologist* 40(1):33–41.

Murphy, James L.

1996 Comments on the Composition of Catlinite and Ohio Pipestone. *Ohio Archaeologist* 46(1):10–11.

Noble, William C.

1979 Ontario Iroquois Effigy Pipes. *Canadian Journal of Archaeology* 3:69–90.

1992 Neutral Iroquois Smoking Pipes. In *Proceedings of the 1989 Smoking Pipe Conference,* edited by Charles F. Hayes III, Connie C. Bodner, and Martha L. Sempowski, 41–49. Research Records No. 22. Rochester Museum and Science Center, Rochester, N.Y.

O'Brien, Michael J.

1994 *Cat Monsters and Head Pots: The Archaeology of Missouri's Pemiscot Bayou.* Univ. of Missouri Press, Columbia.

Paper, Jordan

1988 *Offering Smoke: The Sacred Pipe and Native American Religion.* Univ. of Idaho Press, Moscow.

1992 The Iroquoian and Pan-Indian Sacred Pipes: Comparative Ritual and Symbolism. In *Proceedings of the 1989 Smoking Pipe Conference,* edited by Charles F. Hayes III, Connie C. Bodner, and Martha L. Sempowski, 163–169. Research Records No. 22. Rochester Museum and Science Center, Rochester, N.Y.

Parker, Arthur C.

1907 *An Erie Indian Village and Burial Site at Ripley, Chautauqua County, New York.* Bulletin 117:459–547. New York State Museum, Albany.

1918 A Prehistoric Iroquoian Site on the Reed Farm, Richmond Mills, Ontario County, N.Y. *Researches and Transactions of the New York State Archaeological Association* 1(1):5–41.

1922 *The Archaeological History of New York.* Bulletin Nos. 235–236. New York State Museum, Albany.

Pendergast, James F.

1980 Huron–St. Lawrence Iroquois Relations in the Terminal Prehistoric Period. *Ontario Archaeology* 44:23–39.

1992 Some Notes on Ceramic Smoking Pipes from St. Lawrence Iroquoian Archaeological Sites. In *Proceedings of the 1989 Smoking Pipe Conference,* edited by Charles F. Hayes III, Connie C. Bodner, and Martha L. Sempowski, 51–70. Research Records No. 22. Rochester Museum and Science Center, Rochester, N.Y.

Penman, J. T., and James N. Gundersen

1999 Pipestone Artifacts from Upper Mississippi Valley Sites. *Plains Anthropologist* 44(167):47–57.

Phillips, Philip, and James A. Brown

1978 *Pre-Columbian Shell Engravings from the Craig Mound at Spiro, Oklahoma,* pt. 1. Peabody Museum Press, Cambridge, Mass.

1984 *Pre-Columbian Shell Engravings from the Craig Mound at Spiro, Oklahoma,* pt. 2. Peabody Museum Press, Cambridge, Mass.

Pollack, David, and A. Gwynn Henderson
1984 A Mid-Eighteenth Century Historic Indian Occupation in Greenup County, Kentucky. In *Late Prehistoric Research in Kentucky,* edited by David Pollack, Charles D. Hockensmith, and Thomas N. Sanders, 1–24. Kentucky Heritage Council, Frankfort.

Pollack, David, Cheryl Ann Munson, and A. Gwynn Henderson
1996 *Slack Farm and the Caborn-Welborn People.* Education Series No. 1. Kentucky Archaeological Survey, Lexington.

Potter, Stephen R.
1989 Early English Effects on Virginia Algonquian Exchange and Tribute in the Tidewater Potomac. In *Powhatan's Mantle: Indians in the Colonial Southeast,* edited by Peter H. Wood, Gregory A. Waselkov, and M. Thomas Hatley, 151–172. Univ. of Nebraska Press, Lincoln.

Quimby, George I.
1966 The Dumaw Creek Site. A Seventeenth Century Prehistoric Indian Village and Cemetery in Oceana County, Michigan. *Fieldiana: Anthropology* 56(1):1–91.

Redmond, Brian G., and Robert G. McCullough
2000 The Late Woodland to Late Prehistoric Occupations of Central Indiana. In *Late Woodland Societies: Tradition and Transformation across the Midcontinent,* edited by Thomas E. Emerson, Dale L. McElrath, and Andrew C. Fortier, 643–683. Univ. of Nebraska Press, Lincoln.

Ritchie, William A.
1954 *Dutch Hollow, an Early Historic Period Seneca Site in Livingston County, New York.* Research Records No. 10. Rochester Museum of Arts and Sciences, Rochester, N.Y.

Rountree, Helen C.
1993 The Powhatans and Other Woodland Indians as Travelers. In *Powhatan Foreign Relations, 1500–1722,* edited by Helen C. Rountree, 21–52. Univ. Press of Virginia, Charlottesville.

Rutsch, Edward S.
1973 *Smoking Technology of the Aborigines of the Iroquois Area of New York State.* Associated Univ. Presses, Cranbury, N.J.

Salter, Andrew H.
1977 Catlinite Calumets: Artifactual Clues to Late Prehistoric and Historic Interactions in Eastern North America. Unpulished honors thesis, Harvard University Department of Anthropology, Cambridge, Massachusetts.

Sempowski, Martha L.
1994 Early Historic Exchange between the Seneca and the Susquehannock. In *Proceedings of the 1992 People to People Conference,* edited by Charles F. Hayes III, Connie C. Bodner, and Lorraine P. Saunders, 51–64. Research Records No. 23. Rochester Museum and Science Center, Rochester, N.Y.

Sempowski, Martha L., and Lorraine P. Saunders
2001 *Dutch Hollow and Factory Hollow: The Advent of Dutch Trade among the Seneca.* Research Records No. 24. Vol. 3, Charles F. Wray Series in Seneca Archaeology. Rochester Museum and Science Center, Rochester, N.Y.

Shetrone, Henry C.

1926 The Campbell Island Village Site and the Hine Mound and Village Site. In *Certain Mounds and Village Sites in Ohio,* vol. 4, pt. 1, edited by William C. Mills. F. J. Heer, Columbus.

Sigstad, John S.

1973 The Age and Distribution of Catlinite and Red Pipestone. Ph.D. dissertation, Univ. of Missouri, Columbia.

Skinner, Alanson

1926 An Unusual Canadian Disc Pipe. *Indian Notes* 3:39–41.

Smith, David G.

1992 Stylistic Variation in Middleport Smoking Pipes. In *Proceedings of the 1989 Smoking Pipe Conference,* edited by Charles F. Hayes III, Connie C. Bodner, and Martha L. Sempowski, 15–30. Research Records No. 22. Rochester Museum and Science Center, Rochester, N.Y.

Smith, Marvin T., and David J. Hally

1992 Chiefly Behavior: Evidence from Sixteenth Century Spanish Accounts. In *Lords of the Southeast: Social Inequality and the Native Elites of Southeastern North America,* edited by Alex W. Barker and Timothy R. Pauketat, 99–109. Archaeological Papers No. 3. American Anthropological Association, Washington, D.C.

Smith, Marvin T., and Julie B. Smith

1989 Engraved Shell Masks in North America. *Southeastern Archaeology* 8(1):9–18.

Spielmann, Katherine A.

1983 Late Prehistoric Exchange between the Southwest and the Southern Plains. *Plains Anthropologist* 28(102, pt. 1):257–272.

Stothers, David M.

2000 The Protohistoric Time Period in the Southwestern Lake Erie Region: European-Derived Trade Material, Population Movement and Cultural Realignment. In *Cultures before Contact: The Late Prehistory of Ohio and Surrounding Regions,* edited by Robert Genheimer, 52–94. Ohio Archaeological Council, Cincinnati.

Sullivan, Lynne P.

1996 The Ripley Site: Domestic or Ceremonial? In *Reanalyzing the Ripley Site: Earthworks and Late Prehistory on the Lake Erie Plain,* edited by Lynne P. Sullivan, 120–128. Bulletin No. 489. New York State Museum, Univ. of the State of New York, State Education Dept., Albany.

Sullivan, Lynne P., and Gwenyth Ann D. Coffin

1996 Mortuary Customs and Society. In *Reanalyzing the Ripley Site: Earthworks and Late Prehistory on the Lake Erie Plain,* edited by Lynne P. Sullivan, 99–119. Bulletin No. 489. New York State Museum, Univ. of the State of New York, State Education Dept., Albany.

Sullivan, Lynne P., Eleazer D. Hunt, and Richard G. Wilkinson

1996 History of Investigations. In *Reanalyzing the Ripley Site: Earthworks and Late Prehistory on the Lake Erie Plain,* edited by Lynne P. Sullivan, 28–52. Bulletin No. 489. New York State Museum, Univ. of the State of New York, State Education Dept., Albany.

Thruston, Gates P.
1897 *The Antiquities of Tennessee and the Adjacent States and the State of Aboriginal Society in the Scale of Civilization Represented by Them.* 2d ed. Robert Clarke, Cincinnati.

Tooker, Elisabeth
1964 *An Ethnography of the Huron Indians, 1615–1649.* Bulletin 190. Bureau of American Ethnology, Washington, D.C.

Trigger, Bruce G.
1986 *Natives and Newcomers: Canada's "Heroic Age" Reconsidered.* McGill-Queen's Univ. Press, Kingston, Ontario.

Turgeon, Laurier
1990 Basque-Amerindian Trade in the Saint Lawrence during the Sixteenth Century: New Documents, New Perspectives. *Man in the Northeast* (40):81–87.
1997 The Tale of the Kettle: Odyssey of an Intercultural Object. *Ethnohistory* 44(1):1–29.

Vietzen, Raymond C.
1974 *The Riker Site.* Sugar Creek Valley Chapter of the Archaeological Society of Ohio.

Waselkov, Gregory A.
1989 Seventeenth-Century Trade in the Colonial Southeast. *Southeastern Archaeology* 8(2):117–133.

Weber, Joann C.
1970 Types and Attributes in the Study of Iroquois Pipes. Unpublished Ph.D. dissertation, Dept. of Anthropology, Harvard Univ., Cambridge, Mass.
1971 Types and Attributes in Iroquois Pipes. *Man in the Northeast* 2:51–65.

Wedel, Mildred M.
1959 Oneota Sites on the Upper Iowa River. *Missouri Archaeologist* 21(2–4):1–180.

West, George A.
1934 Tobacco, Pipes, and Smoking Customs of the American Indians. *Bulletin of the Public Museum of the City of Milwaukee* 17:1–994.

White, Marian E.
1978 Erie. In *Northeast,* edited by Bruce Trigger, 412–417. Handbook of North American Indians, vol. 15. Smithsonian Institution Press, Washington, D.C.

White, Richard
1991 *The Middle Ground: Indians, Empires, and Republics in the Great Lakes Region, 1650–1815.* Cambridge Univ. Press, Cambridge.

Witthoft, John, Harry Schoff, and Charles F. Wray
1953 Micmac Pipes, Vase-Shaped Pipes, and Calumets. *Pennsylvania Archaeologist* 23(3–4):89–107.

Wray, Charles F., Martha L. Sepowski, and Lorraine P. Saunders
1991 *Tram and Cameron: Two Early Contact Era Sites.* The Charles F. Wray Series in Seneca Archaeology, vol. 2, Research Records No. 21. Rochester Museum and Science Center, Rochester, New York.

Wray, Charles F., Martha L. Sepowski, Lorraine P. Saunders, and Gian C. Cervone
1987 *The Adams and Culbertson Sites.* Charles F. Wray Series in Seneca Archaeology, vol. 1, Research Records No. 19. Rochester Museum and Science Center, Rochester, New York.

4. Men and Women, Pipes and Power in Native New England

Michael S. Nassaney

The development and expansion of the world-economic system in the age of exploration and its impact on the cultures of indigenous peoples is one of the most enduring research problems in historical and anthropological inquiry (Deetz 1977:5; Orser 1996:26–28; Wallerstein 1974; Wolf 1982). While the responses of the subaltern are now seen as more varied and complex than ever, the fact remains that European exploration, discovery, and settlement in North America and elsewhere had profound implications for both natives and newcomers. To claim that their histories became intertwined is not to say that cultural differences disappeared. The literature is replete with examples illustrating how the clash of Old and New World practices and ideologies created new conditions that transformed social relations and social reproduction.

Although Native Americans influenced European lives in innumerable ways, in this chapter I focus on the adjustments and accommodations that Amerindians made during the first century of sustained contact in southeastern New England. I do not claim that native peoples were passive victims of an inevitable process, but I must acknowledge that they were repeatedly forced to relinquish power in their struggles with the English (Trigger 1986:263). Perhaps foremost among the challenges that Native Americans faced were their declining numbers brought about by disease and warfare (Crosby 1988; Ramenofsky 1987). The introduction of new land use patterns and land tenure practices impeded earlier native activities (Cronon 1983; Thomas 1976). Religious and other ideological beliefs also contributed to the cultural divide in the Contact period, forcing us to consider the problem of communication across this conceptual chasm. For example, misunderstandings were bound to occur between groups that subscribed to reciprocal as opposed to market principles of exchange. This is not to deny that interaction and exchange took place, but merely to underscore the idea that these encounters necessarily required accommodations that often led to contradictions and conflicts within social structure and worldview (for example, see White 1991). Witness Sharp's (1952) now classic case of "Steel Axes for Stone Age Australians" to appreciate what can happen when a few alien objects fall into the "wrong" hands.

Of course, borrowing was by no means unidirectional. One indisputably indigenous North American practice that Europeans adopted wholeheartedly was tobacco smoking and its associated paraphernalia (Spinden 1950; von Gernet 1988; Winter, ed. 2000). Spanish and Portuguese explorers returning from the New World introduced the plant to their homelands in the early sixteenth century, and its use spread rapidly throughout Europe and Asia; the habit was well established in Japan by 1595 (Corti 1996:50, 145). Significant for this study, the English and the Dutch "reciprocated" by producing and distributing the inexpensive, white clay pipes that, I will argue, contributed to profound changes in the practice of tobacco consumption among natives peoples in southeastern New England and elsewhere in North America. Fragile yet durable, these ubiquitous chronological and social markers litter most post–Contact period archaeological sites throughout the world.

My research into tobacco pipes began with the recovery of several pipes from a seventeenth-century Narragansett Indian cemetery in Rhode Island, including a native produced steatite specimen. I use the material record of native and imported pipes from this site and other contemporaneous cemeteries in the region, along with oral accounts and other ethnohistorical documentation to argue that New England natives and Europeans used and viewed tobacco in fundamentally different ways. Moreover, changes in native tobacco use and associated paraphernalia led to heightened tensions between men and women. In this chapter I address three related questions: (1) What influence did Europeans have on pipe smoking and tobacco use in seventeenth-century southeastern New England? (2) How are these changes evident in the archaeological record? (3) What lessons can be drawn about pipes and tobacco that may have implications for contemporary practice?

A Brief Overview of Native New England before and after Contact

The economic, sociopolitical, and ideological lives of sixteenth- and early-seventeenth-century Native Americans in southeastern New England can be understood through the use of archaeological and ethnohistoric evidence (for example, Bragdon 1996; Brenner 1988; Crosby 1988; Johnson 1999, 2000). At the time of contact, most groups in the region practiced a mixed hunting, gathering, and horticultural subsistence strategy that involved seasonal movement, with some variation between coastal and interior upland areas (Bragdon 1996:77–79). As is typical throughout much of native North America, age and gender formed the basis for the division of labor.

Native women in southeastern New England planted, cultivated, and harvested the crops and gathered wild plant foods. They also produced a variety of domestic objects including pottery, baskets, clothing, and textiles and were responsible for cooking, serving meals, and childcare. Women literally made and kept house, though men often assisted by cutting the poles that framed these dwellings. Men, on the other hand, were charged with hunting and fishing, though the latter was sometimes a communal activity. Male contributions to agriculture were confined to clearing the fields and cultivating tobacco. Men were responsible for producing wooden implements such as bowls, bows, and handles for various objects. They also employed a lapidary industry that involved the production of smoking pipes (Turnbaugh 1976). Stone pestles, however, were female objects that may have been made by women. Men were also involved in political decision making, warfare, and creating alliances.

Within a hereditary lineage-based kinship system, groups identified themselves as members of a local community that were occasionally integrated into larger confederacies that formed for purposes of alliance (Johnson 2000). Both men and women held positions of political leadership in the seventeenth century. There were also a number of religious specialists in native societies who could seek spiritual power through visions and encounters with otherworldly beings (Simmons 1986:41–64). These included powwows that exhibited many shamanic traits, as well as herbalists and a range of other religious practitioners. Their roles were generally to ensure the physical, social, and spiritual well-being of the community. While these activities were not confined exclusively to men or women, it is interesting to note that tobacco, which was an important element of shamanic practice, was cultivated exclusively by men, according to Roger Williams (1973), and was apparently confined to ritual use. Though Williams (1973:126–127) claimed that pipe smoking was prevalent among Narragansett men, not all males smoked, which suggests it was not universal. While its frequency of occurrence is difficult to assess prior to contact, there appears to have been a link between men, ritual, and tobacco at the time of contact, with increasing use over time.

Various authors have commented on the notion of whether the activities of men and women constituted separate spheres (see Shoemaker 1995:3–5), which may have implications for female tobacco use. Male and female roles were interdependent and generally more flexible than their European counterparts (but compare Shoemaker 1998), though the English invariably characterized women as having lower status than men had. Both William Wood and Edward Winslow, for example, commented on the "most slavish life" of women and how more industrious and laborious they were than their lazy husbands. Such negative reports have generally been dismissed as due to a lack of understanding, though they may point to inequities that were developing, if not already in place, after contact. While I am inclined to see men and women's roles as complementary, there is also evidence for social asymmetry along gender lines (Bragdon 1996:181).

Male and female roles also changed as they were drawn into exchange relations with the English. For example, I have argued elsewhere that women were spending less time in agricultural pursuits as they expanded wampum production, which was potentially more profitable and would allow them greater control over their surplus production (Nassaney 2003). This is one way in which women asserted their agency and actively countered colonization. Seldom discussed is the extent to which new economic activities and an uneven flow of European goods may have created or exacerbated tensions between men and women.

It is no longer tenable to use simple models of acculturation to characterize native responses to the European presence. Earlier approaches to culture contact advocated a process of gradual and inevitable change in native societies that led to replacement or assimilation based on disease, warfare, and the technological superiority of European goods. Anthropologists now realize that natives were active agents who made variable and complex choices in daily life. They resisted as well as accommodated cultural changes and new conditions, often leading to decisions that had unintended consequences.

For example, native peoples were selective in their adoption of European commodities (Hamell 1983). They often chose those that were consistent with aboriginal conceptual domains. They also employed goods in different ways than Europeans had intended. These brief examples point to the creativity and agency of Amerindians. Nevertheless, certain objects may have led to subtle and not so subtle changes in daily practice and beliefs. Just the act of engaging in commodity exchange and a cash economy had the potential to transform native ideas about reciprocity and social relationships (Nassaney 1989). Moreover, access to resources was never completely egalitarian, and some individuals could use certain classes of imports obtained through mercantile exchange with Europeans to mark newly emergent political statuses (Brenner 1988; Nassaney 2000). These statuses were frequently marked in death by associating men, women, and children with particular types of goods (Brenner 1988). By the mid-seventeenth century, native peoples were facing and seeking to rationalize a rapidly changing economic, social, and political order (Nassaney 2000:419). A closer look at the archaeological and ethnohistorical evidence can provide a deeper understanding of the ways in which men and women were adjusting their traditional beliefs to achieve "a better balance between the old and the new order" (Turnbaugh 1993:147). The distribution and depositional contexts of tobacco pipes and other ritually charged artifacts are particularly informative.

Tobacco, Pipes, and Power

The discovery and excavation of a Narragansett Indian cemetery in Rhode Island in the early 1980s has led to an increased interest in the Contact period of southeastern New England over the past two decades (for example, Brenner 1988; Carlson, Armelagoes, and Magennis 1992; Handsman 1990; Johnson 1993; Nassaney 1989, 2000, 2003; Robinson 1990; Robinson, Kelley, and Rubertone 1985; Rubertone 1989, 1994; Tuma 1985, 1992; Turnbaugh 1984, 1992). A number of these studies have used mortuary data to demonstrate that ritual acts and ideologically charged objects were significant elements in native responses to the changing social and political conditions of the seventeenth century (for example, Nassaney 1989; Robinson, Kelley, and Rubertone 1985; Rubertone 2001; Turnbaugh 1993; Volmar 1992; Zymroz 1997). Not surprisingly, tobacco pipe smoking was directly implicated. The following observations and interpretations are based on archaeological data in conjunction with oral, documentary, and ethnographic accounts.

Evidence regarding the timing of the introduction of tobacco *(Nicotiana rustica)* into the Northeast is lacking (Wagner 2000). Its antiquity is inferred from its widespread use at the time of contact and the presence of elbow pipes in pre-Columbian archaeological components similar to those used at contact throughout the region (MacNeish 1952:50; Willoughby 1935), particularly west of the Hudson River and in the Mid-Atlantic states. Documentary sources suggest that the cultivation of tobacco was a male activity in southern New England, particularly among the Narragansett, and throughout much of North America (see, for example, McGuire 1899:417 cited in Turnbaugh 1975:63; von Gernet 2000:70). For example, Spinden (1950:66) described the use of wild tobacco by the Thompson Indians of the Interior Plateau at the end of the nineteenth century: "there was a special ceremony for gathering the herb and in the old days only men smoked, or such women as had shamanistic power. Later smoking became general and mostly for pleasure." Tobacco was similarly confined to male use among the Huron and the Hidatsa. Edward Winslow (cited in Simmons 1986:47) "informs us that the men smoked much tobacco, but it was inappropriate for younger boys to do so" in southeastern New England, implying its restricted use.

Though seldom explicitly stated, I would argue that men, tobacco, and ritual were often associated in native North America prior to European contact; whether Narragansett men used it exclusively is suggested but difficult to demonstrate. What is likely is that smoking became more widespread in native society by the mid-seventeenth century as men, women, and children adopted it (Nassaney 2000:424; Turnbaugh 1980:21).

William Turnbaugh (1975, 1980, 1992) was among the first to suggest that tobacco use and pipe smoking became less socially restricted among Algonquian groups after the Contact period. He argued that the expansion of the practice was facilitated by the introduction of widely available European-manufactured white clay pipes, which quickly became disseminated among women and children. Further support for this pattern comes from a pathological analysis of the interments at RI-1000 that showed a high prevalence of tubercular skeletal lesions (30 percent of the population) among children, adolescents, and adults of both sexes (Robinson, Kelley, and Rubertone 1985:118–119). The increased frequency of this condition, as compared to pre-Contact times, was attributed to several physical and cultural factors, including respiratory complications resulting from wood smoke inhalation. Given the lack of evidence for changes in wood-burning activities, tobacco smoke inhalation across age and gender lines could have exacerbated this pathological condition and contributed to the observed pattern (Dena Dincauze, personal communication 2001).

Imported pipes were also accompanied by the introduction of a new species of tobacco from the Caribbean *(Nicotiana tabacum)* that was used alongside of *Nicotiana rustica* (Turnbaugh 1975:66). There is some debate about the characteristics of each of these species. Turnbaugh (1975:66, 1980:21) argued that the imported variety, *N. tabacum,* which was favored by the Europeans, was more palatable and less harsh. Pego et al. (1999:250) claim that it was "initially too strong for North American Indians," whereas von Gernet (1988:7) refers to *N. rustica* as the "potent" form "capable of producing major dissociative states." *N. rustica* apparently has a higher nicotine content than *N. tabacum* (Winter 2000:99). It was the Caribbean variety that was cultivated for commercial purposes in the Tidewater region of Virginia by the English. What is clear is that these two species had different attributes and sources that may have contributed to their use in different contexts.

In an earlier examination of this issue, I agreed with Turnbaugh (1980:21) that "casual tobacco smoking even extended to native American women and children." And I suggested that this might have occurred in imitation of Europeans who had fully adopted the practice by the beginning of the seventeenth century (Nassaney 2000:424–425). Both English women and children were well acquainted with the custom. An English host told a French traveler in 1672 (Fairholt 1968:116–117) "that when the children went to school, they carried in their satchel, with their books, a pipe of tobacco, which their mother took care to fill early in the morning, it serving them instead of a breakfast; and that at the accustomed hour, everyone laid aside his book to light his pipe, the master smoking with them, and teaching them how to hold their pipes and draw in the tobacco; thus accustoming them to it from their youths, believing it absolutely necessary for a man's health."

By the third quarter of the seventeenth century, casual tobacco use was prevalent among the English, and natives may have imitated this recreational practice, ascribing tobacco consumption with new, secular meanings. If tobacco use had previously been a male activity confined to ritual contexts, smoking it for pleasure would have led to social tensions particularly between men and women by undermining an activity that had once served to reproduce gender relations and ideologies. As Turnbaugh (1980:21) stated, "the traditional employment of the tobacco pipe as a socially significant male-only activity was losing ground." I would agree that tobacco was more widespread in native society by the mid-seventeenth century, as this appears to be supported by an increase in the frequency of pipes in the archaeological record. However, I suspect that the reasons for the expansion of the practice were more complex than mere emulation of European usage. I contend that tobacco had different meanings and contexts of use for native men, native women, and Europeans, and these meanings were not simply transcended by the exchange of tobacco and pipes in native New England (compare von Gernet 1988).

The archaeological record clearly indicates that English and Dutch white clay pipes were adopted in native New England (Brenner 1988:Table 4.1; Turnbaugh 1992:117; see also von Gernet 1988:Table 6.1). These artifacts are best known from several mortuary sites in the region where they have sometimes been linked to individuals of known sex. As expected, they are associated with males in most cases, though there are exceptions (see Nassaney 2003). While white clay pipes were clearly acquired from the English, it is more difficult to determine how much tobacco was obtained through exchange. Von Gernet (1988:Table 5.1) provides a selective list of English dispensations of tobacco to Amerindians that show the recipients were most often Iroquoian groups in the seventeenth century. This suggests that the Narragansett and other New England natives were not receiving much (if any) of their tobacco from the English; presumably they cultivated their own. Furthermore, the English in New England had not embraced the practice wholeheartedly; there was clearly "puritanical ambivalence over the habit" (von Gernet 1988:372–373). References to English smoking behavior in seventeenth-century New England are conspicuously absent from the literature, to my knowledge. From secondary sources we learn that "John Eliot, the dominant English missionary in the seventeenth century, . . . denounced tobacco" (von Gernet 1988:372), and "the Puritans . . . abhorred the fume of the pipe" (Fairholt 1968:111). New England was not Virginia!

If Amerindians were not imitating their European counterparts and the archaeological record strongly suggests that pipes were overwhelmingly associated with men, at least for their journey to the afterlife, can the idea that tobacco smoking became more widespread in society be supported? It is important to emphasize that among "Indians, the 'spirit power' of tobacco dictated a prescribed use that transcended mere indulgence or pleasure" (Turnbaugh 1980:18). The power of the pipe is illustrated in a seventeenth-century oral account collected in the late nineteenth century, as well as contemporary treatment of traditional smoking paraphernalia (see Nassaney 2000). Let me elaborate.

The RI-1000 cemetery contained nine clay pipes (one a native product), in addition to a unique steatite or soapstone pipe of native manufacture that was associated with an adult male. While the details of the context of the stone pipe have been described elsewhere (Nassaney 2000), suffice it to say that the discovery of this artifact aroused much interest. Prior to its removal, the Narragansett tribal representative conducted a solemn ceremony at the graveside that involved the placement of several offerings near the burial. While the full significance of the pipe and the ceremony surrounding it remain poorly understood, the native community treated this artifact differently than any other find in the cemetery. Perhaps not unimportant, the pipe lay at the base of an intrusive pit that reunited the artifact with its owner after the original interment.

In an effort to understand the postmortem deposition of this object, I encountered an interesting oral account entitled "The Silver Pipe" (see Veit and Bello, this volume, for a full quotation of this account). The narrative was recorded by Hezekiah Butterworth of Boston in 1892, and the story was told to her by Mrs. Zerviah Gould Mitchell (circa 1805–1895), a Wampanoag who claimed descent from the seventeenth-century sachem Massasoit. Several messages can be interpreted from the account. First, smoking was a male activity, from which women were restricted. Second, women (and men?) desired to smoke from powerful pipes, perhaps to enhance their spiritual well-being. And, third, all pipes were not alike and different pipes were used for various purposes (see Fletcher and La Flesche 1992 cited in Norder 1999).

It is apparent that activities surrounding tobacco ritualism had a strong male orientation but were not confined to men by the later half of the seventeenth century, despite the archaeological association between men and their pipes. Pipes were prescribed for male use in the afterlife as the mortuary record suggests; the oral account of the Silver Pipe served to codify and pass on to subsequent generations the lessons of ideal social roles and relations. The question remains as to why women may have challenged these social roles and rules in the dynamic social and political environment of the seventeenth century.

A number of recent analyses have emphasized female agency in attempting to rationalize the demographic, social, and political upheavals that native communities experienced (for example, Handsman 1988; Nassaney 2003; Volmar 1992; Zymroz 1997). They point to new artifact forms and changing mortuary patterns that signal an attempt to ameliorate the imbalances that Europeans had brought to America. For example, Zymroz (1997:246) argued that the use of symbolically charged objects in mortuary rituals at supernaturally strategic locations on the landscape was an effort "to secure and increase their individual and social physical and spiritual well-being." The concentration of certain classes of spiritually powerful grave goods with children, especially young females, underscores their importance in social reproduction and the biological survival of the group. This pattern occurs at a number of Contact period cemeteries in southeastern New England including Long Pond in Connecticut (Kevin McBride, personal communication 2000), RI-1000 (Turnbaugh 1984; Rubertone 2001:140–158), and Titicut in Massachusetts (Zymroz 1997).

Pipes are not the only artifacts that had ideological significance. Effigy pestles, which are long cylindrical stones with a sculptured representation at one end, were made and used during the Contact period in the greater Northeast (Volmar 1992). The recurrent association of these artifacts with women in death and in folk tales, and the symbolism of the animals depicted, suggest that these artifacts are symbols of female power that were developed in the seventeenth century. Furthermore, the creatures they depict evoke "mythological symbols of supernatural beings . . . to reify women's social position in Algonquian society" (Volmar 1992: 22). In the onslaught of a crumbling social order that challenged the predictability of roles and relations, I contend that individuals developed new ways to make contact with other worldly forces and beings as a way to rectify an unstable situation represented through mortuary ritual and effigy pestles.

Another tactic was an increase in the use of tobacco in native society, again only superficially in imitation of Europeans, and more likely in an attempt to connect with the cosmological forces that could help restore balance in an increasingly unintelligible world of death, animosity, and conflict. This would explain the use of tobacco and clay pipes by women and children and perhaps by men who had previously used them only sparingly. Tobacco use increased to benefit society. In the process, ritual became less institutional and more personal as the efficacy of religious specialists was questioned and their roles were being challenged. Von Gernet (2000:78, 80) arrived at a similar interpretation, which he referred to as "democratized shamanism" in which all members had the potential to acquire spiritual power for themselves and their community. The practice became popular among those who circumvented the hegemony of the shaman and sought their own direct communication with spirit beings.

Men who once controlled the use of tobacco and access to ritual knowledge (for example, powerful shamans?) also responded to the social disruptions brought about by the English and the tensions created by recreational smoking or attempts to use tobacco to usurp their authority in dealings with the supernatural. According to Turnbaugh (1977:67), one possible response to the wider dissemination of the practice was to idealize native pipes and reemphasize smoking as a ritual activity. In 1634, William Wood (1977:80 cited in Turnbaugh 1992:119) observed that the Narragansett employed European metal tools to manufacture "their great stone pipes, which will hold a quarter of an ounce of tobacco." While these pipes may have been produced prior to sustained European contact, they seem to have experienced a renaissance or revitalization in the seventeenth century (Turnbaugh 1975, 1992). The preference for pipes of native manufacture for ritual purposes among natives has been documented elsewhere on the frontier of eastern North America in the eighteenth century, suggesting that the pattern was not confined to southeastern New England (see Trubowitz 1992). By maintaining a decided preference for using their own pipes like the soapstone specimen at RI-1000 as opposed to those introduced by trade, some men may have sought to limit tobacco use for themselves. This may support the idea that "*native* pipes filled with *native* tobacco" *(Nicotiana rustica)* were spiritually most effective (see Turnbaugh 1980:21).

Summary and Conclusions

Few would deny the profound impact that European societies had on native groups. What remains to be understood are the ways in which indigenous groups and individuals incorporated, rationalized, resisted, ideologically transformed, and responded to the new goods, services, and practices that were introduced in the turbulent seventeenth century. Tobacco smoking was indisputably an Amerindian practice, but one that Europeans adopted, modified, and reintroduced to the Colonies. The practice came back to native New Englanders in the form of foreign clay pipes and a new tobacco species that permeated society in new ways. To argue that natives imitated Europeans or that a pipe/tobacco/smoking complex emerged that was a product of native and European interaction fails to take into account the subtle meanings that persisted or were actively created through native tobacco use (compare von Gernet 1988). There was no calumet ceremony in seventeenth-century New England in which natives and newcomers agreed on a common pipe form and a context for sharing a smoke (see Blakeslee 1981; Brown 1989; Salter 1977; compare Trubowitz 1992). The calumet developed among native groups on the edge of the prairie and spread to neighboring groups in the Eastern Woodlands and Plains in the eighteenth and nineteenth centuries in the context of ritual and economic exchanges between partners of relatively equal power, as among the French and their allies. The English never saw themselves as equal to the people they sought to dispossess; they were unwilling to share power or the pipe in seventeenth-century New England and only begrudgingly engaged in the calumet ceremony in the eighteenth century.

Despite the cultural boundary that pipe smoking reinforced in New England, there appears to be good evidence that tobacco use spread to new segments of indigenous society in the seventeenth century. This expansion may have created or exacerbated existing tensions along gender lines. Women and children began to use tobacco to enhance and appropriate lines of communication with the supernatural to ensure spiritual and physical well-being. While the Narragansetts avoided the decimating plague of 1616–1619, other diseases likely impacted them later in the seventeenth century (for example, the smallpox epidemic of the 1630s). Traditional healers were ineffective against this biological onslaught (and may have actually contributed to its spread); this may have led some segments of society to challenge established authority and search for new ways to secure their own earthly or heavenly salvation. This is a common theme in Contact period studies, as Brotherton (2000:365) has recently noted for the Northwest coast in the nineteenth century:

> Widespread deaths during smallpox epidemics challenged beliefs in Native healers. After the epidemics of 1836–39, . . . there was a massive increase in conversions. The bishop of Alaska . . . described how the ineffectiveness of the shamans in preventing deaths . . . helped to attract new converts. The severity of the devastation and widespread death was unlike anything the Tlingit had ever seen and undermined beliefs in the power of the shaman.

The material evidence suggests that beliefs among New England natives may have suffered a similar crisis; however, rather than wholesale conversions to Christianity, there was an attempt to expand and redefine aspects of native ritual activity to rectify a declining social and spiritual order. A more democratized shamanism entailed a shift to new forms of supernatural communication expressed in more widespread smoking practices and the elaboration of stone pestles to represent and placate benevolent creatures possessed with power (see also Nassaney 2003). As men and women employed new artifact forms to symbolize their increasingly personal relationships with otherworldly forces, conflicts invariably cropped up as they redefined their gender identities. The shift from communal to individualized ritual practices was reinforced in other realms by an economic mentality that silently eroded reciprocity and egalitarianism (see Nassaney 1989; Turnbaugh 1993).

Yet, these new activities did not go unchecked, as efforts to revive earlier social relationships were actively expressed in the material world and oral accounts of the period. The placement of pipes almost exclusively with a limited number of men to accompany them into the afterlife and the oral tradition of the Silver Pipe are explicit attempts to codify idealized roles and deny, mask, or ameliorate the struggles along gender and intercultural lines among the living. They represent a desire for the world to be as it once was in the afterlife and in the future. Individual efforts to counter colonialism proved to be ineffective at restoring well-being, and, since King Philip's War, native peoples of southeast New England have rediscovered and successfully employed communal collective action to reassert and express their distinctive ethnic identities.

In conclusion, culture contact had profound consequences for native societies in southeast New England that led to changes in gender roles and relationships with the supernatural. But just because the Narragansett, their neighbors, and the English all smoked tobacco and many even used European white clay pipes does not mean that these societies had shared beliefs in regards to smoking. Neither did they participate in a unified pipe/tobacco/smoking complex so long as they maintained different ideas about the social and spiritual significance of the smoking act. I have tried to show that native ideas about smoking and tobacco were not imitations of English beliefs, even though it appears that their ideas became intertwined with the English.

The ethnohistoric study of native tobacco use can also inform understandings of this practice among contemporary American Indians. For example, the distinction between the secular and sacred use of tobacco that continues to this day in native communities probably originated in the seventeenth century when new forms of tobacco were introduced into the Northeast and the prevalence of white clay pipes availed the practice of smoking to a wider segment of society. Aboriginal tobacco *(Nicotiana rustica)* was often in short supply, whereas trade tobacco *(Nicotiana tabacum)* could be readily obtained "in exchange for furs, but it belonged symbolically in the secular, European realm" (Pego et al. 1999: 252). There is no evidence that the English recognized these different contexts of use. Tobacco smoking is seen almost exclusively as a recreational activity in mainstream society today, following the English tradition. Yet, so long as native peoples continue to recognize their ritual functions, tobacco and its associated paraphernalia will serve as visible material symbols of ethnic identity that have persisted since the turbulent seventeenth century.

Acknowledgments

The arguments in this paper have benefited from the comments of and conversations with numerous colleagues, including John Brown, Dena Dincauze, Eric Johnson, Paul Robinson, Patricia Rubertone, William Simmons, Pamela Stone, William Turnbaugh, and Michael Volmar. Thanks to Sean Rafferty and Rob Mann for organizing the original Society for American Archaeology symposium in which an earlier version this paper was presented and for inviting me to contribute to this volume. Finally, this research was supported by a research fellowship from the John Nicholas Brown Center for the Study of American Civilization at Brown University and an award from the Western Michigan University Faculty Research and Creative Activities Support Fund.

References Cited

Blakeslee, Donald J.
1981 The Origin and Spread of the Calumet Ceremony. *American Antiquity* 46(4):759–768.

Bragdon, Kathleen J.
1996 *Native People of Southern New England, 1500–1650.* Univ. of Oklahoma Press, Norman.

Brenner, Elise M.

1988 Sociopolitical Implications of Mortuary Remains in Seventeenth-Century Native Southern New England. In *The Recovery of Meaning,* edited by M. P. Leone and P. B. Potter Jr., 147–181. Smithsonian Institution Press, Washington, D.C.

Brotherton, Barbara

2000 Tlingit Human Masks as Documents of Culture Change and Continuity. In *Interpretations of Native North American Life: Material Contributions to Ethnohistory,* edited by M. S. Nassaney and E. S. Johnson, 358–397. Society for Historical Archaeology and the Univ. Press of Florida, Gainesville.

Brown, Ian W.

1989 The Calumet Ceremony in the Southeast and Its Archaeological Manifestations. *American Antiquity* 54(2):311–331.

Butterworth, Hezekiah

1893 The Silver Pipe. In *Exercises under the Auspices of the Thalia Club, Warren, R. I.,* 16. Massasoit Monument Association, Providence.

Carlson, Catherine C., George J. Armelagoes, and Ann L. Magennis

1992 Impact of Disease on the Precontact and Early Historic Populations of New England and the Maritimes. In *Disease and Demography in the Americas,* edited by J. W. Verano and D. H. Ubelaker, 141–154. Smithsonian Institution Press, Washington, D.C.

Corti, Count

1996 *A History of Smoking.* Random House, London. Originally published 1931, George G. Harrap & Co. Ltd., London.

Cronon, W.

1983 *Changes in the Land: Indians, Colonists, and the Ecology of New England.* Hill and Wang, New York.

Crosby, Constance A.

1988 From Myth to History, or Why King Philip's Ghost Walks Abroad. In *The Recovery of Meaning,* edited by M. P. Leone and P. B. Potter Jr., 183–209. Smithsonian Institution Press, Washington, D.C.

Deetz, James

1977 *In Small Things Forgotten: The Archaeology of Early American Life.* Anchor Press/Doubleday, Garden City, New York.

Fairholt, Frederick W.

1968 *Tobacco: Its History and Associations.* Singing Tree Press, Detroit. Originally published 1859, Chapman and Hall, London.

Fletcher, Alice C., and Frances La Flesche

1992 *The Omaha Tribe.* Vols. 1–2. Univ. of Nebraska Press, Lincoln.

Hamell, George R.

1983 Trading in Metaphors: The Magic of Beads. In *Proceedings of the 1982 Glass Trade Bead Conference,* edited by C. F. Hayes III, 5–28. Research Records No. 16. Rochester Museum & Science Center, Rochester, N.Y.

Handsman, Russell G.

1988 Algonquian Women Resist Colonialism. *Artifacts* 16(3–4):29–31.

1990 Corn and Culture, Pots and Politics: How to Listen to the Voices of Mohegan Women. Paper presented at the annual meeting of the Society for Historical Archaeology, Tucson, Ariz.

Johnson, Eric S.

1993 *"Some by Flatteries and Others by Threatenings": Political Strategies among Native Americans of Seventeenth-Century Southern New England.* Ph.D. dissertation, Dept. of Anthropology, Univ. of Massachusetts, Amherst.

1999 Community and Confederation: A Political Geography of Contact Period Southern New England. In *The Archaeological Northeast,* edited by M. A. Levine, K. E. Sassaman, and M. S. Nassaney, 155–168. Bergin & Garvey, Westport, Conn.

2000 The Politics of Pottery: Material Culture and Political Process among Algonquians of Seventeenth-Century Southern New England. In *Interpretations of Native North American Life: Material Contributions to Ethnohistory,* edited by M. S. Nassaney and E. S. Johnson, 118–145. Society for Historical Archaeology and Univ. Press of Florida, Gainesville.

MacNeish, Richard S.

1952 The Archaeology of the Northeastern United States. In *Archaeology of Eastern United States,* edited by J. B. Griffin, 46–58. Univ. of Chicago Press, Chicago.

McGuire, J. D.

1899 Pipes and Smoking Customs of the American Aborigines, Based on Material in the U. S. National Museum. *Annual Report of the United States National Museum, 1896–97,* 351–645. Smithsonian Institution, Washington, D.C.

Nassaney, Michael S.

1989 An Epistemological Enquiry into Some Archaeological and Historical Interpretations of Seventeenth Century Native American-European Relations. In *Archaeological Approaches to Cultural Identity,* edited by S. J. Shennan, 76–93. Unwin Hyman, London.

2000 Archaeology and Oral Tradition in Tandem: Interpreting Native American Ritual, Ideology, and Gender Relations in Contact-Period Southeastern New England. In *Interpretations of Native North American Life: Material Contributions to Ethnohistory,* edited by M. S. Nassaney and E. S. Johnson, 412–431. Society for Historical Archaeology and Univ. Press of Florida, Gainesville.

2003 Native American Gender Relations and Material Culture in Seventeenth-Century Southeastern New England. Manuscript on file, Dept. of Anthropology, Western Michigan Univ., Kalamazoo, Michigan.

Norder, John W.

1999 Coming to Terms with the Native American Pipe in Eastern North America. Paper presented at the annual meeting of the American Society for Ethnohistory, Mashantucket, Conn.

Orser, Charles E., Jr.

1996 *A Historical Archaeology of the Modern World.* Plenum Press, New York.

Pego, Christina M., Robert F. Hill, Glenn W. Solomon, Robert M. Chisholm, and Suzanne E. Ivey

1999 Tobacco, Culture, and Health among American Indians: A Historical Review. In *Contemporary Native American Cultural Issues,* edited by D. Champagne, 245–262. Altamira Press, Walnut Creek, Calif.

Ramenofsky, Ann

1987 *Vectors of Death: The Archaeology of European Contact.* Univ. of New Mexico Press, Albuquerque.

Robinson, Paul A.,

1990 *The Struggle Within: The Indian Debate in Seventeenth Century Narragansett Country.* Ph.D. dissertation, Dept. of Anthropology, Binghamton Univ.

Robinson, Paul A., Marc A. Kelley, and Patricia E. Rubertone

1985 Preliminary Biocultural Interpretations from a Seventeenth-Century Narragansett Indian Cemetery in Rhode Island. In *Cultures in Contact,* edited by W. W. Fitzhugh, 107–130. Smithsonian Institution Press, Washington, D.C.

Rubertone, Patricia E.

1989 Archaeology, Colonialism, and Seventeenth-Century Native America: Towards an Alternative Interpretation. In *Conflict in the Archaeology of Living Traditions,* edited by R. Layton, 32–45. Unwin Hyman, London.

1994 Grave Remembrances: Enduring Traditions among the Narragansett. *Connecticut History* 35:22–45.

2001 *Grave Undertakings: An Archaeology of Roger Williams and the Narragansett Indians.* Smithsonian Institution Press, Washington, D.C.

Salter, Andrew Harvey

1977 *Catlinite Calumets: Artifactual Clues to Late Prehistoric and Historic Interactions in Eastern North America.* Honor's thesis, Harvard Univ.

Sharp, Lauriston

1952 Steel Axes for Stone Age Australians. *Human Organization* 11(2):17–22.

Shoemaker, Nancy

1995 Introduction. In *Negotiators of Change: Historical Perspectives on Native American Women,* edited by N. Shoemaker, 1–25. Routledge, New York.

Shoemaker, Robert B.

1998 *Gender in English Society, 1650–1850.* Longman, London.

Simmons, William S.

1986 *Spirit of the New England Tribes: Indian History and Folklore.* Univ. Press of New England, Hanover.

Spinden, Herbert Joseph

1950 *Tobacco Is American.* New York Public Library, New York.

Thomas, Peter A.

1976 Contrastive Subsistence Strategies and Land Use as Factors for Understanding Indian-White Relations in New England. *Ethnohistory* 23:1–18.

Trigger, Bruce G.

1986 Ethnohistory: The Unfinished Edifice. *Ethnohistory* 33:253–267.

Trubowitz, Neal L.

1992 Thanks, but We Prefer to Smoke Our Own: Pipes in the Great Lakes–Riverine Region during the Eighteenth Century. In *Proceedings of the 1989 Smoking Pipe Conference: Selected Papers,* edited by C. F. Hayes III, 97–111. Research Records No. 22. Rochester Museum & Science Center, Rochester, N.Y.

Tuma, S. John

1985 *Contact Period (1500–1675) Burials in Southeast New England.* Unpublished master's thesis, History and Historical Archaeology Program, Univ. of Massachusetts, Boston.

1992 Contact Period Mortuary Practices of the Massachusett and Narragansett Speakers. Paper presented at the 32d annual meeting of the Northeastern Anthropological Association, Bridgewater, Mass.

Turnbaugh, William A.

1975 Tobacco, Pipes, Smoking, and Rituals among the Indians of the Northeast. *Quarterly Bulletin of the Archaeological Society of Virginia* 30(2):59–71.

1976 The Survival of a Native Craft in Colonial Rhode Island. *Man in the Northeast* 11:74–79.

1977 Elements of Nativistic Pipe Ceremonialism in the Post-Contact Northeast. *Pennsylvania Archaeologist* 47(4):1–7.

1980 Native American Smoking Pipes. *Archaeology* 33(1):15–22.

1984 *The Material Culture of RI-1000, a Mid-Seventeenth-Century Narragansett Indian Burial Site in North Kingstown, Rhode Island.* Dept. of Sociology and Anthropology, Univ. of Rhode Island, Kingston.

1992 Post-Contact Smoking Pipe Development: The Narragansett Example. In *Proceedings of the 1989 Smoking Pipe Conference: Selected Papers,* edited by C. F. Hayes III, 113–124. Research Records No. 22. Rochester Museum and Science Center, Rochester, N.Y.

1993 Assessing the Significance of European Goods in Seventeenth-Century Narragansett Society. In *Ethnohistory and Archaeology: Approaches to Postcontact Change in the Americas,* edited by J. D. Rogers and S. M. Wilson, 133–160. Plenum Press, New York.

Volmar, Michael Allen

1992 *The Conundrum of Effigy Pestles.* Unpublished master's thesis, Dept. of Anthropology, Univ. of Massachusetts, Amherst.

von Gernet, Alexander D.

1988 *The Transculturation of the Amerindian Pipe/Tobacco/Smoking Complex and I ts Impact on the Intellectual Boundaries between "Savagery" and "Civilization," 1535–1935.* Ph.D. dissertation, Dept. of Anthropology, McGill Univ., Montreal.

2000 North American Indigenous *Nicotiana* Use and Tobacco Shamanism: The Early Documentary Record, 1520–1660. In *Tobacco Use by Native North Americans: Sacred Smoke and Silent Killer,* edited by J. C. Winter, 59–80. Univ. of Oklahoma Press, Norman.

Wagner, Gail E.

2000 Tobacco in Prehistoric Eastern North America. In *Tobacco Use by Native North Americans: Sacred Smoke and Silent Killer,* edited by J. C. Winter, 185–201. Univ. of Oklahoma Press, Norman.

Wallerstein, Immanuel.

1974 *The Modern World-System: Capitalist Agriculture and the Origins of the European World-Economy in the Sixteenth Century.* Academic Press, New York.

White, Richard

1991 *The Middle Ground.* Cambridge Univ. Press, Cambridge.

Williams, Roger

1973 *A Key into the Language of America.* Edited by J. J. Teunissen and E. J. Hinz. Wayne State Univ. Press, Detroit.

Willoughby, Charles C.

1935 *Antiquities of the New England Indians with Notes on the Ancient Cultures of the Adjacent Territory.* Peabody Museum of Archaeology and Ethnology, Harvard Univ., Cambridge, Mass.

Winter, Joseph C.

2000 Botanical Description of the North American Tobacco Species. In *Tobacco Use by Native North Americans: Sacred Smoke and Silent Killer,* edited by J. C. Winter, 87–127. Univ. of Oklahoma Press, Norman.

Winter, Joseph C. (editor)

2000 *Tobacco Use by Native North Americans: Sacred Smoke and Silent Killer.* Univ. of Oklahoma Press, Norman.

Wolf, Eric

1982 *Europe and the People without History.* Univ. of California Press, Berkeley.

Wood, William

1977 *New England's Prospect.* Reprint of 1634 ed. Univ. of Massachusetts Press, Amherst.

Zymroz, Desiree D.

1997 *The Titicut Site Burials: An Alternative Perspective on Native Actions and Experiences in Southern New England during the Contact Period.* Unpublished master's thesis, History/Historical Archaeology Program, Univ. of Massachusetts, Boston.

5. Smoking Pipes: An Archaeological Measure of Native American Cultural Stability and Survival in Eastern North America, A.D. 1500–1850

Neal L. Trubowitz

This smoking pipe research has been part of my professional interest in the interaction between peoples of different cultures in the Western Hemisphere. Just over five hundred years ago, European explorer Christopher Columbus, while seeking the coast of Asia, stumbled upon an island shore in the Caribbean. There he met some of the people whose ancestors had been living in the Americas for thousands of years, whom he mistook and mislabeled as Indians. This encounter set in motion both a destructive upheaval for the peoples of the Americas and the so-called Columbian Exchange between the human populations of the earth's two hemispheres. The subsequent movements of populations and products, including foods, fibers, and manufactured goods, are so much a part of our everyday lives that most people do not realize how our existence today has been, and our future will be, shaped by the accelerating pace of worldwide cultural interaction that began on a sandy beach in 1492. Thereafter, as expressed in the theme of the Hall of North American Indians at the Peabody Museum of Archaeology and Ethnology at Harvard University, there has been a simultaneous time line of continuity and change in the cultures of the people living in the Americas.

Tobacco possibly was the most widely and rapidly distributed item of the Columbian Exchange. There is no doubt that a number of different species of tobacco plants were first cultivated by prehistoric Native Americans (see Winter 2000); tobacco smoking was unknown to the rest of the world until European explorers learned of it from Native Americans and took it back to the Eastern

Hemisphere. Tobacco and smoking pipes were spread around the world within a couple hundred years of Columbus's island landfall (see Laufer 1924a, 1924b; Laufer, Hambly, and Linton 1930). While here in the United States we have officially recognized the health hazards of tobacco use and have begun to try to discourage its consumption, cigarette filters are reported to be the number one most common form of litter here (just walk anywhere and you will see this confirmed for yourself). Travelers outside the United States can testify to how ubiquitous tobacco use is. Recently on National Public Radio, a commentator described Europe as "one big ashtray." Tobacco consumption is still climbing worldwide, even if you cannot smoke in many restaurants and public buildings in the United States.

In the 1980s while I was on the faculty at Indiana University–Indianapolis, I investigated the Columbian Exchange on a series of contemporary eighteenth-century Native American and European sites on the central Wabash River near Lafayette, Indiana (Trubowitz 1992a). That work revealed a complex pattern of cultural interaction in which technology and natural products were being exchanged in both directions, but when it came to smoking pipes, it seemed that there was little interest by the Native Americans in the European white clay version of smoking pipes. Review of the archaeological literature indicated that this was part of an overall cultural preference of Native Americans for their own pipes throughout the Great Lakes region during the 1700s. European pipes did not predominate over or replace native stone and ceramic pipes among native peoples until the next century, when Indians lost control of most of the land to growing numbers of American and Canadian migrants. The archaeological and ethnohistoric data on pipes reflected different cultural or ethnic uses of pipes and tobacco over time (Trubowitz 1992b).

A 2000–2001 Hrdy research grant from the Peabody Museum of Archaeology and Ethnology at Harvard University afforded me the opportunity to revisit and expand the prior investigations. This chapter is a progress report on my Hrdy grant study on smoking pipes and tobacco use in eastern North America, mostly east of the Great Plains, between A.D. 1500 and 1850. The data used were the pipe collections in the Peabody Museum and the resources of the Tozzer Library. I focused on archaeological data but also referenced some ethnohistoric material. I found an overwhelming body of archaeological data in the library, and the museum collections included thousands of pipes of many varieties.

My study differed from early pipe research that surveyed broad geographic areas (McGuire 1899; West 1934) in its search for evidence of changing pipe use and the inclusion of pipe information from ethnic European and African archaeological sites in North America. In addition, I had the advantage of not only the accumulation of more data but also chronological (both synchronic and diachronic) information that was not available to earlier pipe researchers. My goal was to peruse as much time-bracketed data as possible during my stay at

Harvard. Of the many researchers who have investigated pipes, there were two scholars whose research efforts and writings in many ways paralleled my work in the 1980s and at Harvard: Alexander D. von Gernet's studies, including his 1988 Ph.D. dissertation, and the work of William A. Turnbaugh, which includes a paper on post-Contact pipe use in southern New England (Turnbaugh 1992).

Von Gernet concluded that the traditional academic models of culture contact, including the concepts of acculturation (which has acquired a connotation of unilateral change for native peoples in the face of eventual European dominance) and revitalization, did not fit the exchange of the pipe/tobacco/smoking complex between native Americans and Europeans. Rather, he preferred the term *transculturation* to denote that the cultures in contact combined native and newcomer elements of the pipe/tobacco/smoking complex into the same interactive entity. As both sides copied pipe styles from one another, it was "an archaeological challenge to discover who was making and trading what to whom" (von Gernet 1988:303).

I took up that challenge to learn if archaeological data demonstrated ethnic preferences in smoking pipe and tobacco use in eastern North America from first contact through 1850. By 1850, many Native American communities had been annihilated and/or removed from their traditional homelands, leaving much smaller native populations among the European immigrants. The persistence of native pipes in many places throughout this 350-year time span, in the face of the "near-total replacement of other material culture with European counterparts" (von Gernet 1988:304), most likely reflected the continuity of Native American beliefs involved in the use of tobacco and other smoking materials (Engelbrecht 1993). I would also examine whether the presence or absence of pipes, contexts in which they were deposited, and kinds of pipes found on European and African sites in North America would document their user's ethnicity and different functions for tobacco smoking.

The Exchange of Tobacco and Smoking Pipes

As Europeans first began to meet and interact with Native Americans, they observed that Indians utilized tobacco in a variety of ways. Pipes and tobacco, sometimes in combination with other vegetal fibers, were used in medicinal practice, to counter hunger and thirst, to focus intellectual consideration, in the torture and execution of enemies, and also for recreation or relaxation. Smoking and other forms of tobacco use or pipe ceremonialism, served as a means of communication in several ways, from person to person, group to group, and from the group or individual to the supernatural or spiritual world. Pipe ceremonialism helped to establish fictive or symbolic kin ties that could give safe passage, assuage wars or blood feuds, permit trade, and create and maintain alliances (Trubowitz 1992b). Pipes and tobacco were important to Native peoples in both sacred and profane aspects of their lives (Linton 1924; Turnbaugh 1975). Some pipes, usually made of stone, were reserved only for special ceremonial or sacred functions, while others were personal possessions used more frequently in mundane contexts (Paper 1992).

Observing these practices, Europeans experimented with tobacco for medicinal and aphrodisiac uses but soon largely settled upon using it as a recreational herb. Early accounts of smoking referred to its use as "drinking smoke." Most western European elites had become acquainted with tobacco by the third quarter of the 1500s. Smoking and other means of taking tobacco quickly became a ubiquitous component of European relaxation, usually accompanied by drinking alcoholic or other beverages in social circles, public houses, and in the home or workplace. The prototype for the first European manufactured pipes created by the English was most likely a native style found in the Tidewater region between Maryland and North Carolina.

The manufacture of white clay pipes was established in England by the 1580s and soon spread into northern Europe, first to the Dutch, into the Germanic states and central Europe, and later into France (Laufer 1924b). By the mid-1600s there were thousands of pipe manufacturers in Europe (which makes it time consuming for pipe researchers to identify pieces that have decorations or makers' marks molded on them). The northern Europeans brought their white clay pipes back to North America, where they were introduced to native peoples. These white clays are ball clays, and, as pointed out by Ian Walker more than thirty years ago (Walker 1977), archaeologists have been misidentifying them as kaolin clay, which they are not. White clay or white ball clay is the proper way to refer to these artifacts.

In the 1600s English colonists in New England and the Tidewater regions imported European molds and manufactured terra-cotta pipes from local reddish and brown clays (see Agbe-Davies, this volume, and Capone and Downs, this volume). Sometimes these clays were mixed with white clays to produce what is termed an agate paste. Evidence was recently uncovered of locally manufactured pipes at Jamestown, Virginia, in a deposit dating only three years after the 1607 founding of the first successful English colony in North America. These were probably made by a tobacco-pipe maker, Robert Cotton, who arrived at Jamestown in the first month of 1608 (Kelso and Straube 2000:40–41). The Europeans also imported pipes made from pewter and other metals in small numbers compared to their ceramic types (see Veit and Bello, this volume). Metal pipes joined stone pipes as important means of establishing communication and relations between Native Americans and Europeans.

Native peoples and Europeans experimented with each other's pipes and different varieties of tobacco. At first contact, on the mainland in eastern North America, yellow flowered *Nicotiana rustica* (L.) was the universal species of tobacco grown by native peoples, while pink-flowered *Nicotiana tabacum* (L.) was cultivated in the Caribbean, Mexico, and Central and South America. The Europeans introduced the southern species into North America, and it rapidly became the predominant tobacco species grown by the Europeans in their colonies. By the mid-1600s, North American Indians were insistent that tobacco they received in trade or gifts from Europeans (including the Dutch, French, and English), be *N. tabacum* grown by the Portuguese in Brazil (von Gernet 1988).

Collections Research

At the start of my research year, the computer database at the Peabody Museum, EmbARK, contained more than 300,000 object records. First, I reduced the electronic database sample to all pipes from North America, yielding some 2,340 catalog numbers. This smaller database was further refined for pipes that had geographic provenience by state or province. These searches yielded 1,440 pipe catalog numbers from forty-two states/provinces and the District of Columbia in eastern North America. Each of the catalog numbers may represent one or more objects. Thus, the catalog number total was an underestimate of the total number of pipe pieces in the electronic database. I found as many as fifty-seven pipe fragments assigned to an individual catalog number.

According to Archaeology Collections Manager Gloria Greiss, at the time of the study a conservative estimate figure for the number of pipe pieces compared to catalog numbers was a ratio of 4:1. This multiplied out to 5,760 pipe artifacts, including both archaeological and ethnographic specimens. There were additional pipes identified from particular regions, such as the Great Lakes or North America, which did not have state or province provenience.

I decided to concentrate on expanding research first in the areas closest to my prior work on the Great Lakes with the Mid-Atlantic and New England states. These areas included three of the four largest state collections of pipes in Ohio, New York, and Massachusetts. The EmbARK records were compared against Native American Graves Protection and Repatriation Act (NAGPRA) reports and files compiled by the repatriation staff to determine if there were any pipes from funerary contexts that could be affiliated with a Native American tribe. Small numbers of artifacts were identified as such, and letters were sent to designated representatives of the Iroquois tribes, the Wampanoag, and the Delaware, informing them of the research project and that no destructive methods of investigation would be utilized. Their input and/or comments were invited, and there were no objections.

Another step was to eliminate pipes that did not fall within the time span under study. This disqualified most of the pipes from Georgia, the southern state with the most pipes, which had come from Etowah and dated to the Mississippian occupation prior to 1500. Many of the Ohio pipes were earlier Hopewell objects and were excluded. Most of the other Ohio pipes were from Madisonville and previously were studied and described (Drooker 1997), so they were not revisited for lack of time. Pipes from New York, Massachusetts, Pennsylvania, and a few from Maine, New Jersey, Indiana, and Wisconsin were examined to determine whether they needed to be excluded or to be moved to a study location at the museum annex. For example, the New York sample of 222 catalog numbers was reduced to about 100 archaeological catalog numbers that needed to be pulled. I ended up taking measurements in detail on about 138 pipes from New Jersey north to Maine, and west to Wisconsin. Unfortunately, most of these artifacts did not have site-specific provenience information.

The Peabody pipe collections spanned the study time interval. There were native pipes dating to the 1500s that were in use into the early 1600s. Native ceramic pipes with very fine stippled decorations from Trenton, New Jersey, had stylistic elements common along the Atlantic coast into the Carolinas in the 1600s. There has been some argument in the past about whether such decorative motifs had been created by enslaved Africans brought to North America, but recent research clearly demonstrated that these decorative techniques predated the importation of slaves and originated with Native Americans (Magoon 1999). It is still not clear whether Europeans and enslaved Africans copied these kinds of pipes and/or obtained them in trade.

One New Jersey site, a Dutch Trader's House, yielded a red pipestone disk pipe. This may be one of the most eastern known finds of this type of pipe, which originated on Oneota sites in the Upper Great Lakes in the 1500s and was one of the earliest forms of pipes with a separate stem that may have been used as a calumet. The calumet ceremony (in which the decorated stem played a critical role) was used in cross-cultural interaction. The ceremony was well established in the upper Great Lakes and upper Mississippi Valley regions when the French first visited in the mid-1600s, and it was a near universal practice among the Indians of the lower Mississippi Valley by the end of that century (Brown 1989). A red pipestone disk pipe in the Peabody Museum collection found at Liberty, Wisconsin, had its date of discovery, "1847," scratched onto one side.

Per Gundersen (1993), I note that the assignment of the term *catlinite* to pipes cannot be made without chemical analysis of trace elements. The quarry at Pipestone Monument in Minnesota, where the argillite was named catlinite in honor of George Catlin, the early-nineteenth-century artist whose account made this place famous, is only one of several ancient mines that furnished red stone for making pipes. In the absence of tests to identify specific quarries, "red pipestone" should be used to refer to these artifacts.

The eighteenth- and nineteenth-century calumet pipe bowls with separate stems developed out of the disk pipe form. Peabody collections included an elbow pipe calumet form from Muscota, Wisconsin. Among the later type sometimes called a modified "T," was a beautiful lead inlaid piece; it looks nineteenth century in age and western in origin but had a Suffield, Connecticut, provenience attribution.

The Peabody collections included a variety of both early and late Iroquoian pipes, some acquired in research expeditions led by M. R. Harrington in the early 1900s to sites in New York State. There were classic trumpet bowl forms of ceramic elbow pipes, as well as some examples of ceramic animal and human effigy elbow pipes.

Along the Lake Erie shore margins of western New York State are the Ripley and Silverheels sites, which might be affiliated with the Erie Confederacy (Grumet 1995; Guthe 1958; Sullivan 1996). Ripley may have several components, which extend into the late 1500s/early 1600s. Some early ceramic styles recovered in 1904 at Ripley included so-called mamillary noded pipes and simple elbow pipes. There were also stone pipe bowls in several styles, including the vasiform variety. Such pipes required a separate reed stem. One of the Ripley specimens in the Peabody collections is a brown stone piece that may be from a broken disk pipe. Engraving on the top represents a long-tailed creature with scales on its back, possibly a mythological underground or underwater panther more typical of Upper Great Lakes Indian cosmology (Eric Hollinger, personal communication 2001). Arthur Parker conducted New York State Museum excavations at Ripley in 1906, recovering more separate-stem stone pipes, including an animal or mythical beast effigy that faces away from the smoker, and ceramic elbow pipe forms of trumpets and animal and human effigies that faced the smoker (Parker 1907).

Jordan Paper (1992) argued that the separate-stem stone Iroquoian pipes were reserved for intertribal ritual and the welcoming of alien visitors, compared to the one-piece ceramic forms that were personal pipes. He postulated that the difference in orientation in the facing-out stone effigies compared to the facing-in ceramic effigies reflected their different functions.

Silverheels is dated between the end of the sixteenth century to some burials that may have been interred between 1625 and 1650 (Guthe 1958). Most of the pipes were variations of ceramic elbow pipes in the ring bowl form that is typical of western New York Iroquois sites in the early 1600s. One of these had iron deposit stains and clearly was buried in association with a piece of imported European metal. Harrington also excavated in the Mohawk Valley on Garoga and Ganada No. 2, two large Mohawk villages that date from 1525–1580 (Funk 1967; Snow 1995). Ceramic elbow pipe forms were most common on these sites.

Early contact with Europeans provided new materials for use in traditional forms of pipes. Glass beads appeared as eyes in Iroquoian ceramic effigy pipes, and Massachusetts Indians used copper or brass to repair stems and bowls of native stone and ceramic elbow pipes (Willoughby 1935). The Peabody Museum had examples of such pipes with metal, dating to the early 1600s from sites in Chelsea, Revere, and Ipswich, Massachusetts. There was a native style pipe from Revere that was made by rolling a piece of lead into an elbow tube.

In the early 1600s, with European metal tools in hand, the Iroquois and other northern Indians had a burst of creative art in the design and decoration of stone, wood, and bone artifacts, including pipes. Perishable materials rarely survive on eastern North American archaeological sites, but they are indicated by a few whole artifacts, and remnants of decorative elements such as shell inlay. For an inlay example, see the Seneca Adams site in New York (Wray et. al. 1987). Metal components like cuprous bowl liners may also serve as evidence (as on the Oneida Thurston site in New York; see Pratt 1976). A rare wooden pipe inlaid with lead in the Peabody collection was attributed to the Mohawk Valley in New York. This was in the form of a hand, palm up, holding the decorated bowl. Charring inside the bowl indicates this pipe was well used. In 1998, Elizabeth Chilton's Harvard excavations at the Lucy Vincent site on Martha's Vineyard, Massachusetts, recovered a wooden hand pipe. According to Chilton (personal communication 2001), this specimen was possibly carved onsite with imported, nonlocal persimmon wood. The pipe came from a seventeenth-century Wampanoag component that also contained native ceramic elbow and European white clay pipes. The hand effigy may have been an important image to northeastern Indians. The Peabody had an undated red pipestone hand pipe that only has a general Massachusetts provenience.

Native pipes remained prominent when pipes of European manufacture (mostly white clay but also metal) were also being acquired, starting around 1610 in the Northeast. In seventeenth-century southern New England, metal tools permitted the carving of more elaborate stone effigy pipes, such as a Narragansett pipe from the Burr's Hill site in Rhode Island, in Brown University collections (Turnbaugh 1992). At another Narragansett site, RI-1000, a pipe maker's kit of iron files and an unfinished pipe were found (Turnbaugh 1984). Europeans may have tried to imitate these effigies in metal. The Peabody museum has a pewter pipe, found on the Pennsylvania side of the Delaware River Valley, near Trenton, New Jersey. This pipe was very similar to an effigy pipe found in a seventeenth-century Delaware-Munsee cemetery near Montague, New Jersey, in the Delaware River Valley. That dog effigy pipe was recovered in 1914 by the Heye and Pepper expedition sponsored by the Museum of the American Indian (Heye and Pepper 1915). The surviving piece of a lip on the Peabody specimen indicates that it too may have once had an effigy on the bowl facing the smoker, and there is a small equal-armed cross on the back of the bowl, facing the smoker. The New Jersey cemetery also had both Iroquois effigy and Susquehannock "tulip" bowl ceramic elbow pipes, an unusual native angular red pipestone pipe, and European clay pipes.

The Peabody had an European white clay pipe from a New Jersey Indian site, with the "EB" mark of Amsterdam pipe maker Edward Bird, whose wares dating from 1635 to 1665 have been found on many Iroquois sites in New York. Bird's initials were also on a number of white clay pipes in the Peabody collections from the Dutch Trader's House in New Jersey. This site also yielded seventeenth-century terra-cotta European pipes manufactured in North America and white clay European pipes dating from the seventeenth through nineteenth centuries (Veit and Bello 1999). The Peabody collections included a very early European white clay pipe that came from a shell heap on Keene's Point, along Muscongus Sound at Bremen, Maine. A variety of as yet unanalyzed European pipes were in the collections from Damariscove Island, Boothbay Harbor, Maine. The Mohawk Ganada No. 1 site dates to 1755–1776, and the separation of two hundred years in time but not space from Ganada No. 2 showed in the presence of European white clay pipes and absence of native pipes. The later Mohawk reoccupation coincided with a time of great change, from the French and Indian War to the early years of the American Revolution. Most Mohawks had to leave their ancient valley homeland, as they were allied with the British and were invaded and burned out by the Americans (Snow 1995).

In the 1700s native-style stone pipes from the Great Lakes became more popular in the Northeast (including the so-called Micmac and developing calumet styles), and European-invented metal pipe-tomahawks were introduced and found favor (Peterson 1971). Micmac pipes, like an eighteenth-century-style specimen from Indiana at the Peabody, had separate reed stems. A hole in the base was usually drilled to permit a tie attachment to the stem, as with a nineteenth-century-pipe from Oldtown, Maine, that still had some of the ribbon tie on both the bowl and stem. An early stone elbow calumet pipe in the Peabody collections came from Nassau Hall at Princeton, New Jersey.

The English, French, and Spanish all developed distinctive styles of pipe-tomahawks, which are represented in both archaeological and ethnographic collections across the East. Several pipe-tomahawks in the Peabody collections spanned dates from 1750 to 1850. These included both iron and brass styles, all probably of Anglo manufacture. Pipe-tomahawks were readily accepted by Native Americans due to their resemblance to the calumet, which had a dual symbolic function as an instrument that could be used in making either war or peace. When European artists and later photographers made portraits of Native Americans, the Indians often chose to be portrayed holding their most important pipes, both calumets and pipe-tomahawks.

Pipe-tomahawks were sometimes imitated in stone by native artisans, as with an undated piece in the Peabody collections from New York, which had a Cherokee attribution. From the late eighteenth century into the early twentieth century the Cherokee carved many object, animal, and human forms of effigy pipes. A very finely carved stone flintlock pistol-pipe, an eighteenth-century weapon style, had an Indiana provenience in the Peabody records and also may have originated among the Cherokee. To smoke it, one would have placed the barrel of the pistol in his mouth. Besides the pipe-tomahawk version of the calumet, Europeans also carved copies of native calumets in red pipestone. One Peabody collection pipe from Indiana may have been modified if not created by Europeans. The stem hole portion of the elbow may have been reworked after a break, and a human profile wearing a plains-style feather headdress was scratched on one side. Such designs were usually done by Europeans as they were not a common native motif.

Examples in the Peabody collections of nineteenth-century pipes included white clay pipes excavated at American Fort Independence in Boston Harbor (Clements 1989), and both a white clay stem and a terra-cotta separate-stem pipe, found on an American house site built on a mound at the ancient Mississippian community at Cahokia, Illinois. The ribbed style of terra-cotta separate-stem pipe probably was made by the Akron Smoking Pipe Company and could have come from its factories in Ohio or at Pamplin, Virginia, between 1890 and 1919 (Sudbury 1986:23). These so-called stub-stemmed forms of terra-cotta pipes were first manufactured on the East Coast in the late eighteenth century, probably by immigrant pipe makers from central Europe, such as the Moravian artisans at Bethabara, North Carolina (South 1999; Walker 1980). They had copied this style of pipe from the Turks, who had developed their new pipe forms from European white clay styles. Turkish pipes (not in the Peabody collections) were recovered from the 1696 wreck of the HMS *Sapphire* at Bay Bulls, Newfoundland (Walker 1980).

Library Research

In my library research on published sources, the literature spanned over a century of reporting. There was considerable change in research standards, the level of detail given, and the focus of the writers. As of this progress report I had compiled information from some four hundred archaeological components spanning the 350 years from 1500 to 1850. (More than seven hundred will be included in the final monograph report.) Most of the components were single-occupation sites, but some sites had multiple ethnic occupations that fell within the project study interval. There were components ranging from a single Native American burial or single European trash pit to large Indian villages or European pipe manufacturing waste dumps. As the sample size was large, it helped ameliorate uncertainties caused by variability in the quality of reporting, the nature of the sites, and their geographic distribution. I note where some sampling problems must be considered.

In terms of time expanse, the library data sample included 38 components (10 percent) from the 1500s, 30 (7 percent) spanning the 1500–1600s, 111 (28 percent) from the 1600s, 64 (16 percent) spanning the 1600–1700s, 83 (20 percent) from the 1700s, 44 (11 percent) spanning the 1700–1800s, and 33 (8 percent) components in the first half of the 1800s.

My prior research area and ease of data recording influenced the geographic distribution of the library data recorded. Sources that were more time consuming to interpret and extract relevant pipe data had to be set aside in an effort to increase the total component sample size. Thus, there were data gaps and variability in geographic sample size that were not filled for lack of time. These included native sites in northern New England and the Ohio/West Virginia/Kentucky area. I did not record any library data from the District of Columbia, Kentucky, Iowa, and Missouri as of April 2001, which was the cut off point for this progress report. However, some data gaps also reflected the variability in the intensity of occupation across different geographic regions over time, as well as the variable history of archaeological research in different areas, thereby providing different potential databases in each state or province. For example, there are many more known seventeenth-century native American archaeological sites in Virginia (Hodges 1993) compared to only a few in Maine (Spiess 1995), as a result of greater historic Indian populations, a history of more numerous archaeologists, and greater amounts of archaeological research and reporting in Virginia.

Most of the sites represented Native American occupations with 274 components (69 percent). There were 117 (29 percent) components of European origin, including colonial sites with African (both enslaved Africans and escaped slaves) and later American and Canadian loci. Five of the sites (1 percent) had mixed Native American and European occupations, and another 5 (1 percent) could not be positively assigned to an Indian, European, or mixed ethnic community. Indeed, as one reviews data from more recent archaeological sites, it becomes progressively difficult to identify Native American components where there are declines in the presence of artifacts of Indian manufacture, unless there are documentary data to assign an ethnic affiliation. The ethnic affiliations assigned to Native American sites by the original researchers were highly variable, ranging from assignment to archaeological phases, generic historic era native peoples, or one of fifty-six specific tribes, sometimes from historically verified named villages.

The 117 components of European origin were further refined to 127 different ethnic situations. Ten of these components (8 percent) were Spanish or Basque (2 sites), 4 (3 percent) were Dutch, 21 (16 percent) were French, 64 (50 percent) were British/English/Canadian, 21 (16 percent) were American, and 9 (7 percent) were African. American sites were separated from the British starting with the American Revolution in 1775. Among the French sites there was Ste. Marie I in Ontario, a 1639–1649 Jesuit mission, where there was a large resident Huron population immediately adjacent (Kidd 1949). British sites included an American Revolution military encampment in New York, with Hessian mercenary soldiers as well as English troops (Calver and Bolton 1950), a Quaker residence in Maryland (Cox, Kavadias, and Luckenbach 2000), and Moravian pipe makers in North Carolina (South 1999). Scotch-Irish was the ethnic assignment for several American components assigned to the early Virginia educational institution that is now Washington and Lee University (McDaniel, Russ, and Potter 1979).

Sites were categorized on the basis of the presence or absence of Native American or European styles of pipes. Due to the variability in the kinds of sites represented, the quality of excavations and the data recovered, and different standards of reporting, detailed quantitative comparisons of pipe numbers was not attempted. Some native cultural variations could be discerned, for example, in the difference between Iroquois village sites that have yielded hundreds of pipe fragments, compared to contemporary native communities in the Southeast, where far fewer pipes are generally found. Smoking was clearly more common among the Iroquois.

It was important to record sites where no pipes were found, to help round out the picture of pipe usage in general, and how it might reflect ethnic variability in particular. For example, the Gemelli foundation in Scituate, Massachusetts, was an American domestic site inhabited by ship carpenter Luther Tilden's family from 1818 to 1848. Bette DeVeuve (1992:39) noted that "conspicuous by their absence were clay tobacco pipe sherds and alcoholic beverage bottles, indicative perhaps of cultural ideology or economic status of site occupants." Since neither tobacco pipes nor alcohol were cost prohibitive at that time, it is likely that the absence of pipes and alcohol, which are often associated on other European sites, was a reflection of the religious and/or ethnic status of the Tildens. That site had sufficient excavation to be confident that the lack of pipes reflected usage. In another case, small sample size may be responsible for the lack of pipes reported in the ongoing research at the Dutch Fort in Branford, Connecticut, dating between 1623 and the 1640s (Pfeiffer 2000).

Overall, 67 (17 percent) of the components had no pipes present. Native pipes were found exclusively in 96 (24 percent) components, 110 (27 percent) components had both native and European style pipes, and 128 (32 percent) had only European style pipes. Of the Native American components, 57 (21 percent) had no pipes, 93 (34 percent) had only native style pipes, 80 (29 percent) had both native and European style pipes, and 44 (16 percent) had only European style pipes. The statistic for native sites without pipes was slightly skewed, as many of those native components consisted of isolated burials. That overweighed the isolated graves compared to larger cemeteries and domestic sites. On an overall individual basis most Native American graves did not have pipes, but they were not uncommon and were most often associated with adult males. On the European components, 10 (9 percent) had no pipes, only 1 (1 percent) had only native style pipes, 25 (21 percent) had both native and European style pipes, and 81 (69 percent) had only European style pipes. Of the five mixed-occupation components, one site had only native style pipes and four had both styles.

There were some immediate observations drawn from these data. Only 9 percent of the European sites had no pipes, compared to 57 percent of the Native American sites. Again, there may have been some skewing of the statistic due the lone native burials that had no pipes. However, the predominant presence of pipes on European sites of northern European ethnicity was a firm conclusion, overwhelming the exceptions like the Tilden home. Pipes were even found on Quaker (Cox, Kavadias, and Luckenbach 2000) and Shaker sites (Starbuck 2001), where tobacco use was officially taboo. The other few European sites without pipes mostly reflected ethnic affiliations with southern rather than northern Europe.

Though the Spanish were the first Europeans to encounter tobacco and smoking, it was in the Caribbean where Native Americans consumed tobacco in the form of cigars made out of rolled leaves rather than smoking it in pipes. Thus, the tobacco usage that the Spanish initially brought back to southern Europe was less likely to be found in the debris of an archaeological site. Neither the Basque fishing station at Red Bay, Labrador, used between 1550 and 1600, or the 1565 shipwrecked *San Juan* in that harbor have produced any pipe finds (Grenier 1988). Religious restrictions may have reduced the likelihood of pipes appearing on mainland Spanish sites where the native smoking tradition included pipes. In Florida the Spanish San Luis Fort and San Francisco de Oconee Mission sites, occupied between 1633 and 1704, had no pipes (Smith 1956). The Spanish Mission Santa Catalina de Guale in Georgia was occupied into the 1600s and produced both native and European style pipes (Uricheck, personal communication 2001).

As this mission was closer to English sources of pipes, the residents may have acquired the European style of pipe smoking sooner, compared to other Spanish sites. Native residents or visitors rather than the Spanish might have done the pipe smoking there. Except for the few failed French settlement attempts of the 1500s, from South Carolina to the Gulf of Mexico, the Spanish presence may have forestalled the introduction of European pipes until the French and English began to displace the Spanish in the 1700s. Other Spanish sites in the Southeast in this sample did not show European pipes in any quantity until after the first quarter of the eighteenth century, such as at Pensacola (including the brief period of Spanish resurgence during the American Revolution [Bense 1999]) and at Fort Mose, Florida. Fort Mose was a settlement first inhabited from 1738 to 1740 by enslaved Africans who had escaped from English settlements in Georgia and were permitted by the Spanish to settle north of St. Augustine as an early-warning buffer community against English attack (Deagan and Landers 1999).

The several slave sites in the sample from eighteenth-century South Carolina and nineteenth-century Florida had a few European pipes appropriate to the time period they were occupied. A probable African adult female in a wooden coffin grave was discovered at the Virginia Kingsmill plantation; she was buried with an eighteenth-century English white clay pipe beneath her left arm (Kelso 1984: 108–109). European slaveholders were the likely source for these pipes associated with Africans. There were no pipes in the nineteenth-century slave component at the Deshazo site in Texas (Story 1982). The lack of artifacts of African origin on slave sites may reflect active suppression of African culture and/or the poverty of slavery. In contrast, the Dominican Republic community of Maniel de Jose Leta was a "Cimarron" town of escaped slaves before it was destroyed by the Spanish in 1666 (Deagan and MacMahon 1995). Excavations there produced reed-stemmed clay pipes with African designs, indicating African modification of European pipe styles.

The European preference for pipes of their own manufacture is also a firm conclusion. The French were most likely of the Europeans to have native style pipes present with 33 percent of their components. Of the British sites 23 percent had native style pipes, followed by the Americans with 19 percent, and the Spanish with 11 percent. The most British sites with native style pipes were in the Mid-Atlantic in Maryland and Virginia. These Tidewater areas had the earliest association with native style pipes and became home to European tobacco plantations. In the Great Lakes area, British occupations often succeeded the French regime, but French civilians remained in residence. Even when both Native and European pipes were found on European sites, the European forms far outnumbered the native styles, often by hundreds if not thousands of fragments.

The only purely European site where the only pipe was a native style was one of the earliest European sites, Fort Raleigh in North Carolina (Harrington 1962). Fort Raleigh's ruins revealed the failed first English attempt at North American settlement from 1585 to 1587. In the earthen fort's ditch, a single Native American pipe was found in a context that dated to the English occupation. The English would soon be manufacturing their own clay pipes on both sides of the Atlantic.

The appearance of European pipes on native sites corresponded with the general historical sequence of northern European penetration into North America. The earliest European pipes on native sites in my sample were on Virginia components, dating between 1575 and 1625. European pipes appeared on Iroquoian sites in New York dating between 1600 and 1625 and in Pennsylvania dating between 1610 and 1625, with New Jersey sites also showing pipes in the early 1600s. New England native sites showed pipes possibly as early as 1620 in Rhode Island and Connecticut, and 1650 in Massachusetts. In the South, European pipes appeared on native sites as early as 1660 in North Carolina, 1670 in South Carolina, 1675 in Florida, 1682 in Alabama, and during the 1600s in Georgia. In the Great Lakes area, the appearance of European pipes on native sites was as early as 1670 in Wisconsin, 1683 in Illinois, and 1691 in Michigan. My sample shows a number of places having their first evidence of native use of European pipes in the 1700s. In the South these included Alabama and Tennessee around 1700. They appeared in Canada in Ontario in 1700 and New Brunswick in 1731. Indiana native sites had European pipes as early as 1715 and in Minnesota in 1731. Also across the Mississippi River, Louisiana had native components with European pipes as of 1731, Nebraska had villages with European pipes as of 1775, and in Arkansas there were European pipes on 1790–1835 components of immigrant Cherokee and Delaware. The latest first evidence of European pipes on a native site was the Leavenworth Arikara village in South Dakota. It was founded around 1800 and was visited by the Lewis and Clark expedition four years later as it ascended the Missouri River (Bass, Evans, and Jantz 1971; Krause 1972; O'Shea and Ludwickson 1992). Lewis and Clark carried a pipe-tomahawk with them to use in interaction with the Indians they met.

The sample of archaeological sites showing the latest presence of Native American pipe styles was a more variable pattern than the first appearance of European pipes on native sites. The East Coast, with the earliest European presence, also showed the earliest dates for the latest native components with native pipes still present—that is, native style pipes disappeared from the archaeological record there sooner than elsewhere: 1680 in Rhode Island and 1685 in Virginia. In the Great Lakes the "earliest" latest native pipes were on components dating to 1780 in Minnesota and 1791 in Indiana. Native pipes do persist on archaeological components in a number of states into the 1800s. In states and provinces bordering the Great Lakes, the latest components found thus far were 1809 in Ontario, 1820 in Michigan and Wisconsin, and 1830 in Illinois and New York. Across the Mississippi there were archaeological components with native pipes dating to 1832 in South Dakota, 1841 in Texas, and 1845 in Nebraska. As we know that Native American use of native style pipes continues in many of these places into the present (particularly on the many reservations in Oklahoma), these dates for the latest archaeological presence of native pipes must be used only as a general overview rather than for state- or tribal-specific conclusions.

It is expected that many of these dates, both the earliest presence of European pipes and latest presence of native pipes on Native American archaeological sites, would be altered by the accumulation of further published information, which time did not permit me to review. The details are likely to be modified, but the larger trend in the archaeological record will prevail: the Native American pipe/tobacco/smoking complex was highly resistant to abandonment compared to other aspects of Native American culture that has material manifestations that can be recovered as archaeological remains. The later nineteenth-century dates for Native American pipes on archaeological components, such as in New York and Texas, reflected Indian populations that were still living on remnants of their original homelands, as compared to other states where most of the Native American population had been removed. The sample in this study showed that Delaware and Cherokee immigrants passing through Arkansas on their way to reservations in Oklahoma had adopted European pipe styles. With the absence of Native style pipes as well, this may reflect the upheaval in their lives caused by forced removal from eastern homelands.

Conclusions

The library research showed general trends supporting the premise that smoking pipes were a most persistent form of Native American material culture through the mid-nineteenth century to survive the changes brought by the Columbian Exchange. There was time variation between the coastal areas, where direct contact came earlier, and the interior native groups, where direct contact was later, but the overall pattern held up. Differences between regions appeared to be in detail rather than overall trend. Eventually European pipe styles appeared on Native American sites throughout eastern North America, but they usually remained a minority or did not totally replace Native American pipe styles until long after first contact and under circumstances of population loss, geographic displacement, and severe changes in Native American lifeways.

The pronounced persistence of native forms of pipes despite the incorporation of many other aspects of European technology into native life reflected the central importance and survival of sacred themes of the pipe/tobacco/smoking complex. The appearance of European pipes on native sites alongside native forms may indicate the use of these smoking devices for everyday recreation and pleasure rather than use in sacred contexts, for which Native stone pipes were retained. Native American cultural and personal identity was evident in the pipe debris recovered on archaeological sites for the first 350 years of culture contact with Europeans.

The Europeans learned the pipe/tobacco/smoking complex from Native Americans, reinterpreted the pipes into new forms of their own manufacture, and introduced smoking to Africans, some of whom were enslaved and brought to North America. In the interaction between Europeans and Native Americans, transculturation took place in the imitation of sacred forms of stone pipes with the European invention of metal pipe-tomahawks. Both parties found this form of pipe fit their needs for developing cross-cultural communication, trade, and alliance. Europeans and Africans favored European derived clay pipes for profane recreational use. The European clay pipe became almost ubiquitous on their archaeological sites dating to this time interval. It was not until post-1850 that the popularity of briar and other woods and materials began to relegate the white clay and terra-cotta clay smoking pipes to a more restricted presence among lower social ranks in America. However, even then they still reflected ethnicity as well as economic status (see Reckner 2001).

Review of data from across eastern North America clearly indicated that smoking pipe debris on archaeological sites is an important marker of European, African, and Native American ethnicity and often reflected the stability or survival of Native American cultural identity and sacred practices. The archaeological context in which pipes are found may offer clues to ethnicity where it might otherwise be uncertain. Pipes have been found in Native American and African graves, but there was no evidence of them having been placed in European burials. European burials generally had no grave offerings and showed no archaeological objects other than the remains of the clothing and/or shroud and coffin in which the body was buried, and occasionally some personal jewelry such as wedding rings.

The Peabody Museum pipe collections included many of the Native American and European pipe styles dating from 1500 on and exemplified both the sacred and profane uses of the smoking pipe. My research skimmed the details of the Peabody Museum collection and outlined general trends. Additional collections and library research can only add to the depth of this portrait and help us understand how humans behave or react when they come into contact with new people of different cultures.

It is a story worth studying, for the repercussions of the Columbian Exchange will long continue to affect our future, a future in which each new day brings the world's diverse humans into easier and more frequent communication and contact. The modern world must cope with the changes that cultural exchanges will bring and must be concerned with how quickly old infectious diseases like hoof-and-mouth, or new ones like AIDS, may be able to spread from one hemisphere to another. Understanding the history of contact between different peoples, including the spread of the pipe/tobacco/smoking complex from North America to the rest of the world and back again, can only help us in our shared future.

Acknowledgments

In my thirty-three years of work in archaeology, I have variously been a full-time university teacher, a museum administrator, and a researcher utilizing archaeological contract projects and field schools as the means of my investigations. The Hrdy Visiting Research Curator position at the Peabody Museum of Archaeology and Ethnology at Harvard University afforded me an unparalleled opportunity to focus my studies without any simultaneous responsibilities or distractions at the office, such as administrative obligations or student papers to grade. It was probably a once-in-a-lifetime experience that will be fondly recounted after I return to the normal round of multiple workday obligations. While my Hrdy year has ended, I have continued to work on a book-length manuscript as an affiliate of the Peabody Museum.

Therefore, I acknowledge all those who contributed to my work at the Peabody Museum. First, my thanks go to Director Rubie Watson, Director of Collections Steven LeBlanc, and the selection committee, for the grant position as the Hrdy Visiting Research Curator in North American Archaeology, and to Senior Collections Manager David Schafer, who facilitated much of my research at the museum. Second, I thank all the staff in the museum and Tozzer Library, who patiently introduced me to the administrative and practical complexities of working at Harvard and provided a museum office with a computer, as well as access to collections, archives, NAGPRA reports, and library resources. Please accept my gratitude collectively.

My thanks go to Rob Mann and Sean Rafferty for inviting me to participate in the original Society for American Archaeology symposium they organized and for including this paper in the published volume.

References Cited

Bass, William M., David R. Evans, and Richard L. Jantz

1971 *The Leavenworth Site Cemetery: Archaeology and Physical Anthropology.* Univ. of Kansas Publications in Anthropology 2. Lawrence.

Bense, Judith A.

1999 Archaeology of Late Colonial Pensacola. In *Archaeology of Colonial Pensacola,* edited by Judith A. Bense, 121–206. Univ. Press of Florida, Gainesville.

Brown, Ian W.

1989 The Calumet Ceremony in the Southeast and Its Archaeological Manifestations. *American Antiquity* 54(2):311–331.

Calver, William L., and Reginald Pelham Bolton

1950 *History Written with Pick and Shovel: Military Buttons, Belt-Plates, Badges, and Other Relics Excavated from Colonial, Revolutionary, and War of 1812 Camp Sites by the Field Exploration Committee of the New York Historical Society.* New York Historical Society, New York.

Clements, Joyce M.

1989 The Maturation of the American Military: A Case Study from Fort Independence, Boston, 1800–1820. Unpublished master's thesis, Dept. of Anthropology, Univ. of Massachusetts, Boston.

Cox, C. Jane, Dennis Kavadias, and Al Luckenbach

2000 Skipworth's Addition (1664–1682): Limited Testing at a Seventeenth Century Quaker Homelot, Anne Arundel County, Maryland. *Maryland Archeology* 36(1):1–10.

Deagan, Kathleen, and Jane Landers

1999 Fort Mose: Earliest Free African-American Town in the United States. In *"I, Too, Am America": Archaeological Studies of African-American Life,* edited by Theresa A. Singleton, 261–282. Univ. Press of Virginia, Charlottesville.

Deagan, Kathleen, and Darcie MacMahon

1995 *Fort Mose: Colonial America's Black Fortress of Freedom.* Univ. Press of Florida, Florida Museum of Natural History, Gainesville.

DeVeuve, Bette F.

1992 The Gemelli Foundation: The Archaeological Testing of Oral Tradition. Unpublished master's thesis, Dept. of History/Historical Archaeology, Univ. of Massachusetts, Boston.

Drooker, Penelope Ballard

1997 *The View From Madisonville: Protohistoric Western Fort Ancient Interaction Patterns.* Memoirs of the Museum of Anthropology, Univ. of Michigan No. 31. Ann Arbor.

Engelbrecht, William

1993 Review of *Proceedings of the 1989 Smoking Pipe Conference. Journal of Middle Atlantic Archaeology* 9:172–173.

Funk, Robert E.

1967 A Late Prehistoric Iroquois Village in the Mohawk Valley. In *Iroquois Culture, History, and Prehistory: Proceedings of the 1965 Conference on Iroquois Research,* edited by Elisabeth Tooker, 81–84. Univ. of the State of New York, State Education Dept., New York State Museum and Science Service, Albany.

Grenier, Robert

1988 Basque Whalers in the New World: The Red Bay Wrecks. In *Ships and Shipwrecks of the Americas: A History Based on Underwater Archaeology,* edited by George F. Bass, 69–84. Thames and Hudson Ltd., London.

Grumet, Robert S.

1995 *Historic Contact: Indian People and Colonists in Today's Northeastern United States in the Sixteenth through Eighteenth Centuries.* Univ. of Oklahoma Press, Norman.

Gundersen, James N.

1993 "Catlinite" and the Spread of the Calumet Ceremony. *American Antiquity* 58(3):560–562.

Guthe, Alfred K.

1958 *The Late Prehistoric Occupation in Southwestern New York: An Interpretive Analysis.* Rochester Museum and Science Center Research Records No. 11. Rochester, N.Y.

Harrington, Jean Carl

1962 *Search for the Cittie of Ralegh: Archeological Excavations at Fort Raleigh National Historic Site, North Carolina.* Archeological Research Series No. 6. National Park Service, U.S. Dept. of the Interior, Washington, D.C.

Heye, George G., and George H. Pepper

1915 *Exploration of a Munsee Cemetery near Montague, New Jersey.* Contributions from the Museum of the American Indian 2(3). Heye Foundation, New York.

Hodges, Mary Ellen N.

1993 The Archaeology of Native American Life in Virginia in the Context of European Contact: Review of Past Research. *The Archaeology of Seventeenth-Century Virginia,* edited by Theodore R. Reinhart and Dennis J. Pogue, 1–65. Archeological Society of Virginia Special Publication No. 30, Courtland.

Kelso, William M.

1984 *Kingsmill Plantations, 1619–1800: Archaeology of Country Life in Colonial Virginia.* Academic Press, New York.

Kelso, William M., and Beverly A. Straube
2000 *Jamestown Rediscovery VI.* Association for the Preservation of Virginia Antiquities, Richmond, Va.

Kidd, Kenneth E.
1949 *The Excavation of Sainte-Marie I.* Univ. of Toronto Press, Toronto, Ontario.

Krause, Richard A.
1972 *The Leavenworth Site: Archaeology of an Historic Arikara Community.* Univ. of Kansas Publications in Anthropology 3. Lawrence.

Laufer, Berthold
1924a *Tobacco and Its Use in Asia.* Field Museum of Natural History, Anthropology Leaflet No. 18. Chicago.
1924b *The Introduction of Tobacco into Europe.* Field Museum of Natural History, Anthropology Leaflet No. 19. Chicago.

Laufer, Berthold, Wilfrid D. Hambly, and Ralph Linton
1930 *Tobacco and Its Use in Africa.* Field Museum of Natural History, Anthropology Leaflet No. 29. Chicago.

Linton, Ralph
1924 *Use of Tobacco among North American Indians.* Field Museum of Natural History, Anthropology Leaflet No. 15. Chicago.

Magoon, Dane T.
1999 "Chesapeake" Pipes and Uncritical Assumptions: A View from Northeastern North Carolina. *North Carolina Archaeology* 48:107–126.

McDaniel, John M., Kurt C. Russ, and Parker B. Potter
1979 A Description and Analysis of Tobacco Pipes Excavated at Liberty Hall. *Quarterly Bulletin of the Archeological Society of Virginia* 34(2):83–92.

McGuire, Joseph D.
1899 Pipes and Smoking Customs of the American Aborigines, Based on Material in the U.S. National Museum. *Report of the U.S. National Museum for 1897* 1:351–645. Government Printing Office, Washington, D.C.

O'Shea, John M., and John Ludwickson
1992 *Archaeology and Ethnohistory of the Omaha Indians: The Big Village Site.* Univ. of Nebraska Press, Lincoln.

Paper, Jordan
1992 The Iroquoian and Pan-Indian Sacred Pipes: Comparative Ritual and Symbolism. In *Proceedings of the 1989 Smoking Pipe Conference: Selected Papers,* edited by Charles F. Hayes III, Connie Cox Bodner, and Martha L. Sempowski, 163–169. Rochester Museum and Science Center Research Records No. 22. Rochester, N.Y.

Parker, Arthur C.
1907 *Excavations in an Erie Indian Village and Burial Site at Ripley, Chautauqua Co., N.Y.* New York State Museum Bulletin No. 117. New York State Education Dept., Albany.

Peterson, Harold L.
1971 *American Indian Tomahawks.* Contributions from the Museum of the American Indian, Heye Foundation 19. Rev. ed. New York, N.Y.

Pfeiffer, John

2000 Bentley Locus and Other Dutch Settlements in Branford, Connecticut. At http://www.mohawk.net/~dpope/bentleylocus.html#D. Wesleyan Univ.

Pratt, Peter P.

1976 *Archaeology of the Oneida Iroquois, Volume 1.* Occasional Publications in Northeastern Anthropology No. 1. Man in the Northeast, Inc., George's Mills, N.H.

Reckner, Paul E.

2001 Negotiating Patriotism at the Five Points: Clay Tobacco Pipes and Patriotic Imagery among Trade Unionists and Nativists in a Nineteenth-Century New York Neighborhood. *Historical Archaeology* 35(3):103–114.

Smith, Hale G.

1956 *The European and the Indian: European-Indian Contacts in Georgia and Florida.* Florida Anthropological Society Publications No. 4. Gainesville.

Snow, Dean R.

1995 *Mohawk Valley Archaeology: The Sites.* Institute for Archaeological Studies, State Univ. of New York.

South, Stanley

1999 Historical Archaeology in Wachovia: Excavating Eighteenth-Century Bethabara and Moravian Pottery. Kluwer Academic/Plenum Publishers, New York, N.Y.

Spiess, Arthur

1995 Early Contact Period Context. *Maine Archaeological Society Bulletin* 35(2):1–20.

Starbuck, David R.

2001 Canterbury Shaker Village. *Council for Northeast Historical Archaeology Newsletter* No. 48:6.

Story, Dee Ann (editor)

1982 *The Deshazo Site, Nacogdoches County, Texas. Volume 1. The Site, Its Setting, Investigation, Cultural Features, Artifacts of Non-Native Manufacture, and Subsistence Remains.* Texas Antiquities Permit Series No. 7. Texas Antiquities Committee, Austin.

Sudbury, Byron

1986 An Illustrated 1895 Catalogue of the Akron Smoking Pipe Co. *Historic Clay Tobacco Pipe Studies* 3:1–42. Byron Sudbury, Ponca City, Okla.

Sullivan, Lynne P. (editor)

1996 *Reanalyzing the Ripley Site: Earthworks and Late Prehistory on the Lake Erie Plain.* New York State Museum Bulletin No. 489. Univ. of the State of New York, State Education Dept., Albany.

Trubowitz, Neal L.

1992a Native American and French on the Central Wabash. In *Calumet and Fleur-de-Lys: Archaeology of Indian and French Contact in the Midcontinent,* edited by John A. Walthall and Thomas E. Emerson, 241–264 Smithsonian Institution Press, Washington, D.C.

1992b Thanks, but We Prefer to Smoke Our Own: Pipes in the Great Lakes–Riverine Region during the Eighteenth Century. In *Proceedings of the 1989 Smoking Pipe Conference: Selected Papers,* edited by Charles F. Hayes III, Connie Cox Bodner, and Martha L. Sempowski, 97–112. Rochester Museum and Science Center Research Records No. 22. Rochester, N.Y.

Turnbaugh, William A.

1975 Tobacco, Pipes, Smoking, and Rituals among the Indians of the Northeast. *Quarterly Bulletin of the Archeological Society of Virginia* 30(2):52–71.

1984 *The Material Culture of RI-1000: A Mid-Seventeenth-Century Narragansett Indian Burial Site in North Kingstown, Rhode Island.* Dept. of Sociology and Anthropology, Univ. of Rhode Island, Kingston.

1992 Post Contact Smoking Pipe Development: The Narragansett Example. In *Proceedings of the 1989 Smoking Pipe Conference: Selected Papers,* edited by Charles F. Hayes III, Connie Cox Bodner, and Martha L. Sempowski, 113–121. Rochester Museum and Science Center Research Records No. 22. Rochester, N.Y.

Veit, Richard, and Charles A. Bello

1999 "A Unique and Valuable Historical and Indian Collection": Charles Conrad Abbott Explores a Seventeenth Century Dutch Trading Post in the Delaware Valley. *Journal of Middle Atlantic Archaeology* 15:95–123.

von Gernet, Alexander D.

1988 The Transculturation of the Amerindian Pipe/Tobacco/Smoking complex and Its Impact on the Intellectual Boundaries between "Savagery" and "Civilization," 1535–1935. Unpublished Ph.D. dissertation, Dept. of Anthropology, McGill Univ., Montreal, Quebec.

Walker, Ian C.

1977 *Clay Tobacco-Pipes, with Particular Reference to the Bristol Industry.* History and Archaeology No. 11A. National Historic Parks and Sites Branch, Parks Canada, Dept. of Indian and Northern Affairs, Ottawa, Ontario.

1980 The Central European Origins of the Bethabara, North Carolina, Clay Tobacco-Pipe Industry. In *The Archaeology of the Clay Tobacco Pipe, IV. Europe I,* edited by Peter Davey, 11–70. British Archaeological Reports International Series No. 92, Oxford.

West, George A.

1934 *Tobacco, Pipes, and Smoking Customs of the American Indians.* Bulletin of the Public Museum of the City of Milwaukee No. 17. Milwaukee, Wis.

Willoughby, Charles C.

1935 *Antiquities of the New England Indians.* Peabody Museum of American Archaeology and Ethnology, Harvard Univ., Cambridge, Mass.

Winter, Joseph C. (editor)

2000 *Tobacco Use by Native North Americans: Sacred Smoke and Silent Killer.* Univ. of Oklahoma Press, Norman.

Wray, Charles Foster, Martha L. Sempowski, Lorraine P. Saunders, and Gian Carlo Cervone

1987 *The Adams and Culbertson Sites.* Rochester Museum and Science Center Research Records No. 19. Rochester, N.Y.

6. Smokescreens: Tobacco, Pipes, and the Transformational Power of Fur Trade Rituals

Rob Mann

On a 1709 trip to the Carolinas, John Lawson found trading with the Native Americans there a baffling endeavor. "If a Man give [*sic*] them any thing of a Present," he wrote, "they think it obliges him to give them another . . . till he has given all he has" (Lawson in Murray 2000:27). He concluded that "their way of Living is so contrary to ours, that neither we nor they can fathom one anothers [*sic*] Designs and Methods" (Lawson in Murray 2000:27). When the French and native groups of the Great Lakes region encountered one another in the seventeenth century, they, too, found that the other possessed desirable objects. And like Lawson they found that these objects of exchange—furs and European goods—were enmeshed within conflicting estimations of value and disparate motivations for exchange (Murray 2000:46–47; Thomas 1991:31).

In order for exchange to proceed, the two groups had to arrive at "some common conception of suitable ways of acting" (White 1991:50). I argue here that because of the tension between global market forces and local models of exchange, the traffic in furs and European goods between French traders and the Native American groups of the Wabash Valley during the eighteenth and nineteenth centuries was rife with ambiguities and contradictions. Whereas native groups typically operated under an ideology of reciprocity and framed exchange in terms of the transfer of inalienable things, European traders typically operated under the ideology of capitalism and framed exchange in terms of the transfer of alienable things. Successful trading hinged on mitigating this basic contradiction.

Fur trade rituals provided the mechanisms that allowed each side to find commonalties in the behavior of the other. Because of its enormous ritual potency, smoking tobacco played a central role in fur trade rituals, helping to bring about the mental and material transformations that made cross-cultural exchange possible. Archaeological investigations at the Cicott Trading Post site, a *Canadien* fur trader's post located on the Wabash River near the present-day village of Independence in Warren County, Indiana provide an opportunity to examine the material residues of cross-cultural exchange during the late fur trade era (Map 6.1). I argue that the stone tobacco pipes recovered from the Cicott Trading Post site were constitutive components of nineteenth-century fur trade rituals that linked Great Lakes fur trade society to both the expanding Western market system and the kin-ordered world of Great Lakes native societies by effecting the transformation of gifts into commodities and commodities into gifts. In so doing, they reproduced the local material and social relations of fur trade society. Understanding why such transformations were necessary to the reproduction of fur trade society requires that we examine the historical particulars of capitalist and indigenous forms of exchange.

Commodities, Fetishism, and *Besoins*

Marx (1906:41) opens Book 1 of *Capital* with two assertions; that the capitalist mode of production "presents itself as 'an immense accumulation of commodities'" and that therefore the investigation of capitalism must "begin with the analysis of a commodity." A commodity, he says, is "an object outside us, a thing that by its properties satisfies human wants of some sort or another" (Marx 1906:41). This is the commonsensical definition of a commodity—a product of human labor that so far as it is useful has a use-value, and since it can be exchanged for other products (or money) has an exchange-value (Appaduri 1986; Kopytoff 1986:64).

This definition of a commodity has been widely applied to the products presented and acquired by Europeans during exchanges with indigenous populations at the peripheries of the capitalist world system. From a world-systems perspective, production on the indigenous side of the equation is often characterized as petty commodity production (for example, Delâge 1993; Dunaway 1996, 1994; Kardulias 1990; Pickering 1994; Wolf 1982). The products of indigenous labor, though, differed socially and conceptually from "commodities" produced under capitalism, even if the objects were in fact the same (Taussig 1980:25). Thus, to label the furs, hides, and skins produced by native hunters and hide processors "commodities" ignores not only Marx's (1906:82) elaboration of the "mystical character" of commodities under capitalism but also obscures the nature of exchange between capitalist and indigenous societies.

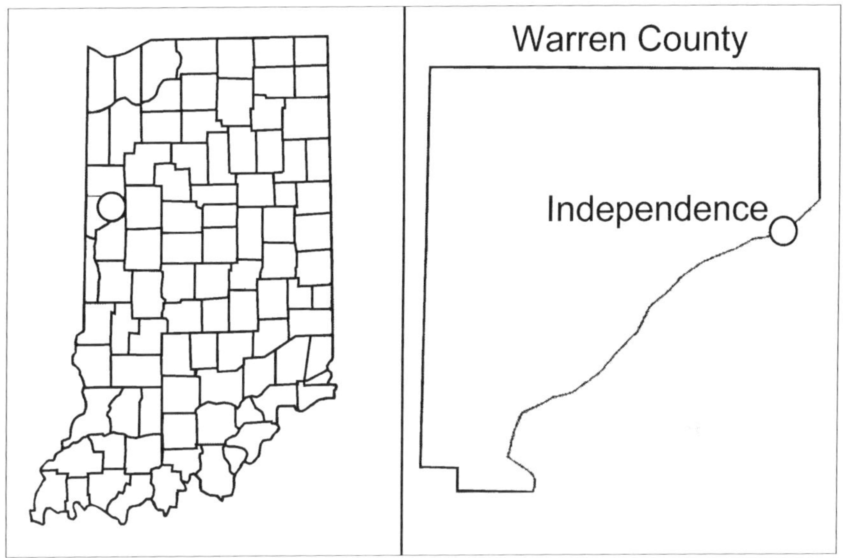

MAP 6.1. ▸ *Location of Independence in Warren County, Indiana.*

We are dealing here with two different ideologies of exchange, often conceptualized in Maussian terms as a "precapitalist" gift economy versus a commodity market economy (for example, Jaenen 1985; Rotstein 1972; White 1982; compare Gregory 1982; Murray 2000; Thomas 1991). The *Canadien* view of commerce corresponded to the latter. *Canadien* traders approached the objects they received in trade with Native Americans in the detached way described by Marx. But the ideological significance of this position only becomes clear once we follow up on Marx's seemingly unproblematic definition of a commodity. In a move typical of his method of analysis and style of writing, Marx reveals that under capitalism a commodity is not the "very trivial thing" he has just demonstrated it to be (Marx 1906:81). It is in reality "a very queer thing, abounding in metaphysical subtleties and theological niceties" (Marx 1906:81).

This is, of course, Marx's (1906:83) notion of commodity fetishism, whereby the valuation and exchange of the products of human labor—"a definite social relation between men" (and/or women)—assumes "the fantastic form of a relation between things." This produces a "phantom objectivity" that obscures the true roots of the products of human labor, abstracts them from social life, and in so doing denies or mystifies the social construction of reality (Taussig 1980:4–5). In a market economy things appear to move freely from individual to individual, and "people experience their interest in commodities as a desire to appropriate goods"

(Strathern 1988:143). But this is illusory, not the natural state of the world. Thus, under capitalism a "commodity" entails certain "historical and social preconditions" peculiar to the capitalist mode of production (Gregory 1982:8). Unfettered from the social relations that brought them into being, these fetishized commodities operate as alienable objects, things apparently disassociated from their producers or former users (Gregory 1982:20; Taussig 1980:4; Thomas 1991:39; compare Weiner 1992). Capitalist commodity exchange obscures the relations between exchange partners and naturalizes the notion that the relationship is one between the objects exchanged (Gregory 1982:19; Marx 1906:83; Murray 2000:39; Strathern 1988:143).

For the native groups of the Wabash Valley, however, exchange proceeded from a different logic. Marx well understood this kind of logic and saw that the "whole mystery of commodities" and "all the magic and necromancy that surrounds the products of labour as long as they take the form of commodities, vanishes therefore, so soon as we come to other forms of production" (in Taussig 1980:10). Because the "new epistemology" of the commodity had not been assimilated by the indigenous peoples of the Great Lakes during the fur trade era, we must "liberate ourselves from the fetishism and phantom objectivity with which (capitalist) society obscures itself" and "take issue with the ether of naturalness that confuses and disguises social relations" (Taussig 1980:5–6) in order to understand not only capitalist exchange but also the cross-cultural exchange of the Great Lakes fur trade.

Among the native groups of the Great Lakes, exchange with *Canadien* traders was based on a familial model that conceptualized the French as "Fathers" (White 1991:112). The role of a "father" was to provide for his "children." These societies spoke of exchange in terms of their *besoins*—their needs or necessities (White 1991:129; see also Murray [2000:28–29]; Rich [1960]; Vibert [1997]; White [1982]). The goal was not to profit or to maximize one's material advantage, but rather to "excite pity and thus deserve aid" (White 1991:98, 129; see also Gregory [1982:51]; Vibert [1997:144–156]).

The concept of pity is key to understanding indigenous ideologies of exchange (Vibert 1997:147; White 1982:62). Among the Ojibwa, for instance, to pity was "to give a gift without thought of immediate return" (Vibert 1997:147). Begging, weeping, and other demonstrative behaviors were culturally appropriate ways of exciting pity in hopes of establishing long-term relationships with persons or groups who could supply one's *besoins* (on the weeping ceremony, see Blakeslee [1977:84–85]). From a native perspective, profit was not a motivation for exchange. "They gave away their last food to a visiting stranger and did not hesitate to beg for food from the French who came among them. The underlying logic of such exchange patterns was that *besoins* took precedence over profits" (White 1991:131). These competing ideologies of exchange were a source of tension throughout the colonial period.

What Europeans characterized as destitution and "beggarly" conduct were actually part of indigenous modes of exchange that emphasized the creation of relationships with those perceived to be more powerful or who had access to desired goods (Vibert 1997:155). When seeking to establish such a relationship, to "be humble was the appropriate way of asking" for one's *besoins* (Vibert 1997: 155). Though immediate material concerns were certainly important, "the desire to forge or reaffirm" social relationships, with an eye toward future considerations, was perhaps even more important (Vibert 1997:155–156). Unlike capitalist exchange, where immediate profit was the primary motivation for exchange, the creation of relationships between exchange partners was crucial to indigenous modes of exchange. If no relationship was seen to exist, one had to be created (White 1991:98). The French learned this lesson early on. Jesuit missionary Paul Le Jeune wrote in 1634 that though they are "very generous among themselves and even make a show of not loving things . . . they are as ungrateful as possible towards strangers" (in Murray 2000:35). He concluded that should they "conduct themselves thus toward our French, and towards other strangers, it is because . . . we do not wish to ally ourselves with them as brothers, which they would very much desire" (in Murray 2000:35–36).

Once a relationship had been established, exchange partners were expected to act as kin and each side was expected to the supply the *besoins* of the other (White 1991:129; see also Comer [1996:5, 21]; Mann [1999b]; Mauss [1990:13–14]). The things given and received were viewed as gifts, and their exchange was seen as the transfer of "inalienable things between persons who are in a state of reciprocal dependence" (Gregory 1982:18–19; White 1991:98). The social relations of production of these objects remained transparent, not fetishized, and exchange established or maintained social relationships (see Pickering 1994:59).

Because of these fundamental differences, I contend that the traffic in furs and European goods between *Canadien* traders and the Native American groups of the Wabash Valley during the eighteenth and nineteenth centuries was rife with ambiguities and contradictions. As Nicholas Thomas (1991:31) notes, cross-cultural exchange is "inevitably a politicized field entailing compromise, subordination, acquiescence, refusals, and so on." When indigenous North Americans took European goods in exchange for furs, they became part of a still emerging world economy. But because these "moments of exchange" were profoundly local and face-to-face, the fur trade could never be completely divorced from the wider spectrum of French–Native American relations it was embedded within, and a "straightforward domination" of the local village world by the market never emerged (Murray 2000:3; White 1991:94–95; see also Rotstein 1972).

As a result, successful trading hinged on mitigating the basic contradiction between alienable and inalienable things. Understanding how this was accomplished requires that we examine, as David Murray (2000:2) has recently put it, "the process of exchange itself, with its swirl of oppositions and transformations."

We must also abandon the essentialist idea that categories of material objects—for example, gift, commodity, utilitarian, nonutilitarian, etc.—and the meanings attached to them, are fixed and immutable (Thomas 1991:28; White 1994:395–396; for an archaeological perspective, see Upton 1996). Appadurai's (1986) notion of the "social life of things" emphasizes the mutability of objects, and, as Thomas (1991:29) asserts, this "permits us to examine the transformation of gifts into commodities and vise versa" (see also Gosden and Marshall 1999; Kopytoff 1986; Peers 1999).

Fur Trade Pipe/Tobacco/ Smoking Rituals

When they worked properly, fur trade rituals could effect such transformations and allow Native Americans to conceive of the fur trade as a "system designed to satisfy their *besoins*" and the *Canadiens* to think of it as a source of profit (White 1991:141; see also Comer 1996:144). Douglas Comer (1996) has examined the role of ritual in the formation of new identities and relationships at Bent's Old Fort. Bent's Old Fort, the largest trading post on the southwestern Plains, was operated by the Bent and St. Vrain Company, a large fur trade concern second only in the United States to John Jacob Astor's American Fur Company (Comer 1996:27).

Drawing on the work of Mircea Eliadc (for example 1958, 1959), Comer (1996:7) examines how disparate groups came together at Bent's Old Fort and employed rituals "to form a common world for a time." In this view the trading post was much more than just an economic institution; it was a social space where relationships and identities were forged. This was accomplished through trade or, more precisely, "through rituals associated with trade" (Comer 1996:20). Ritual trade occurred "at the nexus of subjectivity and objectivity, where the individual is especially receptive to socially assigned meanings" (Comer 1996:23). During rituals associated with exchange, individuals were influenced not only by verbal expressions but also by actions and nonverbal information, which affected not only how the participants thought but also how they *felt*—about their exchange partners, themselves, and the objects exchanged (Comer 1996:23). It was the performance of ritual that created and/or sustained social relationships and identities.

Trading, therefore, was a key component in the ethnogenesis of fur trade society. "Those who participated in the exchange, then, were proclaiming a common mythical ancestry and, thereby, establishing fictive kinship relations. Profit may have been a consideration but was not paramount in importance . . . . Most important was the establishment of social relationships" (Comer 1996:129). Drawing on the Maussian (1990:3) idea that a "power resides in the object given that causes its recipient to pay it back," Comer (1996:135) asserts that the "object itself has no 'power' or 'meaning' (and, for that matter, no 'value' in the abstract modern sense, either), power is culturally inscribed—and inscription, for the most part, is achieved through the *ritual* that accompanies both gifting and the reciprocation of the gift." The material objects of exchange (that is, furs and European goods) acquired meaning through ritual and came to represent the social relationships created by the process of cross-cultural trade (Comer 1996: 130). But ritual also transformed the meanings of the objects of exchange as they crossed the liminal ideological space between members of a gift economy on the one hand and members of a commodity or market economy on the other.

The question becomes, how was this transformation brought about? Among most Native American societies, tobacco was a spiritually charged substance of great ideological importance (for example, Drooker, this volume; Irwin, this volume; Nassaney, this volume; Paper 1988; Rafferty, this volume; Springer 1981; Trubowitz, this volume; West 1970; Winter 2001; von Gernet 1988, 1992). Smoking tobacco was often equated with praying. Okanagan Chief Nkwala told Hudson's Bay Company (HBC) trader Archibald McDonald in 1827 that he smoked from the same motivation that "moves the white people to look in the Great Fathers Book" (that is, the Bible) (in Vibert 1997:153). In the twentieth century an Ojibwa man told ethnographer Inez Hilger that lighting his pipe was "the same as praying" (in White 1982:63). Significantly, the efficacy of tobacco was enhanced when smoked in either native clay or stone pipes (Nassaney 2000 and this volume; Trubowitz 1992 and this volume; Turnbaugh 1977, 1992).

Scholars have long recognized the importance of pipes, tobacco and smoking in fur trade rituals (for example, Blakeslee 1977, 1981; Brown 1989; Comer 1996; Dempsey 1972; Green 2002; Hall 1977; Klein 1993; Nekich 1977; Peach 1993; Reid 1995; Rich 1960; Rotstein 1972; Smith 1991; Springer 1981; Sutton 1995; Thorne 1996; Trubowitz 1992 and this volume; Turnbaugh 1979, 1992; Vibert 1997; von Gernet 1988, 1992; White 1991). The "regular smoking match" that preceded and accompanied ritual exchange between traders and natives was one of the key "precapitalist" political economic practices that European traders learned was "essential to the maintenance of smooth relations" (Vibert 1997:152; Klein 1993; see also von Gernet 1988:242–243). The act of smoking tobacco was itself a form of gift exchange (Vibert 1997:152). The ritual practice of smoking replicated the "primorial state" and created, if only temporarily, a fictive kinship between smokers that was based on a "common mythical ancestry" (Comer 1996:129).

During the early years of contact between traders and natives fur trade rituals were often formal ceremonies. These sometimes lasted for days and minimally included the exchange of gifts, the firing of salutes, a banquet or feast, and smoking of the calumet, a stone (usually catlinite) pipe with an elaborately decorated stem (Blakeslee 1977:78; Rotstein 1972:15–16). HBC trader Edward Umfreville described the role of the calumet ceremony in ritual exchange during the late eighteenth century (Rotstein 1972:18–19). His description is a detailed account of how elaborate fur trade rituals could be when large native trading expeditions traveled to the grand fur trading posts of the HBC. As Blakeslee (1977:84–85) notes, though, fur trade rituals were active sites of negotiation throughout the colonial period, and Europeans constantly worked to modify them so that they more closely fit European models of exchange.

By the nineteenth century the formal calumet ceremony had, in many places, given over to a more "degraded" or "fugitive" form of the ritual sometimes known as "smoking over" the trade or trading "under the pipe" (Comer 1996:110, 142, 144). Fugitive ritual is less prescribed than formal ritual and may not even be recognized as such by the participants (Comer 1996:23). Nonetheless, fugitive ritual is still effective and imparts meaning(s) and value(s) to the objects of exchange (Comer 1996:144). According to Comer (1996:152), "the affective response shared by the participants (of fur trade rituals) renders the material culture employed important to the participants, in a symbolic sense. It becomes a symbol of their renewed social relationship and, therefore, of slightly altered but essentially stable identities." I would argue further that since the tobacco and the stone pipes it was smoked in were ritually powerful paraphenalia, they were not merely symbolic of the resulting social relationships and cultural identities but were also *constitutive* of those relationships and identities. As Thorne (1996:63) has recently put it, "Kinship was the metaphor, and pipes (and tobacco) were the medium of establishing trade, peacable congress, and proper social relations."

The power of tobacco seems to lie primarily in its ability to facilitate "*communication* with (and *transformation* into) the spirit world" (von Gernet 1992:173, emphasis in original). It is this transformational power that I am most concerned with here. The power of what von Gernet (1988, 1992) calls the pipe/tobacco/smoking complex to produce transformations, however, was not restricted to the spiritual realm. It could and did facilitate social and material transformations as well. For example, Thorne (1996:30) notes that pipe rituals were used to "make relatives," transforming ethnically and linguistically distinct "strangers" into kin (see also Green 2002; Springer 1981:225). Like the calumet ceremonies that accompanied ritual trade, these pipe "dances" often lasted for days and also included feasting, dancing, and gift exchange. During the ceremony an elaborately decorated pipe stem was given by a "father" to a "son," creating a fictive kinship between the two parties that "was allegedly stronger than blood" (Thorne 1996:30). Regardless of the antiquity of these practices—and the debate over the origins of all such "calumet" ceremonies has generated a voluminous literature (for example, Blakeslee 1981; Brown 1989; Drooker, this volume; Irwin, this volume; Rafferty, this volume; Turnbaugh 1979)—it is clear that the pipe/tobacco/smoking complex provided Native American societies with an indigenous system for dealing with European "strangers," as well as a mechanism for "integrating them as trading partners and kin" (Thorne 1996:35; see also von Gernet 1988, 1992).

The *Canadiens,* Native Americans, and métis of the Great Lakes region had been generally successful at such integration by the eighteenth century. Great Lakes fur trade society was a unique social formation based on a unique lifestyle that included particular skills, knowledge, and aptitudes (Dickason 1985; Edmunds 1985; Faragher 1998; Kardulias 1990:32; Murphy 2000; Peterson 1982, 1985; Sleeper-Smith 1994, 2001; Thorne 1996). But the process of ethnogenesis is never complete, static, or free of contradiction. Thus, fur trade society had to be produced and reproduced through material social processes, the daily practices of life, including, of course, trade and exchange. These processes were part of the "work" necessary to create and maintain fur trade society and were carried out by individual men, women, and children at native villages and jackknife posts throughout the Great Lakes region.

Pipes and Fur Trade Rituals at the Cicott Trading Post

Zachariah Cicott, a *Canadien* from Detroit, established just such a post on the central Wabash River in the first quarter of the nineteenth century. Zachariah married Pe-say-quot, the sister of a local Potawatomi clan leader, sometime early in the nineteenth century. This marriage established the kin relations so crucial to the trade. But as Thorne (1996:61) points out, kinship networks could not "ultimately guarantee enduring peaceful relations or material reciprocity." These had to be maintained through the rituals of trade (Comer 1996).

Evidence for these rituals comes from the stone smoking pipes and pipe fragments recovered at the Cicott Trading Post site, Indiana state site number 12Wa59. The site is situated atop a precipitous bluff overlooking the Wabash River in present-day Warren County, Indiana. The Warren County Park Board (WCPB) purchased the property containing the site and converted it into a historical and recreational park. The Cicott Trading Post Project, initiated in 1990, is a long-term archaeological and ethnohistorical investigation of the material conditions of daily life at a *Canadien* jackknife post during the late fur trade era in the Wabash Valley. Archaeological investigations sponsored by the WCPB were undertaken in 1990, 1991, 1992, and 1997 (see Mann 1994, 1999a, 2003). I served as the project supervisor from 1991 until 1993 and as the project director from 1997 until 1998.

Tobacco-related items, including white clay pipes, stone smoking pipes (including stone pipe-making debris), and other clay pipes (redware and stoneware stub-stemmed pipes) have been recovered across the site from both feature and sheet midden contexts. Table 6.1 shows the totals of the smoking pipes recovered during the 1991, 1992, and 1997 field seasons. A quick glance at this table reveals that European-made white ball clay pipes dominate the smoking pipe assemblage. A total of 274 white clay pipes—mostly undecorated stem fragments (n = 185)—

TABLE 6.1 ▸ Smoking Pipes Recovered at the Cicott Trading Post Site, 1991, 1992, 1997

	White Clay Pipes	Stone Pipes*	Other Pipes
1991	55 (84%)	3 (5%)	7 (11%)
1992	154 (90%)	6 (4%)	11 (6%)
1997	65 (81%)	8 (10%)	7 (9%)

Note: *Including pipe-making debris.

were recovered. These represent 87 percent of the smoking pipe assemblage. Stone pipes and stone pipe-making debris (n = 17) make up 5 percent of the pipe assemblage. Other clay pipes (n = 25) make up the remaining 8 percent of the smoking pipe assemblage.

The stone pipe assemblage consists of broken finished pipes, miscues—pipes discarded in various stages of manufacture—and stone pipe-making debris (Figure 6.1). Recognizable types of stone pipes, either finished or miscues, include elbow pipes (Figure 6.1A–C) and skeuomorphs—stone imitations of European white clay pipe forms (Figure 6.1D). Stone elbow pipes have a conical bowl set at a right angle to a short shank that is designed to accommodate a reed or wooden stem. At least one variety of stone elbow pipe has been recognized. It is a keeled stone elbow pipe recovered in 1991 (Figure 6.1C). This nearly finished miscue was found on top of a large circular trash pit feature. This pipe is similar to the Micmac pipes commonly used in the region during the eighteenth century and has a hole drilled through the keel, which allowed the pipe to be worn around the neck when not in use (see Trubowitz 1992 and this volume).

The second type of stone pipe found on the site is skeuomorphs. A specimen recovered in 1991 is mimetic of heeled (or spurred) nineteenth-century (circa 1800–1830) European white clay pipes and consists of most of the bowl and heel and a portion of the stem or shank. A second skeuomorph, recovered in 1997, consists of a portion of the stem, heel, and bowl of a stone pipe also made to imitate the appearance of a heeled (or spurred) nineteenth-century (circa 1800–1830) European white clay pipe (Figure 6.1D). Eighteenth-century examples of this phenomenon were recovered from the Wea village site, located not far up the Wabash River from the Cicott Trading Post site (Trubowitz 1992:104). Although the 1997 skeuomorph exhibits no visible signs of use-wear, this well-executed specimen appears to have been functional prior to being broken and discarded.

Most of the stone pipes recovered at the trading post, however, are miscues discarded in various stages of manufacture. The majority of the stone pipes are made from a soft, green limestone that outcrops in the immediate vicinity. Tool marks on the pipes clearly indicate that metal saws, drills, and files were used in

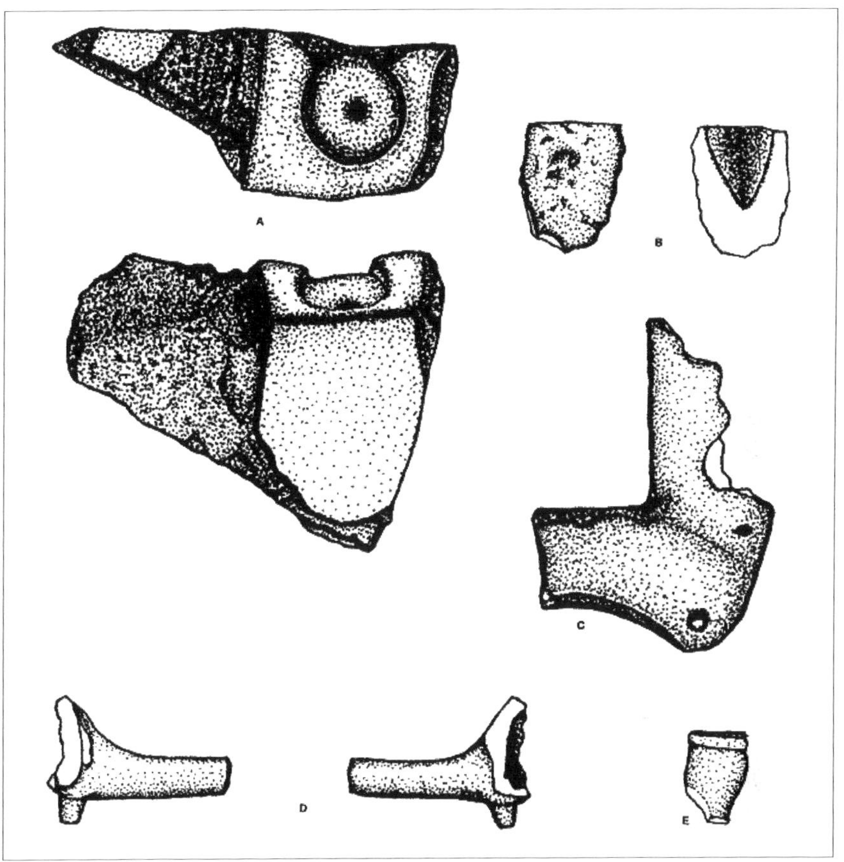

FIG. 6.1. ▸ *Smoking-pipe types from the Cicott Trading Post site.*

the manufacturing process (see Elliott 1972:149–150; Turnbaugh 1992; compare West 1970:351–352). Stone pipes were typically made in four steps: (1) sawing a square-cut blank; (2) sawing the blank into a preform; (3) drilling the preform with an iron drill and/or clasp knife; and (4) finishing the pipe by grinding and polishing (Elliott 1972:149). We have recovered losses or miscues from each of these technological stages.

It seems profitable to view the stone pipes recovered at the trading post as active components in the construction and reproduction of fur trade society. The low frequency of finished specimens suggests that stone pipes were highly curated (Peach 1993:103) and perhaps were not used in the same manner as the more ubiquitous white clay and stub-stemmed pipes found across the site. The greater frequency of white clay and stub-stemmed pipes is not only an indicator of greater availability but also of their use in different—but no less social—contexts (for example, Dallal, this volume; Reckner, this volume). White clay pipes were inexpensive, short-lived, essentially disposable objects. They were easily broken and easily replaced. Individual white clay pipes probably did not hold much personal significance for the smoker, a fact attested to by the thousands of white clay pipes recovered from trading posts throughout the Great Lakes, including Cicott's post.

This is not so in the case of stone pipes. The relative rarity of finished pipes at the Cicott Trading Post site suggests that stone pipes were likely not thought of as "disposable." Trubowitz (1992:107) suggested that the great variety of decorative motifs on the Wea village stone pipes was indicative of the highly personal nature of these objects. It was "as if in many cases it was the pipe's owner who completed its decoration according to personal experiences, desires, and needs" (Trubowitz 1992:107). Likewise, Stahl (2001:142; 2002:838–839) has, in an African context, drawn a connection between "morphological and stylistic diversity" and the individuation of the owners of locally produced pipes. Here it is important to consider the social relations of production as they pertain to pipe making. Both Native Americans and *Canadien* traders produced stone pipes throughout the Great Lakes and beyond, and it seems likely that they exchanged and gifted these *locally made* products to each other (Morand 1994; Peach 1993; Trubowitz 1992). Unlike the productive relations of the homogenous, mass-produced white clay pipes, the local relations of stone pipe-production remained transparent and stone pipes were not fetishized. This becomes significant when we consider that both stone pipes and white clay pipes were smoked in a variety of social contexts.

Thus, although Turnbaugh (1977:5) has postulated that white clay pipes were fine for casual or recreational smoking and that stone pipes were reserved for "sacred business" (compare von Gernet 1988:306–307), such a rigid distinction between the sacred and profane use of stone pipes probably was not recognized in the Great Lakes. Nineteenth-century artist George Winter, for example, often depicted the Wabash Potawatomi leisurely smoking both clay and stone pipes (Cooke and Ramadhyani 1993). In his journal he noted that tobacco "is a 'weed' of great importance and significance. It is not only used by them (the Potawatomi) as a medium of recreative [*sic*] pleasure in smoking. But is used also, symbolically—for ceremonial, religious and votive offerings" (Cooke and Ramadhyani 1993:94; on Potawatomi tobacco use and pipe smoking, see Wagner 2003.).

Nonetheless, following Turnbaugh (1977), Trubowitz (1992), and Nassaney (2000), I suggest that stone pipes were more likely *preferred* over the common white clay pipe during cross-cultural exchange—when social relations were created or renewed through the practice of fugitive rituals. The lack of finished stone pipes at the Cicott Trading Post site suggests that stone pipes functioned in more formal contexts. Finished stone pipes were made to be used, valued, and saved rather than used and discarded.

Stone pipes were constitutive components of fur trade society and thereby helped to give meaning to and maintain the social relations between individuals from capitalist, commodity-oriented cultures on the one hand and individuals from kin-ordered, gift-oriented cultures on the other. Cross-cultural exchange at the post was always potentially fraught with misconceptions and conflict and thus was always a "sacred business." The transformative power of tobacco smoked in stone pipes assuaged these tensions and enabled Cicott and his native customers to conceptualize the outcomes of exchange within their own cultural frameworks.

Conclusion

I have argued that Europeans and Native Americans agreed that the other had desirable objects and that in order to access these objects some sort of social relationship was necessary. But discordant conceptions of the objects of exchange and conflicting motivations for exchange fostered disagreement over the nature of the relationship and how it was to be created. For Native Americans the creation of social relations could not be divorced from the objects of exchange themselves. For Europeans exchange was predicated on the notion that the "economic" *was* divorced from the social.

In order to turn strangers into kin, commodities had to first be converted into gifts, and in order to keep the economic separate from the social, gifts had to be converted into commodities. This was accomplished through trade rituals, especially those that involved smoking tobacco. The resulting social relations (both real and fictive) were the result of the resolution of this fundamental contradiction. But the resolution was never final. It was in fact a smokescreen that temporarily covered the contradiction and made possible the actual process of exchange. The work of reproducing Great Lakes fur trade society was thus never complete. The social relations and material transformations that were the foundations of this society had to be ritually reconstituted whenever exchange took place. The finished stone smoking pipes and the evidence for their production at the Cicott Trading Post site are the material manifestations of these ritually charged "moments of exchange."

Acknowledgments

This chapter has benefited from the keen insights of several readers, including Marvin T. Smith, Donald J. Blakeslee, Michael Nassaney, and Diana Loren. My wife, Amy, produced the stone pipe illustrations that appear in this chapter, and I am grateful for her artistic talent and support. I am indebted to my coeditor, Sean Rafferty, for shouldering much of the burden of preparing this volume for publication. Finally, I thank Mr. John Henry for introducing me to the Cicott Trading Post site.

References Cited

Appadurai, Arjun

1986 Introduction: Commodities and the Politics of Value. In *The Social Life of Things: Commodities in Cultural Perspective,* edited by Arjun Appaduri, 3–63. Cambridge Univ. Press, Cambridge.

Blakeslee, Donald J.

1977 The Calumet Ceremony and the Origin of Fur Trade Rituals. *Western Canadian Journal of Anthropology* 7(2):78–88.

1981 The Origin and Spread of the Calumet Ceremony. *American Antiquity* 46(4):759–768.

Brown, Ian

1989 The Calumet Ceremony in the Southeast and Its Archaeological Manifestations. *American Antiquity* 54(2):311–331.

Comer, Douglas

1996 *Ritual Ground: Bent's Old Fort, World Formation, and the Annexation of the Southwest.* Univ. of California Press, Berkeley and Los Angeles.

Cooke, Sarah E., and Rachel B. Ramadhyani (compilers)

1993 *Indians and a Changing Frontier: The Art of George Winter.* Indiana Historical Society, Indianapolis.

Delâge, Deny

1993 *Bitter Feast: Amerindians and Europeans in Northeastern North America, 1600–64.* UBC Press, Vancouver.

Dempsey, Hugh A.

1972 Western Plains Trade Ceremonies. *Western Canadian Journal of Anthropology* 3(1):29–33.

Dickason, Olive Patricia

1985 From "One Nation" in the Northeast to "New Nation" in the Northwest: A Look at the Emergence of the Métis. In *The New Peoples: Being and Becoming Métis in North America,* edited by Jacqueline Peterson and Jennifer S. H. Brown, 19–36. Univ. of Manitoba Press, Canada.

Dunaway, Wilma A.

1994 The Southern Fur Trade and the Incorporation of Southern Appalachia into the World-Economy, 1690–1763. *Review* 17(2):215–242.

1996 *The First American Frontier: Transition to Capitalism in Southern Appalachia.* Univ. of North Carolina Press, Chapel Hill.

Edmunds, R. David

1985 "Unacquainted with the Laws of the Civilized World": American Attitudes toward the Métis Communities in the Old Northwest. In *The New Peoples: Being and Becoming Métis in North America,* edited by Jacqueline Peterson and Jennifer S. H. Brown, 185–193. Univ. of Manitoba Press, Canada.

Eliade, Mircea

1958 *Rites and Symbolsof Initiation.* Harper and Row, New York.

1959 *The Sacred and Profane: The anture of Religion: The Significance of Religious Myth, Symbolism, and Ritual within Life and Culture,* translated by Willard R. Trask. Harcourt Brace Jovanovich, New York.

Elliott, Jack

1972 Tobacco Pipes among the Hivernant Hide Hunters: A.D. 1860–1882. *Western Canadian Journal of Anthropology* 3(1):146–157.

Faragher, John Mack

1998 "More Motley than Mackinaw": From Ethnic Mixing to Ethnic Cleansing on the Frontier of the Lower Missouri, 1783–1833. In *Contact Points: American Frontiers from the Mohawk Valley to the Mississippi, 1750–1830,* edited by Andrew R. L. Cayton and Fredika J. Teute, 304–326. Univ. of North Carolina Press, Chapel Hill.

Gosden, Chris, and Yvonne Marshall

1999 The Cultural Biography of Objects. *World Archaeology* 31(2):169–178.

Green, William

2002 *Hides and Pipes, Traders and Relatives: Interethnic Relationships in the Midwest as Seen from Iowaville, 1770–1810.* Paper presented at the 2002 Annual Meeting of the American Society for Ethnohistory, Quebec City, Quebec, Canada.

Gregory, C. A.

1982 *Gifts and Commodities.* Academic Press, London.

Hall, Robert L.

1977 An Anthropocentric Perspective for Eastern United States Prehistory. *American Antiquity* 42(4):499–518.

Jaenen, Cornelius

1985 The Role of Presents in French-Amerindian Trade. In *Explorations in Canadian Economic History: Essays in Honor of Irene Spry,* edited by D. Cameron, 231–250. Univ. of Ottawa Press, Ottawa.

Kardulias, P. Nick

1990 Fur Production as a Specialized Activity in a World System: Indians in the North American Fur Trade. *American Indian Culture and Research Journal* 14(1):25–60.

Klein, Alan M.

1993 Political Economy of the Buffalo Hide Trade: Race and Class in the Plains. In *The Political Economy of North American Indians,* edited by J. H. Moore, 133–160. Univ. of Oklahoma Press, Norman.

Kopytoff, Igor

1986 Cultural Biography of Things: Commoditization as Process. In *The Social Life of Things: Commodities in Cultural Perspective,* edited by Arjun Appadurai, 64–91. Cambridge Univ. Press, Cambridge.

Mann, Rob

1994 Zachariah Cicott Nineteenth-Century French Canadian Fur Trader: Ethnohistoric and Archaeological Perspectives of Ethnic Identity in the Wabash Valley. Unpublished master's thesis, Ball State Univ., Muncie, Indiana.

1999a *The 1997 Archaeological Excavations at the Cicott Trading Post Site (12Wa59).* Reports of Investigations Number 520, IMA Consulting, Minneapolis.

1999b The Silenced Miami: Archaeological and Ethnohistorical Evidence for Miami–British Relations, 1795–1812. Ethnohistory 46(3):399–427.

2003 *Colonizing the Colonizers:* Canadien *Fur Traders and Fur Trade Society in the Great Lakes Region, 1763–1850.* Unpublished Ph.D. dissertation, State Univ. of New York at Binghamton.

Marx, Karl

1906 *Capital: A Critique of Political Economy.* Edited by Frederick Engels. Translated by Ernest Untermann. Random House, Modern Library, New York.

Mauss, Marcel

1990 *The Gift: The form and Reason for Exchange in Archaic Societies.* Translated by W. D. Hall. W.W. Norton and Co., New York.

Morand, Lynn L.

1994 *Craft Industries at Fort Michilimackinac, 1715–1781.* Mackinac State Historic Parks, Mackinac Island, Mich.

Murphy, Lucy Eldersveld

2000 *A Gathering of Rivers: Indians, Métis, and Mining in the Western Great Lakes, 1737–1832.* Univ. of Nebraska Press, Lincoln.

Murray, David

2000 *Indian Giving: Economies of Power in Indian-White Exchanges.* Univ. of Massachusetts Press, Amherst.

Nassaney, Michael S.

2000 Archaeology and Oral Tradition in Tandem: Interpreting Native American Ritual, Ideology, and Gender Relations in Contact-Period Southeastern New England. In *Interpretations of Native North American Life: Material Contributions to Ethnohistory,* edited by Michael S. Nassaney and Eric S. Johnson, 412–427. Univ. Press of Florida, Gainesville.

Nekich, Sandra

1977 The Feast of the Dead: The Origin of Indian-White Trade Ceremonies in the West. *Western Canadian Journal of Anthropology* 4:1–20.

Paper, Jordan

1988 *Offering Smoke: The Sacred Pipe and Native American Religion.* Univ. of Idaho Press, Moscow.

Peach, A. Kate

1993 Ethnicity and Ethnic Markers: A Fur Trade Example. *Manitoba Archaeological Journal* 3(1–2):97–124.

Peers, Laura

1999 “Many Tender Ties”: The Shifting Contexts and Meanings of the S BLACK Bag. *World Archaeology* 31(2):288–302.

Peterson, Jacqueline

1982 Ethnogenesis: The Settlement and Growth of a New People in the Great Lakes Region. *American Indian Culture and Research Journal* 6(2):23–64.

1985 Many Roads to Red River: Métis Genesis in the Great Lakes Region, 1680–1815. In *The New Peoples: Being and Becoming Métis in North America,* edited by Jacqueline Peterson and Jennifer S. H. Brown, 37–71. Univ. of Manitoba Press, Canada.

Pickering, Kathleen

1994 Articulation of the Lakota Mode of Production and the Euro-American Fur Trade. In *The Fur Trade Revisited: Selected Papers of the Sixth North American Fur Trade Conference, Mackinac Island, Michigan, 1991,* edited by Jennifer S. H. Brown, W. J. Eccles, and Donald P. Heldman, 57–67. Michigan State Univ. Press, Mackinac Island.

Reid, C. S. "Paddy"

1995 The "Sacredness" of Carved Stone Pipes in the Ojibwa-Cree Area of the Northern Mid-Continent: A Spatial and Temporal Dilemma. *Wisconsin Archaeologist* 76(3–4):399–422.

Rich E. E.

1960 Trade Habits and Economic Motivation among the Indians of North America. *Canadian Journal of Economics and Political Science* 26:35–53.

Rotstein, Abraham

1972 Trade and Politics: An Institutional Approach. *Western Canadian Journal of Anthropology* 3(1):1–28.

Sleeper-Smith, Susan

1994 Silent Tongues, Black Robes: Potawatomi, Europeans, and Settlers in the Southern Great Lakes, 1640–1850. Unpublished Ph.D. dissertation, Univ. of Michigan, Ann Arbor.

2001 *Indian Women and French Men: Rethinking Cultural Encounter in the Great Lakes.* Univ. of Massachusetts Press, Amherst.

Smith, Erica

1991 Something More than Mere Ornament: Cloth and Indian-European Relationships in the Eighteenth Century. Unpublished master's thesis, Univ. of Winnipeg/Univ. of Manitoba.

Springer, James Warren

1981 An Ethnohistoric Study of the Smoking Complex in Eastern North America. *Ethnohistory* 28(3):217–235.

Stahl, Ann Brower

2001 *Making History in Banda: Anthropological Visions of Africa's Past.* Cambridge Univ. Press, Cambridge.

2002 Colonial Entanglements and the Practices of Taste: An Alternative to Logocentric Approaches. *American Anthropologist* 104(3):827–845.

Strathern, Marilyn

1988 *The Gender of the Gift: Problems with Women and Problems with Society in Melanesia.* Univ. of California Press, Berkeley.

Sutton, Wendy

1995 Tea Wares and Stone Pipes: Construction of Métis Ethnicity Through Consumer Behavior. Paper presented at the Annual Meeting of the Society for Historical Archaeology Conference on Historical and Underwater Archaeology, Cincinnati, Ohio.

Taussig, Michael

1980 *The Devil and Commodity Fetishism in South America.* Univ. of North Carolina Press, Chapel Hill.

Thomas, Nicholas
1991 *Entangled Objects: Exchange, Material Culture, and Colonialism in the Pacific.* Harvard Univ. Press, Cambridge.

Thorne, Tanis C.
1996 *The Many Hands of My Relations: French and Indians on the Lower Missouri.* Univ. of Missouri Press, Columbia.

Trubowitz, Neal L.
1992 Thanks, but We Prefer to Smoke Our Own: Pipes in the Great Lakes–Riverine Region during the Eighteenth Century. In *Proceedings of the 1989 Smoking Pipe Conference: Selected Papers,* edited by Charles F. Hayes III, 97–112. Rochester Museum and Science Center, Rochester, N.Y.

Turnbaugh, William
1977 Elements of Nativistic Pipe Ceremonialism in the Post-Contact Northeast. *Pennsylvania Archaeologist* 47(4):1–7.
1979 Calumet Ceremonialism as a Natavistic Response. *American Antiquity* 44(4):685–691.
1992 Post-Contact Pipe Development: The Narragansett Example. In *Proceedings of the 1989 Smoking Pipe Conference: Selected Papers,* edited by Charles F. Hayes III,. 113–124. Rochester Museum and Science Center, Rochester, N.Y.

Upton, Dell
1996 Ethnicity, Authenticity, and Invented Traditions. *Historical Archaeology* 30(2):1–7.

Vibert, Elizabeth
1997 *Traders' Tales: Narratives of Cultural Encounters in the Columbia Plateau, 1807–1846.* Univ. of Oklahoma Press, Norman.

von Gernet, Alexander D.
1988 The Transculturation of the Amerindian Pipe/Tobacco/Smoking Complex and Its Impact on the Intellectual Boundaries between "Savagery" and "Civilization," 1535–1935. Unpublished Ph.D. dissertation, McGill Univ., Montreal, Quebec.
1992 Hallucinogens and the Origins of the Iroquoian Pipe/Tobacco/Smoking Complex. In *Proceedings of the 1989 Smoking Pipe Conference: Selected Papers,* edited by Charles F. Hayes III, 171–185. Rochester Museum and Science Center, Rochester, N.Y.

Wagner, Mark J.
2003 In All the Solemnity of Profound Smoking: Tobacco Smoking and Pipe Manufacture and Use Among the Potawatomi of Illinois. In *Stone Tool Traditions in the Contact Era,* edited by C. R. Cobb, 109–126. The Univ. of Alabama Press, Tuscaloosa.

Weiner, Annette B.
1992 *Inalienable Possessions: The Paradox of Keeping-While-Giving.* Univ. of California Press, Berkeley.

West, George A.
1970 *Tobacco, Pipes, and Smoking Customs of the American Indians, Parts 1 and 2.* Greenwood Press Publishers, Westport, Conn.

White, Bruce M.

1982 "Give Us a Little Milk": The Social and Cultural Meanings of Gift Giving in the Lake Superior Fur Trade. *Minnesota History* 48:60–71.

1994 Encounters with Spirits: Ojibwa and Dakota Theories about the French and Their Merchandise. *Ethnohistory* 41(3):369–405.

White, Richard

1991 *The Middle Ground: Indians, Empires, and Republics in the Great Lakes Region, 1650–1815.* Cambridge Univ. Press, Cambridge.

Winters, Joseph

2001 *Tobacco Use by Native Americans: Sacred Smoke and Silent Killer.* Univ. of Oklahoma Press, Norman.

Wolf, Eric R.

1982 *Europe and the People without History.* Univ. of California Press, Berkeley.

7. "Neat and Artificial Pipes": Base Metal Trade Pipes of the Northeastern Indians

Richard Veit and Charles A. Bello

In 1643, while writing about his Narragansett neighbors, Roger Williams made a passing comment regarding their metalworking talents. In his words, "They have an excellent art to cast our pewter and brass into neat and artificial pipes" (Williams 1936:45). Although archaeologists working on seventeenth- and eighteenth-century Native American sites in the Northeast have uncovered base-metal pipes made from pewter, lead, brass, copper, and iron, most scholars have logically assumed that these finds had a European origin (Trubowitz 2001:5). Here we examine these enigmatic artifacts, focusing particularly on the lead and pewter pipes in their cultural and historical contexts. Although our interpretations are preliminary, we hope to better define the geographic, cultural, and temporal ranges of these unusual pipes. We provide a basic descriptive typology of the pipes and make some general statements regarding their manufacture and possible manufacturers. What the pipes may have meant to those who made and smoked them is also discussed. We conclude with some suggestions for further research.

Methodology

Tobacco pipes are artifacts of exceptional interest to archaeologists. Their analysis can provide information about past belief systems (Hall 1977; Otto 1992: 1–13; von Gernet and Timmins 1987), craft specialization (Turnbaugh 1984), trade networks (Becker 1985:1–4), culture change (Matlack 1992:66–73), and potting

FIG. 7.1. ► *A pewter pipe found near Bethlehem, Pennsylvania. Decorated with an avian effigy, it measures eleven centimeters long (Object #14031). Photograph reproduced courtesy of the University of Pennsylvania Museum, Philadelphia (NEG. #S4.143924).*

traditions. Perhaps most important, because of their association with potent narcotics and the spirit world, pipes often figured prominently in religious ceremonies (Kearsley 1996:62; Turnbaugh 1977, 1979; von Gernet 1992). Tobacco was also smoked in pipes for enjoyment, during diplomacy—particularly at the signing of treaties—and to treat various ailments (Springer 1984:219).

Historical archaeologists have employed tobacco pipes as dating tools (Harrington 1954; Binford 1962; Noël Hume 1969) and to explore trade networks and ethnic pride. Their iconography may even provide a glimpse of past political movements (Cook 1989, 1997).

Our focus here is on pipes that span the divide between prehistory and history; pewter and lead tobacco pipes recovered from seventeenth- and eighteenth-century Native American sites in the eastern, and particularly northeastern, United States (Figure 7.1). Here we refer to these pipes simply as base-metal pipes. Although pipes were made from other base metals, including copper, brass, and iron (see Noël Hume 1969:308; Neumann and Kravic 1997:244; Pratt 1976:129)—particularly the famous tomahawk pipes—they form distinct categories, were manufactured in different ways, and are not treated here. It is worth noting that all of these metal pipes were less fragile than clay pipes and hence of particular value to hunters and travelers (Noël Hume 1969:308).

For the purposes of this discussion no distinction is made between pewter and lead tobacco pipes. The terms appear to have been used interchangeably and rather arbitrarily by the archaeologists and curators who excavated and cataloged the pipes we examined. According to metallurgy expert John Light, lead is a "very heavy, soft, malleable and slightly ductile metal. When the surface is freshly exposed it is silvery-blue in color, but the oxide which forms fairly quickly is dull gray" (Light 2000:12). Pewter is formed when lead is alloyed with tin (Light 2000:10). The interchangeable use of the terms *pewter* and *lead* in reference to these pipes probably comes from the fact that one of the primary components of colonial pewter was lead. Spectroscopic analysis of surviving museum samples could help resolve the exact chemical composition of the pipes.

Pewter and lead base metal pipes are quite rare; less than 150 are currently known to exist. Generally, they form only a token portion of the archaeological assemblages on the sites where they are found. Often they are overshadowed by clay and stone pipes (see Turnbaugh 1980) produced by Native Americans and white ball-clay trade pipes of Dutch and English manufacture.

Although numerous previous researchers have noted the presence of base-metal pipes on Contact period sites in the Northeast (see Cadzow 1936:80; Hammell 1979; Heye and Pepper 1915; Hulse 1977; Kraft 1978; McGuire 1898:460), to date there has been only one detailed study of such pipes (Anderson 1992). This lack of attention is surprising given the interesting iconography and manufacturing techniques embodied by the pipes. Perhaps pipes such as these have been overlooked because they are scattered in museum collections up and down the East Coast, making it that much more challenging to synthesize what little is known about them.

We examined a total of thirty-three pipes for this study. They are held by several major research institutions, including Harvard University's Peabody Museum of Archaeology and Ethnology, the University of Pennsylvania Museum, the Smithsonian Institution, the North Museum at Franklin and Marshall College, Carnegie

TABLE 7.1 ▸ REPOSITORIES HOLDING BASE METAL PIPES

Repository	Number of Base Metal Pipes
New Jersey State Museum	1
New York State Museum	10
Pennsylvania State Museum	15
Carnegie Museum	5
North Museum	5
University of Pennsylvania Museum	1
Natural Museum of the American Indian	3
Smithsonian Institution	1
Peabody Museum	2
Total	**43**

Museum of Natural History, Pennsylvania State Museum, New York State Museum, and New Jersey State Museum (Table 7.1). A substantial collection held by the Rochester Museum and Science Center has not yet been examined.

Although we are aware of others, the total number of these unusual pipes surviving in museum collections and private cabinets is probably under 150. Undoubtedly, other specimens survive elsewhere and presumably unexcavated in the ground—though they appear to have a finite life span when buried in acidic soils. Nevertheless, we believe that the thirty-three pipes discussed here make up a representative sample from which to draw some preliminary conclusions.

Geographic Distribution

Base metal lead and pewter tobacco pipes have been found on sites from Brant County in Ontario, Canada, in the north (Canadian Institute 1891:67), to North Carolina in the south (Carnes 1987:154). They have also been found in Rhode Island, Massachusetts (McGuire 1898:463), New York (Beauchamp 1903:13), Pennsylvania (Cadzow 1936:80; Kent 1993:287), New Jersey (Heye and Pepper 1915:50–51; Kraft 1986:208; Philhower 1934), and Virginia (Cotter 1994:57). They are, however, most common on Seneca sites in upstate New York and Susquehannock sites from south-central Pennsylvania. This distribution may reflect the fact that Seneca and Susquehannock cemeteries from the seventeenth century have been systematically studied, while those of other groups have not (George Hamell, personal communication 2001). Interestingly, these two groups maintained an adversarial relationship for much of the seventeenth century (Dickens, Ward, and Davis 1987:89). Smaller quantities are known from Ohio, Indiana, and Michigan (Cleland 1971; Hulse 1977).

All but two of the pipes were found on Native American sites. The exceptions are from Jamestown, Virginia (Cotter 1994:57), discussed below, and the French Azilum (Rob Mann, personal communication 2000), a site in central Pennsylvania (circa 1794–1817) associated with refugees from the French Revolution. The pipe from the French Azilum differs considerably in form and decoration from those found on Native American sites and may be a toy pipe or European import.

Although no full-sized pewter pipes have been recovered in the Netherlands, miniature metal tobacco pipes were found there (Jan Baart, personal communication 2000). They may have been used as toys. Nevertheless, the larger North American pipes are sometimes termed Dutch pewter pipes. Although the possibility of manufacture in the Netherlands cannot be ruled out, our research generated no clear evidence that the Dutch made the pipes.

Not only do most of the pipes come from Native American sites, but almost all were recovered from burial contexts. A disproportionately large number of those found came from the burials at the Strickler (36La3) and Byrd Leibhart (36La6) sites in Lancaster County, Pennsylvania, and the Dann and Marsh sites, located in Monroe and Ontario Counties, New York. The examples from the Munsee Cemetery in northern New Jersey, Bristol, Pennsylvania (Veit and Bello 2001), and Rhode Island (Chapin 1927:19; William Turnbaugh, personal communication 2000) also come from burials. Although most of these sites were excavated in the late nineteenth or early twentieth centuries with minimal regard for archaeological provenience, it is worth noting that most of the pipes came from the graves of adult males.

Simply put, these artifacts are unusual. Most archaeologists who have found them commented on their use, production, and possible associations. For instance, John Cotter, who recovered two lead tobacco pipe fragments from a mid- to late-seventeenth-century deposit in Jamestown, Virginia, wrote: "Associated with Structure 19A fill are other metal objects including a brass spoon bowl, a brass thimble, a brass and silver button, a copper pot lid, lead came fragments, and two fragments of a unique lead tobacco pipe (marking one unhappy experiment which we know was not again repeated at Jamestown and we hope never again in America!)" (Cotter 1994:57). Unbeknownst to Cotter, many more of these unusual pipes were present upriver in the settlements of the Susquehannocks.

Based on the currently available information, it appears that base metal (pewter/lead) tobacco pipes provided an alternative to the more common clay and stone pipes of the time and were used primarily by Iroquoian peoples and, to a lesser degree, Algonquians in the Northeast. Wooden pipes, sometimes elaborately decorated, were also used but have not survived in large numbers.

Dating the Pipes

In his article "A Pewter Effigy Pipe from Pennsylvania in the Collections of the University Museum of Archaeology and Anthropology, University of Pennsylvania," David Anderson assigns these pipes a date range of 1650–1750 (Anderson 1992:76) (see Figure 7.1). Herbert Kraft, discussing trade goods from the Minisink site in Warren County, New Jersey, has argued that pewter pipes were used there between 1614 and 1750 (Kraft 1978:45–50). Charles Wray, in his *Manual for Seneca Iroquois Archaeology*, assigns them to a period between 1660 and 1700 (1973:30). Furthermore, Barry Kent notes the presence of metal pipes on Native American sites in central Pennsylvania between 1575 and 1743 (1993:292). Unfortunately, Kent does not specify whether these dates refer to copper, iron, or pewter/lead pipes.

Our research indicates that while base metal pipes were employed between the early seventeenth century and the mid-eighteenth century, they were, in fact, most common between 1645 and 1680. In Pennsylvania, pewter/lead pipes were particularly common at the Strickler site, occupied between 1645 and 1665 (Kent 1993:367). In New York State, the pipes are most common at the Dann and Marsh sites (dated respectively 1660–1675 and 1650–1670) (Wray, Sempowski, and Saunders 1991:4–5). At the Frederick site in North Carolina, two pipes were found in burials dated to the 1670s (Carnes 1987:154).

Form and Ornamentation

The pipes vary considerably in size, form, and ornamentation (Figure 7.2). One of the smallest is from Warwick, Rhode Island, and measures only 8 cm in length (William Turnbaugh, personal communication 2000). Its form is typical of a European ball clay pipe. The other extreme is provided by a 76.5 cm long example in the collection of the North Museum at Franklin and Marshall College. The aver-

FIG. 7.2. ▸ *(Right) A small and simple example of a lead/pewter pipe (catalog no. 15207). Reproduced courtesy of the New York State Museum, Albany, N.Y.*

FIG. 7.3. ▸ *(Below) A flanged form bowl with a distinct foot. This lead/pewter pipe was recovered from the Dann site in Monroe County, New York (catalog no. 21136). Reproduced courtesy of the New York State Museum, Albany, N.Y.*

age length is 36.43 cm. However, because many of the pipes are today broken accurate measurements are difficult to obtain. It is possible that some of the pipes were broken or ritually killed prior to their burial; others may have been broken simply by the weight of the overlying soil. Again, if more information were available on the archaeological contexts from which the pipes were recovered, it might be possible to determine their condition at burial.

The form of the pipes is variable but typically the bowl rests at an obtuse angle to the stem, which is generally round. The bowls come in several different forms including small "belly bowls," conical bowls, squared bowls, and flanged bowls (Table 7.2). The squared bowls were most common in the Susquehanna and Delaware Valleys, while flanged bowls were more common on Seneca sites in western New York (Figure 7.3). Colin Doak, in his thesis titled "Towards a Semiotic Analysis of Huron Smoking Pipes," has argued that the four corners of coronet form pipe bowls may equate with the four cardinal directions, and the pipes' smoking chamber, with the world center (Doak 1993). This interpretation may hold true for the pewter pipes with squared bowls.

Several of the pipes also are ornamented with elaborate effigies (Figure 7.4). The effigies either rest on the distal side of the bowl or stand on a spur or pedestal extending out from the distal top of the bowl. Typically the effigies face back toward the smoker or are self-directed. Avian, ursine, and lupine motifs are all present. The birds are almost all raptors. Owls are most common, followed by monkeys, hawks, bears, and dogs. One spectacular, albeit broken, owl effigy pipe

TABLE 7.2 ▸ PIPE FORMS AND EFFIGIES

Bowl Form/Iconography	Number of Examples
Belly/footed bowl	6
Trade pipe	4
Flanged bowl	3
Square	6
Calumet	1
Micmac	1
Incised	1
Bear/otter	1
Dog/wolf	2
Duck	1
Hawk	2
Ape/monkey	2
Owl	3
Total	**33**

FIG. 7.4. ▸ *(Left) An ambiguous quadruped, possibly a panther, peers over the bowl of this lead/pewter tobacco pipe. Recovered from a site in Lancaster County, Pennsylvania, the pipe is in the collections of the North Museum (catalog no. GF 21252-1). Reproduced courtesy of the North Museum, Franklin and Marshall College, Lancaster, Pennsylvania.*

FIG. 7.5. ▸ *(Right) One of the most elaborate effigies found on a lead/pewter pipe. This owl, which once decorated a pipe, has two inlaid blue-glass seed beads as eyes. The owl was found at the Dann Site in Monroe County, New York (catalog no. 21078). Reproduced courtesy of the New York State Museum, Albany, N.Y.*

was inset with pale blue seed beads for eyes (Figure 7.5). All of these identifications are tentative, as in most cases decay has rendered the carvings ambiguous. The monkey or ape effigies are particularly interesting, as neither apes nor monkeys were known to the indigenous people of eastern North America. Perhaps these pipes were the products of a European craftsman or of Native Americans who had been to Europe or knew of these animals from Europeans' pets or from artwork. A unique pipe in the collections of the North Museum displays a goose's head carved from wood and inlaid with copper attached to a long base metal shaft. Although not in the collections that we examined, we are aware of three mixed-media pipes made of wood with extensive lead inlays. Two of these pipes are curated by Rochester Museum and Science Center and came from Seneca sites dated between 1670 and 1687. The third example was excavated from the Frederick site in North Carolina and dates from the 1670s. Both the William Penn Museum in Harrisburg, Pennsylvania, and the North Museum in Lancaster, Pennsylvania, hold soapstone pipes with elaborate inlaid lead decoration.

Secondary motifs or decoration present on some of the pipes include fine cross-hatched lines, patterns, or inscribed dots and, in one case, a cross. All these patterns are reminiscent of similar designs on Contact period brass bracelets, clay tobacco pipes, and shell effigies (see Cowin 2000:1–14; Sempowski 1989:81–112).

Regional Variation

The pipes show only minimal regional variation. In our sample, flanged bowl pipes are only present on Seneca pipes. Squared bowls are more common on sites from the Delaware Valley (Figure 7.6). Calumet form pipes are present in Indiana and Michigan (Figure 7.7), while a Micmac form pipe bowl curated by the Carnegie Museum is cataloged with a likely provenience of Ohio. More research and an expanded sample may reveal further regional variations. Unfortunately, too little is known about the dates of the pipes to discuss whether or not their forms evolved through time.

FIG. 7.6. ▸ *(Above) A squared bowl pipe, lead/pewter pipe from Bristol, Pennsylvania. The small nub protruding from the distal side of the bowl may have supported an effigy figure (catalog no. 88-34-10/46151). Photograph reproduced courtesy of the President and Fellows of Harvard College, Peabody Museum (photo no. N33441).*

FIG. 7.7. ▸ *(Left) A calumet-style pipe made from lead/pewter of uncertain provenience, possibly Indiana (catalog no. 1186). Reproduced courtesy of the Carnegie Museums of Pittsburgh.*

Manufacture

One major unresolved issue is how the pipes were made. A single example in the collections of the Peabody Museum at Harvard University was clearly manufactured by wrapping a sheet of lead around a form (Dincauze 1974:Plate vi-2). The technology employed in making the others is less evident. One would assume that they were cast in molds. Colonists and Native Americans made and used simple molds, often carved from stone, to cast musket balls, buttons, and ornaments (see Hamell 1979:6; Rumrill 1988:19–25; Willoughby 1935). The complex, three-dimensional carving on many of the pipes suggests that two-piece molds or perhaps lost wax casting methods were employed. Presumably this would have left mold scars or seams on the finished products. All of the pipes cataloged for this study were carefully examined for mold scars. Although many are so badly decayed that it would be impossible to tell if seams were present, others were exceptionally well preserved. None showed evidence of mold seams.

If the pipes had been cast in molds, one would expect identical or nearly identical pipes to be present in the collections. Although the badly decayed condition of many of the pipes makes this difficult to assess, we believe that the owl effigies, apes, and the calumet form pipes are similar enough that they may have been cast in the same molds. Other pipes are clearly unique, so if they were made in molds the molds may literally have broken or been discarded after the first casting.

Interestingly, ethnohistoric sources note that Native Americans were casting tobacco pipes in the mid-seventeenth century. Roger Williams, amateur ethnographer and the founder of Rhode Island, in the quotation that forms the title of this chapter, clearly states that Native Americans were casting pipes (Williams 1936:44). An even earlier reference to metal being used by Native Americans to make tobacco pipes is provided by Dutch explorer David Pietersen de Vries. In 1632 he questioned a Native American regarding the massacre of some Dutch settlers at Swanendael, Delaware. During the questioning, he learned that the settlers had "set up a column, to which was fastened a piece of tin, wheron the arms of Holland were painted. One of their chiefs took this off for the purpose of making tobacco pipes, not knowing that he was doing amiss" (Myers 1912:16–17).

Writing a few years later, in the 1640s, William Bradford, governor of the Plymouth colony, noted that the Indians had "moulds to make shot of all sorts, as musket bullets, pistol bullets, swan and goose shot, and of smaller sorts" (Bradford cited in Malone 1993:93). Somewhat later, in the 1670s, William Harris wrote that "they [Native Americans] are Admirable witty & they use to reach anything they have a minde to presently as to be Smithes coopers Carpenters braysers yea one that I knew turned coyner of money . . . & did make some of pewter like Spanish money but teached another his skill whoe not being wary put away soe much was discoured for which they whipt them in ye Massachusetts" (Harris cited in Fairbanks and Trent 1982:84). Of course, the art of casting pipes presumably would not have been beyond the skill of a colonial pewterer or silversmith.

One very interesting source hints at an Old World origin for the pipes. In 1892 Mrs. Zerviah Gould Mitchell (circa 1805–1895), a Wampanoag, told the following story to Hezekiah Butterworth of Boston (Nassaney 2001:12). Titled "The Silver Pipe," the story is reprinted in William Scranton Simmons's *Spirit of the New England Tribes:*

> King James of England, on hearing of the goodness and virtues of Massasoit, once sent him a present of a silver pipe. The chieftain prized it highly as a gift from his "white brother over the sea." But one of his warriors did a deed of valor that so won his heart that he resolved to make him a present of the pipe as his choice treasure. The warrior, finding himself about to die, charged his squaw to put the silver pipe into his grave at the burial, but she, out of regard to the treasure, hid it, and covered the grave without it. One evening she went to the place where she had hidden the royal present, resolving to smoke from the pipe alone, and to hide it again. She put out her hand to take the pipe, but it moved away from her. Again, but it moved away, and again and again, but a dead hand was moving it. Then she bitterly repented of her disobedience, and promised to bury the pipe if she were able. At this resolution, the pipe lay still, and she opened the grave, fulfilled the warrior's command, and was enabled to smoke in peace of mind and conscience, we may hope, the rest of her days. (Butterworth 1893 cited in Simmons 1986:124)

Was the "silver pipe" referred to in this oral tradition in fact made from pewter or lead? We may never know, but in this case, at least, a metal pipe with a European provenance came to be seen as an item of great power in a Native American community.

An alternative explanation is that the pipes were not molded but cold hammered or carved. Lead is a very soft metal and can be carved with iron tools. Perhaps Native craftsmen carved the pipes from bars of lead traded to them for the manufacture of musket balls. The methods employed would have been largely identical to those used to carve steatite and other soft stones into pipes and bannerstones during the prehistoric period. In fact, in New England impressive stone pipes became more common after the introduction of European metal tools (McGuire 1898:433; Turnbaugh 1977:3). Men probably carved these pipes and other stone sculptures during the Late Woodland period (Bragdon 1996:119).

Roger Williams described the tools employed in the manufacture of stone pipes as "steele drills and other instruments" (Williams 1936:55). If lead were substituted for stone, the carving process would remain basically the same. Blocking with a sharp knife or chisel would have provided the basic shape, which could have been further refined by filing and eventually burnished to a bright sheen.

At first glance this method of manufacture seems improbable. However, it is worth noting that complete lead bars, long enough to support the manufacture of several pipes, have been recovered on Seneca sites in upstate New York. Although other scholars have noted that these bars were sometimes reworked into lead effigies (de Roever 1996:81). The possibility that they formed the raw material for pipes has not been previously examined.

It is common to think of Native Americans as having a "stone-age" existence; however, copper and other native metals had been worked by Native Americans since the Late Archaic period. It is also clear that Native Americans rapidly adopted those European technologies that they found useful. For example, archaeologists have found evidence for Native Americans acting as stonemasons and building European-style fortifications in New England (Malone 1993:99–101). Moreover, at sites in Pennsylvania and New York archaeologists have found caches of tools and gunparts, presumably the stores of Native American gunsmiths (Hamilton 1960; Malone 1993:95; Robinson, Kelley, and Rubertone 1991). Metal tools also expedited the production of wampum and other shell ornaments made by both Native Americans and European colonists during the historic period (Becker 1980; Williams and Flinn 1990).

The almost exclusive use of native motifs, often drawn directly from earlier stone examples, also hints that Native Americans made the pipes. Ronald Kearsley notes that certain talented craftsmen specialized in the manufacture of liturgical implements, such as turtle shell rattles, within the Iroquoian community (Kearsley 1996:107). Perhaps a few of these specialists are responsible for these fine pipes. If Native Americans did not make the pipes, then the colonists who did were certainly attuned to their customers' needs and artistic sensibilities. Moreover, if the pipes were made by Native Americans, they would appear to be only one of many singularly artistic items produced during this time of incredible cultural foment. With new tools and materials, some skilled craftsmen began to interpret and use new materials in different, unintended, and challenging ways. Things were different in the translation, as witnessed by Henry Hudson when he saw Lenape men wearing spoons as ornaments upon their breasts, or as seen in the reworking of European kettles into thunderbird icons, bracelets, beads, rattles, and other ornaments (Bradley 1987:130–135; Groce 1980:114–116). Even iron axes, certainly a challenging medium even for skilled metallurgists, were reworked into a variety of lesser tools such as wedges (see Bradley 1980). Native American craftsmen also produced intricate brass hair ornaments during the same period (Fairbanks and Trent 1982:84), not to mention handsomely carved bone combs (Baart 1996:175–187). A bright new pewter pipe, whether cast or carved, must have been an impressive sight. Even today, bent and decayed, they are striking artifacts.

Iconography

Although most of the pipes were made in familiar European forms, roughly one-third of those that were examined for this study are effigy pipes, identical but for their material to other Native American pipes of the period carved from wood, stone, and modeled in clay. Zena Pearlstone Matthews's study of approximately fifteen hundred Iroquoian effigy pipes provides some useful baseline information regarding these intriguing artifacts. According to Mathews, effigy pipes were scarce before 1500 and increase dramatically after contact (1980:297). She also divides the pipes into two categories: zoomorphic and anthropomorphic forms. In the case of the base metal pipes, with only a handful of exceptions, anthropomorphic pipes are absent.

The motifs displayed on the pipes are strikingly similar to those used by Native Americans to ornament shell pendants (Wray 1964:17). Most of the creatures depicted were prominent in the cosmologies of northeastern Native Americans. Almost all of the animals depicted are native to the area: bears, hawks, lizards, owls, panthers, and wolves. The puzzling exceptions to these two rules are the aforementioned pipes decorated with effigies of apes or monkeys. Europeans may have made them.

Bird effigies, especially hawks and owls, are particularly common. Raptors held a special place in the cosmology of many Native American groups. Writing in the eighteenth century, David Zeisberger, a Moravian missionary, described the forked tailed hawk: "The Indians call it Chauwalanne, forked eagle, from the fact that its tail is forked . . . If it approaches the dwellings of the Indians, they always look upon it as a sign of change of weather or rain" (Hubert and Schwarze 1996:67). Alternatively, these birds may be swallow-tailed kites. George Hamell notes, "The Hurons associated swallows with thunder [and lightning] due to their presence in numbers just before and following late spring and summer thunderstorms" (personal communication 2001).

Zeisberger also noted that "if an Indian hunter hears an owl screech in the night he immediately throws some tobacco into the fire, muttering a few words at the same time. Then they promise themselves success for the next day for the owl is said to be a powerful spirit" (Hubert and Schwarze 1996:139). Kathleen Bragdon states that "in many parts of the world, shamans are linked through a multiplicity of symbols to birds, or to those animals who shift between environments or mediate between disparate states. Birds are likewise linked to the experience of drug-induced 'flight,' a linkage marked by the common association in

Native North America between birds, tobacco, and smoking pipes" (Bragdon 1996:205). Bears were also seen as having special spiritual power because they resembled human beings (Kraft 1986:157). Panthers similarly held special spiritual significance (Hamell 1998:258–291).

It is worth noting that some of the animals on the pipes were totemic animals of various social units (Swanton 1946:661). The species represented on Hopewell pipes, though produced hundreds of years earlier in Ohio, are quite similar (Otto 1992:5). This is true even to the degree that both Hopewell and base metal owl effigy pipes have inlaid eyes. Clearly the roots of this iconography stretched back well into the past. But clan symbols do not suffice to explain the range of species represented on the pipes. Several clans found among the Iroquois, such as the deer and turtle, do not appear in the pipe's iconographic vocabulary.

As previously noted, many of the pipes are self-directed. Ted Brasser, writing about effigy pipes, notes that "ethnographic information from the Iroquoian tribes and their Algonkian neighbors indicate that smoking of the pipe was a mental device used by the smoker to concentrate his thoughts upon a given subject . . . the self-directed aspects of many effigy pipes related to the spiritual communication between men and their guardian spirits, cultivated by means of meditation while contemplating the representation of those spirits" (Brasser 1980:96). Moreover, ethnohistoric sources note that exhaled smoke could be blown back along the top of the stem toward the effigy, thus invoking the spirits represented there (Paper 1992: 8, 24, 39; Lafitau 1977:178). It is our belief that the base metal pipes discussed here were symbolically charged objects, which, in the case of the effigy pipes may have represented men's guardian spirits.

Suggestions for Further Research

Considerable additional research could be done on the base metal pewter and lead pipes of the colonial Northeast. A complete inventory and catalog of the pipes should be made, particularly as many of these artifacts have not been conserved or, if conserved, were incorrectly treated and are rapidly decaying. The application of two relatively simple analytical techniques could also help unravel the production of these unusual smoking pipes. X-rays of surviving intact pieces might reveal the presence of mold seams obscured by careful polishing and reveal whether the pipes were made in molds or carved by hand. Spectroscopic analysis of the pipe metal could reveal whether the pipes were made from pewter, lead, or a combination of the two. If multiple pipes show the same chemical signatures, it might also show that they were made by the same craftsman and at the same time. The alloys employed in the pipes might also be compared with other lead and pewter artifacts in an effort to further trace the origins of these items.

Conclusions

Are the "neat pipes" described by Roger Williams and the elaborate base metal pipes found by archaeologists in the Northeast one and the same? Who made them? Why did they make them? Many questions remain unanswered or are incompletely answered. For now we can say that a wide variety of carefully crafted base metal pipes were used by Native Americans in the Northeast during the late seventeenth century. Their motifs and general absence from European sites seem to argue for Native manufacture and an association with shamanism. The animals represented on the pipes may represent the guardian spirits that "all Iroquoians had until at least the 18th century" (Tooker 1964:92 n). Ethnohistoric sources confirm that Native Americans in this region were engaged in metalworking, including the casting of pipes. Manufacture by colonists or in the Netherlands, France, or England is also possible. When new and brightly burnished, lead and pewter must have been impressive symbols of power.

The base metal pipes were most common at a time when other innovative types of tobacco pipes were manufactured, including the famous Chesapeake terra-cotta pipes. The latter were apparently made by Native Americans, African Americans, and Europeans (Emerson 1988; Henry 1979; Mouer 1993). Like the latter, they were popular at a time when supply lines with the Old World were strained, resulting in increased local production. Unlike the latter, and more like stone pipes, they were rarely casually discarded. Almost all have been recovered from graves where they were carefully interred. Some display carefully manufactured effigies of creatures revered by many northeastern Native Americans. They are material reminders of a world that we only imperfectly understand, when cultures previously separated by vast distances, languages, and beliefs came together on the first American frontier.

Acknowledgments

We would like to thank Rob Mann and Sean Rafferty from SUNY Binghamton for organizing the symposium titled "The 'Sot-weed Factor': Recent Development in the Archaeology of Smoking and Tobacco Pipes" at the annual meeting of the Society for American Archaeology in 2001. Our research and interpretations benefited considerably thanks to the assistance provided by several colleagues presenting in the session, particularly Neal Trubowitz and Michael Nassaney. George Hamell commented extensively and constructively on an earlier draft of this manuscript. We greatly appreciate his help and insights. Researching and writing this paper would have been impossible without the assistance of several talented and helpful curators, the unsung heroes of museum research. The following individuals provided valuable help: Lucy Fowler Williams and Melissa Elsberry at the University of Pennsylvania Museum; Stephen G. Warfel from the William Penn Museum–Pennsylvania State Museum; Karen Flinn from the New Jersey

State Museum; Bradley Smith of the North Museum; Gloria Greis from the Peabody Museum of Archaeology and Ethnology at Harvard University; Penelope Drooker from the New York State Museum; Verna Cowen from the Carnegie Museum of Natural History; Betty Prisch from the Rochester Museum and Science Center; Linda Carnes from the Research Laboratories of Anthropology, University of North Carolina; Richard L. George, staff archaeologist/archaeology collection manager, Carnegie Museum; and Dennis Curry from the Maryland Historical Trust. William Turnbaugh from the Department of Sociology and Anthropology at the University of Rhode Island graciously shared his insights into the production and meaning of Native American stone pipes. Gary Fogelman told us of pewter pipes in private collections. Kathy Earhardt from Montclair State University discussed her knowledge of Native American metalworking with us. Jan Baart, from the City of Amsterdam's Archaeological Department, provided us with important information about the presence of pewter pipes in the Old World. A hearty thank you to all of these individuals and anyone we may have forgotten. Any errors of fact or omission remain, of course, our own.

References Cited

Anderson, David

1992 *A Pewter Effigy Pipe from Pennsylvania in the Collections of the University Museum of Archaeology and Anthropology, University of Pennsylvania.* Pennsylvania Archaeologist 62(1):73–78.

Baart, Jan

1996 Kammen/Combs. In *One Man's Trash Is Another Man's Treasure.* Edited by Alexandra van Dongen, 175–188. Museum Boymans-van Beuningen, Rotterdam.

Beauchamp, William M.

1903 Metallic Ornaments of the New York Indians. *New York State Museum Bulletin* 73(8):1–120.

Becker, Marshall J.

1980 Wampum: The Development of an Early American Currency. *Bulletin of the Archaeological Society of New Jersey* 36:1–11.

1985 A Crested Blackstone Pipe from Bucks County, Pennsylvania. *Pennsylvania Archaeologist* 55(3):1–4.

Binford, Lewis

1962 A New Method of Calculating Dates from Kaolin Pipe Stem Samples. *Southeastern Archaeological Conference Newsletter* 9(1):19–21.

Bradley, James A.

1980 Ironwork in Onondaga: 1550–1650. In *Studies on Iroquoian Culture,* edited by Nancy Bonvillain, 109–118. Occasional Publications in Northeastern Anthropology, Dept. of Anthropology, Franklin Pierce College.

1987 *Evolution of the Onondaga Iroquois: Accommodating Change, 1500–1655 A.D.* Syracuse Univ. Press, Syracuse, N.Y.

Bragdon, Kathleen J.

1996 *Native People of Southern New England, 1500–1659.* Univ. of Oklahoma Press, Norman.

Brasser, T. J.
1980 Self-Directed Pipe Effigies. *Man in the Northeast* 19:95–104.

Cadzow, Donald A.
1936 *Archaeological Studies of the Susquehannock Indians of Pennsylvania.* Safe Harbor Report No. 2, Archaeological Section. Pennsylvania Historical Commission, Harrisburg.

Canadian Institute
1891 *Fourth Annual Report of the Canadian Institute.* Warwick and Sons, Toronto, Canada.

Carnes, Linda F.
1987 Euroamerican Artifacts from the Fredericks, Wall, and Mitchum Sites. In *The Siouan Project: Seasons I and II,* edited by Roy S. Dickens Jr., H. Trawick Ward, and R. P. Stephen Davis Jr., 84–154. Research Laboratories of Anthropology Univ. of North Carolina, Monograph Series No. 1, Chapel Hill, N.C.

Chapin, Howard M.
1927 Indian Graves: A Survey of the Indian Graves That Have Been Discovered in Rhode Island. *Rhode Island Historical Society Collections* 20(1):14–32.

Cleland, Charles E. (editor)
1971 *The Lasanen Site: An Historic Burial Locality in Madison County, Michigan.* Publications of the Museum, Michigan State Univ., East Lansing. Anthropological Series 1, No. 1.

Cook, Lauren, J.
1989 Descriptive Analysis of Tobacco-Related Material from the Boott Mills Boardinghouses. In *Interdisciplinary Investigations of the Boott Mills, Lowell, Massachusetts. Volume III: The Boardinghouse System as a Way of Life.* Cultural Resource Management Study 21. U.S. Dept. of the Interior, National Park Service, North Atlantic Regional Office, Boston.
1997 "Promiscuous Smoking": Interpreting Gender and Tobacco Use in the Archaeology Record. *Northeast Historical Archaeology* 26:23–38.

Cotter, John C.
1994 *Archaeological Excavations at Jamestown, Virginia.* 2d ed. Archaeological Society of Virginia, Special Publication No. 32.

Cowin, Verna L.
2000 Shell Ornaments from Cayuga County, New York. *Archaeological of Eastern North America* 28:1–14.

de Roever, Margriet
1996 Koopmanschappen voor Nieuw Nederland. Een blik op de Nederlandse handelsartikelen voor de inheemse bevolking van Noord-America/Merchandises for New Netherland. A look at Dutch articles for barter with the native American population. In *One Man's Trash Is Another Man's Treasure.* Edited by Alexandra van Dongen, 71–94. Museum Boymans-van Beuningen, Rotterdam.

Dickens, Roy S., Jr., H. Trawick Ward, and R. P. Stephen Davis Jr. (editors)
1987 *The Siouan Project: Seasons I and II.* Research Laboratories of Anthropology Univ. of North Carolina, Monograph Series No. 1, Chapel Hill, N.C.

Dincauze, Dena
1974 An Introduction to Archaeology in the Greater Boston Area. *Archaeology of Eastern North America* 2(1):39–67.

Doak, Colin James

1993 Towards a Semiotic Analysis of Huron Ceramic Smoking Pipes: The Le Caron, Robitelle, and Ball Assemblages. Unpublished master's thesis in anthropology, Trent Univ., Peterborough, Canada.

Emerson, Matthew Charles

1988 Decorated Clay Tobacco Pipes from the Chesapeake. Unpublished Ph.D. dissertation, Dept. of Anthropology, Univ. of California, Berkeley.

Fairbanks, Jonathan L., and Robert F. Trent

1982 *New England Begins: The Seventeenth Century, Introduction Migration and Settlement.* Museum of Fine Arts, Boston.

Groce, Nora

1980 Ornaments of Metal: Rings, Medallions, Combs, Beads and Pendants. In *Burr's Hill: A Seventeenth Century Wampanoag Burial Ground in Warren, Rhode Island.* Edited by Susan G. Gibson, 108–113. Haffenreffer Museum of Anthropology, Brown Univ.

Hall, Robert L.

1977 An Anthropocentric Perspective for Eastern United States Prehistory. *American Antiquity* 42(4):499–518.

Hamilton, T. M. (editor)

1960 Some Gun Parts from Seventeenth Century Seneca Sites. In *Indian Trades Guns. Missouri Archaeologist* 22:103–107.

Hamell, George R.

1979 Of Hockers, Diamonds and Hourglasses, Some Interpretations of Seneca Archaeological Art. Paper presented at the Iroquois Conference, Albany, New York.

1998 Long-Tail: The panther in Huron-Wyandot and Seneca myth, ritual, and material culture. In *Icons of Power: Feline Symbolism in the Americas,* edited by Nicholas J. Saunders, 258–291. Routledge, London and New York.

Harrington, J. C.

1954 Dating Stem Fragments of Seventeenth and Eighteenth Century Clay Tobacco Pipes. *Quarterly Bulletin, Archaeological Society of Virginia* 9(1).

Henry, Susan L.

1979 Terra-Cotta Tobacco Pipes in Seventeenth-Century Maryland and Virginia: A Preliminary Study. *Historical Archaeology* 13:14–37.

Heye, George G., and George H. Pepper

1915 *Exploration of a Munsee Cemetery near Montague, New Jersey.* The Museum of the American Indian, Heye Foundation, New York.

Hubert, Archer Butler, and William Nathaniel Schwarze (editors)

1996 *David Ziesberger's History of the Northern American Indians.* Originally published 1910. Wennawoods Publishing, Lewisburg, Pa.

Hulse, Charles A.

1977 Archaeological Evaluation of Fort St. Joseph: An Eighteenth Century Military Post and Settlement in Berrien County, Michigan. Master's thesis in anthropology, Michigan State Univ.

Kearsley, Ronald Glenn

1996 Pinched-Face Human Effigy Pipes: The Social Mechanisms That Conditioned Their Manufacture and Use in Seventeenth Century Iroquoia. Unpublished master's thesis in anthropology, Trent Univ., Peterborough, Ontario, Canada.

Kent, Barry C.

1993 *Susquehanna's Indians.* Anthropological Series No. 6. Commonwealth of Pennsylvania, Pennsylvania Historical and Museum Commission, Harrisburg.

Kraft, Herbert C.

1978 *The Minisink Site: A Reevaluation of a Late Prehistoric and Early Historic Contact Site in Sussex County, New Jersey,* Archaeological Research Center, Seton Hall Univ., South Orange, N.J.

1986 *The Lenape: Archaeology, History, and Ethnography.* New Jersey Historical Society, Newark, N.J.

Lafitau, Joseph-Francois, S. J.

1977 *Customs of the American Indians Compared with the Customs of Primitive Times.* 2 vols. Edited by William N. Fenton and Elizabeth L. Moore. Originally published 1724. Publications of the Champlain Society, Nos. 48–49, Toronto.

Light, John D.

2000 A Field Guide to the Identification of Metal. In *Studies in Material Culture Research,* edited by Karlis Karklins, 3–19. Society for Historical Archaeology, California Univ. of Pennsylvania, California, Pa.

Malone, Patrick M.

1993 *The Skulking Way of War: Technology and Tactics among the New England Indians.* Johns Hopkins Univ. Press, Baltimore.

Mathews, Zena Pearlstone

1980 Of Man and Beast: The Chronology of Effigy Pipes among Ontario Iroquoians. *Ethnohistory* 27(4):295–307.

Matlack, Harry A.

1992 Development of the McFate Culture of North-Central Pennsylvania: The Monongahela–Shenks Ferry Connection. *Pennsylvania Archaeologist* 62(2):55–73.

McGuire, Joseph D.

1898 Pipes and Smoking Customs of the American Aborigines, Based on Material in the U.S. National Museum. In *Annual Report of the United States National Museum, 1896–1897,* 351–645. United States National Museum, Washington, D.C.

Mouer, L. Daniel

1993 Chesapeake Creoles: The Creation of Folk Culture in Colonial Virginia. In *The Archaeology of Seventeenth-Century Virginia,* edited by Theodore R. Reinhart and Dennis J. Pogue, 105–166. Archaeological Society of Virginia, Richmond.

Myers, Albert Cook (editor)

1912 *Narratives of Early Pennsylvania, West New Jersey, and Delaware, 1630–1707.* Charles Scribner's Sons, New York.

Nassaney, Michael S.

2001 Men and Women, Pipes and Power in Native New England. Paper presented at the annual meeting of the Society for American Archaeology, New Orleans.

Neumann, George C., and Frank J. Kravic

1997 *Collector's Illustrated Encyclopedia of the American Revolution.* Scurlock Publishing Co., Texarkana, Tex.

Noël Hume, Ivor

1969 *A Guide to Artifacts of Colonial America.* Alfred Knopf, New York.

Otto, Martha Potter
1992 A Prehistoric Menagerie: Ohio Hopewell Effigy Pipes. In *Proceedings of the 1989 Smoking Pipe Conference, Selected Papers,* edited by Chares F. Hayes III, Connie Cox Bodner, and Martha L. Sempowski, 1–13. *Research Records No. 22,* Rochester Museum and Science Center, Rochester, N.Y.

Paper, Jordan
1992 The Iroquoian and Pan-Indian Sacred Pipes: Comparative Ritual and Symbolism. In *Proceedings of the 1989 Smoking Pipe Conference: Selected Papers,* edited by Charles F. Hayes III, Connie C. Bodner, and Martha L. Sempowski, 163–170. *Research Records 22,* Rochester Museum and Science Center, Rochester, N.Y.

Philhower, Charles A.
1934 *Indian Pipes and Use of Tobacco in New Jersey.* Archaeological Society of New Jersey Leaflet No. 3.

Pratt, Peter P.
1976 *Archaeology of the Oneida Iroquois, Vol. 1.* Occasional Publications in Northeastern Anthropology, No. 1. Man in the Northeast, George's Mills, N.H.

Robinson, Paul, Marc A. Kelley, and Patricia Rubertone
1991 Preliminary Biocultural Interpretations from a Seventeenth-Century Narragansett Indian Cemetery in Rhode Island. In *Cultures in Contact: The Impact of European Contacts on Native American Cultural Institutions,* A.D. *1000–1800,* edited by William W. Fitzhugh, 119–124. Smithsonian Institution Press, Washington, D.C.

Rumrill, Donald A.
1988 Art Form or Artifact Type. *Bulletin of the New York State Archaeological Association* 96:19–25.

Sempowski, Martha L.
1989 Fluctuations through Time in the Use of Marine Shell on Seneca Iroquois Sites. In *Proceedings of the 1986 Shell Bead Conference, Selected Papers,* edited by Chares F. Hayes III and Lynn Ceci, 81–96. *Research Records No. 20.* Rochester Museum and Science Center, Rochester, N.Y.

Simmons, William S.
1986 *Spirit of the New England Tribes: Indian History and Folklore, 1620–1984.* Univ. Press of New England, Hanover and London.

Springer, James W.
1984 An Ethnohistoric Study of the Smoking Pipe Complex in Eastern North America. *Ethnohistory* 28(3):217–235.

Swanton, John R.
1946 *The Indians of the Southeastern United States.* Bulletin 137. Smithsonian Institution, Bureau of American Ethnology, Washington, D.C.

Tooker, Elisabeth
1964 *An Ethnography of the Huron Indians, 1615–1649.* Smithsonian Institution Bureau of American Ethnology Bulletin 190, Washington, D.C.

Trubowitz, Neal L.
2001 The Sacred and Profane Smoking Pipe: A Reflection of Ethnicity in Eastern North America, A.D. 1500–1850. Lecture presented at the Peabody Museum of Archaeology and Ethnology, April 20, 2001.

Turnbaugh, William A.

1977 Elements of Nativistic Pipe Ceremonialism in the Post-Contact Northeast. *Pennsylvania Archaeologist* 47(4):3–7.

1979 Calumet Ceremonialism as a Nativistic Response. *American Antiquity* 44(4):685–691.

1980 Native American Smoking Pipes. *Archaeology* 33(1):15–22.

1984 Cloudblowers and Calumets. In *Plains Indian Seminar in Honor of Dr. John C. Ewers,* edited by George P. Horse Capture and Gene Ball, 54–72. Buffalo Bill Historical Center, Cody, Wyo.

Veit, Richard, and Charles A. Bello

2001 Tokens of Their Love: Interpreting Native American Grave Goods from Pennsylvania, New Jersey, and New York. *Archaeology of Eastern North America* 29:47–66.

von Gernet, Alexander

1992 Hallucinogens and the Origins of the Iroquoian Pipe/Tobacco/Smoking Complex. In *Proceedings of the 1989 Smoking Pipe Conference,* edited by Charles F. Hayes III, Connie Cox Bodner, and Martha L. Sempowski, 171–182. Research Records No. 22, Rochester Museum and Science Center, Rochester, N.Y.

von Gernet, Alexander, and Peter Timmins

1987 Pipes and Parakeets: Constructing Meaning in an Early Iroquoian Context. In *Archaeology as Long Term History,* edited by Ian Hodder, 31–182. Cambridge Univ. Press, Cambridge.

Williams, Lorraine E., and Karen A. Flinn

1990 *Trade Wampum: New Jersey to the Plains.* New Jersey State Museum, Trenton.

Williams, Roger

1936 *A Key into the Language of America.* Reprint of 1643 edition. Rhode Island and Providence Plantations Tercentenary Commission, Providence.

Willoughby, Charles C.

1935 *Antiquities of the New England Indians.* Harvard Univ., Peabody Museum of Archaeology and Ethnology, Cambridge.

Wray, Charles F.

1964 The Bird in Seneca Archaeology. *Proceedings of the Rochester Academy of Science* 11(1):1–56.

1973 *Manual for Seneca Iroquois Archaeology.* Cultures Primitive, Rochester, N.Y.

Wray, Charles F., Martha L. Sempowski, and Lorraine P. Saunders

1991 *Tram and Cameron, Two Early Contact Era Seneca Sites.* The Charles F. Wray Series in Seneca Archaeology. Vol. 2 , edited by C. F. Hayes III. *Research Records No. 21.* Rochester Museum and Science Center, Rochester, N.Y.

8. The Tudor Rose and the Fleurs-de-lis: Women and Iconography in Seventeenth-Century Dutch Clay Pipes Found in New York City

Diane Dallal

In 1984, nearly ten thousand clay tobacco pipe fragments were recovered from the Broad Financial Center site in lower Manhattan. Five hundred and fifty-two pipes contained distinctive makers' marks that could be attributed to ten cities, regions, or states in four different countries. One of the pipes was marked "IAK" on the base of the heel (Figure 8.1). Bowl morphology and quality of "finish" established that the pipe had been made in Gouda during the late seventeenth century. A search of the literature revealed that only one Gouda pipe maker had used this mark—Suzanna Jacobse circa 1686–1695 (Duco 1981:322). Suzanna Jacobse's pipe was duly noted and described in the site report but ultimately treated as a curiosity (Dallal in Grossman 1985:VII-49).[1] This was the first time a pipe made by a seventeenth-century Dutch woman had been reported at an archaeological site in the United States.

Women have always been active in the pipe-making industry—as wives and widows, as decorators and finishers, as pipe firers and proprietors, and as independent crafts persons. Women manufactured pipes for most of the year while their husbands soldiered and sailed and for all of the year when their husbands died. Women were also represented in the iconography of the pipe as symbols of England, Home, War, and Peace.

This correlation of tobacco, pipes, and pipe making with feminine iconography is striking. The icons speak of the Tudor Rose and the fleurs-de-lis, of pipe makers' wives and "Good Queen Bess." They provide familiar historical, religious, and mythical associations with the Virgin Mary and the Virgin Queen. Fleurs-de-lis

FIG. 8.1. ▸ *Pipe made by Suzanna Jacobse of Gouda, working circa 1686–1695 and marked "IAK." Broad Financial Center site. Courtesy of the South Street Seaport Museum, New York.*

are not simply commonplace decorations but motifs chosen and applied by pipe makers (women and men). Each time one picks up a pipe, women can be heard whispering in the background—in the clay, in the pipe bowls, in the icons, and in the ground.

Pipes exist in at least two dimensions. The first is strictly utilitarian—the pipe is designed to hold tobacco that is then smoked. The second is social—all the relevant variables that enable one to define it as a pipe impart to it a complex social meaning that is interpretable by the maker, the consumer, and the group to which he or she belongs. Smoked or displayed in an emblematic way, pipes can indicate variations in class, ethnicity, and group affiliation (Cook 1989; Dallal 1994). Pipes can also communicate ideological values (Alexander 1986; Reckner 2001). Some marks acknowledge mythical and historical events of the past, and by marking pipes, pipe makers commit buyers to loyalty in the future.

Traditionally, archaeologists have focused on the chronological aspects of clay tobacco pipes. Clay pipes were easily broken, which made their period of utilization short. This made them useful temporal indicators of site occupation periods. Seventeenth-century pipe makers marked their pipes in a distinctive manner, the most common being a tiny icon stamped onto the underside of the heel with a small stamp "engraved in a piece of hard iron and mounted in a wooden handle" (Duco 1980:188). The selection of the mark by the pipe maker was a matter of personal choice. These early makers' marks were nearly invisible; these hidden icons not easily observed. But if the marks were nearly invisible, then to whom were they "speaking"? Perhaps, during this early period, pipe makers in the Netherlands were talking amongst themselves.

The first pipe-making shops in the Netherlands were small cottage industries. According to Duco (1980:416), boys rolled the clay, men did the molding, and women finished and glazed the pipes. If it was a smaller operation, women played a more active role. Pipe makers communally used potters' kilns to fire their pipes, and it is likely that pipes were distinctively marked to differentiate one pipe maker's product from another's in the kiln. Evidence for this kind of behavior has been reported by Buhler-Oppenheim (1971), who documented the use of bread stamps that allowed one's loaves to be distinguished from those of a neighbor in the communal oven.[2]

Makers' marks also derive from numismatic traditions. Some coins from the reign of James I, for example, bear marks and mintmarks identical to the heel marks on pipes (McCashion 1992). And the use of "pellets" (circular bosses or a series of dots in relief) is a borrowed numismatic tradition. These raised dots, called *parelcircels,* or circles of pearls by the Dutch, often surround the heel mark on Dutch pipes. The marks are also similar to tradesmen's tokens, which represented legal currency throughout England circa 1648–1672, more than half a century after the introduction of pipe making (Akerman 1969). The similarity in appearance of tokens and heel marks suggest a tradition and style of marking that was probably based on coins.

Early makers' marks were applied to pipes as signs of authorship, as signs of quality in the tradition of medieval craftsmen (hallmarks), and as signs of group solidarity. When the marks shifted to the bowl in the latter part of the century, they took on an additional function. While maintaining their link with quality and authorship, the "conversation" widened to include the consumer. A purchased item is "consumed in its image" as well as through usage (Barthes 1957: 150). This shift in the placement of the mark signaled a fundamental change in the way business was conducted. The advent of the Dutch pipe makers' guilds and the institution of a formalized pipe market with its institutions of credit (the *pijpenprand)* signified a major transformation in commodity production and in methods of sale. A discussion of this transformation is beyond the scope of this study, however, and will have to await further exploration.

During the seventeenth century, ornamentation was occasionally added to pipe stems, and elaborately decorated "theme" pipes were also manufactured. Pipe makers often stamped their products with their own initials or names or with special (often playful) marks, or with the place of manufacture. These makers' marks can be traced through archival documents to pipe makers who were in business during finite time periods and have been considered the best evidence for "authorship" as defined by Wobst (1977). But therein lies the rub. Makers' marks can only be traced to individuals who owned their own mark.

By the mid-seventeenth century, one earned the right to a maker's mark by serving an apprenticeship of three to four years and,[3] in some cities, by undergoing a Guild examination.[4] A master was legally entitled to open a pipe-making shop *(pijpmakerswinkel)* and to have his own mark(s). These (male) makers' marks have been used to date pipes from archaeological assemblages and the (male) pipe makers' names associated with these marks have been perpetuated in the literature. Thus pipes marked "EB" are said to have been manufactured by Edward Bird despite the fact that others, often family members, were involved in the production sequence. As Rita Wright (1991:199) has concluded about ceramic production, the archaeological literature supports the myth that pipe making "is a male activity" when it is actually an activity conducted by both sexes. Such language in the literature (Duco 1980:200) as "the pipemaker's workshop was also his selling place," or seventeenth century pipemaking shops employed "3–4 men," when women played a key role in the making and selling of pipes, distorts reality and renders women invisible. One such bias relates to the way women were accounted for in historic documents—that is, as nameless widows of named pipe makers: Widow Johannes van Bovene, for example, or Widow Lucas Krijne, if they were mentioned at all. "The civil law tradition operative in the Netherlands, Old and New, mounted numerous barriers for women looking to be active in the wider economy or in the courtroom" (Shaw 2001:10).[5] One legal document, however, cited in Duco (1981:437), alludes to women's importance in the pipe industry while revealing ways in which they were concealed.

In 1662, wheel maker Daniel de Wit petitioned the Leiden Court for permission to open a pipe-making workshop. Arguing that his wife "was familiar with pipe making, having helped her father in his pipe shop for twenty-six years," De Wit reasoned that he could learn pipe making (ostensibly with his wife as teacher) during those periods when he was unemployed and eventually become a pipe maker himself. He asked that his *wife* be allowed to take the guild test. The court was sympathetic and ruled that his wife could open a pipe-making shop,[6] but only with a (male) workman who had already taken and passed the test. This case highlights the restrictions placed on women in the workplace. Superior knowledge and skill did not guarantee a woman entry into the guild or allow her to operate her own pipe-making shop.[7] It also prevented her from owning a maker's mark that might show up three hundred years later at an archaeological site in New York City. This court case, however, also illustrates one way in which these restrictions could be circumvented.

Several kinds of sources were examined to derive the data from which to make inferences about women's actions in the Dutch pipe-making industry. In 1980, pipe historian Don Duco published a treatise on clay pipe manufacturing processes in the Netherlands. In 1981, he published histories of early pipe making industries in towns and cities throughout the Netherlands. Duco's research was based primarily upon marriage, burial and house tax registers, wills, and notary and police administration records, which revealed the names, occupations, and countries of origin of many of the country's first pipe makers. Duco (1978, 1982) also published "guidebooks" that listed and illustrated makers' marks owned and used by pipe makers.[8]

In 1987, Margriet de Roever demonstrated ways in which original Dutch documents such as probate inventories could be used to reconstruct the household and relative wealth of seventeenth-century pipe maker Edward Bird.[9] Duco and de Roever were used to reconstruct the lives of Edward Bird's first and second wives and to further illustrate ways in which women could contribute to the archaeological record yet remain *invisible*.

The other data set was composed of the pipes themselves. Seventeenth-century clay tobacco pipe assemblages from three archaeological sites in New York City were selected for analysis: the Seven Hanover Square site (Rothschild and Pickman 1990), the Stadt Huys Block site at 85 Broad Street (Rothschild, Rockman, and Boesch 1987), and the Broad Financial Center site at 33 Whitehall Street (Grossman 1985). The pipes were used in two ways. First, to determine the kinds of pipes New Yorkers were smoking, and, second, to construct a data set to supply information for the analysis, contextualization, and deconstruction of the iconography of early- to mid-seventeenth-century "Dutch" clay pipes.

Four types of makers' marks and motifs common to early- to mid-seventeenth-century Dutch pipes were selected for analysis. These represented examples of popular makers' marks, motifs, and iconographic "themes" of the time period and represented typical marking locations. The marks and motifs chosen for study included a picture icon located on the underside of the heel (Tudor Rose); a "theme" pipe encompassing the bowl and stem (Sir Walter Raleigh and the crocodile); stem decoration (fleur-de-lis); and a set of initials stamped into the underside of the heel ("EB").

Makers' marks were often *stolen*—that is, plagiarized—suggesting that certain symbols were more *powerful* than others. The Tudor Rose mark, for example, represented a constellation of ideas about *Englishness* and *quality* that were bound up within a tiny icon. The Tudor Rose mark *stylistically* communicated the position of the group—in this case, English pipe makers/foreigners/mercenaries—relative to that of greater Dutch society. It set them apart.

The Tudor Rose

Against the backdrop of the Inquisition, the Dutch war with Catholic Spain, and a reformation movement led by Calvinists and Puritans in the Netherlands, religious refugees, immigrants, and English soldiers introduced pipe making to the Netherlands in the late sixteenth century.[10] They brought with them the "Mistery" and "Art of Makeing Tobacco Pipes" and monopolized the Dutch pipe industry for more than fifty years (Walker 1977:1000; Duco 1981:371, 413).[11] Many soldiers remained in the Netherlands, married, and resumed their former occupations when hostilities ceased. Soldiers supplemented their pay by making pipes while their wives took over when "the men were in the army during spring, summer and autumn" (Duco 1981:408). This suggests that *women* (not men) were making pipes for most of the year and were among the earliest pipe makers in the Netherlands.

The Tudor Rose stamped into the base of the heel was one of the earliest symbols used to mark pipes and during the seventeenth century it was the most popular mark (Duco 1981). The significance of the rose in this context derives from the end of the Wars of the Roses (1485) when the white rose representing the House of York and the red rose of the House of Lancaster were pictorially combined in a single, dual-colored flower, the Tudor Rose (Neubecker 1988:133). To pipe makers/soldiers and refugees who left England for military, economic, or religious reasons, bringing their craft with them to the Netherlands, the Tudor Rose was a symbol of "Good Queen Bess"[12] and an age when smoking and pipe making were free of the harsh restrictions imposed by James I.[13] As English pipe makers came to the Netherlands, the crowned Tudor Rose was transformed into "a symbol for freedom and prosperity" (Duco 1981:397).

What compelled early pipe makers to choose one motif over another? Approximately seventeen pipe makers were working in Amsterdam prior to 1620. Of these, ten were English. The remainder came from northern Germany, an area occupied by Dutch citizens who had fled the Spanish (Duco 1981). In these early years, there appears to have been strong competition among the pipe makers, as is evidenced by the growing number of complaints involving rights to the use of the crowned rose as a symbol to mark pipes. The records of these early pipe makers of Amsterdam are located in the Chapel of the Begijnhof,[14] and the earliest reference (1607) to a pipe maker describes an English printer, William Boseman, who "now maketh tobacco pipes" (Duco 1981:391). Pipe maker Thomas Lourens (Lawrence) of Bedfordshire, England, was also noted when he and his wife, Mercy Fuller, purchased a house they named *"de Engelsche Roos"* (Duco 1981:391).[15] The house name suggests that Thomas and Mercy Lawrence were stamping their pipes with the Tudor Rose mark.

The first Gouda pipe maker was also an Englishman—William Baernelts (Barends), who introduced the crowned Tudor Rose mark to the city in 1617 and is generally credited with its popularity (Duco 1981:413). Evidence of the power of the Tudor Rose mark as a symbol is documented in a series of civil cases that chronicle the contentious bickering over rights to its use. When English soldier/ pipe maker Willem Hoppe used the crowned rose mark in 1625, William Barends signed a formal complaint against him in civil court (Duco 1978:40). When Hoppe returned to army service, his wife, Magdaleentje (now in charge of the business and in defiance of a court order), began to mark her pipes with the crowned rose. She was ordered to delete the rose or the crown to differentiate her pipes from

Barends's products (Duco 1981:414). This implies that in the decades before the formation of the pipe makers' guilds, civic authorities were attempting to regulate the use of makers' marks. Beginning in 1629, a six-guilder fine was instituted for imitating another's mark.

Barends's partner, Willem Flud (William Flood), filed a complaint against another English pipe maker working in Gouda. Robert Jaxon (Jackson) was discovered using the crowned rose mark illegally in 1629. The police confiscated Jackson's pipes and ordered him to use the *uncrowned* rose instead. Flud married his partner's widow, Martintje Jaspers van der Goude, and they continued to use the crowned rose mark while living and working in a house they named *"inde Vergulde Roosen"* (Duco 1978:6, 39; 1981:415).[16] Martintje later married yet a third pipe maker, Jan Jacobs Verheij, and this new domestic partner used the crowned rose mark until his own demise. This sequence of marriages and deaths suggest that the crowned rose mark was the property of Martintje Jaspers-Barends-Flood-Verheij, and it was only through marriage to her that the mark could be legitimately used.

In 1641, pipe makers of Dutch ethnicity attempted to establish a guild in Gouda. The event stressed the growing animosity between two disparate and increasingly antagonistic communities of pipe makers. The Dutch proposed the total exclusion of soldiers from guild membership, from taking apprentices, and from owning workshops (Duco 1981:416). In most cities there was a visible connection between soldiering and the production of pipes; there was also an undercurrent of hostility directed toward foreign mercenaries billeted in towns. In Breda, for example, soldiers who boarded with Govaert Goyaerden, raped his wife and then "smoked tobacco downstairs in her kitchen" (Duco 1981:408). It is hard to determine which was the greater crime, the rape itself or the smoking of tobacco in the kitchen, because laws prohibiting the smoking of tobacco or other weeds were soon enacted in Breda. It would not be surprising if soldiers (that is, foreigners, pipe makers) were associated with smoking and depravity in the national psyche, however.

The wives of approximately fifty English soldier/pipe makers garrisoned near Gouda, however, were vehemently opposed to the establishment of a guild. They argued that the English had brought the pipe industry to Gouda and were responsible for the city's prosperity. They further contended that to deny English soldiers membership in the guild would result in depriving the *women* of their livelihood (Duco 1981:417). Gouda's civic authorities evidently agreed, and the establishment of the Gouda pipe makers' guild was shelved for another twenty years. In this way, the soldiers' wives were responsible for subverting the establishment of the Gouda guild.

Between 1630 and 1660, the number of pipe makers remained relatively constant, although the industry was still dominated by the English, who continued to pour into the Netherlands. Complaints about the unauthorized use of the crowned

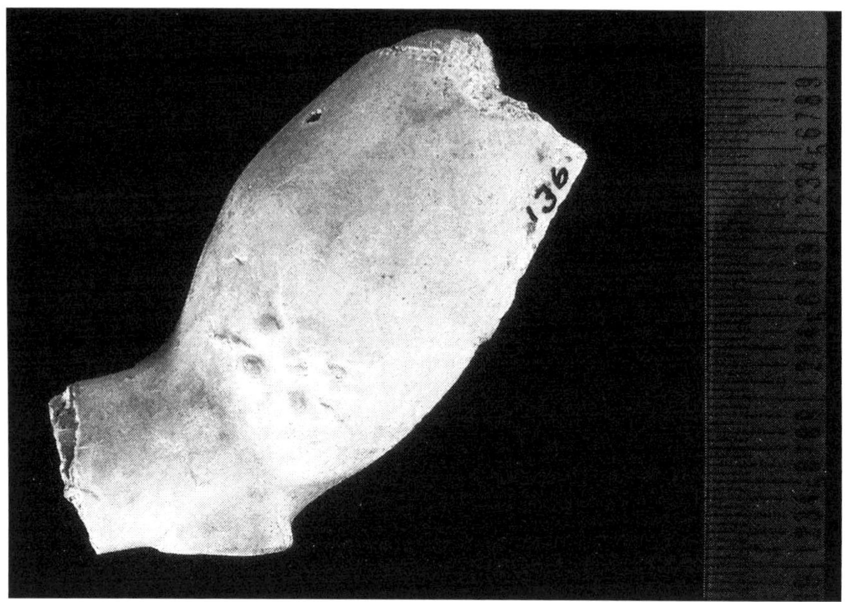

FIG. 8.2. ▸ *Tiny belly bowl decorated on each side with five-petaled rose composed of dots. Made in the western Netherlands circa 1640–1670. Broad Financial Center site. Courtesy of the South Street Seaport Museum, New York.*

rose mark continued unabated. The crowned Tudor Rose "continued to be a symbol for freedom and prosperity" until circa 1660 when English pipe makers were no longer in the majority and the Tudor Rose was supplanted by other marks (Duco 1981:397).

A survey of seventeenth-century pipe assemblages from three archaeological sites in New York City revealed that eighteen pipes marked with the Tudor Rose were recovered during excavations. Three pipes were decorated with a "dotted" Tudor Rose in relief on each side of the bowl, and fifteen were stamped on the base of the heel. This confirms that the Tudor Rose was used as a "trademark" during the seventeenth century as well as a decorative motif.

Three general types of rose marks were recovered at the sites: a rose created from dots in relief on the base of the heel, sometimes with leaves; a Tudor Rose on the base of the heel, sometimes crowned; and a dotted rose in relief on either side of the bowl.

Five pipes marked with the Tudor Rose mark were recovered at the Broad Financial Center site. Four were marked on the base of the heel and a fifth was decorated with a Tudor Rose on either side of the lower portion of the bowl. Three of the four containing the Tudor Rose on the heel were recovered from the cobbled

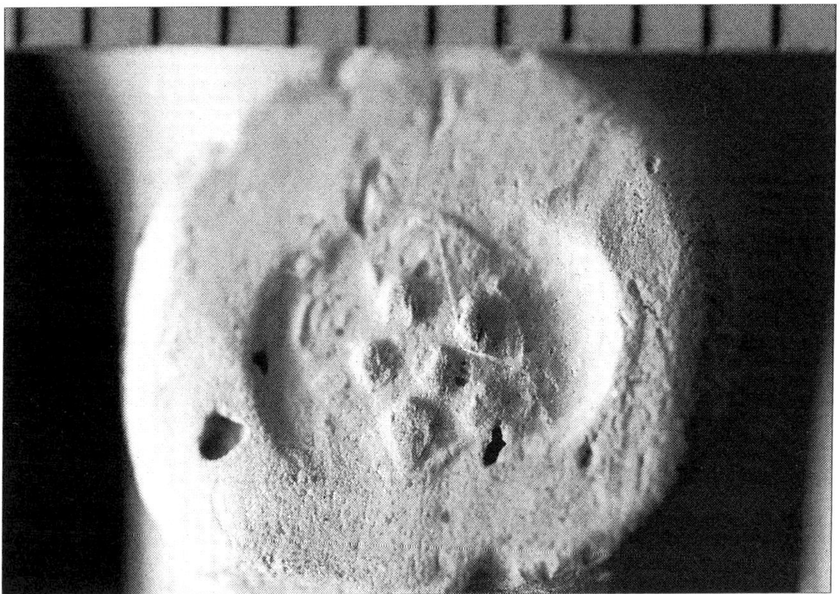

FIG. 8.3. ▸ *Close-up of dotted rose mark on base of heel. Probably made in Amsterdam circa 1640–1660. Broad Financial Center site. Courtesy of the South Street Seaport Museum, New York.*

floor of Augustine Heermans's warehouse built sometime prior to 1651 and predating the establishment of pipe makers' guilds in Holland (Dallal in Grossman 1985:VII-16; Innes 1902). The other examples were recovered from disturbed contexts but ascribed seventeenth-century dates based on their morphology.

The pipes from the cobblestone floor included a tiny belly bowl from the western Netherlands that dated between circa 1640 and 1670 (Figure 8.2). Decorated on each side with a five-petaled rose composed of five dots surrounding a dotted sepal, the stem-bore diameter was 8/64 of an inch. This pipe was similar to several found at the Stadt Huys Block and Seven Hanover Square sites. The second pipe found on the cobblestone floor consisted of a double conical bowl with partial rouletting around the rim and a 7/64-inch stem-bore diameter. The heel mark was nearly illegible and broken but consisted of a portion of a Tudor Rose. The third pipe was completely rouletted, suggesting a higher quality product,[17] while the bowl shape suggested that the pipe had been made in Amsterdam circa 1645–65. It was also apparent that a crowned Tudor Rose had once adorned the broken heel.

A fourth pipe was found in a disturbed context but had all the attributes of a seventeenth-century pipe—that is, a belly bowl of the shape made in Amsterdam between 1640 and 1660, a rouletted rim, and a 7/64-inch bore. A five-petaled

FIG. 8.4. ▸ *Dutch and English Walter Raleigh pipes, circa 1620–1640, from Brongers 1964.*

rose composed of five dots in relief around a dotted sepal was located on the bottom of the heel (Figure 8.3). Leaves surrounded the flower. This mark was identical to one recovered from the Stadt Huys Block site, although the Stadt Huys example was considerably smaller. It is significant that the Stadt Huys Block pipe was recovered from an early- to mid-seventeenth-century ground surface deposit.

The fifth pipe, a double conical bowl made in Amsterdam between 1630 and 1659 (Duco 1981) was also found in a disturbed context but contained a Tudor Rose mark on the heel. It was rim rouletted and had a 7/64-inch bore diameter. The off-center, sloppily applied heel mark consisted of a tiny, dotted five-petaled rose with surrounding leaves and was nearly identical to the one described above.

Eight pipes with Tudor Rose marks were recovered from the Stadt Huys Block site. Two contained bowl marks nearly identical to those described for the Broad Financial Center site (dotted Tudor Roses on either side of the bowl), and six were marked on the base of the heel. Of the heel-stamped pipes, one was recovered from the demolition debris of the most recent structure on the block, the second from a seventeenth-century deposit. Four pipes marked with a Tudor Rose on the heel were recovered from "a late 17th century ground surface" deposit with a *terminus post quem* (TPQ) of 1670 and a Binford (1962) mean date of 1660, based on fifty-one stem-bore diameters. Another came from the "early–

mid 17th ground surface" of Stone Street, one of the earliest paved streets in New Amsterdam (Rothschild, Rockman, and Boesch 1987:314). This pipe, with a 7/64-inch bore diameter, was decorated with a Tudor Rose mark consisting of a five-petaled rose with a large stamen.

Although the TPQ of this deposit was 1670, the pipe mean date was 1654 based on 170 bore diameters (Rothschild, Rockman, and Boesch 1987). Two additional Tudor Rose pipes marked on the heel were recovered from a refilled—that is, disturbed—trench on Stone Street (Rothschild, Rockman, and Boesch 1987: 313). Of these, one consisted of a tiny belly bowl with rouletting around the rim and a 7/64-inch bore diameter. The deeply impressed heel mark was composed of five dots surrounding a dotted stamen. Based upon the shape of the bowl, it is suggested that the pipe was made in Amsterdam circa 1630–1650.

Five pipes with Tudor Rose marks were recovered from the Seven Hanover Square site. All marks were located on the base or underside of the heel. Four of the pipes dated to the seventeenth century, but a fifth, postdated 1739, had an eighteenth-century shape and will not be discussed here. One pipe, recovered from a landfill deposit, was worthy of note. The mark consisted of a Tudor Rose within a beaded circle that had been stamped onto the large, rather square heel of a belly bowl with a 7/64-inch stem bore diameter.[18] The rest of the pipes were identical to those described above.

Walter Raleigh Pipes

The second type of pipe examined in depth was a "theme" pipe known as a "Walter Raleigh" (Figure 8.4). A Walter Raleigh pipe consists of a bowl in the shape of the head of a seventeenth-century gentleman that juts out of the open mouth of a crocodile, which forms the stem. Although the legend that the pipe perpetuates is of unknown origin, several layers of meaning are encapsulated in this small piece of smoking paraphernalia. In brief, Sir Walter Raleigh (brilliant courtier, enemy of Spain, favorite of Queen Elizabeth I, founder of the Virginia colonies, and world-renowned for his nicotine addiction and his shameless promotion of the joys of smoking) falls overboard during a voyage of exploration to South America and is swallowed by a crocodile. Because he reeks of the stench of tobacco, the crocodile spits him out.

The resemblance to the biblical story of "Jonah and the Whale" is unmistakable. Jonah flees from God into exile. While aboard ship, a colossal storm arises. Jonah is blamed for the misfortune and is cast into the sea, where he is swallowed by a whale. The creature spits him out. The similarity of the tales and a review of the pipe literature (Walker 1977; Duco 1981) suggest that Walter Raleigh pipes originated with "Jonah" pipes. There are several ambiguities, however. Although resembling contemporary portraits of Raleigh, the visage on the Walter Raleigh pipe stem, with its long face and pointy beard, might be any well-groomed seventeenth-century gentleman. Duco (1981:381) has pointed out that "in Christian iconography, Jonah is depicted with a beard and a mustache." He is also often represented with a crown of seaweed. Although some early Raleigh pipes bear crowns of seaweed, most crowns have been reduced to a dashed line around the upper part of the bowl (Duco 1981:380). This degeneration of the seaweed crown into a single row of rouletting implies that early Walter Raleigh pipes are derivative of Jonah pipes. The representation of the crocodile on the Walter Raleigh pipe is also ambiguous. The sharp teeth appear to be those of a crocodile but might equally represent those of any toothed whale. Leviathans caught the imagination at the beginning of the seventeenth century, and the story of "Jonah and the Whale" had a resurgence in paintings and tin-glazed earthenware tiles (Duco 1981; Frank 1993). A wide variety of fanciful sea monsters were also represented. Similar to the crocodiles and whales depicted on Raleigh and Jonah pipes, few were realistic or anatomically correct portraits, despite the fact that beached sperm whales and smaller toothed whales had been illustrated in natural history books since the 1550s (Frank 1993). This apparent confusion in depictions of crocodiles and whales may simply be part of an artistic tradition that used the category of "sea monsters" interchangeably.

Several of the crocodiles on Raleigh pipes have forked tongues. To modern observers, the forked tongue is characteristic of a serpent. In seventeenth-century iconography, however, the forked tongue was crudely used to represent the spouting of a whale (Duco 1981:380). "Jonah and the Whale" became a symbol of the Resurrection early in the Christian era (Pierpont Morgan Library 1940–1941). As such, "Jonah became a symbol for help in periods of need and danger," and these nautical and biblical themes of regeneration and rebirth prevailed among sailors and proliferated in port towns (Duco 1981:381). Jonah pipes have been recovered frequently in ports on the Zuiderzee such as Enkhuizen and Hoorn, also the location of some of the earliest pipes in the Netherlands. Plain white pipes were the most common finds, but others had green or yellow lead glazes. They also bore the name "JONAS" or "JONIS" and 1630s dates stamped on the stem (Duco 1981:411). A pipe similar to those found in North America, England, and the Netherlands is currently in the Pritchard Collection at the Bristol City Museum (Walker 1977:20). The bowl is in the shape of a man's head, and the ubiquitous crocodile decorates the stem. The name "JONAS" is inscribed on the left side of the stem, and the date "1638" is inscribed on the right. The superior workmanship of the pipe suggests it is Dutch (Duco 1981). Although identical in appearance to a Walter Raleigh pipe, this example in the Bristol Museum represents Jonah, as is indicated by the name on the stem. What appears to be a crocodile is undoubtedly a whale. The fact that the two "sea monsters" were used interchangeably lends credence to the hypothesis that the story of Raleigh and the crocodile had its origins in the Book of Jonah.

The larger questions remain, however. Why was Sir Walter Raleigh commemorated in this manner, and why were Raleigh pipes popular during the early part of the seventeenth century?

Raleigh's life has been the subject of several excellent biographies (Lacey 1973; Rowse 1962; Thompson 1936), and in brief the facts are these. Walter Raleigh (also spelled Ralegh) was born in Devon circa 1552 and educated at Oxford. He left school to join a band of gentlemen volunteers who were aiding the Huguenots in France and returned to England in 1578 to participate in a voyage to America. Raleigh was summoned to court in 1581 and became a favorite of Queen Elizabeth I. By 1584 he had been knighted.

Raleigh financed several expeditions to the New World. His colonists landed in North Carolina and explored the coastline as far as Florida. He subsequently named the entire region "Virginia" in honor of his patroness. Tobacco was grown commercially in Virginia, and Raleigh's popularization of the herb might have helped Jamestown to survive as a colony. Tobacco steadily gained popular favor under the tolerance of the queen during the Elizabethan reign, and Raleigh was known to have smoked in her presence (Rowse 1962). In 1595 Raleigh made his first unsuccessful voyage to South America in search of El Dorado. It may be here that the origin of the myth began.

If Raleigh was the "patron of smoking," then James I was its antithesis (Rowse 1962:259). Elizabeth's successor hated and feared Raleigh and imprisoned him in the Tower of London for thirteen years. Raleigh was released in 1616 after consenting to lead another expedition in search of the fabled city. He was ordered to avoid confrontation with the Spaniards, but a skirmish ensued that resulted in the death of Raleigh's son. He subsequently returned to England, where he was sentenced to death. Sir Walter Raleigh smoked his last pipe in the Tower of London just prior to his execution in 1618. As might be expected, this flamboyance in the face of death held great appeal and helped perpetuate the myth of the great Sir Walter Raleigh. "This event inspired pro-Tudor pipe makers to raise a monument in memory of Sir Walter, which, although small in size, was so widely spread that it has been preserved to the present day. They made special pipes according to the model of the day but the bowl was in the shape of Sir Walter's face" (Werner 1922:34).

It is interesting in light of Raleigh's relationship with James I that the king was widely regarded as the "snake . . . (who) devoured Tudor power" (Duco 1981: 380). The snake has a forked tongue, and a forked tongue implies duplicity. Sir Walter Raleigh was "swallowed" by James I in the guise of a serpent/crocodile who also swallowed Tudor/Protestant/Raleigh power. If we superimpose Raleigh's relationship with the queen and the tobacco trade and stir in the tale of Jonah and the

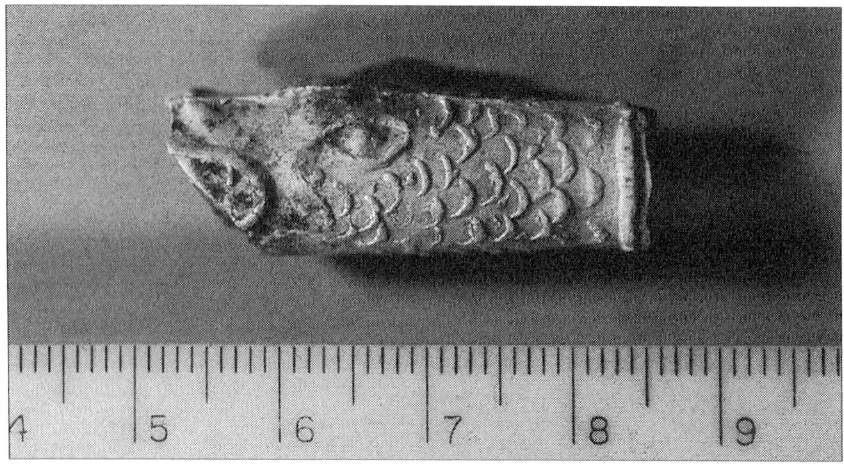

FIG. 8.5. ▸ *Walter Raleigh pipe missing its head. Seven Hanover Square site.*

Whale, it becomes easier to understand how symbolic themes become conflated and transformed into emblems to be carried about, tucked into pockets, and blown in peoples' faces.

Only two Walter Raleigh pipe fragments were found in archaeological assemblages in New York City. One was recovered from the Stadt Huys Block site (Rothschild, Rockman, and Boesch 1987) and the other from the Seven Hanover Square site (Rothschild and Pickman 1990). The single Walter Raleigh stem excavated from the Stadt Huys Block site was 43 mm long, embellished with the wide-open mouth of a crocodile, and had scales, sharp-pointed teeth, and large eyes (Figure 8.5). Raleigh's head is missing. The example from the Seven Hanover Square site was a well-made 35-mm-long fragment decorated with a crocodile's head, scales, sharp teeth, and large eyes. Similar to the first pipe, the head was missing.

The scarcity of Raleigh pipes in New York City is not surprising. They peaked in popularity in port towns along the coast of the Netherlands circa 1630 and diminished after 1640. They were no longer fashionable by the time the Seven Hanover Square, Broad Financial Center, and Stadt Huys Block sites were created. The Tudor Rose, fleur-de-lis, and EB marks had longer life spans. The Seven Hanover Square site, for example, was landfilled beginning in 1687. Although landfill is composed of re-deposited materials and theoretically may contain artifacts from the entire period of colonial settlement, circa 1624 to the date of the landfilling episode, the population of New Amsterdam during the first half of the century was low. Rosenwaike (1972) has estimated the population to be approximately 270 people in 1636. It is therefore expected that artifact density would be also low. Ornately decorated pipes such as the Walter Raleigh were considered kitsch by midcentury and even called "farmer" pipes (Duco 1981:382). The word *farmer* had the same connotation as the word *hick*. In light of these facts, the likelihood of Raleigh pipes reaching New Amsterdam at the height of their popularity was minimal.

Fleurs-de-lis

Fleur-de-lis is the French name for a variety of lily. Although its origin is obscure, the lily is a symbol of purity in Christian iconography (Cirlot 1993). It is the symbol of the Virgin Mary, who, according to legend, sent a lily as a mark of favor to Clovis, king of the Franks, at his baptism (Lillywhite 1972). "The *fleur-de-lys* as the symbol of the Virgin Mary was the chief emblem of the kings of France" (Neubecker 1988:132). Adopted as the heraldic lily on the old royal French coat of arms in the twelfth century, it was incorporated into the English royal insignia circa 1341 when Edward III assumed the throne of France (Neubecker 1988:35). The use of the fleur-de-lis in art as a symbol of the "female principle" is longstanding (Cirlot 1993:189).

There is often a considerable difference between a natural flower and its heraldic representation. "The heraldic lily is constructed symmetrically," three vertical petals bound below midpoint by a horizontal band (Neubecker 1988: 132). Fleur-de-lis marks on pipe stems are customarily situated within a diamond-shaped cartouche. In heraldic terms, this diamond, consisting of a rhombus standing on its point, is called a lozenge (Neubecker 1988:46). Western European heraldic tradition calls for a woman's arms (specifically spinsters and widows) to be represented on a lozenge instead of a shield.[19] The shield was used in war and therefore peculiar to men. It is clearly the representation of the man's right to bear arms and to be the bearer and defender of his lineage. Women, who did not inherently have the right to bear arms, used the lozenge instead. The side panels of a triptych by the Dutch painter Lucas van Leydan, for example, illustrate a young woman carrying "the lozenge shield customary for her sex in the Netherlands" (Neubecker 1988:234–235).

But why the lozenge shape? It is likely that the elongated shape of the lozenge is an allusion to the spindle or distaff, generally associated with women (Pimbley 1908). According to Cirlot (1993:194), the lozenge shape represents "the intercommunication between the inferior and the superior." The lozenge and the shield signify man's relationship to woman and define their separate spheres. Fleur-de-lis motifs on seventeenth-century pipe stems are confined by the lozenge, the shape in heraldry, traditionally confined to women.

"Everywhere, creative elements are transforming signs, changing their meanings slightly or radically, and thus creating new systems of order" (Buhler-Oppenheim 1971:8). Alfred Dunhill (1925 in Tatman 1985:369–371) has suggested that certain pipe makers might have adapted the fleur-de-lis "symbol to idealize tobacco plants." The similarity of the lily to the flower of the tobacco plant lends credibility to such a hypothesis. A transformation of the lily into a tobacco flower is conceivable given the long association of the fleur-de-lis with Catholicism and France, those hereditary enemies of Protestant England and Holland—the bastions of the burgeoning clay pipe industry. The transformation of the fleur-de-lis can be explained, in part, as an attempt to reduce the hostile symbolism associated with this motif. The association of tobacco with Queen Elizabeth, during whose reign tobacco gained popular favor, is another.

If we accept that the fleur-de-lis (a symbol of the "female principle") was transformed by (English) pipe makers into a sign for tobacco, while remaining mindful that the fleur-de-lis is both a symbol of royalty and purity, we can superimpose Elizabeth Tudor (the "Virgin Queen") who is female, royal, "pure," and associated (in fact and fictional contexts) with the rise of tobacco, the source of all pipe makers' livelihoods. There are only two heraldic blooms—the lily and the rose. Similar to the Tudor Rose mark, which represented memories of England and home, freedom and prosperity to English pipe makers in Holland, it is reasonable to assume that the fleur-de-lis marks on the long stems of pipes reflected those same inchoate yearnings.

It is likewise intriguing that pipe decoration has traditionally been women's work (Duco 1980). The most popular stem motif during the seventeenth century was the fleur-de-lis circumscribed by the lozenge. Female pipe decorators main-

TABLE 8.1 ▸ Breakdown of Fleur-de-lis Types

Type	Description
Type 1	Single plain *fleur-de-lis*
Type 2	Single *fleur-de-lis* within a beaded lozenge
Type 3	Single *fleur-de-lis* associated with other motifs
Type 4	Multiple, scattered *fleur-de-lis* in a linear pattern
Type 5	Four-in-diamond—i.e., four separate *fleur-de-lis*, each within its own separate lozenge and together composing one large lozenge filled with *fleur-de-lis*
Type 6	Other multiple patterns
Type 7	*Fleur-de-lis* with radiating lines, enclosed within a lozenge
Type 8	Four-in-diamond within a double outlined lozenge and triangular-shaped points radiating outward from the outside of the lozenge

TABLE 8.2 ▸ Breakdown of Fleur-de-lis Types by Site

Type	7 Hanover Square	Stadt Huys	Broad Financial Center
1	16	24	37
2	0	6	30
3	5	3	0
4	7	11	4
5	63	34	22
6	9	22	0
7	0	0	4
8	0	0	4
9	56	127	27

tained this stylistic tradition of repetitive rows of lilies on the stems of pipes for nearly a century (Duco 1980). The fleur-de-lis, therefore, has a long tradition of association with women—as a symbol of the Virgin Mary and the Virgin Queen, emblazoned on the lozenge representing a woman's lineage, and as an expression of women's handiwork.

Although the archaeological literature (Duco 1981; McCashion 1979; Oswald 1960, 1961; Walker 1977) described a fluorescence of fleurs-de-lis and other stem decorations at the beginning of the seventeenth century that all but disappeared by the century's close, the archaeological evidence indicated that the fleur-de-lis retained its popularity in New Amsterdam/New York throughout the entire seventeenth century (Dallal 1995). It is possible that merchants were unloading older or unsalable pipes on the colonies.

The fleurs-de-lis marks from the Stadt Huys Block, Seven Hanover Square, and Broad Financial Center sites were divided into eight categories based upon Bradley and De Angelo's (1981) fleur-de-lis typology, which was then expanded (Dallal 1995). All fleurs-de-lis were enclosed within lozenge-shaped cartouches. A brief description of the various motifs is shown in Table 8.1. Table 8.2 shows the types and percentages of this motif by site.

The Seven Hanover Square Block site sample consisted of fifty-six stems decorated with fleurs-de-lis marks, the majority (63 percent) of which consisted of Type 5 (thirty-six), the four-in-diamond motif (Figure 8.6). A large proportion of stems contained a band(s) of rouletting as an additional design element (Figure 8.7). Sixteen percent of the stems were examples of the Type 1 motif, the single plain lily (Figure 8.8); 5 percent were Type 3, the lily associated with other motifs (Figure 8.9); 7 percent were Type 4, multiple, scattered lilies in a row (Figure 8.10); and 9 percent were Type 6 (not illustrated). Types 2, 7, and 8 were not present at the site. Stem bores measured 5/64" through 8/64", with nearly half (48 percent)

FIG. 8.6. ▸ *(Left) Close-up of four-in-diamond fleur-de-lis, Type 5. Note lozenge-shaped cartouche. Broad Financial Center site. Courtesy of the South Street Seaport Museum, New York.*

FIG. 8.7. ▸ *(Right) Four-in-diamond cartouche with tiny fleurs-de-lis and bisected by lines of rouletting. Broad Financial Center site. Courtesy of the South Street Seaport Museum, New York.*

having a 7/64" bore diameter and 23 percent having a 6/64" bore. The majority of stems in the landfill (deposited beginning circa 1687) were Type 5, while those in river bottom deposits were Type 1. The sample was too small, however, to be of significance.

A total of 127 stems were decorated with fleurs-de-lis motifs at the Stadt Huys Block site. Of these, 24 percent were Type 1, 6 percent Type 2 (Figure 8.11), 3 percent Type 3, and 11 percent Type 4. Similar to the Seven Hanover Square site, the majority (34 percent) was decorated with the four-in-diamond motif (Type 5). Type 6 constituted 22 percent of the sample, and Types 7 and 8 were not present. The majority (35 percent) was associated with the Lovelace Tavern, and Type 5 was the most predominant style found in these Tavern deposits. Types 1, 4, and 6 were also prevalent. Thirty-one percent of the pipes decorated with fleur-de-lis were excavated from the trenches beneath Stone Street. Of these, Type 1, the single plain fleur-de-lis, was most prevalent with Type 6, consisting of other multiple patterns, close behind.

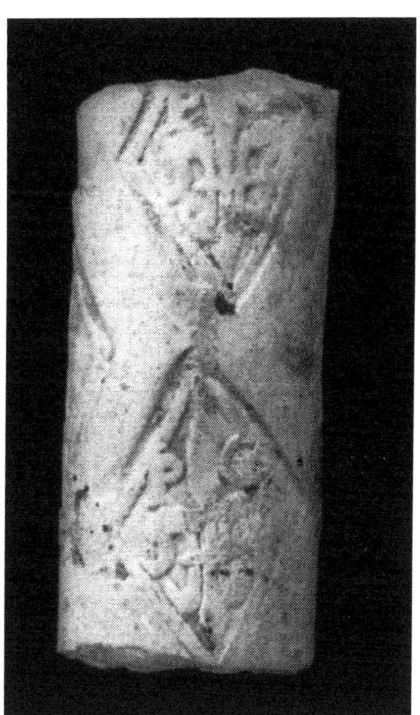

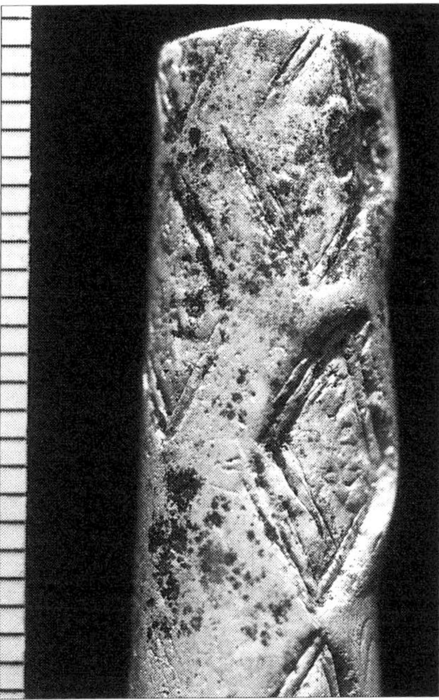

FIG. 8.11. ▸ *Type 2 motif, linear pattern fleurs-de-lis in beaded lozenges. Broad Financial Center Site. Courtesy of the South Street Seaport Museum, New York.*

The Broad Financial Center site sample consisted of twenty-seven stem fragments. Thirty-seven percent were Type 1, 30 percent Type 2, 22 percent Type 5, and 4 percent each of Types 4, 7, and 8. Types 3 and 6 were not extant. The majority of the decorated stems were recovered from deposits associated with the mid-seventeenth-century occupation of the block, and there was no correlation between type and date of deposit. The sample was too small.

"EB" Pipes

The last mark examined in detail was an initial mark. By the mid-seventeenth century, three large pipe-making shops were operating in Amsterdam. One of these concerns was owned and operated by Edward Bird (Evert Burt), an English pipe maker from Surrey, and his wife, Aeltje Govaert.[20] Pipes from the Bird workshop have been recovered in quantity from sites associated with the Dutch occupation of New York (Dallal in Grossman 1985; Huey 1985; Dallal 1995; McCashion 1979), suggesting that Bird and his wife were working "for one or more large pipe merchants who exported pipes to many countries" (Duco 1981:399). As a master pipe maker and owner of his own shop, Bird was entitled to his own mark. If, as Duco (1980:200) suggests, the whole of the master's workforce lived under his roof as a family, it is logical to assume that Bird and his wife provided for their general welfare. With apprentices at least, this would have been in the form of food, clothing, education, instruction in the craft, and a salary (Walker 1977). In addition to working in the shop, Aeltje Govaert would have been in charge of the household as well as her children.[21]

Aeltje Govaert died at the age of forty in December 1658 and left a large inheritance that included real estate (de Roever 1987:56). Her only surviving child was thirteen years old. Six months after her death, Edward Bird married Anna Maria van der Heijden of Oudewater, "widow of Jeremias Lugin" (de Roever 1987:56). We will assume that his new wife's tasks were identical to her predecessor's.

When she lost a child in infancy in 1664, Bird added a codicil to his will giving Anna Maria the right to live in a house he had purchased on one of the canals many years earlier (de Roever 1987). Edward Bird died in 1665. From an inventory of his possessions (see de Roever 1987:57), we learn that he lived and worked in a double house on the Rozengracht with living quarters in one half and a workshop in the other. In the living area, "besides furniture and tableware, there was a fine cabinet with silver. There were fifteen paintings and prints on the walls, including portraits of Bird, his first wife, and his son, as well as two small paintings of deceased infants in the attic" (de Roever 1987:57). Bird also owned books, including an English Bible, suggesting that he was literate. The workshop area consisted of "a small kitchen with a bed and blankets, the front workshop, the rear workshop, a shed, and a clay shed" (de Roever 1987:57).

Evert Bird, the only surviving son, inherited the business and remained a pipe maker until 1683 (de Roever 1987:58). He called his business "the Rose," suggesting that he identified with his English paternal heritage and used the Tudor Rose to mark at least some of his products. The presence of EB pipes in post-1665 contexts in New York City also implies that Evert Bird used the "EB" mark. Adriaen Van der Cruis, a pipe merchant who contracted others to make pipes that were then exported to North America and elsewhere, owned the mark by 1672 (Duco 1981).

Evert Bird's stepmother moved to the house on the Eglantiersgracht, the one provided for in her husband's will. She remarried in 1668. Anna Maria van der Heijden's new husband was Hendrik Gerdes from Wedel, a thirty-six-year-old *suikerbakker* who soon appeared in the records as a pipe maker (de Roever 1987) (Figure 8.12).[22] Through his marriage to Anna Maria, Gerdes acquired a burghership as well as a new trade. It is noteworthy that pipes marked "HG" and "EB" have been discovered in the same seventeenth-century deposits at New York archaeological sites (Dallal in Grossman 1985; McCashion 1979). This suggests that Anna Maria van der Heijden maintained her association with the merchants who were central to the shipping of Edward Bird's products to America. EB and HG pipes are associated not only in time and stratigraphy but also by the woman who was married to both men yet remains invisible in the artifact record.

Fig. 8.12. ▸ *"HG" mark. Hendrik Gerdes of Amsterdam (working circa 1668–1684) married the widow of Edward Bird.*

Pipes made in the workshop of Edward Bird (1630–1665, or possibly his son, widow, or pipe makers working for Adriaen Van der Cruis to 1683) and marked "EB" on the base of the heel were the most abundant of the initial-marked pipes recovered from deposits associated with the Dutch colonial and early English occupation periods of New York City. One hundred thirty-four EB pipes were recovered from three archaeological sites that made up the sample. The archaeological evidence revealed that the Bird workshop produced several styles of pipe and at least eight variations of the EB mark. No correlation could be found linking specific stylistic attributes—that is, bowl morphology, quality (finish), or bore diameter size—with any of the specific EB mark variations. Neither was there a correlation between the type of EB mark and the date of deposit. It should be emphasized, however, that pipes are relatively fragile and usually fragmentary when found. Archaeologists may recover only a heel stamped "EB" and a bit of the stem. It is difficult, then, to correlate bowl style with a maker's mark, especially when the sample is comparatively small. It should be mentioned, however, that Huey (1985) had greater success correlating EB marks with specific date ranges when he attempted a chronological analysis of EB pipes at the Fort Orange site in Albany, New York. Huey found that beaded EB pipes (Figure 8.13) were recovered from strata dating circa 1650–1664, while plain EB pipes (Figure 8.14) were recovered from strata dating circa 1647–1676. The EB mark in concentric circles (Figure 8.15) dated circa 1650–1664, and the EB mark surrounded by sunbursts or cogwheels dated circa 1640–1647 (Figure 8.16). However, neither the crowned EB nor the EB with dots between the letters was recovered at Fort Orange.

As can be seen in Table 8.3, the predominant mark at the Seven Hanover Square and Broad Financial Center sites was the beaded EB, which consisted of the pipe maker's initials surrounded by a circle of pearls or beads. The plain, unadorned EB mark was most frequent at the Stadt Huys Block site.

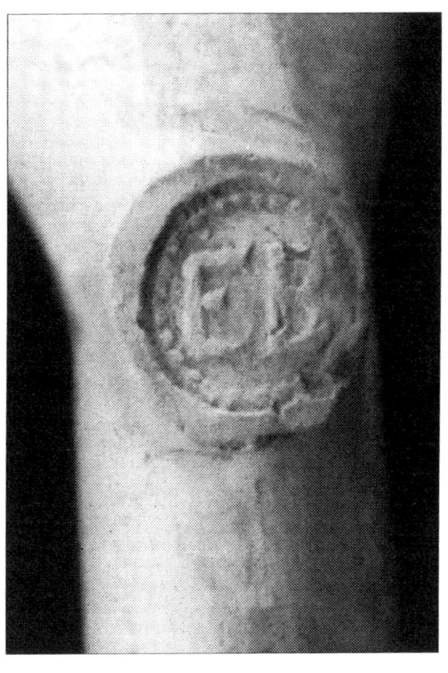

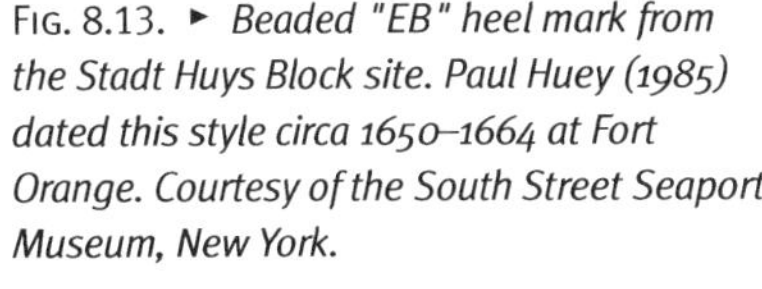

Fig. 8.13. ▸ *Beaded "EB" heel mark from the Stadt Huys Block site. Paul Huey (1985) dated this style circa 1650–1664 at Fort Orange. Courtesy of the South Street Seaport Museum, New York.*

Fig. 8.14. ▸ *Plain "EB" mark from the Broad Financial Center site. Huey (1985) dated these marks circa 1647–1676 at Fort Orange. Courtesy of the South Street Seaport Museum, New York.*

Fig. 8.15. ▸ *"EB" mark in concentric circles from the Broad Financial Center site. Dated circa 1650–1664 at Fort Orange (Huey 1985). Courtesy of the South Street Seaport Museum, New York.*

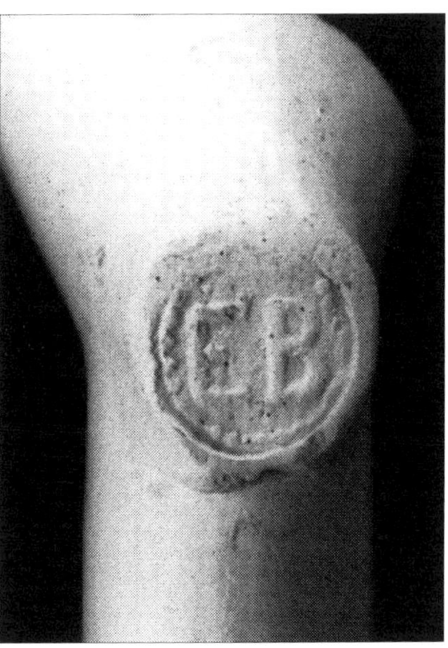

Fig. 8.16. ▸ *"EB" mark within cogwheel from the Seven Hanover Square Site. Dated circa 1640–1647 at Fort Orange (Huey 1985). Courtesy of the South Street Seaport Museum, New York.*

TABLE 8.3 ▸ EB Pipes from All Sites by Type

Type	7 Hanover Square	Stadt Huys	Broad Financial Center
Beaded	55 (71%)	6 (17%)	13 (62%)
Plain	10 (13%)	21 (62%)	3 (14%)
Concentric circles	4 (5%)	2 (6%)	4 (19%)
Dot	1 (1%)	0%	0%
Crown	5 (6%)	5 (17%)	0%
Cogwheel or sunburst	2 (3%)	0%	0%
Beaded and sunburst	0%	0%	1 (5%)
Crown and beaded	1 (1%)	0%	0%

Women in the Industry and Conclusions

Intensive research by Duco (1978, 1981), Laansma (1977), and de Roever (1987) made it possible to identify the names of twenty-seven women involved in the seventeenth-century Netherlands' pipe industry (Table 8.4). A twenty-eighth woman was noted by Duco (1981:447), but her identity was unknown. This total did not include the anonymous soldier/pipe makers' wives of Gouda in 1641 or the nameless daughters, wives, relatives, and servants working alone or in shops around the country. It is significant that several women were described as *baas,* a Dutch term that developed into the word "boss" but also meant "master." Others were noted as *zelfstandig,* or "independent," meaning that they were not in the employ or service of anyone else and were working for themselves (Gehring 2002; Jacobs 2002).

It is important that we recognize the enormity of the contribution of women who have been underrepresented in the written record. Women manufactured pipes, decorated, burnished, and sold them, and were symbolically represented in the icons and makers' marks. As we gaze at Walter Raleigh pipes, we acknowledge his debt to the queen. While studying clay pipe production methods, we can ponder the curious term *Kleimeter* (clay godmother), theoretically a job description for a male but which loosely translates as the person who watches over the clay, tends it, cares for it, nurtures it—a traditionally feminine role (Duco 1980). The primary relationship between the Old World and the New was mercantile, and the invisibility of women has virtually excluded them from any serious economic study outside of the domestic sphere. This study shows that women were participants in the emerging industries of the Old World that made a significant contribution to transatlantic trade.

TABLE 8.4 ▸ Women Working in the Seventeenth-Century Dutch Pipe Industry

Name	Document Dates	Job Notes	Maker's Mark	Comments	Reference
Anonymous	1636	Female tobacco-pipe maker		"at the *Pesten Gasthuis*" (Guesthouse); Zwolle	Duco 1981:447
Andriesz., wife of Daniel	1628	Crowned star		Gouda	Duco 1981:414
Arents, Pietie	1688				Duco 1981:445
Ariensz., widow Simon	1686–1701+	Worked in the business until after 1701		Widow of Frans. Andriesz.; Schoonhoven; Gouda	Duco 1981:316
Basen, Dieuwerie	1668	*Baas* (master or boss)		Gouda	Duco 1978:37; 1981:317
Derx., Geesgen	1662–1672	*Pijpenbakster* (woman pipe firer)		She is a pipe maker and also has her own kiln; Zwolle	Duco 1981:447
Dongen, Lijsbeth	1668–1670	*Baas*		Gouda	Duco 1981:319
Fieler, Anneken	ca. 1636	Inherited first husband's workshop		First husband was Nicolaes Fieler; Schiedam. Then marriedThomas Poostelwith, who becamea pipe maker.	Duco 1981:443

TABLE 8.4 ▸ Women Working in the Seventeenth-Century Dutch Pipe Industry (continued)

Name	Document Dates	Job Notes	Maker's Mark	Comments	Reference
Gerrit, Antie	ca. 1652	Pipemaker with husband Jan Moseliin	I probably 1M	Leewarden	Duco 1981:431–432
Goude, Martin* van der	pre-1625 to after 1638		crowned Tudor Rose	She married pipe makers William Berends, William Flood, and Jan Jacobs. Verheij; Gouda	Duco 1981:414–415
Govaert, Magdalena	before + 1658	Pipemaker; had her own factory		Sister-in-law of Edward Bird; Amsterdam	De Roever 1987:54, 56
Gravier, wife of Jan	ca. 1699–1706			Ran forty-person workshop in Doornik when husband went to Gent to open another shop	Duco 1981:412
Jacobse, Suzanna	c.1686–1695	*Zelfstandig* (independent)	IAK	Gouda Wife of Will em Hoppe; she used the mark illegally; Gouda	Duco 1981:322
Jacobs, Magdaleentje	ca, 1628		crowned Tudor Rose		Duco 1978:6
Jans, Marrigie	until 1705			Widow of Cornelis Pau!us Baeck; Gouda	Duco 1981:322

TABLE 8.4 ▸ Women Working in the Seventeenth-Century Dutch Pipe Industry (continued)

Name	Document Dates	Job Notes	Maker's Mark	Comments	Reference
Jongeian, Widow van	1668	*Baas; zelfstandig*			Duco 1978:42; 1981:322
Maertens, Aegie	from 1679	*Baas*		From 1679 she is *baas* because her husband Jan Gerritz. is at sea; Gouda	Duco 1978:40
Philipszn., wife of Pieter	1670	Sold the shop		Gouda	Duco 1978:43; 1981:325
Pieters, Liisbeth	1628			Lived or worked near pipemllker Willel11 Flood; Gouda	Duco 1978:43
Pieters, Nanne	1686–1712	*Baas*	N	Gouda	Duco 1981:325
Proost, Widow Thie! (Ghiel) Jansz.	1670	*Baas*		Business run by widow from 1670 on. Between 1652–1665, husband was *baas;* Gouda	Duco 1978:43
Rase, Dieuwertje	1670	*Baas*	IW	Widow Willem Tin; prior to 1670, he was *zelfstandig;* Gouda	Duco 1978:43-44
Theunis, Soetie	1686–1691		AI	Gouda	Duco 1981:327

TABLE 8.4 ▸ Women Working in the Seventeenth-Century Dutch Pipe Industry (continued)

Name	Document Dates	Job Notes	Maker's Mark	Comments	Reference
Thonis, Rebecca	1653	*Toebacxpijpe-maeckster (female pipe maker)*		Her factory closed prior to 1660; Amersfoort	Duco 1981:390
Waniaert, Meiisgie	1641			Leiden	Duco 1981:330
Willems, Franchitje (Widow Barent Cornelisz. Hopman)	ca. 1645		crowned marigold?	Gouda	Duco 1978:10
Wit, wife of Daniel de	ca. 1662	She was the experienced pipe maker.		Husband was a wheel maker; Leiden	Duco 1981:436-437
Wittjes, Widow Joost van	1668–1670	*Baas*		Gouda	Duco 1978:45; 1981:328

Notes

1. Duco (1981:322, 323) mentions that she was *Zelfstandig,* or independent.

2. This behavior has been documented in Greece, Italy, Spain, and Switzerland.

3. Until recently, it was believed that only male children could be pipe makers' apprentices, although daughters, wives, and servants often worked in the shop. Alison Bell (1992:61), however, using data from Oswald (1975), has documented six female apprentices in England between 1667 and 1756. Female apprentices have not been recorded in the Netherlands, however.

4. The applicant was required to create a number of perfect pipes from a specified number of rolls of clay.

5. Although civil inheritance laws treated women more equitably in the Netherlands, inheriting a piece of property did not mean that an heiress controlled her inheritance (Shaw 2001:10).

6. Her name is not mentioned in Duco (1980:200); perhaps it is not mentioned in the legal brief, either.

7. Women could become members of the guild if they were widows or inherited a business of renown and were unmarried (Duco, personal communication 2001).

8. Laansma (1977) also published a list of pipe makers working between 1724 and 1865.

9. Bird was working in Amsterdam 1630–1665.

10. English soldiers were dispatched by Elizabeth I to serve in the armies of Prince Maurice of Nassau during the Dutch struggle against Spanish occupation (Duco 1981:371).

11. *De wetenschap van Tabackpijpmaken* (the science of pipemaking) (Duco 1981:393).

12. Elizabeth Tudor.

13. James I published his "Counterblaste to Tobacco" in 1604. According to this Royal, smoking was a "custom loathsome to the eye, hateful to the nose, harmful to the brain, (and) dangerous to the lungs" (quoted in Werner 1922:63).

14. Founded by English immigrants in the Netherlands in 1607 (Haley 1972).

15. The English Rose.

16. In the Gilded Rose.

17. It was more time consuming to carefully apply the rouletting around the entire rim than it was to apply it haphazardly.

18. In Dutch, a *parelcircel,* or circle of pearls.

19. Unmarried daughters bear their paternal arms on a lozenge. When married, the woman shares the shield of her husband. If widowed, this shield is placed on a larger lozenge.

20. Aeltje's sister Margaretha was a pipe maker in her own right and owned her own "factory" (de Roever 1987; Duco 1978). This suggests that Bird's wife might have come from a family of pipe makers and was familiar with pipe-making technology.

21. Between 1632 and 1662 she gave birth to eleven children, ten of whom died young or in infancy (Duco 1981:399).

22. Hendrik Gerdes might have been a sugar refiner, but it is more likely that he worked for one of the large industrial potteries that manufactured ceramic molds used for "baking" loaves of sugar (Van Dongen, personal communication 1994).

References Cited

Akerman, John Yonge

1969 *Tradesmen's Tokens Current in London and Its Vicinity between the Years 1648 and 1672.* Reprinted. Burt Franklin, New York. Originally published 1849, London.

Alexander, L. T.

1986 Clay Pipes with Irish Affiliations. In *Historic Clay Tobacco Pipe Studies,* vol. 3, edited by Byron Sudbury, 69–75. Ponca City, Okla.

Barthes, Roland

1957 La Nouvelle Citroen. In *Mythologies,* edited by Roland Barthes, 191–247. Editions du Seuil, Paris.

Bell, Alison

1992 Widows, Free Sisters, and "Independent Girls": Female Pipemakers in Great Britain, 1640–1920." Paper written for a course in Material Culture, Boston Univ.

Binford, Lewis R.

1962 A New Method of Calculating Dates from Kaolin Pipe Stem Samples. *Southeastern Archaeological Conference Newsletter* 9:19–21.

Bradley, James, and Gordon De Angelo

1981 European Clay Pipe Marks from Seventeenth Century Onondaga Iroquois Sites. *Archaeology of Eastern North America* 9:109–133.

Brongers, George A.

1964 *Nicotiana Tabacum: The History of Tobacco and Tobacco Smoking in the Netherlands.* Joh. Enschede En Zonen, Haarlem.

Buhler-Oppenheim, Kristin

1971 *Zeichen, Marken, Zinken/Signs, Brands, Marks.* Hastings House, New York.

Cirlot, J. E.

1993 *Dictionary of Symbols.* Originally translated by Jack Sage in 1971. Barnes and Noble, New York.

Cook, Lauren J.

1989 Tobacco-Related Material and the Construction of Working-Class Culture. In *Interdisciplinary Investigations of the Boot Mills, Lowell Massachusetts,* edited by Mary C. Beaudry and Stephen A. Mrozowski, 209–230. *The Boarding House System as a Way of Life,* vol. 3, Cultural Resources Management Study No. 21. U.S. Dept. of the Interior, Washington, D.C.

Dallal, Diane

1994 The Pipe Transcendent: A Contextual Analysis of Smoking Pipes from Working-Class Privies in Wilmington, Delaware. Paper presented at the Annual Meeting of the Society for Historical Archaeology, Vancouver, B.C.

1995 “The People May Be Illiterate but They Are Not Blind”: A Study of the Iconography of Seventeenth Century Dutch Clay Tobacco Pipes Recovered from New York City’s Archaeological Sites. Unpublished master’s thesis, Dept. of Anthropology, New York Univ.

Dallal, Diane

1985 Clay Pipes. In *The Excavation of Augustine Heermans’ Warehouse and Associated Seventeenth Century Dutch West India Company Deposits: The Broad Financial Center Mitigation Final Report,* by Joel W. Grossman, vol. 2, VII-1-82. Prepared for HRO International, Ltd., New York, by Greenhouse Consultants, New York.

de Roever, Margriet

1987 The Fort Orange “EB” Pipe Bowls: An Investigation of the Origin of American Objects in Dutch Seventeenth-Century Documents. In *New World Dutch Studies: Dutch Arts and Culture in Colonial American, 1606–1776,* edited by Roderic H. Blackburn and Nancy A. Kelly, 51–61. Albany Institute of History and Art, Albany.

Duco, D. H.

1978 *Goudse Pijpen.* Privately printed, Amsterdam.

1980 Clay Pipe Manufacturing Processes in Gouda, Holland: A Technical and Historical Review. In *The Archaeology of the Clay Tobacco Pipe IV: Europe 1, Part 1,* edited by Peter Davey, 179–217. British Archaeological Reports International Series 92, Oxford.

1981 The Clay Tobacco Pipe in Seventeenth Century Netherlands. In *The Archaeology of the Clay Tobacco Pipe V: Europe 2, Part 2,* edited by Peter Davey, 111–468. British Archaeological Reports International Series 106(ii), Oxford.

1982 *Merken van Goudse Pijpenmakers, 1660–1940.* Uitgeversmaatschappij De Tijdstroom B.V., Lochem.

Dunhill, Alfred

1925 *The Pipe Book.* Black, London.

Frank, Stuart M.

1993 *Delftware: Dutch and Flemish Faience in the Kendall Whaling Museum.* Kendall Whaling Museum, Sharon, Mass.

Grossman, Joel W.

1985 *The Excavation of Augustine Heermans’ Warehouse and Associated Seventeenth Century Dutch West India Company Deposits: The Broad Financial Center Mitigation Report.* Report on file with the New York City Landmarks Preservation Commission.

Harrington, J. C.

1994 Dating Stem Fragments of Seventeenth and Eighteenth Century Clay Tobacco Pipes. *Quarterly Bulletin, Archeological Society of Virginia* 9:9–13.

Haley, K. H. D.

1972 *The Dutch in the Seventeenth Century.* Harcourt Brace Jovanovich, New York.

Huey, Paul R.

1985 Archaeological Excavations in the Site of Fort Orange, a Dutch West India Company Trading Fort Built in 1624. In *New Netherlands Studies: An Inventory of Current Research and Approaches,* Bulletin KNOB, 84:70–72. Bohn, Scheltema and Holkema, Amsterdam.

Innes, J. H.

1902 *New Amsterdam and Its People.* Charles Scribner's Sons, New York.

Laansma, S.

1977 *Pijpmakers en Pijpmerken, 1724–1865.* Gysbers en Van Loon, Arnhem, Netherlands.

Lacey, Robert

1973 *Sir Walter Ralegh.* Athenum, New York.

Lillywhite, Bryant

1972 *London Signs: A Reference Book of London Signs from Earliest Times to About the Mid-Nineteenth Century.* George Allen & Unwin, London.

McCashion, John

1979 A Preliminary Chronology and Discussion of Seventeenth and Early Eighteenth Clay Tobacco Pipes from New York State Sites. In *The Archaeology of the Clay Tobacco Pipe II: The U.S.A.,* edited by Peter Davey, 63–149. British Archaeological Reports International Series 60, Oxford.

1992 The Clay Tobacco Pipes of New York State (Part IV). *The Bulletin: Journal of the New York State Archaeological Association* 103 (spring):1–9.

Neubecker, Ottfried

1979 *A Guide to Heraldry.* McGraw Hill, New York.

1988 *Heraldry: Sources, Symbols, and Meaning.* Macdonald, London.

Oswald, Adrian

1960 The Archaeology and Economic History of English Clay Tobacco Pipes. *Journal of the British Archaeological Association* 23:40–42.

1961 The Evolution and Chronology of English Clay Tobacco Pipes. *Archaeological News Letter* 7:55–62.

1975 *Clay Pipes for the Archaeologist.* British Archaeological Reports No. 14, Oxford, England.

Pierpont Morgan Library

1940–1941 *The Animal Kingdom: An Exhibition of Manuscript Illuminations, Book Illustrations, Drawings, Cylinder Seals, and Binders.* Pierpont Morgan Library, New York.

Pimbley, Arthur Francis

1908 Publisher unknown, Maryland. Online version by James P. Wolf on http://www.digiserve.com.

Reckner, Paul

2001 Negotiating Patriotism at the Five Points: Clay Tobacco Pipes and Patriotic Imagery among Trade Unionists and Nativists in a Nineteenth-Century New York Neighborhood. In *Historical Archaeology* 35(3):103–114.

Rosenwaike, Ira

1972 *Population History of New York City.* Syracuse Univ. Press, Syracuse, New York.

Rothschild, Nan A., and Arnold Pickman

1990 Archaeological Excavations on the Seven Hanover Square Block. Ms. on file, New York City Landmarks Preservation Commission, New York.

Rothschild, Nan A., Diana Rockman, and Eugene Boesch

1987 *Archaeological Investigation of the Stadt Huys Block: A Final Report.* On file, New York City Landmarks Preservation Commission, New York.

Rowse, A. L.
1962 *Sir Walter Ralegh: His Family and Private Life.* Harper Brothers, New York.

Shaw, Susannah
2001 New Light from Old Sources: Finding Women in New Netherland's Courtrooms. In *de Halve Maen: Journal of the Holland Society of New York* (spring):9–14.

Tatman, C.
1985 Stamps and Mouldings on Clay Pipes Found in London. In *The Archaeology of the Clay Tobacco Pipe IX: More Pipes from the Midlands and Southern England, Part II,* edited by Peter Davey, 363–388. British Archaeological Reports International Series 146, Oxford.

Thompson, Edward
1936 *Sir Walter Ralegh: Last of the Elizabethans.* Yale Univ. Press, New Haven.

Walker, Iain C.
1977 Clay *Tobacco Pipes with a Particular Reference to the Bristol Industry.* History and Archaeology, Volumes 11a–11d. National Historic Parks and Sites Branch, Parks Canada, Dept. of Indian and Northern Affairs.

Werner, Carl Avery
1922 *Tobaccoland.* Tobacco Leaf, New York.

Wobst, H. Martin
1977 Stylistic Behavior and Information Exchange. In *Essays for the Director: Research Essays in Honor of James B. Griffin,* edited by Charles E. Cleland, 317–342. Museum of Anthropology Anthropological Paper 61. Museum of Anthropology, Univ. of Michigan, Ann Arbor.

Wright, Rita
1991 Women's Labor and Pottery Production in Prehistory. In *Engendering Archaeology: Women and Prehistory,* edited by Joan M. Gero and Margaret W. Conkey, 194–223. Basil Blackwell, Oxford.

9. Home Rulers, Red Hands, and Radical Journalists: Clay Pipes and the Negotiation of Working-Class Irish/Irish American Identity in Late-Nineteenth-Century Paterson, New Jersey

Paul Reckner

For the beginning is assuredly
the end—since we know nothing, pure
and simple, beyond
our own complexities.
—William Carlos Williams, *Paterson*

During the second half of the nineteenth century the American social landscape underwent a series of dramatic transformations. Rapid expansion of the industrial capitalist economy challenged and threatened the ideal of the small-scale, independent skilled tradesman as the rightful inheritor of the promise of the American Revolution. Because these rightful inheritors were also envisioned as male, white, native born of Anglo-Saxon descent, and Protestant, the massive migrations from Europe and Ireland occurring during this period challenged the very nature of American national identity. This was a period of unprecedented nativist activity. Native-born Americans expressed fears that immigrant groups threatened the moral, physical, and economic well-being of the country, and developed a range of strategies to address the "immigrant problem"—from exclusionary social policies to reformist institutions aimed at inculcating "American" values in recent immigrants to the United States. Immigrants did not passively accept exclusion and acculturation. They struggled against negative stereotypes and the direct oppression perpetrated by nativist groups. By their very presence, recent immigrants challenged the ideology of a single, homogenous American national identity and ideology, and through their struggles they reshaped the country.

Material culture and symbols play a key role in the construction and contestation of ethnic/national identities (Barthes 1988; Bodnar 1992; Hall 1994; Lightfoot,

Martine, and Schiff 1998). Symbols of nationalism and patriotism are material expressions of the discourse on national identity, but by their very nature, the meaning(s) attached to national icons such as flags, crests, or seals are never fixed and singular. Symbols become meaningful within highly specific contexts of use and discourse and are frequently contested. This is especially true of symbols with the visibility of a national flag. Many interest groups, operating within a terrain of unequal power, attempt to co-opt national symbols in order to further their agenda (Bodnar 1992). Through such struggles over meaning, national symbols become tied to wildly different—even contradictory—identities and ideologies. Thus, any effort at understanding the meaning of national symbols must seek out these contexts of contestation (Hobsbawm and Ranger 1983; Kertzer 1988; Paynter and McGuire 1991; Ranger 1993; Scott 1990; Trouillot 1995).

In addressing the question of the meanings of various nationalist motifs, issues of power and class are of foremost concern. Constructions of ethnic and national identity are inherently crosscut by issues of class. Class conflict is especially relevant in the context of the case study of Paterson, New Jersey, that follows, because the vast majority of immigrants arriving in the United States during this period held little in the way of economic and cultural capital and by and large found themselves among the ranks of America's underclass (Miller 1985). This does not hold for all immigrant experiences, but the most widely promulgated ethnic stereotypes of this period were clearly framed in opposition to America's predominantly Anglo-Protestant middle and upper classes (Curtis 1997; Higham 1988; Knobel 1986).

In the latter part of the nineteenth century, Irish immigrants to the United States typically worked as day laborers, domestic servants, porters, piecework seamstresses, and factory operatives in the emerging industrial capitalist economy (Miller 1985). These forms of employment clearly situate these groups in a class position with a minimum of control of the means of production. Although job situations and experiences were frequently gender-specific under the emerging industrial capitalist economic system of the period, all workers relied heavily on the owners of capital for the material means by which they could reproduce themselves socially and biologically.

This context of life and work impacted the meaning of nationalist symbols and demands an exploration of the meanings of these symbols to recent Irish immigrants of Paterson, many of whom worked in the lowest echelons of an exploitative capitalist system. What did they hope to accomplish through associating themselves and their ideologies with national icons, and from a retrospective point of view, what role did Irish nationalist symbols play in the emergence of a distinctly Irish-American working-class identity?

It is frequently asserted that immigrant groups responded in one of two ways to conditions in late-nineteenth-century America. The first holds that by adopting American cultural practices and patriotic motifs, immigrants attempted to acculturate to middle-class American ideals in order to gain access to improved economic circumstances. Alternatively, the rejection of American identity and continued use of nationalist symbols associated with immigrants' countries of origin reflect an effort to maintain traditional ethnic/national identities. However, documentary and archaeological evidence from Paterson points to an alternative trajectory and to the possibility that "traditional" symbols of ethnic identity actually played an active roll in the transformation of ethnic/national identities.

This study takes a conflict-oriented approach to interpreting the meanings of American and Irish nationalist symbols on clay tobacco pipes from blocks 863 and 866 in Paterson, New Jersey. In the late nineteenth century, Paterson, New Jersey, was a small but intensely industrial town with a heavily Irish and working-class population centered in the neighborhood known as "Dublin." This study explores working-class immigrants' use of Irish nationalist symbols in daily struggles defined along axes of ethnicity and class. While many of the contested discourses engaged by recent immigrants focused on ethnic and national identity, aspects of class conflict played an explicit part in these discourses and must not be overlooked. The use or avoidance of nationalist symbols by working-class immigrant groups need not be understood merely as an indicator of acculturation or the resurgence of pride in a distant homeland. The organizations and movements that adopted these symbols where caught up in conflicts in their own present—many structured by class relations. The essential question thus becomes one of how nationalist motifs connected with class struggles. These struggles led to new constructions of both native and nonnative identities and challenged emergent American capitalist ideologies.

Archaeologically recovered household refuse offers a unique opportunity to study the material means by which working-class immigrants attempted to define themselves within the context of a complex American cultural and political landscape (Yamin 2000:91–156). Moving beyond questions of self-definition, immigrants' use of symbolically loaded objects offers a window into the contested arena of American ethnic and national identity. It will be argued that symbols of Irish ethnicity and nationalism, such as the motto "Home Rule" appearing on clay tobacco pipes, must be understood not as simple markers or expressions of an ethnic identity, but as symbols with contingent and contested meanings, actively structuring and structured through the day-to-day interactions of social agents. The study explores the meshing of Irish nationalist symbols and ideologies with late-nineteenth-century American labor union rhetoric in conflicts between organized workers and owners of capital, and the transformations this wrought on immigrant identities as well as on the character of U.S. labor activism. Clay tobacco pipes from Paterson, New Jersey, decorated with Irish nationalist motifs serve as material entry points into discourses on ethnic/national identity and the course of class struggles in late-nineteenth- and early-twentieth-century North America.

Paterson, Pipes, and Politics

Many of the old names and some of the
places are not remembered now . . .

The part of town called Dublin
Settled by the first Irish immigrants. If
you intend residing in the old town you'd
drink of the water of Dublin Spring. The
finest water he ever tasted, said Lafayette.

—William Carlos Williams, *Paterson*

Paterson presents a rich social and historical context in which to explore the tumultuous transformations occurring in urban industrial America during the second half of the nineteenth century. This small town in northern New Jersey underwent the full range of changes typical of the period; rapid industrialization, major economic boom and bust cycles, expansion of wage labor, in-migration from Europe, and an increasingly active and militant labor movement. Paterson figures prominently in the work of historians of labor and immigration (for example, Gutman 1977a; Montgomery 1987; O'Donnell 1987; Scranton 1985; Voss 1993). Archaeological evidence from the "Dublin" neighborhood enriches and refines our understanding of the day-to-day interactions of Irish residents of Paterson and illustrates in concrete ways the struggles and transformations taking place among and between Irish immigrants and American society at large.

At the Falls

Paterson, New Jersey, lies at the fall line of the Passaic River, roughly nineteen miles northwest of New York City (Map 9.1). In 1792, the area around the Great Falls was chosen by the newly chartered Society for the Encouragement of Useful Manufactures (SEUM) as the site of a planned industrial town. Alexander Hamilton organized the SEUM as a private holding company with the express purpose of developing (and profiting from) domestic U.S. manufacturing. The company was granted the power to annex land around the village of Paterson, so named in honor of the New Jersey governor and SEUM investor Thomas Paterson. While private investment in Paterson began almost immediately, it remained under the political jurisdiction of Aquanonck township until 1831 when it was partitioned off as a separate township.

Cotton manufacturing dominated the earliest phase of planned development in Paterson, with the first cotton mill opening in early 1794 (Trumbull 1882:38).

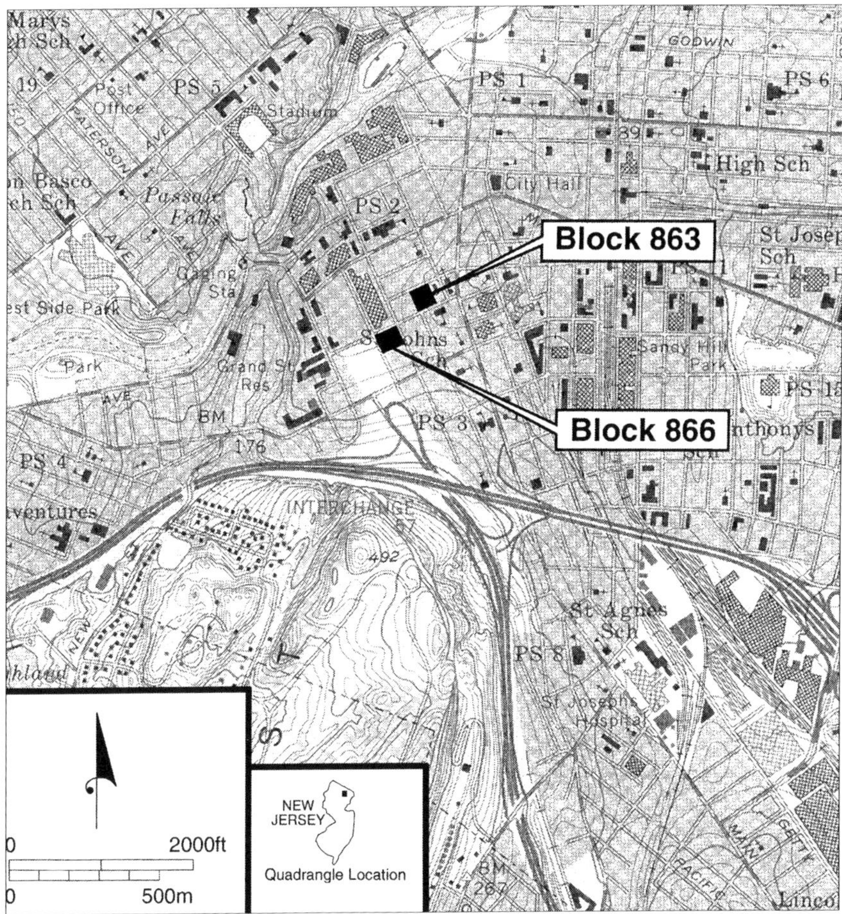

Map 9.1. ▸ *Detail map of Paterson, New Jersey, showing the locations of Blocks 863 and 866, adapted from Patterson, N.J., 7.5 minute quadrangle (USGS 1955 [1981]).*

Financial problems struck the SEUM shortly after, and virtually all cotton production ceased until the end of the first decade of the nineteenth century (Garber 1968:27). Paterson manufacturers experienced a brief boom period during the War of 1812 and immediately after. Easy access to hydraulic power, drawn from the Great Falls of the Passaic, and Paterson's central location within reach of both New York City and Philadelphia markets encouraged additional manufacturers to set up shop in the burgeoning town. The cotton market went into decline in the 1830s, once again driving a number of Paterson mills under and putting many factory workers out of work.

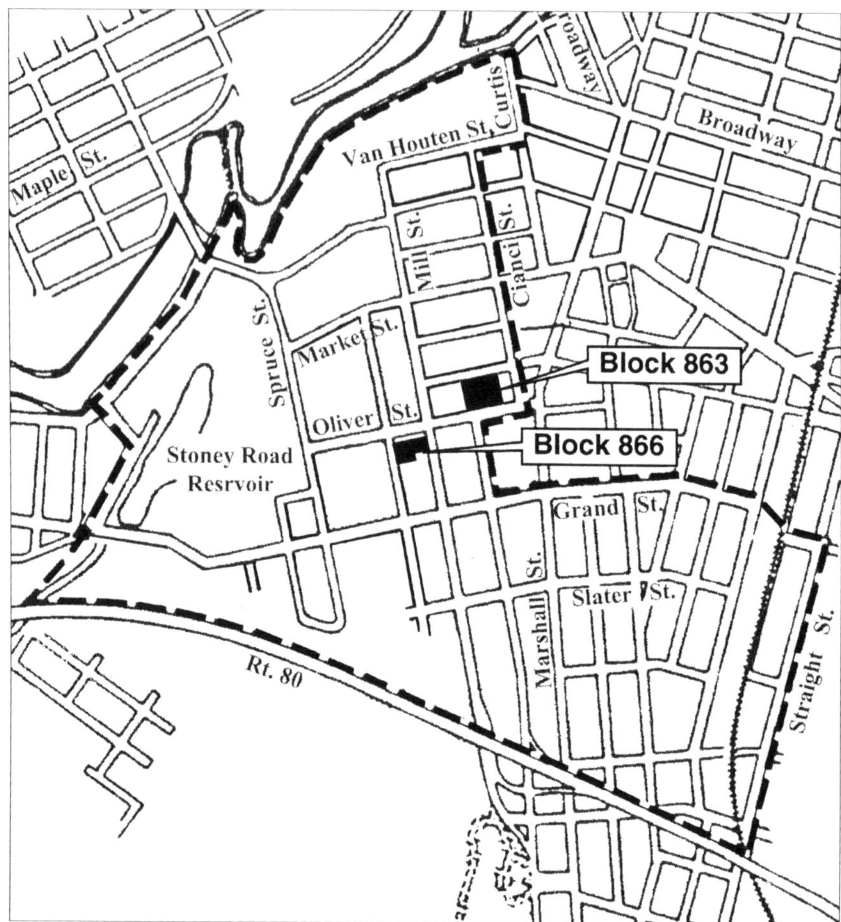

Map 9.2. ▸ *Blocks 863 and 866 in relation to approximate historic boundaries of the "Dublin" neighborhood (adapted from Rutsch 1975).*

In the 1840s, silk manufacturers seized on the opportunity presented by Paterson—a conveniently located industrial center with a stock of underutilized textile factories and a large pool of underemployed factory workers—to establish firms in the town. Silk production came to dominate Paterson's industrial base in the 1860s as a result of tariffs on silk imports that strongly favored domestic manufacturing (Margrave 1985:12–13). Capitalists engaged in the silk industries of New York City and Boston, with connections to the major silk towns in England, began to move their operations to Paterson, building large and technologically advanced factories (Gutman 1977a:239). Paterson became known as "the Silk City," as by

1880 nearly one-third of Paterson's working men were engaged in silk production. The mills also employed many women and children in the community. Women and children constituted as much as 60–70 percent of the overall millworker population in the 1880s. Gutman (1977a:239) indicates that in 1876 fourteen silk ribbon and broad silk factories in Paterson employed approximately eight thousand operatives, of which two-thirds were women and one-quarter were under the age of sixteen.

Many immigrants, skilled and unskilled, arrived in ever-increasing numbers in search of employment in the mills (Scranton 1985; Voss 1993:107). Irish immigrants had been settling in Paterson prior to the Famine-driven waves of the 1840s; some arrived to work on the Morris Canal project during the 1820s and took up residence after its completion, but their numbers grew precipitously in the latter part of the 1840s. Irish immigrants tended to settle in Paterson's South Ward, referred to as "Dublin" from as early as 1824, reflecting the dominant Irish national character of the neighborhood (De Cunzo 1983:15; Cotz, Rutsch, and Wilson 1980:259–260). English and Germanic immigrants were also well represented in the Paterson workforce of this period, and in the latter part of the nineteenth century many Italians made the town their home.

Though the physical and conceptual boundaries of the "Dublin" community were unstable and intangible (as are those of most urban neighborhoods), they can be loosely characterized as encompassing the core of Paterson's original industrial complex, including factory buildings and mill races at its northern end (see Map 9.2). Mixed residential, commercial, and industrial blocks abut the industrial center and cover an irregularly shaped area of approximately ten-by-ten blocks at its greatest extent (Rutsch 1975).

In De Cunzo's (1983:71) archaeological and documentary study of six tax lots located at the northern edge of "Dublin," she found that 84.1 percent of the residents in 1880 identified themselves as having foreign-born parentage, and of these 27.0 percent claimed Irish descent. Census data from blocks 863 and 866 situated in central "Dublin" indicate a far more dense concentration of Irish-born and Irish-descended inhabitants during the decades spanning 1880–1900 (see Table 9.1).

Silk workers predominated in De Cunzo's (1983:71) sample, representing 44.7 percent of employed residents in 1880, followed by metal workers at 26.3 percent and other textile workers at 15.8 percent. This same study revealed that fully 95.1 percent of area residents whose jobs could be identified worked at jobs typically identified as skilled or less skilled manual labor (De Cunzo 1983:75). Again, census and city directory information for blocks 863 and 866 indicate the presence of a large working-class population, many employed in the city's textile industry (Table 9.2).

"Dublin's" Irish working-class social landscape in the closing decades of the nineteenth century included religious institutions and temperance societies

TABLE 9.1 ▸ Demographic Data for Lots in the Paterson Block 863/866 Project Area

Census Year	Total Population of Project Area Lots (N)	Residents Born in Ireland (N)	Residents Born Outside Ireland to Irish-Born Parents (N)	Population of Irish Background (%)	Households with Residents of Irish Background (N/%)
1880	112	48	28	67.8%	19 (79.2%)
1900	127	27	62	70.1%	19 (57.6%)
1910	107	8	22	28.0%	6 (35.3%)

SOURCE: U.S. Bureau of the Census 1880. 1900,1910.

(many of Catholic affiliation), Irish ethnic and national organizations, military clubs, volunteer fire departments, and labor organizations (Cotz, Rutsch, and Wilson 1980:135–141, 148; De Cunzo 1983:93–94; *PLS,* May 13, 1882; Voss 1993:124). These institutions, as well as many informal ones such as neighborhood saloons, shaped and reproduced ethnic and community ties and identities. The majority of such organizations were explicitly (and often exclusively) masculine social venues, and the consumption of tobacco was a common feature of working-class male socializing and identity in this period (Cook 1989; Reckner 2001; Reckner and Brighton 1999; Stott 1990). In the United States' mainstream discourses on and representations of recent immigrants (particularly the Irish), the clay pipe became a signal identifying trait. For the largely white, Anglo-Saxon, Protestant, and native-born American populace, the clay pipe played a central role in stereotypes of the impoverished, immoral, intemperate, and dangerous immigrant (Curtis 1997; Knobel 1986; Reckner 2001; for example, Foster 1990). It is in this context that political slogans on clay tobacco pipes provide insight into the struggles of Paterson's working-class Irish.

The Pipes of "Dublin"

Backyard shaft features (privies, cisterns, and other plumbing-related structures) located on ten tax lots on blocks 863 and 866 were excavated by John Milner Associates, Inc., in 1989 (Yamin 1999). Block 863 is bounded by Ward Street to the north, Oliver Street to the south, Cross Street to the east, and Mill Street to the west (Map 9.3). Block 866 is bounded by Oliver Street to the north, Grand Street to the south, Mill Street to the east, and Jersey Street to the west (Map 9.3). As shown in Map 9.2, these two blocks are located in what was, and is

Table 9.2 ▸ Known Residents of Selected Lots in the Paterson Block 863/866 Project Area by Block and Tax Lot

Block #	Tax Lot	Known Residents (Date and Source)
863	444-1	Donald Brown, molder (1888–1889 City Directory)
		John Delaney, tailor (1888–1889 City Directory)
		Terence Leonard, laborer (1888–1889 City Directory)
		William Pilkington, clerk (1888–1889 City Directory)
		Mary Gaffler, widow, "German" (1900 Census)
		John Gaffler, shoemaker, "German" (1900 Census)
		John Conlon, ribbon weaver, Irish-born (1900 Census)
		James Kane, weaver in silk mill, Irish parentage (1900 Census)
		John Egan, barber, Irish decent (1900 Census)
		Walter Brown, machinist, English parentage (1900 Census)
		Georgia Brown, English decent (1900 Census)
		Mary Roche, silk mill warper, Irish decent (1900 Census)
		Anna and Minna McKaig, silk mill warpers, Irish decent (1900 Census)
		Elizabeth Cline, silk mill warper, French (1900 Census)
863	444-3	James Mackel, machinist, Irish-born (1866–c. 1885 Census)
		Sarah Mackel, "keeps house," Irish-born (1866–c. 1897 Census)
		Mary Mackel, schoolteacher, Irish-born (1866–c. 1897 Census)
		Jenny, Charles, Bell, John, and Willie Mackel, children (1880 Census)
		James Minikin, store clerk, Irish-born (1880 Census)
		Lottie Minikin (1880 Census)
		John Minikin, child (1880 Census)
863	444-8	No Data on Residents Available
866	432	Eleanor Ball, flax worker (1888–1889 City Directory)
		George Dangler, heater (1888–1889 City Directory)
		Charlotte Nichols, widow (1888–1889 City Directory)
		Thomas E. Ruddy, foreman (1888–1889 City Directory)
		Mary Pollitt, head of household, born in Ireland (1889 Census)
		Mary Murphy, flax worker, born in Ireland (1889 Census)
866	433N&S	Michael Connolly (1888–1889 City Directory)
		Samuel McGuinness (1888–1889 City Directory)
		John Tinman, fireman (1888–1889 City Directory)
		Thomas Tinman, machinist (1888–1889 City Directory)
		John O'Neill, laborer, Irish-born (1900 Census)
		Jane O'Neill, "wife," Irish-born (1900 Census)
		Mamie and John O'Neill, children, American-born (1900 Census)
		Ann McPhillips, flax mill worker, Irish-born (1900 Census)
		Daniel Whalen, laborer, Irish-born (1900 Census)
		Annie Whalen, "wife," Irish-born (1900 Census)

TABLE 9.2 ▸ Known Residents of Selected Lots in the Paterson Block 863/866 Project Area by Block and Tax Lot (continued)

Block #	Tax Lot	Known Residents (Date and Source)
		John, Robert, Annie, Daniel, and Margaret Whalen, children (1900 Census)
		Patrick Brown, laborer, Irish-born (1900 Census)
		Mamie Brown, daughter, "keeps house" (1900 Census)
		John Brown, farm worker (1900 Census)
		Agnes and Annie Brown, children (1900 Census)
		John Malone, laborer, Italian-born (1900 Census)
		Julia Malone, "wife" Italian-born (1900 Census)
		Rosie and Marion Malone, children (1900 Census)
		Salvatore Malone, laborer, Italian-born (1900 Census)
866	434N&S	Bernard Cunningham, laborer (1881–1882 City Directory)
		Thomas Dooling, laborer (1881–1882 City Directory)
		Lawrence Farly, laborer (1881–1882 City Directory)
		George Kirk, laborer (1881–1882 City Directory)
		Patrick Moran, laborer (1881–1882 City Directory)
		Kate Dooling, winder (1881–1882 City Directory)
		Joseph Capel, blacksmith (1888–1889 City Directory)
		Thomas McGill, fireman, Irish decent (1895–1911 Census)
		Minnie McGill, "wife," Irish decent (1895–1911 Census)
		Daniel and Richard McGill, children (1895–1911 Census)
		David Monroe, laborer (1895–1911 Census)
		Martha Monroe, "wife," (1895–1911 Census)

SOURCE: Abstracted from Yamin 1999.

often still referred to as, Paterson's "Dublin" neighborhood (Cotz, Rutsch, and Wilson 1980:259–260). The archaeological material considered below relates to the residential use of six of the ten tax lots excavated on blocks 863 and 866 and spans the last quarter of the nineteenth century and the early twentieth century.

During the period of study, residents of blocks 863 and 866 consisted almost exclusively of Irish immigrants and those of Irish descent, with shifting numbers of other nationalities also present (Tables 9.1 and 9.2). In many cases, specific information was available on the type of employment held by residents. The vast majority appear to have been skilled and less-skilled workers, many employed by the numerous silk mills booming in Paterson during the period of study. Clay tobacco pipes bearing motifs associated with Irish nationalist movements were recovered from each of the six tax lots selected. The following sections briefly discuss the significance of clay pipes and smoking culture in Irish working-class life and describe the motifs and movements represented on pipes from blocks 863 and 866.

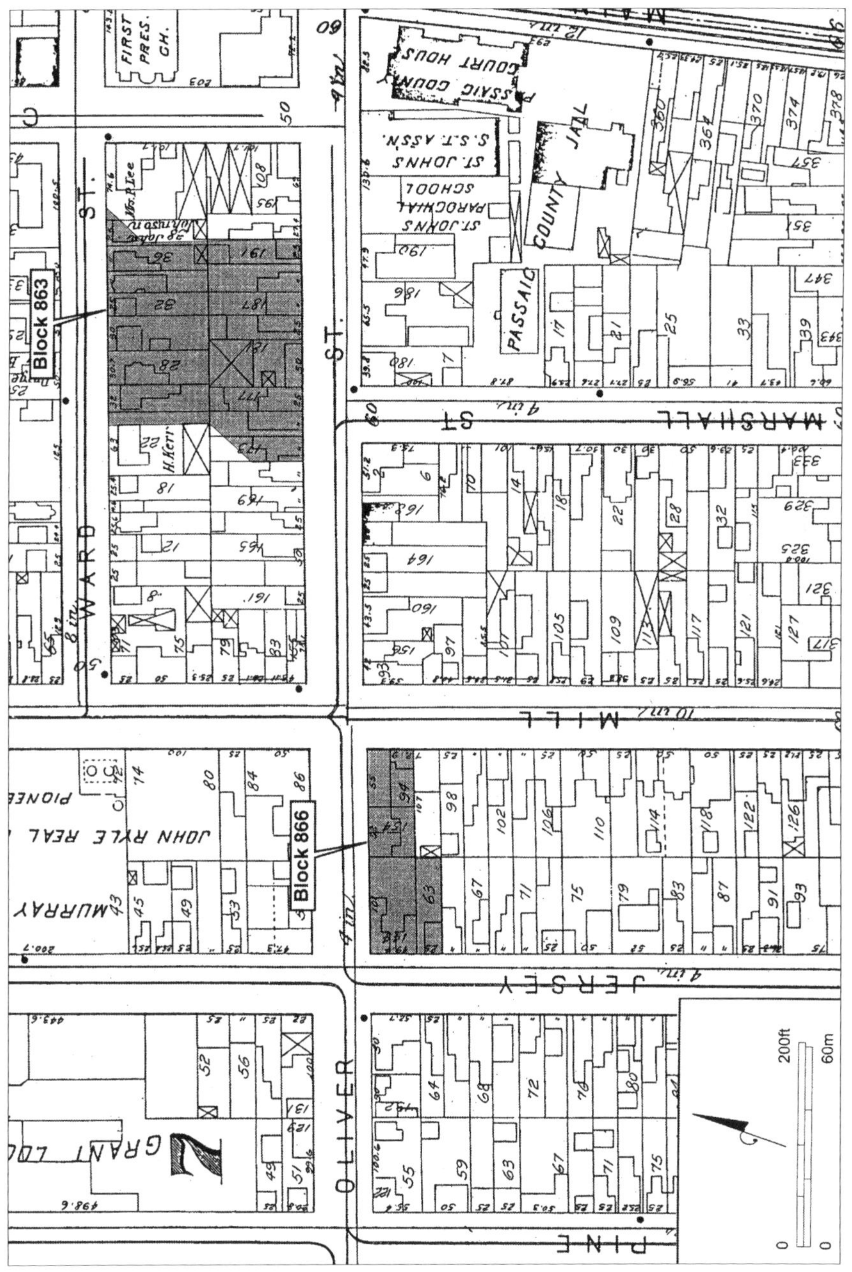

Map 9.3. ▸ *The Block 863/866 project area superimposed on the 1899 Robinson Atlas of Paterson, New Jersey (Robinson Atlas 1899).*

Red Hands and Home Rulers

Many clay tobacco pipe manufacturers of the nineteenth century marketed products that incorporated explicitly nationalist symbols and slogans. Several of the largest pipe makers of the late nineteenth century distributed pipes throughout the world and produced special "export" product lines intended to appeal to various local markets (Walker 1977, 1983; also see the "Irish Price List" of the Duncan McDougall Company reprinted in Sudbury 1980; Anonymous 1885–1893; Westerwald Clay Tobacco Pipe Catalogue n.d., post-1891). Clay pipe makers utilized a startling variety of political references in their products, including actual portraits (and sometimes caricatures) of politicians. Pipe smokers of this period could often choose from a wide range of expressive pipe styles if they desired to endorse a particular point of view through the highly social practice of tobacco use.

Pipes bearing symbols and slogans referencing Irish nationalist and political movements are some of the most frequently encountered "political" pipes in nineteenth-century North American archaeological sites, after the many American nationalist styles (for an overview of Irish motifs on clay pipes, see Alexander 1986; Reckner and Dallal 2000). The Irish clay pipe styles present in the Paterson assemblages represent a range of Irish nationalist factions and ideologies. Interestingly, the Paterson Block 863/866 pipe assemblage includes very few overtly American patriotic motifs (Table 9.3). Based on an estimate of the minimum number of distinct pipes present in the assemblage, pipes decorated with Irish motifs are more common from each block of the site as well as from the site as a whole. There is also a marked difference in the frequency of pipes with Irish versus American nationalist motifs recovered from blocks 863 and 866 (Table 9.4).

The Irish motifs identified in the Paterson Block 863/866 assemblage are discussed below in order to establish their historical associations and to contextualize their use within Irish nationalist political discourses of the late nineteenth century.

Pipes from four contexts on blocks 863 and 866 exhibit variations of the motto "HOME RULE," most commonly appearing in the form of a mold-impressed mark on proximal side of the bowl (Table 9.3 and Figure 9.1A). The slogan was adopted by a wide range of Irish nationalist factions who shared the desire to see Ireland governed by a representative Irish political body. While the sentiment has long been a part of Irish activism, the slogan became extremely popular in the wake of the Fenian movement of the late 1840s (Cruise O'Brien and Cruise O'Brien 1985:106–116). In the late 1870s, the charismatic Irish politician Charles Stewart Parnell lead the Home Rule Confederation of Great Britain and agitated for land reform under the banner of the Land League. William E.

TABLE 9.3 ▸ Distribution of "Irish" Pipe Styles Recovered from the Paterson Block 863/866 Site by Block, Tax Lot, and Feature

Block #	Tax Lot	Feature	Analytical Stratum	TPQ[1]	MCD[2]	Irish Styles Present	Irish Pipes (N)[3]	Pipes from Feature (%)
863	444-1	8	N/A	1891	N/A Triskelion	Hand of Ulster 2	8.3	
863	444-3	63	AS I	1894	1884	Gladstone	2	15.4
863	444-8	86	N/A	1842	1885	Home Rule	1	16.6
866	432/433S	47/36	N/A	1903	N/A Triskelion Gladstone	Home Rule	10	25.0
866	433N	120	AS II	1880	N/A	Home Rule	8	26.7
					Gladstone			
866	434S	10	AS I/II 1887	1906/ 1884	1885/ Hand of Ulster Gladstone	Home Rule	6	26.1

SOURCE: Abstracted from Yamin 1999.

NOTES: [1] *Terminus Post Quem.* [2] Mean Ceramic Date, [3] The number of pipes present in each assemblage was estimated based on a conservative "minimum pipe count" of separate and distinct examples.

TABLE 9.4 ▸ Total Number of Pipes Bearing Irish-Associated Motifs versus American Nationalist Symbols Recovered from all Paterson Block 863/866 Features

Block	Irish Motifs (N)	American Nationalist Motifs (N)	Other Pipes (N)	Total Pipes (N)	Irish Motifs (%)	American Motifs (%)
863	6	4	161	171	3.5	2.3
866	20	2	181	203	9.8	1.0
Total	26	6	342	374	6.9	1.6

Gladstone succeeded in bringing the first Irish Home Rule Bill to a vote in 1886, but the measure was defeated.

The hand and heart motif appears on pipes from two Paterson assemblages (Table 9.3 and Figure 9.1B, C). It frequently takes the form of a hand (palm side out) molded in relief on the left and right faces of the bowl. In some examples, a heart lies in the center of the palm. This motif evokes the symbolism of the Red Hand of Ulster. The origin of this symbol lies in an extremely old Celtic tale of kingly succession, but after the conquest of Ireland by England this icon was

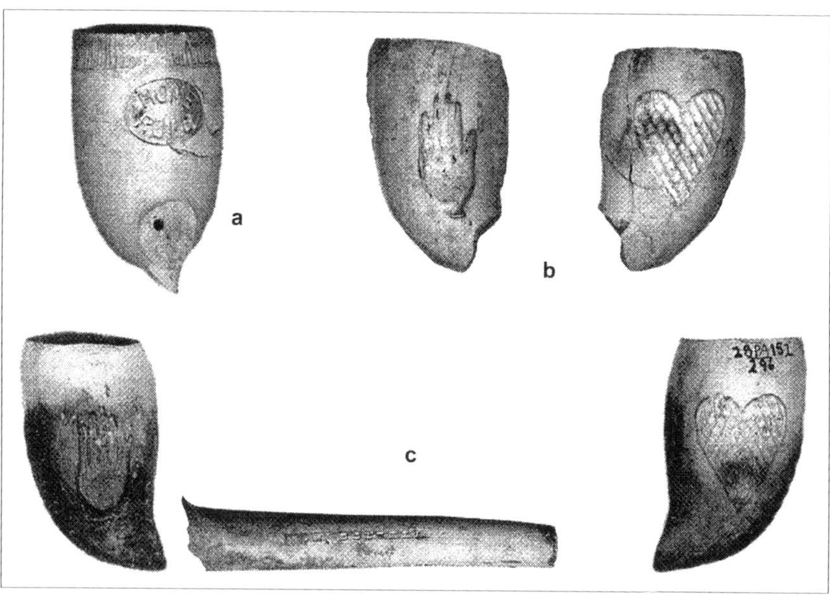

FIG. 9.1. ▸ *Examples of Irish motifs on pipes recovered from the Paterson site.*

FIG. 9.2. ▸ *Pipes with Irish motifs and name references from Paterson (Block 86, Lot 433-N, Feature 120).*

co-opted by English-descended Protestants in Ulster to legitimate their presence in Northern Ireland.

The triskelion of the Isle of Man consists of three human legs, bent at the knee, radiating out from a central point (Figure 9.2B). The symbol derives from early coinage associated with the island, which is located between Ireland, England, and Scotland in the Irish Sea. Davey (personal communication 1996) indicates that many objects manufactured for the Isle's tourist trade in the nineteenth century bore this design. Also referred to as the "Manx triskelion," this motif is present in two Paterson contexts. While there is no distinct political agenda associated with this symbol, it is notable that one example from Paterson also displays the Red Hand motif (Figure 9.2B) .

The distinctive bowl form of the "Gladstone" style was marketed by several European pipe makers (see Figures 9.3 and 9.2A; Anonymous, vol. 52, no. 389; Westerwald Clay Tobacco Pipe Catalogue n.d., post-1891, nos. 29 and 121). The name referred to a leading figure in the Irish Home Rule movement, William Ewert Gladstone. Historically, W. E. Gladstone was instrumental in pushing the 1886 Irish Home Rule Bill to a vote. This first effort, and a second attempt at Home Rule legislation both failed in Parliament (Cruise O'Brien and Cruise O'Brien 1985:131–132). The pipes recovered from the Paterson exhibit the distinctive bowl form common to the "Gladstone" styles illustrated in period pipe catalogs. Other versions also included the stem marking "Gladstone" or "The Gladstone Pipe" and still others depicted a bust of Gladstone himself (Alexander 1986:72, Figure 2D). Gladstone pipes were recovered from four Paterson contexts (Table 9.3).

Situating these symbols within Irish nationalist political movements offers only one level of interpretation and meaning, however. The sections that follow construct a framework for exploring the multiple meanings associated with these symbols within the context of the Irish working-class experience in late-nineteenth- and early-twentieth-century Paterson. Paterson's trade unions and

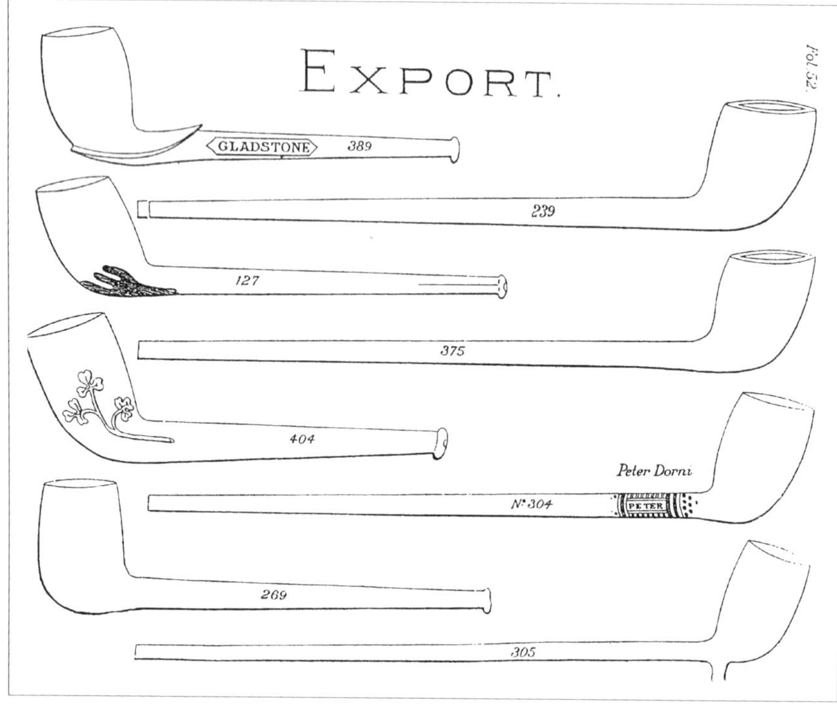

FIG. 9.3. ▸ *Detail from an export catalog of the Dutch pipe manufacturing firm P. Goedewaagen and Son (undated, circa 1885–1893).*

working-class social activists offer an invaluable window into the experiences and conceptions of Irish/Irish American ethnicity and national identity (Emmons 1989; Foner 1978; Miller 1985:524).

Fenians and Socialists in Paterson, New Jersey

The specific historical context of Irish/Irish American working-class labor activism in Paterson, New Jersey, is explored below in order to provide further bases for interpreting the archaeological data. These interpretations lead into a contingent framing of the interrelated transformations of Irish/Irish American ethnicity and national identity. It is argued that the accretion of new meanings and ideologies onto the symbols of the Irish Home Rule movement was tied to the emergence of a distinctly Irish American ethnic identity during the period of study. The meshing of these Irish nationalist symbols with workers' own experiences of working-class labor activism in the United States and with elements of socialist and labor union discourse were fundamental to this transformation. Ironically, and most significant to this study, the very "authentic and traditional" political symbols that defined an Irish national identity became active forces in this transformation. Social agents worked meaningful changes on these icons (and themselves) through the interplay of constructions of Irish/Irish American ethnic identity and workers' struggles in the United States during the Gilded Age.

Paterson Workers in Struggle

Evidence of a nascent working-class solidarity among Paterson's skilled workers exists from as early as 1823, but trade unions and workers' benevolent societies in this era tended to be small and short-lived (Troy 1965:15–16; Voss 1993:106). Major clashes between workers and factory owners are recorded from the second half of the nineteenth century onward, but these early conflicts typically involved only a single shop or trade (Troy 1965:15–26). These included two strikes in Paterson's textile mills, one in 1828 and one in 1835, and a walkout in 1837 staged by the shoemakers' union (Troy 1965:20, 26; Voss 1993:106). These isolated actions and ephemeral trade unions suffered greatly during the economic depressions that plagued nineteenth-century America, and few lasting gains were achieved. Importantly, labor organizations of this period generally consisted of skilled tradesmen—unskilled workers and factory operatives, including many immigrants, women, and children—were not represented (Voss 1993:35). The unskilled were, in fact, frequent targets of trade unions who perceived the incorporation of pieceworkers and operatives into production, through the deskilling and mechanization of traditional artisan crafts, as threatening to skilled workers.

Trade unions in the 1850s struck more frequently and often associated themselves with emerging national trade bodies. The Paterson local of the National Molders Union made its appearance in 1859 (Troy 1965:36–37). Women's trade organizations, such as the Milliners Union of Newark, New Jersey, also formed in this period, but they typically remained separate from male unions, even within the same trade (Troy 1965:36–37; Wilentz 1984:371). Many trade organizations, both male and female, also fragmented along ethnic and national lines, and less-skilled workers remained underrepresented (Wilentz 1984:363–389).

A broad-based labor movement only arose with the formation of the Noble and Holy Order of the Knights of Labor (KOL) in 1869 by a group of six Philadelphia garment cutters (Voss 1993:73). The KOL crossed the Delaware River into New Jersey as early as 1874, marking the beginning of a new era of organized labor in the state (Troy 1965:39). In addition to organizing trade-based locals or incorporating existing locals into a nationwide network, the KOL espoused an inclusive organizing strategy encouraging chapters to recruit unskilled labor, immigrant workers, and women into their ranks. Such organizations represented a watershed opportunity for Paterson's largely unskilled immigrant silk operatives. By 1883, the Knights' ranks numbered approximately fifty thousand (Voss 1993:75).

While the national leadership of the Knights often discouraged or avoided strikes, many of the largely autonomous local chapters of the KOL became embroiled in a bitter struggle with railroad magnate Jay Gould, which they eventually won. This victory reverberated through America's working-class communities, drawing thousands of semiskilled and unskilled laborers into the KOL and kicking off an unprecedented wave of strikes (Voss 1993:75–76). By 1885, 100,000 workers had joined the Knights, and in the year leading up to the "Great Upheaval" of 1886, 120 new KOL chapters formed in New Jersey, more than doubling the total number in the state (Troy 1965:47; Voss 1993:76).

Knights of Labor chapters instigated a third strike against a Gould-owned railroad company in 1886, and publicity brought the Knight's membership to nearly 750,000, representing virtually every nationality and both skilled and unskilled workers, for the first time in U.S. history (Voss 1993:78). The Haymarket bombing on May 1, 1886, triggered an almost immediate reversal of the Knights' meteoric gains. The explosion injured seventy policemen (one fatally), and the surviving officers then opened fire on the crowd, killing an unknown number of demonstrators. In the face of media portrayals of the event and the witch hunt that ensued after the bombing, public sympathy for the Knights turned sour. The Gould strike was called off and the KOL fell into a series of factional squabbles. Ongoing disagreement between the KOL and the American Federation of Labor, which stridently disagreed with the Knights' recognition of unskilled and industrial unions, also took its toll on the organization (Voss 1993:78–80).

The Labor Standard

Many of the sweeping changes in the American labor movement, at the national and local levels, were chronicled in a remarkable socialist newspaper published first in New York City and later in Paterson, New Jersey. Joseph P. McDonnell served as the editor of the paper—originally known as *The Socialist,* then the *New York Labor Standard,* and finally the *Paterson Labor Standard*—from 1876 until his death in 1906 (O'Donnell 1987). A university-educated Fenian activist, McDonnell had a police record that included four arrests and three prison terms by the time he left Ireland (Gutman 1977b:264). The young activist, only twenty-five years old in 1872, also served on the General Council of the International Workers Association, nominated to the position by both Marx and Engels (O'Donnell 1987:123).

Arriving in New York City in 1872, McDonnell quickly fell in with the likes of Samuel Gompers, Peter J. McGuire, and Adolph Strasser—major figures in the American labor movement. In 1876, a group of these activists formed the Central Organization of Trades and Labor Unions of New York, a federation of city unions, and McDonnell became editor of the organization's official English-language newspaper, *The Socialist.* The same paper, renamed *The New York Labor Standard,* was then designated the voice of the newly formed Workingmen's Party of the United States (O'Donnell 1987:127). The pages of the *New York Labor Standard* offered readers a weekly review of domestic and international labor news, editorials, announcements of organizational meetings and boycotts, poetry, and a "letters to the editor" section (*New York Labor Standard,* Aug. 12, 1876–Nov. 11, 1876). In an editorial of August 12, 1876, the paper declared that "the advanced state of American industry and the destructive despotism of capitalistic society, has compelled the working people to found a journal, written by themselves, for the promotion of their material, moral, and intellectual interests . . . In all other respects the services [of the capitalistic press] are worthless for the working people." Struggles internal to the Workingmen's Party pulled the *Labor Standard* to Fall River, Massachusetts, in 1877 to wage the war for eight-hour workday legislation in that state.

McDonnell remained on staff for a short time but returned to New York after disagreements over party policy. Labor unrest in Paterson's silk mills drew his attention, and by October 1878 he had relocated to that city and published the first issue of the *Paterson Labor Standard* (O'Donnell 1987:129). McDonnell immediately became embroiled in a libel suite, the first of two such cases he would face in New Jersey, over the use of the word *scab* (Gutman 1977b:274–277).

Despite, or perhaps because of, his legal troubles, the *Paterson Labor Standard* was extremely well received in the city. Nearly every newspaper agent in town carried the *Standard,* and many local businesses placed advertisements in its pages—one enterprising tobacco dealer, W. P. Allen of 51 Main Street, even advertised his "Labor Standard long cut tobacco" in McDonnell's journal (Gutman 1977b:274; *PLS,* May 29, 1880). McDonnell himself declared the *Standard* "an unprecedented success . . . no paper ever published in this city acquired so large and influential a circulation" (*PLS,* Nov. 23, 1878). The format of the new paper followed very closely that of the old *New York Labor Standard* under McDonnell's editorship. The general tone was overtly oppositional. A banner appearing beneath the paper's masthead announced "the emancipation of the working class must be achieved by the working people themselves" (*PLS,* Nov. 23, 1878).

One of the first major stories to be covered was McDonnell's own trial on charges of libel, but he also covered local strikes in detail, including the 1878 walkout at Adam's mosquito netting factory by female operatives (*PLS,* Dec. 7, 1878). The *Standard* also posted notices of local union meetings, and one issue featured the preamble to the constitution of the Knights of Labor, as well as their bylaws (*PLS*, May 30, 1882). Community events were announced, including Paterson's annual Decoration Day, billed in 1882 as "the fourth annual festival of the working people of Paterson . . . a legal holiday" (*PLS*, May 13, 1882). Victor Hugo's *Les Miserables* was reprinted in serialized form, and critical readings of radical literature from Karl Marx and Henry George frequently appeared in the *Standard*. These critiques of capitalism and private property were explicitly linked to discussions of local and international issues of the day.

Interspersed with the explicitly working-class issues mentioned above, McDonnell actively promoted his own first cause of Irish Home Rule and land reform in the pages of the *Standard*. This becomes particularly evident in the 1880s, with the revitalization of the Irish national struggle through the work of Parnell and Gladstone. Support for the Irish Land League and Parnell was expressed in a brief piece in the October 15, 1881, issue of the *Paterson Labor Standard*, and in December of that same year, McDonnell offered, as an incentive to subscribers, a free map of Ireland entitled "The Carrion of Landlordism in Ireland" (*PLS*, Dec. 24, 1881). The *Standard*'s coverage of the Irish question intensified in 1886 as Gladstone rose to preeminence, only to see his Home Rule bill defeated in Parliament. McDonnell described the situation after the defeat as "Home Rule or Revolution" (*PLS*, May 15, 1886). In his regular column of one-liners on local goings-on, McDonnell quipped (ironically) that "there is no depressing effect on the Irish people of Paterson through the defeat of the Home Rule Bill" (*PLS*, June 12, 1886).

The themes of Home Rule and labor activism merged in an advertisement appearing in the 1 March 1890 issue of the *Standard* urging customers to "use Allen and Dunning's HOME RULE chewing and long cut smoking tobacco—union made cigars." The most literal blending of these two issues comes from McDonnell himself, stating, in a piece entitled "Ireland and America" that "the principles for which the Irish Nationalists are contending are practically the same as those held by the labor reformers in their struggle against capitalistic oppression" (*PLS*, Nov. 22, 1890).

Looking beyond Paterson to the national scene, Foner (1978) has argued that such an overlap of interests characterized American-based agitation promoting the Irish Land League (also see Meagher 1985). His analysis relies heavily on material from the *Irish World* newspaper, headed by Patrick Ford, whose New York office "served as a kind of headquarters for labor leaders and Irish nationalists, ranging from Samuel Gompers to J.P. McDonnell" (Foner 1978:12). Ford consistently attempted to link considerations of the Land League and the Irish question to social issues in the United States—he chided myopic Irish reformers in one editorial by reminding them that "we have a republic here in America, and here in America, too, we have Pittsburgh riots, and Land Grabbers, and Usurers, and slow starvation" (in Foner 1978:14–15). Other individuals figured prominently in both camps. Terrence Powderly served as mayor of Scranton, Grand

Master Workman of the Knights of Labor, and finance chairman for the Clan na Gael, an Irish nationalist organization supporting Home Rule (Foner 1978:25). In 1882, Powderly spoke at Turner Hall on Pittsburgh's industrial South Side on "The Irish Question from the Standpoint of Labor" (Walsh 1981:198).

In arguing that working-class Irish/Irish Americans were conscious of linkages between labor struggles and the Home Rule movement, Foner (1978) cites two extraordinary documents. The first details donations to the *Irish World's* "Spread the Light" fund drive to support free distribution of the *Irish World* throughout Ireland. While the major urban centers donated the greater amount of funds, the "most remarkable concentration of branches oriented toward the *Irish World* lay in the anthracite coal region of northeastern Pennsylvania" (Foner 1978:22). In this region of the United States, Irish workers had already been exposed to bitter labor struggles and "the Land League reflected and helped to shape a developing labor consciousness" (Foner 1978:22).

The second document is a series of three resolutions adopted by the local Land Leaguers of Swatara, Pennsylvania, then a town of only seventy-five families. Their second resolution illustrates the conjuncture of Irish radicalism and socialist ideology: "2. It is the obvious design of the Almighty that every individual man should labor, not that one portion of mankind should perform all the drudgery, slave and suffer that the other may revel in luxury" (in Foner 1978:38). Miller (1985:524) observes that in the post-1870 period "many, perhaps most, working-class Irish-Americans found primary expression of both ethnic and social identities not in bourgeois institutions but in militant labor unions and, to a lesser extent, in radical politics which linked Irish protest traditions to American urban-industrial conditions and grievances." McKivigan and Robertson (1997) see the same developments in New York City's Irish community and trace further social and political transformations among Irish-American workers' radicalism in the early twentieth century. Finally, Ewen (1994:208) states that, for New York's needle trades workers, "ultimately trade union activity created an alternative to Americanization for immigrant women—and particularly for their daughters. If the Americanization movement assumed that it could change the immigrant working class, the trade unions offered a way for them to change America." McKivigan and Robertson (1996) describe a similar trajectory among New York City's Irish-American workers.

In Paterson, New Jersey, the radical Irish American press created an open and influential forum for Irish and working-class issues. Newspapers of this ilk were read widely not only by the Irish but also, as one observer of the *Irish World* noted, "by the 'proletariat' of all nationalities" (Foner 1978:12). The *Paterson Labor Standard* was no exception. Through it, McDonnell offered vocal support for local labor organizations, and the paper served as a means of orchestrating strikes and other actions. The presence of a widely circulated working-class newspaper helped create and reinforce consciousness and solidarity among its readership and countered the hegemonic discourse of what McDonnell termed the "capitalistic press." The direct association of American labor struggles with Irish nationalist activism in the pages of the *Paterson Labor Standard* and other radical media suggests that such political and ideological linkages must be recognized in order to frame the nature of late-nineteenth-century Irish/Irish America identity and the meanings of Irish nationalist symbols.

Radical Becomings

> The Water pouring still
> from the edge of the rocks, filling
> his ears with its sound, hard to interpret.
> A wonder!
>
> —William Carlos Williams, *Paterson*

The elaborate clay pipes from late-nineteenth-century Paterson speak eloquently of the transformation of Irish nationalist rhetoric and symbolism within the oppositional working-class consciousness fostered by J. P. McDonnell through the *Paterson Labor Standard.* Correspondingly, Irish/Irish American working-class identity was transformed. There can be no absolute certainty in associating each Home Rule pipe with a radical Irish-American worker, but neither is it acceptable to deny the possible implications of these symbols, particularly in the context of strike-riddled, industrial Paterson, New Jersey.

The interpenetration of Irish Home Rule rhetoric and American labor union activism shaped and transformed Irish/Irish American working-class lives and identities. It simultaneously drew individuals (many already radicalized by their experiences in Ireland) into a broader critique of their world, while at the same time focusing on highly localized labor issues faced by working-class immigrant communities in the United States. A new constellation of symbols, ideology, identity, and activism offered working-class Irish Americans a framework in which to struggle. And through these struggles, the Irish of Paterson became, simultaneously, more Irish (in the national sense) than their ancestors who fled their homes in Ireland's villages and counties, more American in their direct confrontation of working conditions in the United States, and, in their own experience, they were simply becoming more like themselves.

In light of this process, to describe Irish nationalist symbols on clay tobacco pipes found in association with working-class Irish households simply as expressions of "Irishness" clearly ignores the social and historical context of their use. Such a perspective implicitly calls upon and reinforces a rigidly "traditional" and "authentic" Irish identity. Interpretations of this nature obscure the active role of

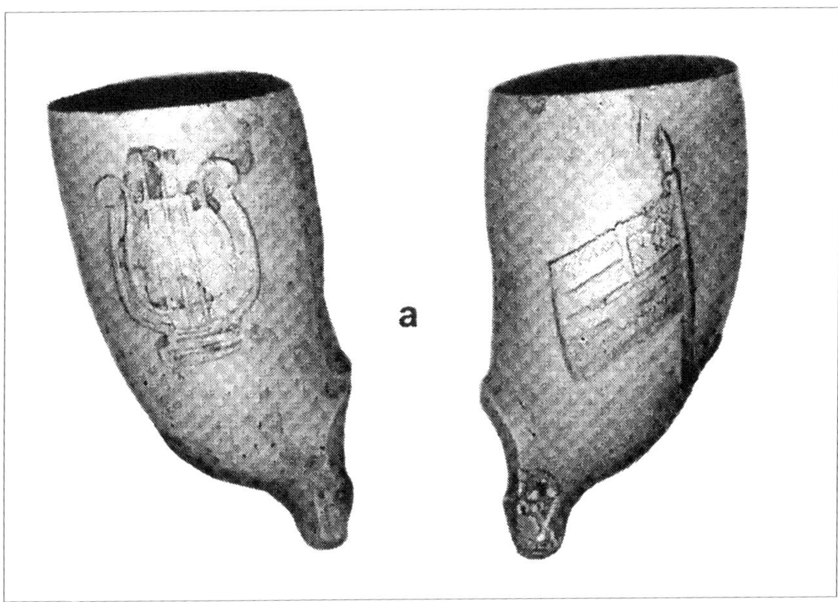

FIG. 9.4. ▸ *Pipe bowl combining Irish and American nationalist symbols recovered from Paterson (Block 866, Lot 432, Feature 36/47).*

Irish/Irish Americans in reshaping American unionism and contesting the exclusivity of nativist-inspired American ethnic and national identity.

The clay tobacco pipes from Paterson raise an interesting question left unresolved in the foregoing discussion, one that adds an additional dimension to the narrative of the radicalization of Irish workers in America. The Irish community in the United States was not a unified and monolithic whole, as evidenced by pipes bearing the Red Hand of Ulster from Paterson. What was the relationship of the Ulster Irish to the many other Irish (and typically Catholic and pro–Home Rule) dominated labor organizations in Paterson and elsewhere. There is no reason to suggest that, based on their religious and political leanings, the Irish workers who smoked Red Hand of Ulster pipes did not take part in the many labor uprisings of the period. However, the divisions within the Irish/Irish American working class suggested by these symbols surely created tensions within labor organizations, illustrating the problematic nature of identity-based collectivities with class-based interests.

Ironically, the very symbols of "traditional" Irish identities—Home Rule, Gladstone, the Red Hand of Ulster, etc.—that were integral in the development of an Irish American working-class identity. While the motifs and slogans remained stylistically stable, they were undergoing their own semiotic transformations in the context of Irish working-class experiences in the United States. A single clay pipe bearing both Irish and U.S. nationalist emblems recovered from Paterson block 866 offers a tantalizing glimpse of a new symbolic construction of Irish American identity (Figure 9.4A). The merging of ideologies of Irish Home Rule, socialism, and working-class radicalism reshaped both the meaning of Irish Home Rule symbols and slogans, and fostered a distinctly Irish American working-class identity.

Postscript: Theory

> A false language. A true. A false language pouring—
> a language (misunderstood) pouring (misinterpreted)
> without dignity, without minister, crashing upon a
> stone ear.
>
> —William Carlos Williams, *Paterson*

The Paterson case study points to a number of noteworthy theoretical issues regarding the nature of ethnicity, its relationship to class struggles and discourses informed by class interests, and the dialectic of continuity and transformation in the reproduction of social identity.

Following Upton (1996:1), it must be emphasized that all ethnic designations are by nature abstractions and generalizations and are, as such, not to be taken as concrete categories. However, the fluidity of ethnic and national identities in no way invalidates them as important and useful areas of study. To the degree that they play a clear role in shaping the life experiences of social agents, it becomes necessary to approach these social categories in a direct (though cautious) manner if we are to paint a truly textured picture of past events and lives.

Identities based on shared practices become active as ethnicity within social contexts where agents possessing distinct sets of behaviors and attributes encounter one another (Barth 1969, 1994). Material culture plays a major and active role in the construction of ethnic identities, and questions of ethnic and national identity have been operative in antiquarian and archaeological research from very early in the history of these fields (Trigger 1989). Unfortunately, archaeological approaches to ethnicity have often operated from an essentializing theory of the relationship between material culture and ethnic identity. If there can be said to be any essential qualities of ethnicity, they would be its fundamentally historical, relational, and emergent nature.

Practitioners of the new archaeology emphasized the identification of individual objects or patterns of material culture which could be associated with the presence of specific ethnic groups (for example, Etter 1980; South 1977). Implicit in the formulations of the new archaeology (and the cultural-historical approach that preceded it) is the notion that particular objects and behaviors possessed an essential connection to a particular ethnic group. For example: opium pipes equal Chinese; shamrocks equal Irish; etc. Processual archaeology's engagements with the ethnicity problem, such as Wobst's (1977) information systems approach to symbolism and ethnicity, were plagued by the same difficulties. Symbols and ethnic groups were constructed with only one distinct and uncontested (and functional) meaning or identity, and these symbolic and ethnic essences were not explicitly rooted within social and historical contexts. Jones (1997:111–112) further criticizes the passivity of material culture in new/processual archaeology.

Postprocessual approaches to ethnicity attempted to move beyond essentializing theories by conceptualizing social identities as semiotic constructs or symbolic discourses (Hodder 1991; see Barthes 1988 and Eco 1979 on semiotics). Ethnic identities also emerge out of material struggles, however, and this aspect of the process cannot be subsumed under concepts of textuality and discourse. It requires attention to daily practices of social agents and the power relations and class struggles that shape (and are shaped by) daily practices (McGuire 1992). Moreover, it is through the daily interactions of social agents that ethnic identities and the meanings of symbols are both *reproduced and transformed* (Bourdieu 1972; Jones 1997; Roseberry 1994).

Jones (1997:87–89), drawing on both Bourdieu (1972) and Giddens (1979), formulates a "practice theory of ethnicity" in which the *habitus*—the persistent dispositions that structure and are structured by social interaction—are the seat of perceptions of affinity and difference that provide cohesion to ethnic groups and associate meanings with ethnic and national symbols. Central to such a perspective on the ethnic question is a recognition that these affinities and differences structure and are structured through actual social relations. Put simply, in order to approach constructions of a particular ethnicity, an awareness of how constructions of that ethnicity were actually "used" (both in an active/intentional and passive/unintentional sense) in daily interactions and struggles is imperative. A historicized perspective on ethnic identity and daily social practice focuses attention on processes of reproduction, continuity, and transformation (Bourdieu 1972; Roseberry 1994). Further, it effectively blurs the untenable distinction between the authentic/traditional and the novel/innovative (Upton 1996). The Paterson case illustrates the ongoing reworking of symbolic meanings and social identities through daily practice and struggle.

A practice approach must also emphasize that social agents are not made up of a series of atomized identities. Rather, they constitute their social worlds from a standpoint that is informed by multiple and *interrelated* social identities and interests—perhaps at times contradictory but by no means separate "lenses" through which social relations are grasped. This issue lies at the heart of the

Paterson example of immigrant working-class identities within the context of labor activism. Asymmetrical power relations, and class conflict in particular, shape the daily lives and interactions of social agents (McGuire 1992; Paynter and McGuire 1991; Wurst 1999). A number of recent studies of ethnicity in the archaeological literature (many under the rubric of creolization) apply theoretically sophisticated concepts of ethnic identity (for example, Lightfoot, Martine, and Schiff 1998; Mouer 1993; Upton 1996). The capacity of marginalized groups to actively and effectively resist and undermine powerful social groups is emphasized in these works, but this is often accomplished at the expense of ignoring or downplaying structures and relations of power and oppression. In contrast, Loren (2001) develops a strand of creolization theory with an acute awareness of power relations. From the literature of historical anthropology, Cohn's (1996) examination of the co-optation and redefinition of symbols of legitimacy and ethnicity in colonial India makes explicit the power dynamics that underlie historical constructions of ethnicity.

In a cogent meditation on the nature of social power and social reproduction, Roseberry (1994:42–45) formulates a historicized, contingently reproduced culture as "socially constituted (it is a product of present and past activity) and socially constitutive (it is part of the meaningful context in which activity takes place)," but it is the "differential access to power [that] is crucial in the determination of control over the means of cultural reproduction." Balancing against this rather pessimistic position, Roseberry (1994:47) adds a new twist to one of Marx and Engel's signature phrases in asserting that "the individuals composing the subordinate class possess among other things consciousness, and therefore think." He goes on to assert that disjunctions, or contradictions, between the meanings and discourses produced by powerful social interests and the day-to-day experiences of ordinary people are inevitable. "In less ordinary circumstances such disjunction may be the focal point for the production of new and alternative meanings, new forms of discourse" and articulate with novel, or previously unrecognized, avenues of action and struggle (Roseberry 1994:47). Such an interplay of discourses and identities, class interests and collective struggle, drove the social transformations of Paterson's "Dublin" Irish at the turn of the twentieth century.

References Cited

Anonymous

n.d. [1885–1893?] Aarden-Tabaks and Sigaren-Pijpen Fabriek P. Goedewaagen and Zoon . Gouda (Holland), Gedeponeerde Fabricksmerken, Export. Illustrated catalog of clay tobacco pipes. Includes cover and 54 pp. Ms. copy in author's personal collection.

Alexander, L. T.
1986 Clay pipes with Irish Affiliations. In *Historic Clay Tobacco Pipe Studies,* vol. 3, edited by Byron Sudbury, 69–75. Byron Sudbury, Okla.

Barth, F.
1994 Enduring and Emerging Issues in the Analysis of Ethnicity. In *The Anthropology of Govers.* Het Spinhuis, Amsterdam.

Barth, F. (editor)
1969 *Ethnic Groups and Boundaries: The Social Organization of Cultural Difference.* Scandinavian Univ. Books, Bergen.

Barthes, Roland
1988 *The Semiotic Challenge.* Translated by Richard Howard. Hill and Wang, New York.

Bodnar, John
1985 *The Transplanted: A History of Immigrants in Urban America.* Indiana Univ. Press, Bloomington.
1992 *Remaking America: Public Memory, Commemoration, and Patriotism in the Twentieth Century.* Princeton Univ. Press, Princeton, N.J.

Bourdieu, Pierre
1972 *Outline of a Theory of Practice.* Cambridge Univ. Press, Cambridge.

Cook, Lauren J.
1989 Tobacco-Related Material and the Construction of Working-Class Culture. In *Interdisciplinary Investigations of the Boott Mills, Lowell, Massachusetts.* Vol. 3, *The Boarding House System as a Way of Life,* edited by Mary C. Beaudry and Stephen A. Mrozowski, 209–230. Cultural Resource Management Study No. 21. North Atlantic Regional Office, National Park Service, Boston.

Cotz, Jo Ann, Mary Jane Rutsch, and Charles Wilson
1980 Salvage Archaeology Project, Paterson, New Jersey, 1973–76, Vol. II: Paterson's Dublin: An Interdisciplinary Study of Social Structure. Ms. prepared for Great Falls Development and the State of New Jersey Dept. of Transportation.

Cruise O'Brien, Máire, and Conor Cruise O'Brien
1985 *Ireland: A Concise History.* Thames and Hudson, New York.

Curtis, L. Perry, Jr.
1997 *Apes and Angels: The Irishman in Victorian Caricature.* Rev. ed. Smithsonian Institution Press, Washington, D.C.

De Cunzo, Lu Ann
1983 Economics and Ethnicity: An Archaeological Perspective on Nineteenth Century Paterson, New Jersey. Doctoral dissertation in American Civilization, Univ. of Pennsylvania, Pittsburgh.

Eco, Umberto
1979 *A Theory of Semiotics.* Indiana Univ. Press, Bloomington.

Emmons, D.
1989 *The Butte Irish: Class and Ethnicity in an American Mining Town.* Univ. of Illinois Press, Urbana.

Etter, Patricia A.
1980 The West Coast Chinese and Opium Smoking. In *Archaeological Perspectives on Ethnicity in America,* edited by R. L. Schuyler, 97–101. Baywood Publishing, Farmingdale, N.Y.

Ewen, Elizabeth
1994 Sweatshops and Picket Lines: European Immigrant Women. In *From Different Shores: Perspectives on Race and Ethnicity in America,* 2d edition, edited by Ronald Takaki, 199–205. Oxford Univ. Press, New York, N.Y.

Foner, Eric
1978 Class, Ethnicity, and Radicalism in the Gilded Age: The Land League and Irish-America. *Marxist Perspectives* 1(2):6–55.

Foster, George G.
1990 *New York by Gas-Light and Other Urban Sketches.* Reprinted. Edited and with an introduction by Stuart Blumen, Univ. of California Press, Berkeley. Originally published 1856, DeWitt and Davenport, New York.

Garber, Morris W.
1968 The Silk Industry of Paterson, New Jersey, 1840–1913: Technology and the Origins, Development, and Changes in an Industry. Unpublished Ph.D. dissertation, Rutgers Univ.

Giddens, Anthony
1979 *Central Problems in Social Theory: Action, Structure, and Contradiction in Social Analysis.* Univ. of California Press, Berkeley.

Gutman, Herbert
1977a Class, Status, and Community Power in Nineteenth-Century American Industrial Cities: Paterson, New Jersey: A Case Study. In *Work, Culture, and Society in Industrializing America,* 234–259. Vintage Books/Random House, New York.
1977b A Brief Postscript: Class, Status, and the Gilded Age Radical: A Reconsideration. In *Work, Culture, and Society in Industrializing America,* 260–292. Vintage Books/Random House, New York.

Hall, Martin
1994 Lifting the Veil of Popular History: Archaeology and Politics in Urban Cape Town. In *Social Construction of the Past: Representations as Power,* edited by G. C. Bond and A. Gillian, 167–184. Routledge, New York.

Higham, John
1988 *Strangers in the Land: Patterns of American Nativism, 1860–1925.* 2d ed. Rutgers Univ. Press, New Brunswick, N.J.

Hobsbawm, Eric, and Terence Ranger
1983 *The Invention of Tradition.* Cambridge Univ. Press, Cambridge.

Hodder, Ian
1991 *Reading the Past: Current Approaches to Interpretation in Archaeology.* 2d ed. Cambridge Univ. Press, Cambridge.

Jones, Siân
1997 *The Archaeology of Ethnicity: Constructing Identity in the Past and Present.* Routledge, London.

Kertzer, David I.
1988 *Ritual, Politics, and Power.* Yale Univ. Press, New Haven.

Knobel, Dale T.
1986 *Paddy and the Republic: Ethnicity and Nationality in Antebellum America.* Wesleyan Univ. Press, Middletown, Conn.

Lightfoot, K. G., A. Martine, and A. M. Schiff
1998 Daily Practice and Material Culture in Pluralistic Social Settings: An Archaeological Study of Change and Persistence from Fort Ross, California. *American Antiquity* 63(3):199–222.

Loren, Diana DiPaolo
2001 Manipulating Bodies and Emerging Traditions at the Los Adaes Presidio. In *The Archaeology of Traditions: Agency and History before and after Columbus,* edited by Timothy R. Pauketat, 58–76. Univ. of Florida Press, Gainesville.

Margrave, Richard D.
1985 Technology Diffusion and the Transfer of Skills: Nineteenth-Century Silk Migration to Paterson. In *Silk City,* edited by Philip B. Scranton, 9–34. Collections of the New Jersey Historical Society, Vol. 19. New Jersey Historical Society, Newark.

McGuire, R. H.
1992 *A Marxist Archaeology.* Academic Press, New York.

McKivigan, John R., and Thomas J. Robertson
1996 The Irish American Worker in Transition, 1877–1914: New York City as a Test Case. In *The New York Irish,* edited by Ronald H. Bayor and Timothy J. Meagher, 301–320. Johns Hopkins Univ. Press, Baltimore.

Meagher, Timothy J.
1985 "Irish All the Time": Ethnic Consciousness among the Irish in Worchester, Massachusetts, 1880–1905. *Journal of Social History* 19(2):273–303.

Miller, Kerby A.
1985 *Emigrants and Exiles: Ireland and the Irish Exodus to North America.* Oxford Univ. Press, New York.

Montgomery, David
1987 *The Fall of the House of Labor: The Workplace, the State, and American Labor Activism, 1865–1925.* Cambridge Univ. Press, Paris.

Mouer, L. Daniel
1993 Chesapeake Creoles: The Creation of Folk Culture in Colonial Virginia. In *The Archaeology of Seventeenth-Century Virginia,* edited by T. R. Reinhart and D. J. Pogue, 105–166. Archaeological Society of Virginia, Charlottesville.

O'Donnell, L. A.
1987 Joseph Patrick O'Donnell (1847–1906): A Passion for Justice. *Éire Ireland* 22(4):118–133.

Paterson Labor Standard (PLS)
1878–1893 J. S. McDonnell, Paterson, N.J.

Paynter, Robert, and Randall H. McGuire
1991 The Archaeology of Inequality: Material Culture, Domination, and Resistance. In *The Archaeology of Inequality,* edited by R. H. McGuire and R. Paynter, 1–27. Blackwell, Oxford.

Ranger, Terence
1993 The Invention of Tradition Revisited: The Case of Colonial Africa. In *Legitimacy and the State in Twentieth-Century Africa: Essays in Honor of A.H.M. Kirk-Greene,* edited by Terence Ranger and O. Vaughan, 62–111. Macmillan Press, London.

Reckner, Paul

2001 Negotiating Patriotism at the Five Points: Clay Tobacco Pipes and Patriotic Imagery among Trade Unionists and Nativists in a Nineteenth-Century New York Neighborhood. *Historical Archaeology* 35(3):103–114.

Reckner, Paul, and Stephen A. Brighton

1999 "Free from All Vicious Habits": Archaeological Perspectives on Class Conflict and the Rhetoric of Temperance. *Historical Archaeology* 33(1):63–86.

Reckner, Paul, and Diane Dallal

2000 The Long and the Short, Being a Compendium of Eighteenth- and Nineteenth-Century Clay Tobacco Pipes from the Five Points Site, Block 160, New York City. Tales of Five Points: Working-Class Life in Nineteenth-Century New York, vol. 6, edited by Rebecca Yamin. Report prepared by John Milner Associates for the General Services Administration, Region 2, New York.

Robinson, E.

1899 *Atlas of the City of Paterson, New Jersey, from Official Records, Private Plans, and Actual Surveys. Compiled under the Supervision of E. Robinson and R. H. Pidgeon Civil and Topographic Engineers. Published by E. Robinson, 84 Nassau St., NY, Engraved by A. H. Mueller, 530 Locust St., Phila.* E. Robinson, New York.

Roseberry, W.

1994 *Anthropologies and Histories: Essays in Culture, History, and Political Economy.* Rutgers Univ. Press, New Brunswick, N.J.

Rutsch, Edward S.

1975 Salvage Archaeology in Paterson, New Jersey, 1973–1975. *Northeast Historical Archaeology* 4 (1, 2).

Scott, J. C.

1990 *Domination and the Arts of Resistance: Hidden Transcripts.* Yale Univ. Press, New Haven.

Scranton, Philip B. (editor)

1985 *Silk City: Studies on the Paterson Silk Industry, 1860–1940.* New Jersey Historical Society, Newark, N.J.

South, Stanley

1977 *Method and Theory in Historical Archaeology.* Academic Press, New York.

Stott, Richard B.

1990 *Workers in the Metropolis: Class, Ethnicity, and Youth in Antebellum New York City.* Cornell Univ. Press, Ithaca, N.Y.

Sudbury, Byron

1980 White Clay Pipes from the Old Connellsville Dump, 36 Fa 140. In *Historic Clay Tobacco Pipe Studies,* vol. 1, edited by Byron Sudbury, 23–46. Byron Sudbury, Okla.

Trigger, Bruce

1989 *A History of Archaeological Thought.* Cambridge Univ. Press, Cambridge.

Trouillot, Michel-Rolph

1995 *Silencing the Past: Power and the Production of History.* Beacon Press, Boston.

Troy, Leo

1965 *Organized Labor in New Jersey.* D. Van Nostrand Co., Princeton, N.J.

Trumbull, Levi R.

1882 *A History of Industrial Paterson.* Carleton M. Herrick, Paterson, N.J.

Upton, Dell
1996 Ethnicity, Authenticity, and Invented Traditions. *Historical Archaeology* 30(2):1–7.

U.S. Bureau of the Census
1880 Federal Census for the Seventh Ward of the City of Paterson, Passaic County, N.J. U.S. Bureaus of the Census. New York Public Library, New York.
1900 Federal Census for the Seventh Ward of the City of Paterson, Passaic County, N.J. U.S. Bureaus of the Census. New York Public Library, New York.
1910 Federal Census for the Seventh Ward of the City of Paterson, Passaic County, N.J. U.S. Bureaus of the Census. New York Public Library, New York.

Voss, Kim
1993 *The Making of American Exceptionalism: The Knights of Labor and Class Formation in the Nineteenth Century.* Cornell Univ. Press, Ithaca, New York.

Walker, Iain C.
1977 *Clay Tobacco Pipes, with Particular Reference to the Bristol Industry.* History and Archaeology, vols. 11a–11d. Parks Canada, Ottawa.
1983 Nineteenth-Century Clay Tobacco-Pipes in Canada. In *The Archaeology of the Clay Tobacco Pipe VIII, America,* BAR-S175, edited by Peter Davey, 1–88. British Archaeology Reports, Oxford.

Walsh, Victor A.
1981 "A Fanatic at Heart": The Cause of Irish-American Nationalism in Pittsburgh during the Gilded Age. *Journal of Social History* 15(2):187–204.

Westerwald Clay Tobacco Pipe Catalog
n.d. post-1891 Catalog of clay tobacco pipes and figurines. Pp. 1–23 (cover missing). The company name does not appear within the catalog but has been attributed to the Westerwald region of Germany. Ms. copy in author's personal collection.

Wilentz, Sean
1984 Chants Democratic: New York and the Rise of the American Working Class, 1788–1850. Oxford Univ. Press, New York.

Williams, William Carlos
1992 *Paterson.* Rev. ed. prepared by C. MacGowan. New Directions, New York.

Wobst, Martin
1977 Stylistic Behavior and Information Exchange. In *For the Director: Research Essays in Honor of James B. Griffin,* edited by C. L. Cleland, 317–377. Univ. of Michigan, Museum of Anthropology, Anthropology Papers No. 61, Ann Arbor.

Wurst, Lou Ann
1999 Internalizing Class in Historical Archaeology. *Historical Archaeology* 33(1):7–21.

Yamin, Rebecca (editor)
1999 With Hope and Labor: Everyday Life in Paterson's Dublin Neighborhood, Vols. 1–2. Report prepared by John Milner Associates, Inc., for the New Jersey Dept. of Transportation Bureau of Environmental Analysis, Trenton, N.J.
2000 A Narrative History and Archaeology of Block 160. Tales of Five Points: Working-Class Life in Nineteenth-Century New York, Volume 1. Report prepared by John Milner Associates, Inc., for the U.S. General Services Administration, Region 2, New York.

10. The Production and Consumption of Smoking Pipes along the Tobacco Coast

Anna S. Agbe-Davies

The earliest references to locally made clay tobacco pipes from colonial sites in the Chesapeake attempted to associate them with one or more past ethnic groups. J. C. Harrington, in his discussion of such pipes from Jamestown, mused:

> Many are obviously of Indian manufacture, but some may have been made by the settlers following Indian styles and techniques . . . some of these pipes which are most Indianlike in character, have well-formed English initials incorporated in the bowl decoration. Is this a case of the Indian copying an European idea; was the maker an "educated" Indian; or did a white man make an "Indian" pipe and put his initials on it? (Harrington 1951:n.p.)

Locally made pipes from the colonial era are most readily distinguished from imported pipes by their clay bodies, the color of which commonly range from pale yellow to dark brown, in contrast with the largely whiter and finer ball clay of European pipes. In their basic construction, the pipes may resemble those manufactured by Native Americans in the pre-Contact era, or those made by Europeans, who first got the idea from observing Native Americans taking tobacco through "pipes made of clay" (Oswald 1975:4). Furthermore, the pipes exhibit a range of decorations including designs common in northern European, pre-Contact Native American, and African repertoires (see, especially, Emerson 1988, 1999; Mouer 1993; Mouer et al. 1999). Thus, as Harrington's commentary suggests, the Chesapeake-made pipes exhibit a unique mix of material, formal and decorative attributes that distinguish them from contemporary clay pipes from other traditions.

Also important to the definition of what are sometimes called "Chesapeake pipes" is their distribution in time and space.[1] For a period of a little more than one hundred years, from the onset of permanent European settlement in 1607 through the first quarter of the eighteenth century, locally manufactured pipes were used alongside the imported variety on sites surrounding the Chesapeake Bay (Deetz 1993:91; Kelso and Straube 2000). According to Matthew C. Emerson (1988:2), the pipes are found only on sites east of the fall line, a physiographic feature that marks the boundary between the inland Piedmont and the coastal Tidewater of Maryland and Virginia. The fall line also marks the limits to which the bay's rivers are navigable by oceangoing vessels and therefore coincides with the limits of early settlement (Middleton 1984:38–39, 41, 101).

Much of the literature that has followed Harrington's initial discussion has continued to emphasize the question of which social group(s) made and smoked Chesapeake pipes. Earlier studies tended to emphasize the "Indian" characteristics of the pipes, particularly those that were not made in molds but rather shaped by hand (Heite 1972:95; Henry 1979:20, 22; Pawson 1969:137–147). Recently, scholars have focused on the "African" elements in the form and decoration of these pipes (Emerson 1988, 1994; Monroe 2002) and also used the pipes to examine the effects of contact between Native Americans, Europeans, and Africans in North America (Deetz 1996:248–251; Mouer 1993:126–146). Still, the question of which social groups produced and used these pipes continues to be a matter of debate among Chesapeake archaeologists (for example, Emerson 1999; Mouer et al. 1999).[2]

A number of theories have been advanced to explain the combination of physical and distributional attributes of locally made pipes. Some archaeologists have suggested that these pipes were evidence of acculturation among Native Americans, who used familiar materials to produce objects that resembled those made and used by their European contemporaries (for example, Heite 1972; Mitchell 1976). Others believed that these artifacts owed their existence to short supplies of imported pipes among European colonists, cut off by unfavorable trade conditions or European wars (for example, Crass 1988; Henry 1979; Miller 1991). Still others suggested that these pipes, particularly in their decoration, signify the arrival of Africans in the region and attribute the pipes' disappearance to the changing modes of bonded labor (for example, Emerson 1988, 1994; Monroe 2002). Yet whether archaeologists have used locally made pipes to discuss cross-cultural exchange, bad year economics, ethnic identity, design symbolism, or culture change, much of this work takes as a given the relationships between pipe *makers* and pipe *users*. Whether one begins with the premise that the pipes were objects of trade, or the idea that a pipe was produced and consumed in a single social context, the key question of how pipes moved from contexts of production to contexts of use has not been the subject of archaeological inquiry itself.

If archaeologists were to demonstrate, for example, that pipes were being produced at the household level, for household consumption, we would make very different arguments about their social significance than if we knew that they were the product of a widely dispersed cottage industry or of full-time specialists. It has long been suspected that the production of locally made pipes did not require sophisticated equipment or industrial organization. Many archaeologists have surmised that Chesapeake pipes were made, consumed, and deposited in the same location (for example, Crass 1988:96; Heite 1972:94), but the recovery of remarkably similar pipes from sites at the extreme northern and southern ends of the bay (Miller 1991:82; Noël Hume 1979:17) seem to contradict this. Yet to date there has been little discussion of the contexts of pipe production and how those relate to contexts of consumption.

After all, tobacco *use* was an important part of Chesapeake society, even though it was the *export* of tobacco that defined the region's place in the world economy (Breen 2001; Kulikoff 1986; Middleton 1984; Morgan 1975). Smoking was introduced to Europeans as a medicine and a novelty, but tobacco soon became a staple consumer good used throughout society (Courtwright 2001). In the seventeenth century there was no consensus about the relative health merits or demerits of smoking (Goodman 1993:61), and there do not seem to have been strong social prohibitions limiting consumption by anyone because of either age or sex.[3] A visitor to the American colonies in the later seventeenth century remarked that "everyone smokes while working and idling. I sometimes went to hear the sermon . . . and when everyone has arrived the minister and all the others smoke before going in . . . they do the same thing before parting . . . It was here I saw that everybody smokes, men, women, girls and boys from the age of seven" (Robert in Goodman 1993:63).

Material evidence demonstrating the universality of pipe smoking can be found at any colonial period site, which is characteristically littered with shattered fragments of the white ball clay pipes that were imported from Britain or the Netherlands. Indeed, because of their very abundance, a number of statistical methods have been developed to best exploit the research potential of the imported clay pipe (Binford 1961; Harrington 1954; Noël Hume 1991:297–302, compare Walker 1977). Ivor Noël Hume wrote that the English tobacco pipe is "possibly the most valuable clue yet available to the student of historical sites, for it is an item that was manufactured, imported, smoked, and thrown away, all within a matter of a year or two" (Noël Hume 1991:296).

Domestically produced pipes have the potential to inform an understanding of local production and exchange as well as tobacco consumption and chronology, yet there has been far less work to date addressing these issues. There have been some important exceptions. For example, in her study of local pipes, Susan Henry (1979) suggested that the boom-and-bust cycle of the tobacco export economy influenced regional pipe production, reasoning that Chesapeake residents could not afford imported pipes when the market was bad. Later, Henry Miller advanced a related hypothesis. He noted that at the Pope's Fort site, Chesapeake pipes often occur with Dutch pipes rather than English specimens and perhaps these two varieties indicate periods during which the colonies were cut off from normal trade with Britain because of the English Civil War (Miller 1991:73, 84).

On the other hand, pipe production may have been one of the many industries with which colonial planters experimented to lessen their dependence on the tobacco market. Green Spring—one of the two sites discussed here—was the residence of Gov. William Berkeley, an advocate of local industry who attempted, among other things, ceramic production and raising silk and flax (Billings 1996; Caywood 1955:312; Crass 1981, 1988:83). Archaeological studies of clay roofing tiles have demonstrated connections between the kiln located at the Page family seat—the other site considered here—with structures built elsewhere by family members and peers (Galucci, Muraca, and McLaughlin 1994:7–8; Metz et al. 1998: 49–50). While we cannot assume that the individuals who made these ceramic products also made pipes, or that they used the same facilities to do so, it makes sense to examine pipe production in the context of regional ceramic production as a whole.

At this point, archaeologists have not explored the extent to which various forms of industry were controlled by local Virginia elites and how much trade was carried out by independent craft specialists. Previous studies of industrial production and distribution, while few in number, have shown the degree to which locally made goods were marketed within the greater Jamestown area (Davidson 1995; Metz 1999; Pittman 1993). Likewise, the positive identification of pipe producers or "workshops" and the analysis of possible trade networks would do much to explain the nature and extent of trade among residents of the colony.

The ongoing research on which this chapter draws uses materials excavated from a selection of contemporary sites in and around James City County, Virginia, to focus on questions concerning the manufacture, distribution, and consumption of locally made pipes. These questions include the following: Can local pipes be traced to a manufacturing location or be grouped by workshop? Do the distributions of these pipes within and across sites indicate their production for on-site use or for trade between producers and consumers? If there is evidence for specialized production, do distribution patterns suggest control by elites or the artisans themselves? In short, what is the potential for these pipes to give archaeologists insight into social life and interaction in the early colonial settlements of the region?

The intent of the present study is to establish criteria suitable for recognizing manufacturing groups. When the data for the larger project has been collected, these criteria will be used to determine whether archaeological assemblages suggest intrahousehold production and consumption of pipes or exchange between producers and consumers. This essay begins with a discussion of strategies for studying Chesapeake-made pipes and an explanation of the strategy applied here. The two sites included in this pilot study are described, along with preliminary findings that suggest that the new approach is justified. The chapter concludes with a discussion of the implications of the preliminary findings and research design.

Problems and Approaches

Upon observing the characteristics that define locally made pipes (local clays, form, decoration, time period, and location), the first issues that suggested themselves to researchers had to do with the difference between these pipes and the imported variety—given that they are often found side by side on seventeenth-century sites—and the particular temporal and spatial limitations to their production. A second important problem confronting archaeologists was the meaning of the decorations found on these pipes: what do these decorations signify? Interest in this question has led to an emphasis on decorative technique and motif in the current literature on Chesapeake pipes (for example, Crass 1988; Emerson 1988; Henry 1979; Mitchell 1976).

Researchers have chosen to approach these questions by, among other things, grouping these artifacts into types. Despite the different questions that concerned them, and the different assemblages they worked with, archaeologists came up with very similar strategies for dealing with these artifacts. A significant number of local pipe analyses used an approach similar to the type-variety method (see Sabloff and Smith 1969). Traditionally, local pipe researchers have used form as the principal organizing attribute, followed by decoration. In some cases (for example, Heite 1972; Pawson 1969), archaeologists adapted categories based on English pipe forms (such as in Atkinson and Oswald 1969 or Oswald 1975). However, it is clear that many locally made pipes do not conform to these ideals. Consequently, other archaeologists have added a range of forms more typical of the Chesapeake tradition (for example, Henry 1979; Emerson 1988). But typological classifications of locally made pipes that are based on form select against highly fragmented specimens, which begs the question: what if the relationship between highly fragmented and more complete artifacts is not random? As will be demonstrated below, it is not (see also Agbe-Davies 2001).

The other common method of studying local pipes uses decoration to distinguish one variety from another. The emphasis on decoration has led to a neglect of undecorated specimens, with implications similar to those cited for the neglect of fragments. While decoration has been used to posit social relationships among artisans (see Deetz 1965; compare Lathrap 1983), decoration is not necessarily the most, or the only, culturally determined feature of an artifact.

The concept of "isochrestic variation," as explained by James Sackett, provides an alternative to classification systems based solely on decorative criteria. Isochrestism holds that stylistic meaning resides not only in decoration but also in all aspects of artifactual variation, that decoration is style rich, but so too are the technical choices made by artisans (Sackett 1990:33–34, 38, 42). Essentially, "style is more often built in, rather than added on, to objects" (Sackett 1990:42). The present project examines decorative style alongside—rather than instead of—what Heather Lechtman (1977) has referred to as the "style of technology" (Figure 10.1). The standardization that is the hallmark of specialized production can be measured by material and metric, as well as decorative, attributes (Blackman, Stein, and Vandiver 1993:61).

So the best classification strategy for dealing with the question of workshop groups would allow for the inclusion of fragmented specimens and the use of technological as well as decorative attributes. In *Prehistory in Haiti: A Study in Method,* Irving Rouse described the value of "modal analysis," also called "analytical classification," in which the constituent attributes, or "modes," of an artifact are the units of analysis rather than the artifacts themselves. Modal analysis is particularly suited for looking at fragments, since it does not require complete objects to derive groupings. Modal analysis is also well adapted to the study of technological and manufacturing attributes—such as firing cores, fabric composition, and construction techniques—attributes that, incidentally, are more readily observed from fragments (Rouse 1939:26, 139–40; see also Rouse 1971) (see Figure 10.1). The end result of modal analysis is not one typology but a series of cross-cutting groupings, each one based on a different "mode" (Rouse 1971: 110–111). In his discussion of the forms of classification to apply to different archaeological problems, Rouse suggests that "modes are the best unit to use in studying cultural distributions. One may trace their persistence and their relative popularity through time . . . or *their diffusion from area to area*" (Rouse 1960:119; italics added), which is key to an archaeological study of exchange.[4]

Classification techniques are of such importance to this study because of the influence that technique has on the categories that underpin one's analysis. Most previous work with locally made pipes has employed taxonomic-typological techniques. With taxonomic typologies, the attributes are ranked hierarchically and the types emerge from a series of branching divisions. For example, one system separated pipes first by clay color, then shape, surface treatment, and decorative motif (Pawson 1969). As with most taxonomic typologies, the order of the attributes within the hierarchy of divisions, and therefore the relationships among the various types, is intuitive, which creates ambiguity in the system (Dunnell 1971:73).

Taxonomic classification requires that one select particular traits or dimensions of variation as primary. With the case of pipes, one could argue that bowl

FIG. 10.1. ▸ *Two views of the same pipe fragment emphasizing (left) decoration and (right) forming technique.*

shape (drawn from sources such as Atkinson and Oswald 1969 and Oswald 1975) might be used as a primary attribute. However, pipe fragments are not always complete enough to determine their similarity to these archetypes. Furthermore, the inclusion of hand-built specimens in the local tradition introduces a variability not seen among the imported (and largely mold-made) pipes, which have been so exhaustively studied. In the population discussed in this chapter (n = 761), only 46 fragments were complete enough to compare to existing schemes, and only 39 conformed to said schemes.

And recall that giving one trait priority over another can produce substantially different results. A concrete example can be drawn from the study of locally made pipes from one of the sites analyzed here. The pipes from Green Spring plantation were included in Emerson's comprehensive study of Chesapeake pipes (Emerson 1988, 1994, 1999), as well as in a study by David Colin Crass devoted exclusively to the pipes (both imported and local) at Green Spring (Crass 1981, 1988). Crass's work identified six types of locally made pipes, differentiated by bowl form, primarily, as well as six aberrant forms in a collection of thirty-six bowls (Crass 1988:89–93). Emerson noted the presence of eight of his types—differentiated by decoration—in a select group of twenty bowls and fragments (Emerson 1988:97–99). The discrepancy in numbers of types is not due to one set of criteria being "right" and another "wrong."[5] Rather, the different conclusions are due to the fact that categories based on different criteria (and using different samples) lead to different outcomes.

The point of the present work is not to correct the previous analyses of locally made pipes, but to ask new questions of the data set, which, therefore, requires different techniques (Brew 1971; Hill and Evans 1972:248–258). The importance of classificatory pluralism was articulated by J. O. Brew, who wrote the following:

> We need more rather than fewer classifications, different classifications, always new classifications, to meet new needs. We must not be satisfied with a single classification of a group of artifacts or of a cultural development, for that way lies dogma and defeat . . . We need have no fear of changing established systems of or designing new ones, for its is only by such means that we can progress . . . We must recognize that any given system in its entirety will probably be applicable only to the given set of problems that it was designed to meet. (Brew 1971:105–106)

Modal attributes, in addition to being amenable to the analysis of fragments, can be applied to the paradigmatic classification of artifacts. Paradigmatic classifications differ from taxonomic systems in that they are nonhierarchical—there is no ordering of divisions from more to less inclusive. Each attribute included is of the same order of magnitude. It follows, then, that there is no ambiguity about the relationships among the classes, which in the case of taxonomies arises from decisions about which attributes out-rank others.

Because of the emphasis on taxonomic classification, researchers have generally selected out highly fragmented specimens, so that discussions of the tradition are based on samples that are a tiny fraction of the original assemblage. The present study demonstrates that samples based on completeness and/or decoration are not representative of the archaeological assemblage, let alone of the corpus of specimens that circulated in the living context of Chesapeake society. So while such samples are useful for characterizing types, they are not proxies for assemblages.

It is important to record information about all of the specimens rather than selecting against the more fragmented ones, because doing so returns a biased sample. While it has been common in other studies to select for bowls and bowl fragments, as these are the most likely to exhibit decoration and readily differentiated formal variation, this study has shown that the range of tools used to execute decoration varies according to the completeness of the pipe being considered. The less complete specimens, as a group, exhibit a more diverse group of decorative strategies, which occur in different ratios than among more complete specimens. For example, of the different kinds of tools used to impress or incise decoration onto the pipe surfaces, twenty-five of the twenty-six identified were observed on the partial fragments, but only nine of the twenty-six were observed in the much smaller sample of fragments counted as "complete" bowls. For both "complete" bowls and other fragments, the majority of the decoration (60–65 percent) was executed using just two types of tools, both used to create a dentate pattern. But the difference between the bowls and stems is even more striking when one examines the remaining decorative repertoire. After the dentate-imparting tools are excluded, the tools used most commonly to decorate complete bowl fragments are tool 3 (25 percent), tool 20 (25 percent), and tool 13 (17 percent). For the population at large, they are tool 3 (15 percent), tool 13 (14 percent), tool 7 (11 percent) and tool 14 (11 percent).

These discrepancies are important because subsequent observations will depend on the representativeness of the sample. For example, of the twenty-six tools used to decorate pipes, four are represented only on artifacts from at the Page site (2, 6, 8, 9), whereas sixteen of them are unique to Green Spring (11–26). Of the two most common tools (1 and 4), 1 dominates the Page assemblage and 4 is most common among the population from Green Spring (Agbe-Davies 2001). If fragmented specimens had been omitted, however, tool 1 would be more common than tool 4 at Green Spring, and vice versa at Page.

When decorated and undecorated pipes are compared, we find that the decorated ones are not representative of the entire population, either, which justifies the collection of data on masses of seemingly undifferentiated fragments. For example, out of all the specimens with bore diameters [n = 665], approximately one-fifth exhibit decoration [n = 136]. Using the mean bore diameter for the entire assemblage (8.017) and for the assemblage of decorated pipes (7.846) as population and sample means, respectively, the standardized normal deviate shows that the probability of obtaining the mean of the decorated pipes as a random sample from the population of pipes at large is between 0.02 and 0.03 (p = 0.0287). So, clearly, decorated fragments cannot stand in for the assemblage as a whole.

Unlike previous studies, the ongoing research incorporates techniques that allow data to be collected on the entire excavated sample rather than focusing on decorated and more complete specimens. Evaluation of other research on ceramic production, and the study of the pipes themselves, has led to the identification of a set of more than forty attributes that appear to be useful in identifying "workshop" groups (see Orton, Tyers, and Vince 1993:145). These include commonly cited characteristics—for example, descriptions of bowl shape—but also the techniques and tools used to form, hollow, and finish said shapes.

There are a number of inferences that can be drawn from ceramic analysis, including when, where, how, why, and by whom an object was made (Kingery 1982:41–42). These can be determined using information about provenience, style, external characteristics, ethnographic observation, relative and absolute dating, chemical composition analysis, and microstructure analysis (Kingery 1982:38–40; Matson 1982:20). Of course, analyses of artifacts alone will not really tell "where" a ceramic object was made, but they will indicate relationships among artifacts. In fact, many, if not most, ceramic studies do not link products to an actual source of raw materials but rather show *relationships among artifacts* that can be demonstrated in other ways to be related, so-called workshop sourcing (Orton, Tyers, and Vince 1993:145). Workshop sourcing works because ceramic objects can be grouped not only based on their source in a common clay bed, but also on the similar processes used by the maker(s) to procure, prepare, and manipulate those raw materials (Neff 1993:33). The goal here is to determine which locally made pipes were made using the same techniques—technological and decorative—with the inference being that these pipes may come from a common "workshop" or (group of) producer(s).

If it is possible to identify particular "workshop groups" of locally made pipes, the second goal is to use the groups' distributions to discuss exchange or the lack thereof. Such a project requires a focus broader than the single site but narrower than the full range of the locally made pipe tradition. Clearly, the present research plan is not sufficient to pin production to particular *geographic* locations. The goal is to associate pipes with production nodes that may be thought of as existing in *social* rather than physical space. What does the ultimate disposition of the pipes tell us about relationships between producers and consumers of pipes? What social and economic networks does the distribution of pipes imply? The point is to learn about the social relationships that characterize the sites that have products from the same workshop(s), rather than the distance that pipes traveled.

Findings

The assemblages selected for this preliminary analysis is the population of red clay pipe fragments from excavations at Green Spring, near Jamestown, and the Page site, in the modern city of Williamsburg (Map 10.1). These sites provided a total of 761 fragments, which were all recorded according to the following series of nominal attributes:

Presence/absence of a heel or spur
Characteristics of heel or spur, if present
Bowl forming technique
Presence/absence of mold scars
Treatment of mold scars, if present
Decorative tool
Decorative motif
Location of decoration

The fragments were also recorded according to the metric traits illustrated (Figure 10.2). These are the most immediately pertinent of the variables that should be useful in identifying manufacturing or "workshop" groups. Many of the metric measurements are those that were used successfully by R. C. Alvey and R. R. Laxton to identify molds used by pipe makers in Nottingham (Alvey and Laxton 1974, 1977).

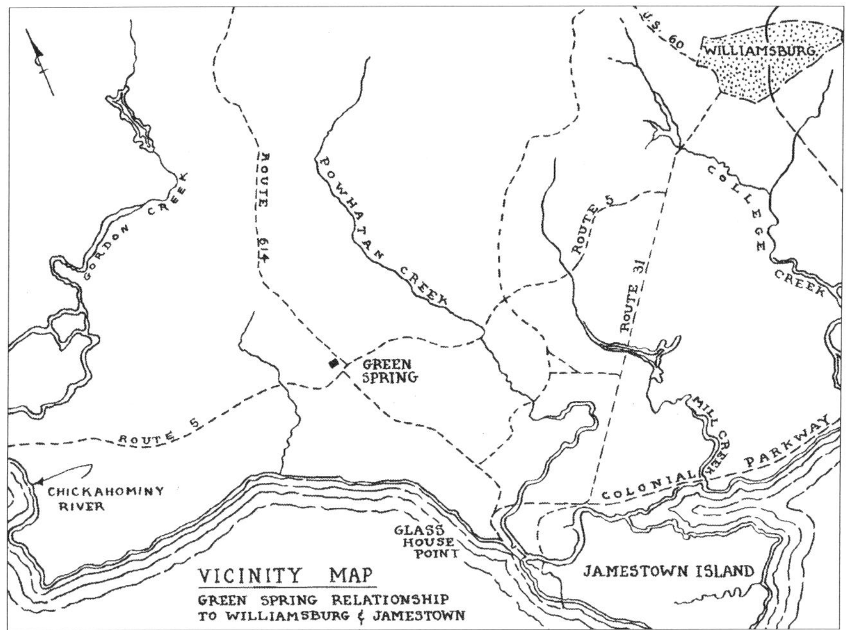

MAP 10.1. ▸ *The locations of Green Spring (44JC9) and the Page site (44WB68 and 44WB70). Illustration by Heather Harvey. Courtesy of the Colonial Williamsburg Foundation, Department of Archaeological Research.*

The two sites discussed here, Green Spring Plantation[6] and the Page site,[7] are both excellent candidates for pipe production centers. Both sites include kilns used in the production of ceramic objects. Pottery from the Green Spring kiln has been found at nearby Jamestown and Governor's Land (Straube 1995: 17). Roofing tiles from the Page kiln have been found throughout Williamsburg and at Jamestown (Metz et al. 1998:49; Galucci Muraca, and McLaughlin 1994). If the production of pipes were a specialized enterprise, where better to anticipate its occurrence? Examination of the pipe fragments demonstrates that they were certainly used at each site. Numerous stem fragments exhibit tooth wear, and charring is evident in a number of the bowls. And if, as has long been argued (notably by Emerson 1988; Henry 1979; and Neiman and King 1999), locally made pipes reflect the exclusion of certain smokers from the market in imported pipes, then we may look to the indentured and enslaved workers known to have lived at these sites (for example, York County 1976:60–62) as the consumers of these pipes, as their producers, or perhaps as both. Finally, both Green Spring and the Page site were occupied during the most active years of local pipe production, circa 1640–1720 (Deetz 1993:91).

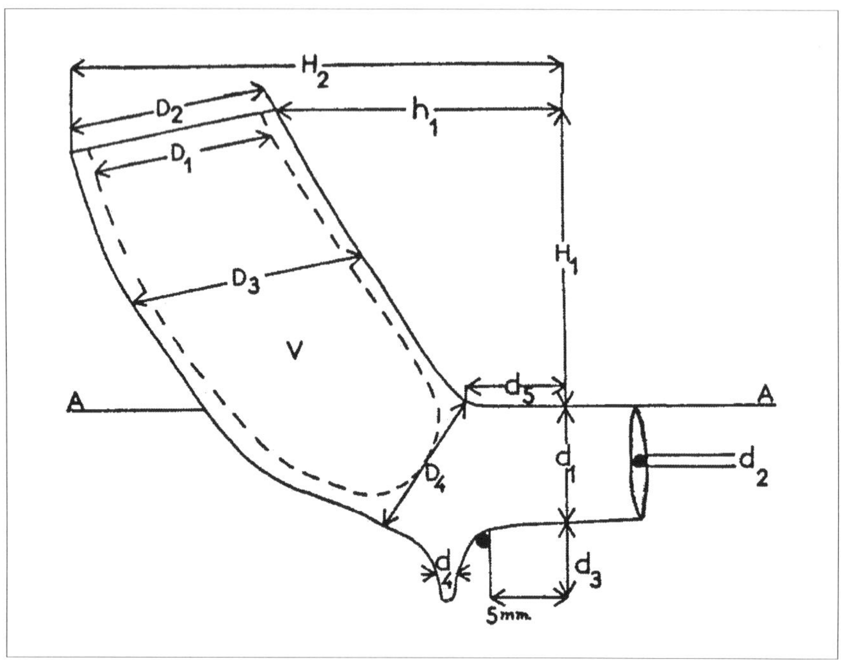

FIG. 10.2. ▸ *Measurements discussed in the text. Illustration by J. Eric Deetz.*

Green Spring

Sir William Berkeley, governor of Virginia, became the first documented owner of Green Spring in the summer of 1643. He received the 984-acre parcel by headright (Carson 1954:9), the kind of allotment one might expect if one had transported twenty individuals into the colony (Morgan 1975:94). Green Spring, located approximately 3.5 miles north and west of the capital city at Jamestown, and 6 miles from the burgeoning suburb of Middle Plantation (later Williamsburg), was Berkeley's primary base of operations during his two tenures as governor, 1641–1652 and 1660–1677. In addition to his political role, Berkeley was also a prominent planter. Eyewitness accounts refer to his acres of tobacco, fruit trees, and rice. His own writings reveal a man always experimenting with alternatives to tobacco planting: lumber, silk, flax, and wine, among other schemes (Billings 1996; Carson 1954:4–5). Pottery from the onsite kiln was found in midden deposits dating to the latter part of his ownership (1660–1680) (Caywood 1955:13; compare Smith 1981:96). Following Berkeley's death, Lady Frances Berkeley married William Berkeley's cousin and political crony, Philip Ludwell. The colony rented Green Spring intermittently for

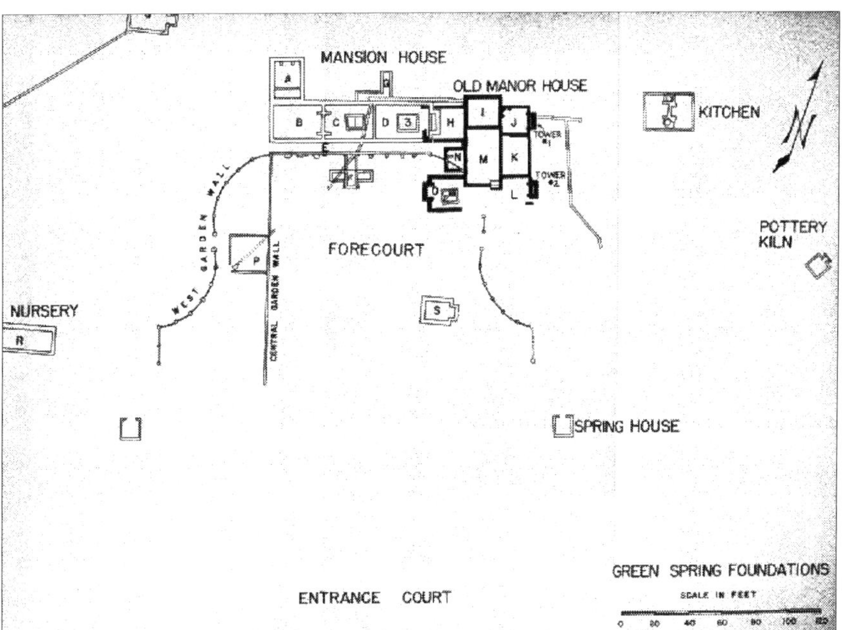

MAP 10.2. ▸ *Archaeological plan of Green Spring. Courtesy of the National Park Service, Colonial National Historical Park, Jamestown Collection.*

the use of subsequent governors over the next several decades, but sometime around 1705 Ludwell's son by a previous marriage took up residence at Green Spring and the property remained in Ludwell hands into the nineteenth century (Carson 1954:6–7; Smith 1993:2).

Major excavations took place at Green Spring in 1928 and 1954–1955. Both of the projects emphasized architectural over other forms of information. They revealed substantial brick and stone foundations with at least two periods of construction. The earliest phase consisted of a large square structure with brick and sandstone foundations. Appended to the western face of that structure was a brick foundation running east-west with a small ell to the rear of the western end. Based on the careful alignment of the two foundations, and an analysis of the brickwork, it seems that they coexisted for a time (Caywood 1955:11–12). By 1781, the older structure was no longer standing, and the later one was described as "ruinous" and was soon pulled down (Caywood 1957:72).

In addition to the main house, excavators uncovered outbuildings interpreted as a jail, greenhouse, pottery kiln, and kitchen, as well as several unnamed structures, drains, garden walls, and middens (Map 10.2). Early twentieth-century landowner Jesse Dimmick was the first to expose the foundations at Green Spring and in the process removed the contents of three of the five cellars associated with the structures (Caywood 1955:18; Dimmick 1929). Although Dimmick published a two-page report and map of his findings, the National Park Service—which now owns Green Spring and its collection—does not possess the documentation or artifacts from that excavation (William Cahoon, personal communication 2000). National Park Service archaeologist Louis Caywood led the re-excavation in the winter of 1954–1955. That project resulted in a collection of 2,948 local and imported pipe fragments, as well as associated documentation. All of the pipes made of local clays that were recovered from Green Spring are included in the present study—with the exception of a small group for which no provenience data survives. The final population of local pipe fragments is 601, which were all described according to the criteria listed above and in Figure 10.2.

The pipes from Green Spring are concentrated in a midden deposit behind the earliest brick house. At this site, unlike several others studied by Fraser Neiman and Julia King (1999), there is no noticeable difference between the distribution of imported pipes and locally made pipes. Of perhaps even greater significance, there was no concentration of locally made pipes associated with the kiln. The excavation records indicate that only a small area around the kiln was excavated, so it is possible that waster piles further away are as yet undiscovered. Nevertheless, the number of fragments from the deposits overlying and within the kiln is quite small: eight in all. Of the eight pipes that could be wasters, based on manner of fracture, incomplete bores, and warping or burning, only one came from the pottery kiln.

The Page Site

John Page was the first Englishman to build a home on the property he purchased at Middle Plantation, now the city of Williamsburg. The large dwelling house was built in 1662 from bricks and tiles manufactured on the property (Metz et al. 1998:4, 39–45). Page was a well-to-do and powerful man who held a number of important local and regional political offices, though he was not a member of Governor Berkeley's inner circle (Metz et al. 1998:31–33; Sprinkle 1992:164). Page owned two other plantations and shares in several merchant ships (York County 1976:60–62). He was often described as a merchant rather than as a planter (McCartney 2000:260–262).

The up-draft kiln and associated facilities located on Page's home lot were used in the production of brick and tiles, not just for the manor house but also for a substantial brick kitchen/quarter and several other structures, one in the heart of Middle Plantation and another at Jamestown, several miles away (Metz et al. 1998 43, 49–50; Galucci, Muraca, and McLaughlin 1994). Page's will makes

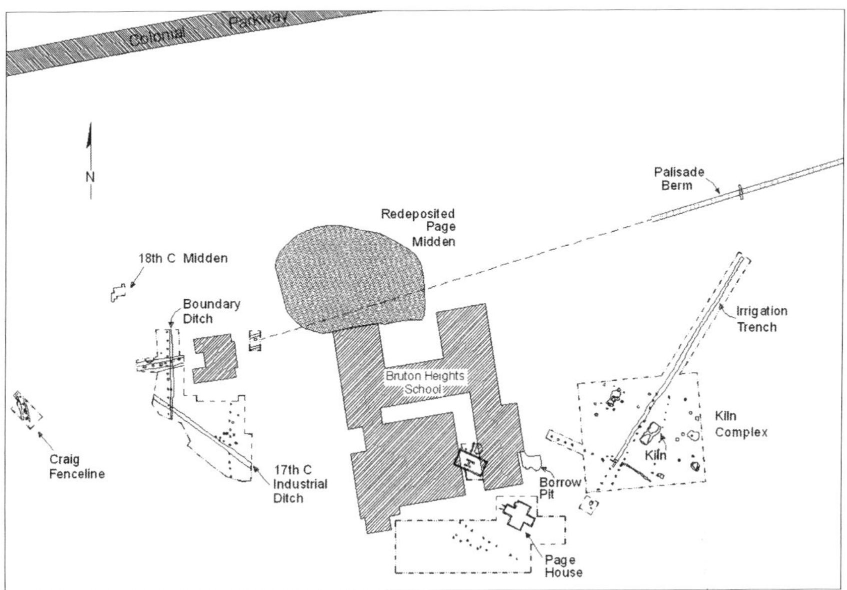

MAP 10.3. ▸ *Archaeological plan of the Page site. Illustration by Heather Harvey. Courtesy of the Colonial Williamsburg Foundation, Department of Archaeological Research.*

clear that during his lifetime, the plantation had been the home of a number of servants and slaves, as well as his family: wife Alice and children Francis, Matthew, and Mary (York County 1976:60–62). The house ultimately descended to Page's great-grandson, also named John Page, who seems to have been the owner when the manor house burned in the late 1720s (Metz et al. 1998:88, 93).

The Page site was excavated between 1992 and 1995 by the Colonial Williamsburg Foundation, with project archaeologists John Metz and Dwayne Pickett leading the excavation teams. The 160 nonball clay pipe fragments were approximately 10 percent of the entire pipe assemblage (Metz et al. 1998:79). Unlike at Green Spring, the greatest number of locally made pipes came from the areas devoted to ceramic production—the kiln, work yard, and borrow pit. A smaller concentration was associated with the kitchen and its transposed midden. The manor house cellar fill contained only three fragments (Map 10.3).

Analysis

The different attributes of the pipe fragments were first analyzed as modes. That is to say, the distributions of the attributes were considered independently of one another and of the artifacts themselves. Second, the attributes were used in

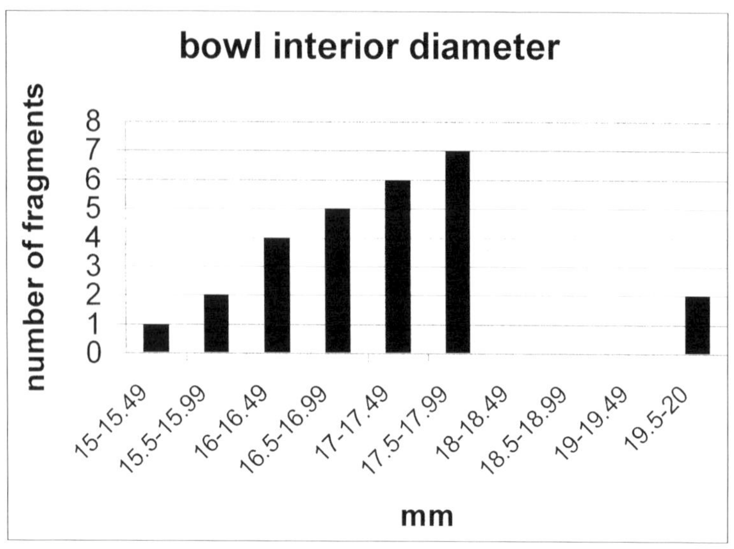

FIG. 10.3. ▸ *Number of pipe fragments by bowl interior diameter.*

a paradigmatic analysis, which examined correlations of attributes with one another at either the artifact level or the site level. For example, of the 110 artifacts for which the presence or absence of a heel or spur could be observed, heelless pipes made up 43 percent of the Green Spring assemblage and 80 percent of the Page population.

One particularly important form of variation examined is the technique used to hollow out the pipe bowls. Of the fifty-eight bowls and bowl fragments with unambiguous marks, forty-six, or 79 percent, show evidence of twisting or reaming while being formed—parallel striations running horizontally across the interior surface of the bowl. This was not the method of choice in England during the seventeenth century, where most pipe makers used machines with a plunger or "stopper" fixed to the mold (Walker 1977:186, 196–197), which would yield marks that run vertically along the bowl interior. Interestingly, the only bowls with such vertical markings do not exhibit overall forms such as those normally found among European ball clay pipes. A number of them resembled those described as aboriginal forms (Henry 1979:20). Furthermore, when the presence or absence of mold scars is taken into account, vertical bowl formation marks are closely associated with unscarred fragments, horizontal marks with the presence of mold scars, demonstrating a clear association between forming technique and overall shape, though not what might be expected given the historical record.

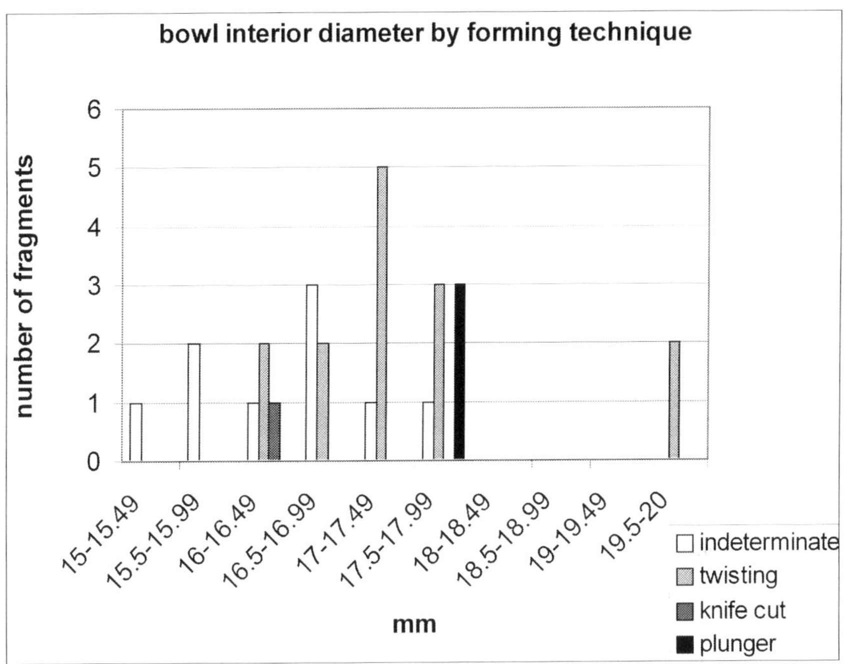

FIG. 10.4. ▸ *Number of pipe fragments by bowl interior diameter and bowl forming technique.*

Rather, we would expect to see mold scars, as the products of the pipe-making machines described above, associated with vertical striations on bowl interiors.

Interestingly, further findings suggest that molds were not the only source of pipe uniformity. When the interior lip diameters of the bowls are compared, there were only slight differences in size throughout the population. Most are between fifteen and eighteen millimeters, with two outliers (Figure 10.3). The coefficients of variation for the types of bowl formation are 5.26 percent for bowls with "indeterminate" forming techniques and 5.78 percent for bowls formed by "twisting." The "plunger" bowls, however, showed a coefficient of variation of only 0.41 percent, quite a narrow range, especially considering that these are what have been called "aboriginal" forms and, furthermore, bear no mold scars. The distribution of interior bowl diameters according to bowl-forming technique returns much more normal-looking curves, suggesting that these reflect significant differences within the attribute range (Figure 10.4).

Another interesting avenue of investigation is variation and standardization among bore sizes. J. C. Harrington's technique for estimating dates using pipe stem bores is well known, as are modifications to that technique by Lewis Binford

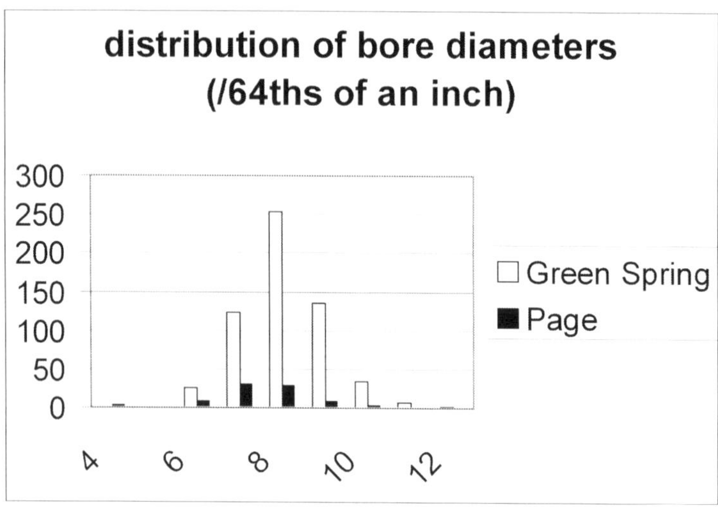

FIG. 10.5. ▸ *Comparison of pipe bore sizes for Green Spring and Page sites.*

and others (Binford 1962; Harrington 1954). Previous work has demonstrated that the formulae and date ranges used by these techniques do not work with Chesapeake-made pipes (for example, Crass 1981:75; Emerson 1988:41–44). However, this does not mean that the *principle* cannot work. Seth Mallios and J. Cameron Monroe have been examining local pipes from sites in James City County, Virginia, and have developed a technique that produces results comparable to those from imported pipes (Mallios et al. 2001). Using their formula, the mean date for Green Spring is 1662. Based on documentary evidence, the median date of occupation for the main house site is 1719, but the median date for *the Berkeleys'* occupation is 1661. The mean formula date for Page is 1687, with the median date of use for the manor house approximately 1696. While the utility of mean dates can be debated (for example, Deetz 1987; Walker 1977:9–12), this new development should become a part of the discussion.

Bore diameters are particularly interesting for what they reveal about standardization and therefore specialization among pipe makers. A comparison of the bore diameters of pipes with mold scars and without reveals, contrary to what one might expect (given the greater precision offered by mold manufacture and the implied access to specialized tools), that the group with clear evidence of mold manufacture has only marginally smaller bores. The mean size of fragments with scars was 7.8/64 of an inch, versus 8.09/64 of an inch. The range of pipes with visible mold scars was 4/64 to 11/64; for unscarred specimens it was 4/64 to 12/64. However, the coefficients of variation within each category are

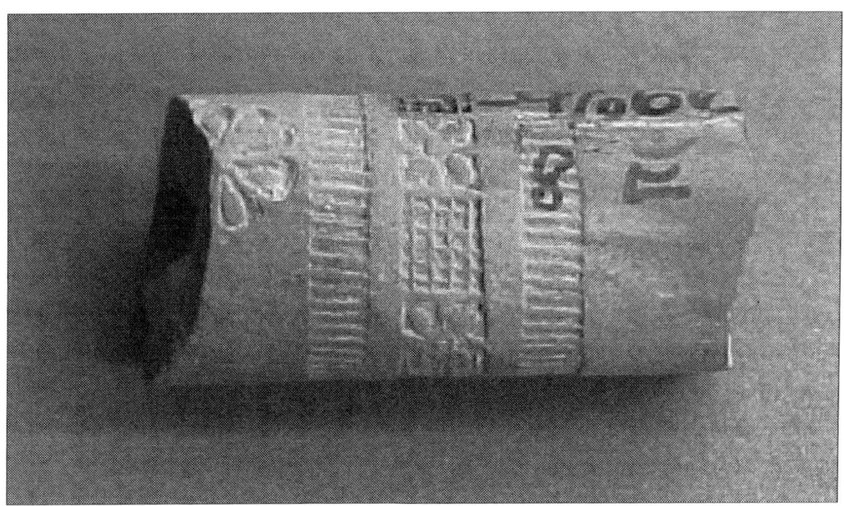

FIG. 10.6. ▸ *The complex stamping pattern shown here has an equivalent in Figure 10.7.*

quite large 13.04 percent and 12.93 percent, respectively, suggesting that some internal variation is still being masked by the groupings. The distributions of bore sizes for Green Spring and Page were different (Figure 10.5), but grouping the fragments by site does not explain the variation. When the fragments were grouped by site *and* presence or absence of mold scars, the Page pipes *with* scars were noticeably more variable with a coefficient of variation of 22.65 percent, whereas the other categories showed coefficients of variation between 11 and 14—still high enough to suggest that there is some additional variability to be accounted for.

Decorative attributes have, of course, been very important in studying the variation in the Green Spring and Page assemblages. As suggested above, it has been important to note not only the designs used in the decoration but also the tools themselves, especially in situations where pipe makers have used a range of tools to execute the "same" decorative motifs. The production of this small, agatized pipe stem required a distinct combination of stamping tools for the compound design (Figure 10.6). Pipes with similar motifs have occurred at other sites throughout the Chesapeake, including Nominy Plantation (Virginia), Martin's Hundred (Virginia), and St. Johns (Maryland) (Henry 1979:Figure 2; Julia King, personal communication 2001; Taft Kiser, personal communication 2001; Al Luckenbach, personal communication 2001; Mitchell 1983:Figure 10; Noël Hume and Noël Hume 2001:Figure 106). However, this study has also identified an alternative version of this decorative pattern, executed at a larger scale, with different

FIG. 10.7. ▸ *Although the person who made this pipe obviously used different tools, the motif is the same as that shown in Figure 10.6.*

tools, clay bodies, and overall proportions (Figure 10.7). While one is clearly patterned on the other, recording these pipes as having the same decoration could preclude, for example, an exploration of the *direction* of the influence. Recording these as two different "types" of pipes could have done the same thing, but by masking their similarities because of the different clays, or scales.[8]

The pipes offer another clear example of the reproduction of a single motif using a range of tools. There are eight pipes that have starburst motifs rendered in dentate lines. Co-occurring with several of these starbursts are square panels.[9] The starbursts are executed with at least three different tools, and a range of different tools are used to form the panels (Figure 10.8). The one starburst that appears on the front of a bowl is also the only one in which the rays consist of a single dentate line. If only the motif itself had been recorded, omitting the manner of execution and location, this correlation might have been overlooked. To lump such examples as identical decoration would mask the very variation that will inform an understanding of how many pipe makers might have shared this decorative style, and it would be just as problematic as focusing exclusively on the tools and ignoring the significant similarity that probably indicates shared knowledge rather than a chance combination of motifs.

These are only a couple of many examples that appear to justify the degree of recording detail and the analytical approach used in this study. When one is considering only two sites, it is difficult to interpret the juxtapositions of similarity and difference. But when one hopes to understand the possible exchange of commodities, it makes sense to pay attention to the isochrestic variation represented. Grouping pipes into heterogeneous "types" can be as problematic as a proliferation of unique "types." Modal and paradigmatic analysis are used here to circumvent the problems associated with an exclusive reliance on taxonomic classification.

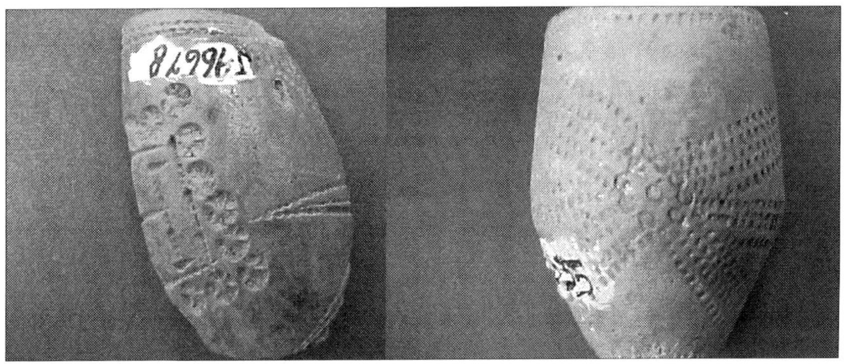

FIG. 10.8. ▸ *Two examples of a "starburst" motif, visible at the right edge of the fragment at left and centered on the fragment shown at right.*

The number of workshop groups represented by the Green Spring and Page assemblages remains to be seen. However, it is clear that the attributes selected are appropriate for examining variation within populations of locally made pipes. As many previous researchers have suggested (Emerson 1988; Henry 1979), locally made pipes are not a monolithic category, and much can be learned from a classificatory method that employs a wide variety of attributes and incorporates all available fragments rather than selecting for particular specimens. At the moment, the variation between the sites at both the modal and paradigmatic levels suggests that the fragments from Green Spring and the fragments from the Page site are not drawn from a single workshop. However, with a sample of two sites, it is not possible to attribute this variation to either household production at each site or to consumption of pipes from different workshops. Clearly, with each site having a kiln and workers skilled in ceramic production techniques, but without any direct evidence such as pipe wasters or manufacturing facilities, either option is still possible. As I add to the range of sites examined, and undertake more sophisticated means of comparison, these patterns should become more clear.

Significance

Tobacco smoking by people other than Native Americans was a function of the connections that characterize the modern world. Europeans popularized tobacco among the people of the Old World, emigrated to the Chesapeake to set up plantations for increased production, and, when the pace of European immigration could not keep up with the demand for labor, conscripted Africans to take their place.

Matthew Johnson describes (European) pipes as "artefact[s] of colonialism as well as of popular resistance [because of their association with alehouses and other hotbeds of radicalism]. Like many other commodities such as tea and sugar, the popularity of these items among ordinary people from the later seventeenth century onwards fueled Imperial trade and colonial domination" (Johnson 1996: 186). The domination of bound laborers—who are often put forward as the makers and/or consumers of Chesapeake-made pipes—is a key dimension to consider. Locally made pipes are often, though not always, concentrated in areas frequented by the slaves and indentured servants on whom the elites of the Chesapeake depended (compare Neiman and King 1999), and the decorative motifs often resemble patterns common among the societies from which they had come.

The planters were subject to an altogether different form of domination: the cycle of credit and debt that characterized most planters' participation in the tobacco trade (Breen 2001; Isaac 1982:27–30; Kulikoff 1986). Perhaps these planters were experimenting with the production (and sale) of Chesapeake pipes as a way to augment their income. They certainly were not making the pipes themselves—that would have been left to their workers. On the other hand, pipes may have been independently produced by plantation laborers and distributed according to *their* wants and needs, completely outside the planter's realm. How to distinguish the product of ideological nonconformity from the product of an "attached" craft specialist? The results presented here suggest that archaeological analyses of locally made pipes can be used to address this question.

The heads of household at Green Spring and the Page site had commercial operations, plantations, and houses throughout the area, several of which have been excavated archaeologically. Future research will include a comparison of the assemblages that could reflect the purchasing or production decisions of a common owner and associated household. Collections from contemporary sites with no known affiliation will clarify the extent to which social networks, as opposed to geography, affect distribution.

Modeling exchange using the archaeological record requires that one establish which patterns should be associated with which types of exchange behavior. When production and consumption are confined to the same household, one would expect to find greater variation among households than within them. One might also expect to find greater variation *within* self-supplying households than within households supplied by a single specialist, due to the tendency of specialized producers to turn out more homogeneous products than producers who exercise their skill less often (Blackman et al. 1993). If there were a one-to-one or one-to-many relationship between a producer and consumer, or consumers, one would expect to find greater assemblage homogeneity between those linked sites than between those sites and ones relying on other producers. If there were a many-to-one relationship between producers and a consumer, one would expect to find greater absolute heterogeneity at the consumer site than at a single, related, producer site. Of course, more complex variants are possible, including itinerant producers, informal sharing, distribution from centralized markets, etc.[10] The main point is to indicate that it is possible to examine underlying exchange networks through the distribution of products.[11] Whether or not the distinctions observed here would have been recognized by the people who made and used Chesapeake-made pipes, the distinctions are analytically informative and to that extent, anyway, real (compare Brew 1971:82; Hill and Evans 1972:233, Ford 1954:42). The attributes and methods discussed here represent an attempt to study local production and consumption through an examination of standardization within assemblages of pipes.

Research has shown that British clay tobacco pipes were one of the few commodities with a high enough value-to-weight ratio to make overland transport within Britain profitable (Crossley 1990:276). In Europe, pipes were sometimes a sideline for professional potters (Weatherill and Edwards 1971) but more often were produced by specialists (Bell 1995). Manufacturing techniques such as burnishing the pipes or rouletting the mouths of their bowls made them more costly, to produce, and to purchase, reflecting a market in which certain makers specialized in higher or lower quality wares (Crossley 1990:277). Little is known, however, about the cost or esteem value of imported pipes vis-à-vis their Chesapeake counterparts. Archaeologists have suggested that the latter were substitutes for when the former became unavailable or too costly (Henry 1979; Miller 1991; Neiman and King 1999).

The above issues demonstrate how fruitful it would be to know if these items were, in fact, produced for sale, or if people made them for their own use. By isolating particular production styles and comparing their distributions, one could conceivably answer this question definitively. The pipes could then inform an understanding of social relations between producers, distributors, and consumers or, alternatively, the nature of household production of a noncommodity.

Like other artifacts, these pipes carry information about social relations beyond the economic ones often emphasized by archaeologists; they are more than just (potential) commodities (Johnson 1996:179). Consider the significance of smoking among the native inhabitants of the Chesapeake. The act was an important component of warfare, diplomacy, medicine, and adult masculinity (Hall 1977; Linton 1924; Rountree 1989:91, 108, 132–136). Since the plant itself and Native American techniques for consuming it influenced European and African habits, one might use Chesapeake pipes to explore how these meanings were transferred to, or transformed by, new smokers. Do locally made and imported pipes have different meanings associated with their use? Do these differ from the meanings we might infer from pre-Contact pipes? (See Magoon 1999.)

Certain "meanings" of local clay pipes will inevitably be linked to the effects of smoking itself. An English merchant in describing the smoking habits of Sierra Leoneans in the early seventeenth century noted that it "seems to be half their food." A later traveler commented, "They are always smoaking Tobacco, which serves to amuse them, and deaden the Appetite" (cited in Walsh 1997:61, 62). Like sugar, tobacco served as a food substitute and drug, binding consumers and producers into tighter and tighter relations while at the same time distracting the laboring classes from their plight (Courtwright 2001; Wallerstein 1980:164). Locally made and consumed pipes are one avenue for exploring the self-medication and addiction of the very people who produced tobacco for the rest of the world economy while also addressing their own consumption within that system.

Many scholars have suggested that historical archaeology approach problems and topics on a number of scales ranging from the individual to the global level (for example, Cleland 1988:13; Johnson 1996:210; Little 1996:46; Orser 1996; Schuyler 1988:41). The above discussion has demonstrated the implications Chesapeake pipes have for studying several different scales, from the world economy of the seventeenth century and the relationship between production and consumption within the Chesapeake to the creation and maintenance of social identities and the impact of tobacco consumption on the lives of individuals. A concept of historical archaeology as the study of the emergence and transformation of the modern world (Schuyler 1997:1) provides a focus for the ongoing research.

Acknowledgments

Many individuals have influenced my thinking on the themes of classification, production, consumption, and meaning that run through this chapter. Here I single out those who have had a direct impact on the material presented in this particular iteration of my research. William Cahoon, David Riggs, and Kelly Ladd provided access to the Green Spring and Page artifact collections and site archives and offered invaluable advice on working with these two assemblages. I have received helpful feedback on the ideas expressed here from a long list of colleagues—David Gadsby, Jillian Galle, Julia King, Taft Kiser, Al Luckenbach, Seth Mallios, Cameron Monroe, Fraser Neiman, William Pittman, and Bly Straube. Close readings of this chapter, and previous versions, by Marley Brown and Robert Schuyler have helped me to clarify my thinking on several key points. These individuals may not agree with everything I say here, but I hope that this piece adds something useful to a continuing conversation.

Notes

1. Also called "terra-cotta," "aboriginal," "local," "Virginia made," "colonoware," and "Colono" pipes (Emerson 1988:1; Henry 1979:14; Monroe 2002).

2. Determining the ethnic identity of the makers and users of Chesapeake pipes is *not* the goal of the present project. However, ethnicity has considerable bearing on this research because the seventeenth century was a period of social flux; ethnic identities

were in a constant state of formation and transformation. Powhatans were becoming Indians, English were becoming Virginians, Ibo were becoming Africans or Negroes, and they were all becoming creoles to one degree or another. Ethnic identities were continually produced and contested by the inhabitants of the seventeenth-century Chesapeake (for example, Deal 1993; Haney López 1995; Isaac 1982; Walsh 1997), and material culture probably played a part in their creation and maintenance, as it often does (Anderson 1991; Bourdieu 1984; Hodder 1987; Palmer 1998).

Recently, research on the ethnic/racial attribution of colonoware was characterized as "a debate headed nowhere" (Singleton and Bograd 1995:26). Of course, arguments that imply "pots [or pipes] equal people" should be avoided; however, it may be that locally made pipes *can* be used to enhance our understanding of "ethnic groups and boundaries" in seventeenth-century Chesapeake, the current standoff notwithstanding.

3. These egalitarian attitudes toward smoking shifted in the eighteenth and nineteenth centuries and were after a time found only among the working classes (Bell 1995:26).

4. Ideally, though, according to Rouse, modal analysis will be a procedure that precedes, but does not replace, the taxonomic classification (1939:112).

5. In fact, work by Henry (1979) demonstrated the correlation of certain decorative motifs with certain forms.

6. 44JC9.

7. 44WB68 and 44WB70.

8. The pattern depicted in figure 10.6 has also shown up as a lip treatment on several pipes, all from a single context at Green Spring.

9. Of the four fragments with panels, two contain impressed initials.

10. Blackman, Stein, and Vandiver make the interesting point that noncentralized production (even by specialists) would lead to a certain amount of diversity, not only from differences in skill or style, but also out of competition in the marketplace (Blackman, Stein, and Vandiver 1993:75).

11. Studies of ceramic pipes made in prehistoric North America, and of postmedieval markets in England, show they are distributed up to fifty miles from their manufacture site (Kuhn 1986:11, 14; Oak-Rind 1980:349, 360).

References Cited

Agbe-Davies, A. S.

2001 Thinking Outside the Box: New Avenues for Research for Locally Made Pipes. Paper presented at the annual meeting of the Jamestown Conference, Jamestown, Va.

Alvey, R. C., and R. R. Laxton

1974 Analysis of Some Nottingham Clay Pipes. *Science and Archaeology* 13:3–12.

1977 Further Analysis of Some Nottingham Clay Pipes. *Science and Archaeology* 19:20–29.

Anderson, B.
1991 *Imagined Communities.* 2d ed. Verso, London.

Atkinson, D., and A. Oswald
1969 London Clay Tobacco Pipes. Oxford Univ. Press, Oxford.

Bell, A.
1995 Widows, "Free Sisters," and "Independent Girls": Historic Models and an Archaeology of Post-Medieval English Gender Systems. *Kroeber Anthropological Society Papers* 78:17–32.

Billings, W. M.
1996 Sir William Berkeley and the Diversification of the Virginia Economy. *Virginia Magazine of History and Biography* 104(4):443–454.

Binford, L. R.
1961 A New Method of Calculating Dates from Kaolin Pipe Stem Samples. *Southeastern Archaeological Conference Newsletter* 9(1):19–21.

Blackman, M. J., G. J. Stein, and P. B. Vandiver
1993 The Standardization Hypothesis and Ceramic Mass Production: Technological, Compositional, and Metric Indexes of Craft Specialization at Tell Leilan, Syria. *American Antiquity* 58(1):60–80.

Bourdieu, P.
1984 *Distinction.* Harvard Univ. Press, Cambridge.

Breen, N.
2001 *Tobacco Culture: The Mentality of the Great Tidewater Planters on the Eve of Revolution.* Princeton Univ. Press, Princeton.

Brew, J. O.
1971 The Use and Abuse of Taxonomy. In *Man's Imprint from the Past: Readings in the Methods of Archaeology,* edited by J. Deetz, 73–107. Little, Brown and Co., Boston.

Carson, J.
1954 *Green Spring Plantation in the Seventeenth Century: House Report.* Report on File, Colonial Williamsburg Foundation, Williamsburg, Va.

Caywood, L. R.
1955 *Green Spring Plantation: Archeological Report.* Colonial National Historical Park, NPS, Yorktown, Va.

Cleland, C. E.
1988 Questions of Substance, Questions that Count. *Historical Archaeology* 22(1):13–17.

Courtwright, D. T.
2001 *Forces of Habit: Drugs and the Making of the Modern World.* Harvard Univ. Press, Cambridge.

Crass, D. C.
1981 *A Formal Analysis of the Clay Pipes from Green Spring.* Master of Arts, College of William and Mary, Williamsburg, Va.
1988 The Clay Pipes from Green Spring Plantation (44 JC 9), Virginia. *Historical Archaeology* 22(1):83–97.

Crossley, D.
1990 *Post-medieval Archaeology in Britain.* Leicester Univ. Press, London.

Davidson, Thomas E.
1995 The Virginia Earthenwares Project: Characterizing 17th-Century Earthenwares by Electronic Image Analysis. *Northeast Historical Archaeology* 24:51–64.

Deal, J. D.
1993 *Race and Class in Colonial Virginia: Indians, Englishmen, and Africans on the Eastern Shore during the Seventeenth Century.* Garland Publishing, New York.

Deetz, J.
1965 *Dynamics of Stylistic Change in Arikara Ceramics.* Univ. of Illinois Press, Urbana.
1987 Harrington Histograms Versus Binford Mean Dates as a Technique for Establishing the Occupational Sequencesof Sites at Flowerdew Hundred, Virginia. *American Archaeology* 6(1):62–67.
1993 *Flowerdew Hundred: The Archaeology of a Virginia Plantation.* Univ. of Virginia Press, Charlottesville, Va.
1996 *In Small Things Forgotten: The Archaeology of Early American Life.* Revised and expanded ed. Anchor Books, New York.

Dimmick, J.
1929 Green Spring. *William and Mary Quarterly,* 2d ser., 9(2):129–130.

Dunnell, R. C.
1971 *Systematics in Prehistory.* Free Press, New York.

Emerson, M. C.
1988 Decorated Clay Tobacco Pipes from the Chesapeake. Unpublished Ph.D. dissertation, Univ. of California at Berkeley.
1994 Decorated Clay Tobacco Pipes from the Chesapeake. In *Historical Archaeology of the Chesapeake,* edited by P. A. Shakel and B. J. Little, 35–49. Smithsonian Institution Press, Washington, D.C.
1999 African Inspirations in a New World Art and Artifact: Decorated Pipes from the Chesapeake. In *I, Too, Am America: Studies in African-American Archaeology,* edited by T. A. Singleton, 47–74. Univ. Press of Virginia, Charlottesville.

Ford, J. A.
1954 On the Concept of Types. *American Anthropologist* 56:42–54.

Galucci, E. A., D. Muraca, and P. McLaughlin
1994 Identifying Producer-Client Relationships at the Bruton Heights Tile Kiln. Paper presented at the Annual Meeting of the Society for Historical Archaeology, Vancouver.

Goodman, J.
1993 *Tobacco in History: The Cultures of Dependence.* Routledge, London.

Hall, R. L.
1977 An Anthropocentric Perspective for Eastern United States Prehistory. *American Antiquity* 42(4):499–518.

Haney López, I. F.
1995 The Social Construction of Race. In *Critical Race Theory: The Cutting Edge,* edited by R. Delgado, 191–203. Temple Univ. Press, Philadelphia.

Harrington, J. C.
1951 Tobacco Pipes from Jamestown. *Quarterly Bulletin of the Archaeological Society of Virginia* 5(4).
1954 Dating Stem Fragments of Seventeenth and Eighteenth Century Clay Tobacco Pipes. *Quarterly Bulletin of the Archaeological Society of Virginia* 9(1):9–13.

Heite, E. F.
1972 American-Made Pipes from the Camden Site. *Quarterly Bulletin of the Archeological Society of Virginia* 27:94–99.

Henry, S. L.
1979 Terra-cotta Tobacco Pipes in Seventeenth-Century Maryland and Virginia: A Preliminary Study. *Historical Archaeology* 13:14–37.

Hill, J. N., and R. K. Evans
1972 A Model for Classification and Typology. In *Models in Archaeology,* edited by D. L. Clarke, 231–273. Methuen & Co., Ltd., London.

Hodder, I.
1987 The Contextual Analysis of Symbolic Meanings. In *The Archaeology of Contextual Meanings,* edited by I. Hodder, 1–10. Cambridge Univ. Press, Cambridge.

Isaac, R.
1982 *The Transformation of Virginia, 1740–1790.* W. W. Norton and Co., New York.

Johnson, M.
1996 *An Archaeology of Capitalism.* Blackwell Publishers, Oxford.

Kelso, W. M., and B. A. Straube
2000 *Jamestown Rediscovery VI.* Association for the Preservation of Virginia Antiquities, Richmond.

Kingery, W. D.
1982 Plausible Inferences from Ceramic Artifacts. In *Archaeological Ceramics,* edited by J. S. Olin and A. D. Franklin, 37–45. Smithsonian Institution Press, Washington, D.C.

Kuhn, R.
1986 Interaction Patterns in Eastern New York: A Trace Element Analysis of Iroquoian and Algonkian Ceramics. *Bulletin and Journal of Archaeology for New York State* 92:9–21.

Kulikoff, A.
1986 *Tobacco and Slaves: The Development of Southern Cultures in the Chesapeake, 1680–1800.* Univ. of North Carolina Press, Chapel Hill.

Lathrap, D. W.
1983 Recent Shipibo-Conibo Ceramics and Their Implications for Archaeological Interpretation. In *Structure and Cognition in Art,* edited by D. K. Washburn, 25–39. Cambridge Univ. Press, Cambridge.

Lechtman, H.
1977 Style in Technology—Some Early Thoughts. In *Material Culture: Styles, Organization, and Dynamics of Technology,* edited by H. Lechtman and R. S. Merrill, 3–20. West Press, New York.

Linton, R.
1924 *Use of Tobacco among North American Indians.* Field Museum of Natural History, Chicago.

Little, B. J.
1996 People with History: An Update on Historical Archaeology in the United States. In *Images of the Recent Past: Readings in Historical Archaeology,* edited by C. E. Orser Jr., 42–78. Alta Mira Press, Walnut Creek, Calif.

Magoon, D.
1999 "Chesapeake" Pipes and Uncritical Assumptions: A View from Northeastern North Carolina. *North Carolina Archaeology* 48:107–126.

Mallios, S. W., J. C. Monroe, and Q. Emmett
2001 A Seventeenth-Century Chesapeake Cottage Industry: New Evidence and a Dating Formula for Colono Tobacco Pipes. Paper presented at the annual meeting of the Jamestown Conference, Jamestown, Va.

Matson, F. R.
1982 Archaeological Ceramics and the Physical Sciences: Problem Definition and Results. In *Archaeological Ceramics,* edited by J. S. Olin and A. D. Franklin, 19–28. Smithsonian Institution Press, Washington, D.C.

McCartney, M. W.
2000 *Documentary History of Jamestown Island.* Vol. 3, *Biographies of Owners and Residents.* Colonial Williamsburg Foundation and the College of William and Mary, Williamsburg, Va.

Metz, J.
1999 Industrial Transition and the Rise of a "Creole" Society in the Chesapeake, 1660–1725. In *Historical Archaeology, Identity Formation, and the Interpretation of Ethnicity,* edited by M. Franklin and G. Fesler, 11–30. Dietz Press, Richmond.

Metz, J., J. Jones, D. Pickett, and D. Muraca
1998 *"Upon the Palisado" and Other Stories of Place from Bruton Heights.* Dietz Press, Richmond.

Middleton, A. P.
1984 *Tobacco Coast: A Maritime History of Chesapeake Bay in the Colonial Era.* Johns Hopkins Univ. Press, Baltimore.

Miller, H. M.
1991 Tobacco Pipes from Pope's Fort, St. Mary's City, Maryland: An English Civil War Site on the American Frontier. In *The Archaeology of the Clay Tobacco Pipe: Chesapeake Bay,* edited by P. Davey and D. J. Pogue. B. A. R. International Series 566, Oxford.

Mitchell, V.
1976 Decorated Brown Clay Pipebowls from Nominy Plantation: A Progress Report. *Quarterly Bulletin of the Archeological Society of Virginia* 31(2):83–92.
1983 The History of Nominy Plantation with Emphasis on the Clay Tobacco Pipes. *Historic Clay Tobacco Pipes* 2:3–38.

Monroe, J. C.
2002 *Negotiating African-American Ethnicity in the Seventeenth-Century Chesapeake.* Archaeology of the Clay Tobacco Pipe XVI, British Archaeological Reports International Series 1042. Archaeopress, Oxford.

Morgan, E. S.
1975 *American Slavery, American Freedom: The Ordeal of Colonial Virginia.* W. W. Norton & Co., New York.

Mouer, L. D.
1993 Chesapeake Creoles: The Creation of Folk Culture in Colonial Virginia. In *The Archaeology of Seventeenth-Century Virginia,* edited by T. R. Reinhart and D. J. Pogue, 105–166. Deitz Press, Richmond, Va.

Mouer, L. D., M. E. N. Hodges, S. R. Potter, S. L. H. Renaud, I. Noël Hume, D. J. Pogue, M. W. McCartney, and T. E. Davidson
1999 Colonoware Pottery, Chesapeake Pipes, and "Uncritical Assumptions." In *I, Too, Am America: Studies in African-American Archaeology,* edited by T. A. Singleton, 75–115. Univ. Press of Virginia, Charlottesville.

Neff, H.
1993 Theory, Sampling, and Analytical Techniques in the Archaeological Study of Prehistoric Ceramics. *American Antiquity* 58(1):23–44.

Neiman, F. D., and J. A. King
1999 Who Smoked Chesapeake Pipes? Paper presented at the Annual Meeting of the Society for Historical Archaeology, Salt Lake City.

Noël Hume, A.
1979 Clay Tobacco Pipes Excavated at Martin's Hundred, Virginia, 1976–1978. In *The Archaeology of the Clay Tobacco Pipe,* edited by P. Davey, 3–36. vol. 60. B. A. R. International Series, Oxford.

Noël Hume, I.
1991 *A Guide to Artifacts of Colonial America.* Vintage Books, New York.

Noël Hume, I., and A. Noël Hume
2001 *The Archaeology of Martin's Hundred.* Univ. of Pennsylvania Museum of Anthropology and Archaeology, Philadelphia.

Oak-Rind, H.
1980 Distribution of Clay Tobacco Pipes Round Their Place of Manufacture, 349–361. In *The Archaeology of the Clay Tobacco Pipe III Britain: The North and West.* British Archaeological Reports International Series 78, Oxford.

Orser, C. E., Jr.
1996 *A Historical Archaeology of the Modern World.* Plenum Press, New York.

Orton, C., P. Tyers, and A. Vince
1993 *Pottery in Archaeology.* Cambridge Univ. Press, Cambridge.

Oswald, A.
1975 *Clay Pipes for the Archaeologist* 14. British Archaeological Reports, Oxford.

Palmer, C.
1998 From Theory to Practice: Experiencing the Nation in Everyday Life. *Journal of Material Culture* 3(2):175–199.

Pawson, M.
1969 Clay Tobacco Pipes in the Knowles Collection. *Quarterly Bulletin of the Archeological Society of Virginia* 23(3):115–147.

Pittman, W. E.
1993 A Survey of Seventeenth-Century Chesapeake Ceramic Typologies. In *The Archaeology of Seventeenth-Century Virginia,* edited by T. R. Reinhart and D. J. Pogue, 357–369. Deitz Press, Richmond, Va.

Rountree, H. C.
1989 *The Powhatan Indians of Virginia: Their Traditional Culture.* Univ. of Oklahoma Press, Norman.

Rouse, I.
1939 *Prehistory in Haiti: A Study in Method.* Yale University Publications in Anthropology 21. Yale Univ. Press, New Haven.
1971 The Classification of Artifacts in Archaeology. In *Man's Imprint from the Past: Readings in the Methods of Archaeology,* edited by J. Deetz, 108–125. Little, Brown and Co., Boston.

Sabloff, J. A., and R. E. Smith
1969 The Importance of Both Analytical and Taxonomic Classification in the Type-Variety System. *American Antiquity* 34(3):278–285.

Sackett, J. R.
1990 Style and Ethnicity in Archaeology: The Case for Isochrestism. In *The Uses of Style in Archaeology,* edited by M. W. Conkey and C. A. Hastorf, 32–43. Cambridge Univ. Press, Cambridge.

Schuyler, R. L.
1988 Archaeological Remains, Documents, and Anthropology: A Call for a New Culture History. *Historical Archaeology* 22:37–42.
1997 Cultural Evolution and the Continuing Attempts to Define Historical Archaeology. Paper presented at the Annual Meeting of the Society for Historical Archaeology, Corpus Christi, Tex.

Singleton, T., and M. D. Bograd
1995 *The Archaeology of the African Diaspora in the Americas.* Guides to the Archaeological Literature of the Immigrant Experience in America, No. 2. Braun-Brumfield, Ann Arbor.

Smith, F. H.
1993 *Eighteenth Century History of the Ludwell Family at Rich Neck Plantation in Williamsburg, Virginia.* Colonial Williamsburg Foundation, Dept. of Archaeological Research.

Smith, J. M.
1981 The Pottery and Kiln of Green Spring: A Study in Seventeenth Century Material Culture. Unpublished master's thesis, Dept. of Anthropology, College of William and Mary, Williamsburg, Va.

Sprinkle, J.
1992 Loyalists and Baconians: The Participants in Bacon's Rebellion in Virginia, 1676–1677. Ph.D. dissertation, College of William and Mary, Williamsburg, Va.

Straube, B. A.
1995 The Colonial Potters of Tidewater Virginia. *Journal of Early Southern Decorative Arts* 21(2):1–40.

Walker, I.
1977 *Clay Tobacco-Pipes, with Particular Reference to the Bristol Industry.* Parks Canada, Ottawa.

Wallerstein, I.
1980 *The Modern World-System.* Vol. 2, *Mercantilism and the Consolidation of the European World-Economy, 1600–1750.* Academic Press, New York.

Walsh, L. S.
1993 Slave Life, Slave Society, and Tobacco Production in the Tidewater Chesapeake, 1620–1820. In *Cultivation and Culture: Labor and the Shaping of Slave Life in the Americas,* edited by I. Berlin and P. D. Morgan, 170–199. Univ. Press of Virginia, Charlottesville.
1997 *From Calabar to Carter's Grove: The History of a Virginia Slave Community.* Univ. Press of Virginia, Charlottesville.

Weatherill, L., and R. Edwards
1971 Pottery Making in London and Whitehaven in the Late Seventeenth Century. *Post-Medieval Archaeology* 5:160–181.

York County
1976 *York County, Virginia Deeds, Orders, Wills, etc., Number 9, 1691–1694.* Compiled by J. F. Dorman. Dorman, Washington, D.C.

11. Red Clay Tobacco Pipes: Petrographic Window into Seventeenth-Century Economics at Jamestown, Virginia, and New England

Patricia Capone and Elinor Downs

Red clay tobacco pipes are found in Colonial period sites in eastern North America, but relatively little is known about their production, technology, or their economic significance. This lack of knowledge about the red clay pipes stands in great contrast to their white clay counterparts, which have received much attention. In this pilot study, petrographic analysis is used to explore the production location, technology, and economic significance of red clay pipes from sites in New England and the Chesapeake, Virginia, area (Map 11.1). We demonstrate that petrographic analysis is a suitable method for examining questions of production and technology of red clay pipes. Results demonstrate that while standardized technology is shared by all samples, production appears to have been localized. This preliminary information is interpreted to suggest a view into the seventeenth-century economic system.

The Chesapeake Area

Red clay pipes from the Chesapeake area have been the focus of relatively more study compared to those from New England (Deetz 1993, 1996; Emerson 1994; Henry 1979; Magoon 1999). Deetz (1996) and Emerson (1994) offer a Chesapeake-based model for production location, technology, and economic significance of red clay pipes:

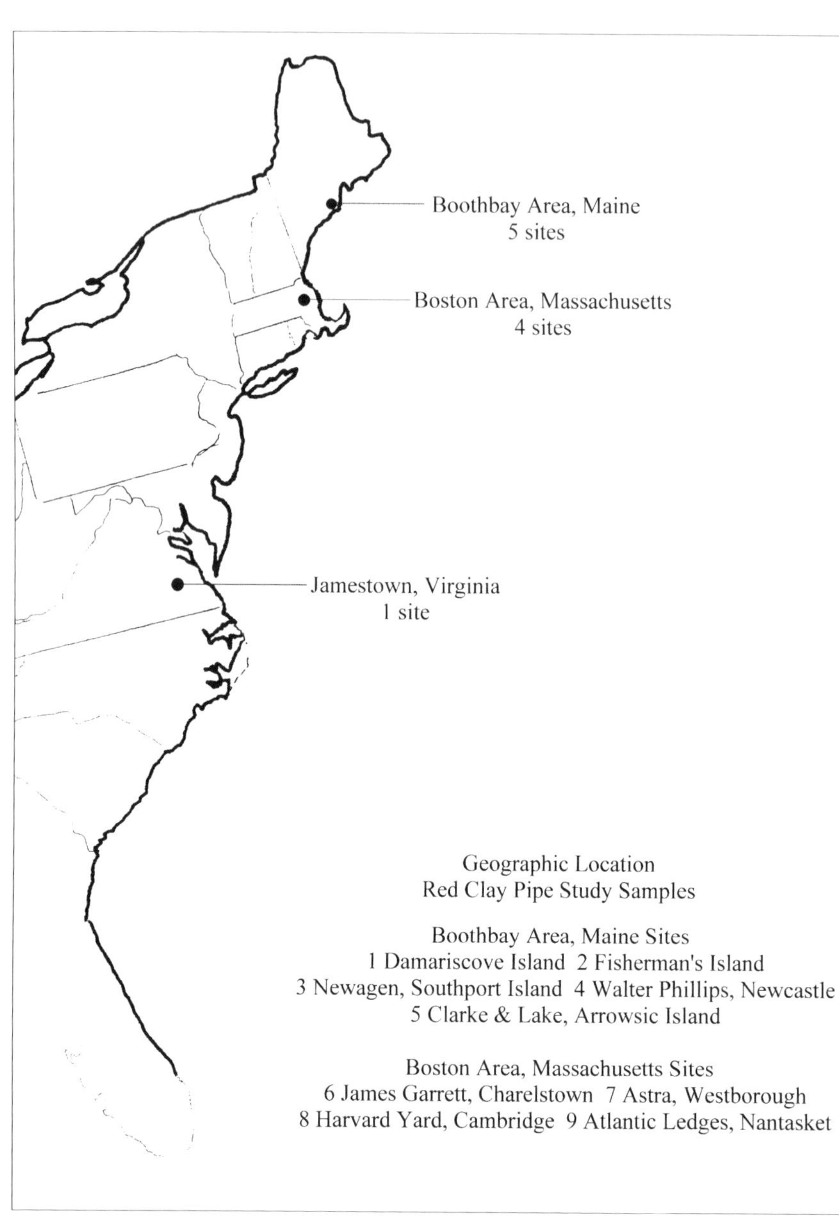

MAP 11.1 ▸ *Location of sites used in analysis.*

- Produced chiefly in the Chesapeake area with local raw materials between approximately 1630 and 1720
- Geographic range in the Chesapeake only, and especially within plantation contexts, and
- Produced and consumed by West Africans (however, see also Agbe-Davies, this volume).

At Jamestown, Virginia, within the Chesapeake area, red clay pipes are found in greater frequency than in New England and constitute about 20 percent of all pipes (Henry 1979:18). Jamestown pipes are variously described as buff, terra-cotta, or brick-red in color, with a variety of bowl shapes, many of which are decorated (Henry 1979). One large group, however, is very similar in color (reddish-yellow) and style (rounded bowl) to the New England red clay pipes (Henry 1979). This similarity may suggest a relationship between the Jamestown pipes and the New England pipes, as implied by the Chesapeake-based production described in Deetz's (1996) and Emerson's work (1994). This project was designed in part to explore this question.

New England

Archaeological contexts of the New England samples in this study contrast with the Chesapeake model of West African plantation contexts for the production and consumption of red clay pipes. Also, the frequency of the red clay pipes in New England assemblages is much lower than in the Chesapeake area. For example, in New England, red clay pipes tend to occur as small clusters in domestic or village settlements or as isolated finds in coastal areas and usually represent less than 4 percent of all pipes in excavated assemblages (Bradley 1997; Faulkner 1991). Additionally, New England red clay pipes are more homogenous in appearance with typical reddish-yellow color and rounded bowl shape. New England red clay pipes especially contrast with their white counterparts in that they have thick stems and lack decoration and makers' marks (Faulkner 1991). No models have been developed for New England red clay pipe economics as they have been for the Chesapeake area. Rather, open questions have developed such as (1) whether New England red clay pipes originated in the purported center of red clay pipe production, the Chesapeake area; and (2) whether they may have been produced at a local center, the James Garrett site in the Boston area (Baker 1985; Bradley 1997; Faulkner 1991). This project was designed in part to explore these specific questions as well as the more general question of seventeenth-century economy.

Sampling and Methodology

The pilot study sample set is small, consisting of twenty-six red clay pipe fragments (bowls and stems) from ten different archaeological sites, four from Jamestown, Virginia, in the Chesapeake area; nine from the Boston area in Massachusetts; and fourteen from the Boothbay area in Maine (Table 11.1). Half of the samples derive from excavations, with the others from surface collections, as indicated in Table 11.1. Direct dating of red clay pipes by size of the bore has not been standardized, as it has been for the white kaolin pipes. Rather, the samples in this study are dated based on historical and archaeological context. Most of the New England and Chesapeake red clay pipes in the study sample fall roughly within a fairly well-defined time range of A.D. 1622–1700 during the early Colonial period. Pipe fragments from two later contexts, namely Astra Farm, Massachusetts (1780), and Harvard Yard, Massachusetts (1795), are also included. The study sample reflects a variety of seventeenth-century colonial contexts such as domestic (urban and agrarian), trading, and fishing settlements and university settings. The sample set was chosen for variation in geographical location and type of site toward observing geographic patterning by production location or site context. These factors were chosen because of their suggested role in the production and use of Chesapeake red clay pipes as described above.

TABLE 11.1 ▸ STUDY SAMPLE OF RED CLAY TOBACCO PIPES

Area Location and Site	Number of Samples	Site Context
Chesapeake Area, VA		
Jamestown	4	Village
Boston Area, MA		
James Garrett	3	Urban, domestic
Atlantic Ledges	1	Fishing settlement?
Astra Farm	1	Agrarian, domestic
Harvard Yard	4	University
Boothbay Area, ME		
Damariscove Island	1	Fishing settlement
Fisherman's Island	1	Fishing settlement
Newagen	9	Trading settlement
Walter Phillips	1	Agrarian, domestic
Clarke & Lake	2	Trading settlement
Total	**27**	

Each sample was examined in thin section under a petrographic microscope. The system of petrographic description used in this study follows that developed by Whitbread (1989) and includes characteristics of fabric texture and raw material composition, both of which are informative for production location and technology. Fabric refers to the arrangement, size, shape, frequency, and composition of its three main components: micromass, inclusions, and voids. Micromass is often regarded as the fired-clay matrix and comprises particles smaller than about fifteen microns. Inclusions are frequently thought of as temper added by the potter, but they may also be naturally occurring particles in the clay that lack plasticity, and are usually larger than fifteen microns. They serve to inhibit cracking of the fabric. Voids are open vesicles in the fabric, which may exhibit distinguishing arrangements, sizes, or shapes. Each of these three components can be a window into geographic location and technology of ceramic production.

The petrographic analysis was conducted initially without knowledge of the provenience or chronological placement of the samples in order to most objectively assess the characteristics. Subsequent to that the petrographic characteristics and the contextual information were considered together for exploration of patterns in the data that might address questions relating to production location and the technology.

Results

This pilot study shows that petrographic analysis provides a useful approach to understanding production location and technology and the economic system in which red clay pipes existed. The fabric of red clay pipes is well suited to petrographic analysis due to its relatively coarse texture, especially when compared to white clay counterparts, whose particle size is too fine for petrographic analysis. A detailed presentation of the petrographic data are available in Table 11.2.

The results of the petrographic analysis of the nine New England samples indicate that production is most likely to be localized rather than centralized. The samples from nearly every New England site are distinct enough from one another to suggest that they were produced in different locations. The simplest explanation for this pattern is localized production rather than import from many different locations. A combination of textural characteristics and mineralogical composition forms the basis of this finding.

For example, the Newagen, Maine, samples are especially coarse compared to those from other sites. This distinction may be due to a difference in raw material source or perhaps to a lesser degree of clay processing (technology). Additionally, high mica concentrations in both the Newagen and Damariscove samples

TABLE 11.2 ▸ Petrographic Descriptionsof Red Clay Pipe Samples in the Study Area

#	Sample Site	State	Petrographic description	Petrographic Group
1	Newagen Beach	ME	Newagen Beach group samples have a higher frequency of coarse fraction (including monocrystalline quartz, and quartz/feldspar rock)than any other samples. Also, the coarse fraction itself is larger in size than the other samples (coarse-sand sized).	Coarse
2	Newagen Beach	ME	Newagen Beach group samples have a higher frequency of coarse fraction (including monocrystalline quartz, and quartz/feldspar rock)than any other samples. Also, the coarse fraction itself is larger in size than the other samples (coarse-sand sized).	Coarse
3	Newagen Beach	ME	Newagen Beach group samples have a higher frequency of coarse fraction (including monocrystalline quartz, and quartz/feldspar rock)than any other samples. Also, the coarse fraction itself is larger in size than the other samples (coarse-sand sized).	Coarse
4	Newagen Beach	ME	Newagen Beach group samples have a higher frequency of coarse fraction (including monocrystalline quartz, and quartz/feldspar rock)than any other samples. Also, the coarse fraction itself is larger in size than the other samples (coarse-sand sized).	Coarse
5	Newagen Beach	ME	Newagen Beach group samples have a higher frequency of coarse fraction (including monocrystalline quartz, and quartz/feldspar rock)than any other samples. Also, the coarse fraction itself is larger in size than the other samples (coarse-sand sized).	Coarse
6	Newagen land	ME	Resembles Newagen Beach group.	Coarse

Table 11.2 ▸ Petrographic Descriptionsof Red Clay Pipe Samples in the Study Area (continued)

#	Sample Site	State	Petrographic description	Petrographic Group
1	Newagen Beach	ME	Newagen Beach group samples have a higher frequency of coarse fraction (including monocrystalline quartz, and quartz/feldspar rock)than any other samples. Also, the coarse fraction itself is larger in size than the other samples (coarse-sand sized).	Coarse
9	Newagen land	ME	Lenses of concentrated mica similar to 106. Hornblende. Very rare feldspar.	Mica lenses
100	Astra, Westborough	MA	Mainly monocrystalline quartz. Remainder too fine to resolve.	No distinguishing characteristics
101	Atlantic Ledges, Nantasket	MA	Subangular monocrystalline quartz medium sand, mica fine sand, hornblende medium sand. Parallel orientation of micas, voids and clay particles.	Quartz, mica, hornblende sand cobine with groundmass characteristics which together distinguish this from other samples.
102	Harvard Yard	MA	Monocrystalline quartz fine and medium sand, patterned birefringence	Fine groundmass, mica rich
103	Harvard Yard	MA	Subangular/round monocrystalline quartz fine sand, hornblende fine sand, mica silt, slightly finer than 101	Fine groundmass, mica rich
104	Harvard Yard	MA	Monocrystalline quartz fine sand, mica silt, hornblende fine sand, finer than 103	Fine groundmass, mica rich
105	Harvard Yard	MA	Similar to 103	Fine groundmass, mica rich
106	Damariscove	ME	Monocrystalline quartz fine sand/ mica silt. Not much mica as 101-105. Lenses of mica concentration.	Mica lenses
107	Newagen Beach	ME	Similar to all	No distinguishing characteristic

TABLE 11.2 ▸ Petrographic Descriptionsof Red Clay Pipe Samples in the Study Area (continued)

#	Sample Site	State	Petrographic description	Petrographic Group
108	Newagen Beach	ME	Similar to all	No distinguishing characteristic
111	James Garrett, Charlestown	MA	Rock fragment, banded. More feldspar than other samples	Rock fragments, medium groundmass
212	Arrowsic Island	ME	Monocrystalline quartz round medium sand, quartz/mica medium grained igneous rock medium sand, fine sand hornblende, mica, feldspar, micaceous groundmass.	Rock fragments, medium groundmass
213	Arrowsic Island	ME	Monocrystalline quartz round medium sand, fine sand hornblende, mica, feldspar, micaceous groundmass.	Rock fragments, medium groundmass
214	Newcastle	ME	Monocrystalline quartz round medium sand, quartz/mica medium grained igneous rock medium sand, fine sand hornblende, mica, feldspar, micaceous groundmass.	Rock fragments, medium groundmass
215	Fisherman's Island	ME	Monocrystalline quartz round medium sand, fine sand hornblende, mica, feldspar, micaceous groundmass.	Rock fragments, medium groundmass
15.2	Jamestown	VA	This sample resembles Jamestown samples 115.2, 215.2 and 315.2. 115.2 notes describe slight difference from that sample, mainly in higher degree of packing of inclusions, similar groundmass. Main inclusion type and size: quartz, bimodal distribution lar	
115.2	Jamestown	VA	See above.	
215.2	Jamestown	VA	See above.	
315.2	Jamestown	VA	See above. Packing: distance apart 2-3 times fine sand size.	

in Maine may reflect a common clay source, a common production location, or a similar clay source available to different production locations. The geographic proximity of Newagen and Damariscove suggests that they may share a common production location.

The Harvard Yard samples were distinctive from the other samples for their fine texture, which is combined with high mica concentration. It may be significant that these samples date approximately one hundred years later than the other samples (1780 and 1795). The samples from the James Garrett House in Charlestown, Massachusetts; the Clarke and Lake trading settlement in Arrowsic, Maine; the Walter Phillips Homestead in Newcastle, Maine; and Fisherman's Island, Maine, all contain types of rock fragment inclusions that differ from one another, each of which might be shown to be characteristic of a distinct production location through further study of a larger sample set. For example, the James Garrett House samples exhibit igneous rock fragments that could be pursued as characteristic of production source.

The sample from Astra Farm, Westborough, Massachusetts, did not exhibit distinguishing characteristics, while the remaining individual sample from the Atlantic Ledges, Nantasket, Massachusetts, shows a combination of characteristics that distinguish it from other samples but may not be suggested as a group based on the single sample.

The results of the Jamestown, Virginia, samples show that the samples share enough characteristics to suggest that they form a group distinct from the New England samples and that they may have been produced at either a single location or at multiple locations with similar raw materials. The main evidence for this is the generally generic quality of the raw materials, quartz inclusions in a micaceous micromass (Figure 11.1). The high degree of similarity among the raw materials and textural features of the Jamestown samples could suggest that geographically limited production is more likely than multiple locations with similar materials. Also, the Jamestown samples differ enough from the New England samples to indicate that Jamestown pipes of this type are not among the New England samples. In particular, the void frequency is notably higher among the Jamestown samples; void size is notably larger among the Jamestown samples, and a notable frequency of opaque minerals is present in the Jamestown samples.

Generalized petrographic patterns shared by all the samples from both the Chesapeake and the New England areas reveal that a common technology was used. In the stem fragments, the concentric patterning of particles such as mica and voids around the bore suggests that all of the stems were produced by a similar technique and that the stems were probably made separately from the bowls. This production technique contrasts with the molded technique common to most white clay pipes. Furthermore, no evidence of mold seams is present in any of the red clay pipes in the study sample. The stem pattern and lack of seam indicates that the stems may have been made either by drawing a coil of clay

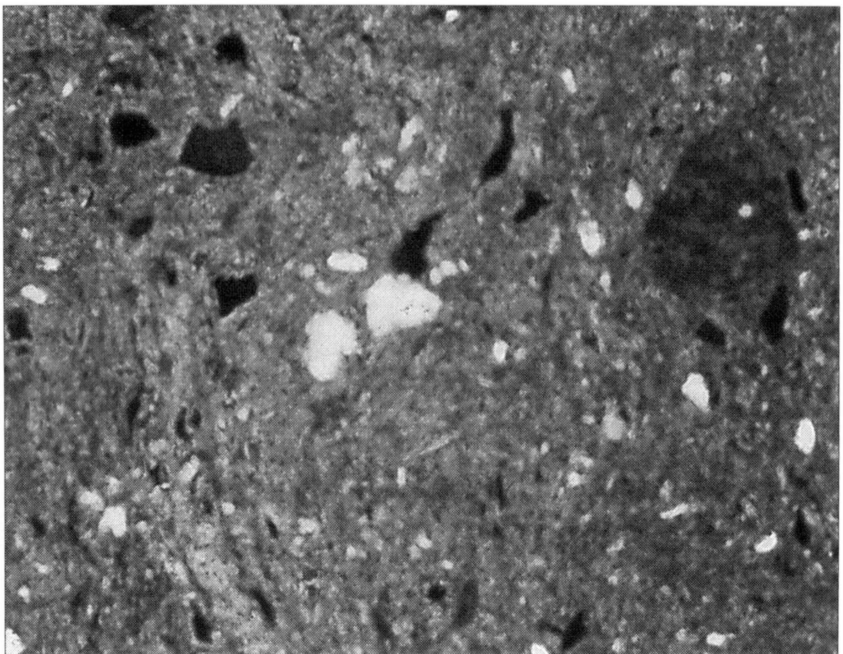

FIG. 11.1. ▸ *Quartz inclusions in a micaceous micromass at the Jamestown, Virginia, site.*

through a die or by rolling a coil of clay and forcing a dowel through to create a bore. The elongation of voids parallel to the bore supports both of these possible construction methods.

These results show that the most common expedient method within petrographic analysis for studying production location of ceramics is not the most useful method for studying these pipes. The most common method focuses on the mineral identification of inclusions and on the composition of the ceramic raw materials, as popularized by Anna Shepard (1965). The problem with this method for red clay pipes arises due to the relative lack of distinctive rock and mineral types in these samples compared to other wares. Rather, the more time-consuming analysis of fabric texture with attention to the arrangement, grain size, shape, and frequency of inclusions and micromass provided most of the results relating to production location and technology, which are presented here. However, once initial patterns have been identified, textural characteristics may be efficiently identified and described.

Petrographic patterns observed in this study sample were influenced most by their geographic locations, less by the date, and probably not at all by site function or whether the pipes were excavated or surface collected.

In sum, the results of this pilot study on red clay pipes show that petrographic analysis is a suitable method for exploring questions of production location, technology, and the economic system they reflect. Analysis of a larger sample group would be desirable in order to draw more firm conclusions about the specific origins of colonial red clay pipes. These preliminary findings provide provisional answers to the questions of production location and economic dependence posed earlier: results do not support implied models for a relationship of economic dependence for red clay pipes by New England on the Chesapeake area or on the James Garrett site in the Boston area. Rather, evidence suggests that production of the New England red clay pipes was local, at numerous locations throughout New England, and not centralized. The extent of distribution could be explored through further study. The results suggest a degree of economic autonomy among seventeenth-century Colonial sites. On the other hand, the technology shared by all samples suggests shared behavior and therefore interaction in some realm. The extent to which this evidence has implications for social boundaries or other aspects of society could be a fruitful focus of future study.

References Cited

Baker, Emerson W

1985 The Clarke and Lake Company: The Historical Archaeology of a Seventeenth-Century Maine Settlement. *Occasional Publications in Maine Archaeology,* No. 4. Maine Historic Preservation Committee, Augusta, Maine.

Bradley, Robert L.

1992 *Analysis of Historic Artifacts Allegedly from the Ark, Cape Newagen, Southport.* Ms. on file at the Maine Historic Preservation Commission, Augusta, Maine.

1997 Report on the Phips Site Survey, 1994–1997. Ms. on file at the Maine Historic Preservation Commission, Augusta, Maine.

Deetz, James

1993 *Flowerdew Hundred: The Archaeology of a Virginia Plantation, 1619–1864.* Univ. Press of Virginia, Charlottesville.

1996 *In Small Things Forgotten: An Archaeology of Early American Life.* Anchor Books, New York.

Emerson, Matthew C.

1994 Decorated Clay Tobacco Pipes from the Chesapeake: An African Connection. In *Historical Archaeology of the Chesapeake,* edited by Paul A. Shackel and Barbara J. Little, 35–50. Smithsonian Institution Press, Washington, D.C.

Faulkner, Alaric

1985 Archaeology of the Cod Fishery: Damariscove Island. *Historical Archaeology* 19(2):57–85.

1991 *Redware Clay Tobacco Pipes from Maine's Seventeenth Century Anglo-Acadian Frontier.* Ms. on file, Dept. of Anthropology, Univ. of Maine, Orono, Maine.

Greene, Frances B.

1906 *History of Boothbay, Southport and Boothbay Harbor—1623–1905, with Family Genealogies.* Loring, Short and Harmon, Portland, Maine.

Henry, Susan

1979 Terra-cotta Tobacco Pipes in Seventeenth-Century Maryland and Virginia. *Historical Archaeology* (13):14–37.

Magoon, Dane T.

1999 "Chesapeake" Pipes and Uncritical Assumptions: A View from Northeastern North Carolina. *North Carolina Archaeology* 48:107–126.

Pendery, Steven R.

1984 *Phase III Chelsea–Water Street Connector Project: Final Report Excavations at the Wapping Street and Maudlin Street Archaeological Districts.* Ms. on file, Peabody Museum of Archaeology and Ethnology, Harvard. Univ., Cambridge, Mass.

Shepard, Anna O.

1965 *Ceramics for the Archaeologist.* Carnegie Institution of Washington, Washington, D.C.

Stubbs, John D.

1992 Underground Harvard: The Archaeology of College Life. Unpublished Ph.D. dissertation, Harvard Univ. University Microfilm International, Ann Arbor, Mich.

Whitbread, Ian

1989 A Proposal for the Systematic Description of Thin Sections toward the Study of Ancient Ceramic Technology. In *Archaeometry, Proceeding of the 25th International Symposium,* edited by Y. Maniatis, 127–138. Elsevier, Amsterdam.

Contributors

ANNA S. AGBE-DAVIES is a staff archaeologist with the Colonial Williamsburg Foundation. Her research on pipes is expanded in her dissertation in anthropology at the University of Pennsylvania. Among the themes it addresses are her current interests in power in plantation societies and issues of artifact classification.

CHARLES A. BELLO is a senior archaeologist and project manager at the Cultural Resource Consulting Group, Highland Park, New Jersey, and a past president and fellow of the Archaeological Society of New Jersey. His research interests include Native American material culture of the Northeast and documenting private archaeological collections.

PATRICIA CAPONE is associate curator at the Peabody Museum of Archaeology and Ethnology, Harvard University. She received a Ph.D. in anthropology from Harvard University in 1995. Her interests include cultural dynamics between Native American and Colonial/Historic European or American cultures, and their manifestations in material culture; materials analysis; and museum/descendant community partnerships.

DIANE DALLAL is curator of archaeology at the South Street Seaport Museum and the director of the museum's urban archaeology center, "New York Unearthed." In addition to tobacco pipes, her research interests include the material culture of seventeenth-century new Amsterdam and early New York and their enslaved populations.

ELINOR DOWNS, M.D., is an independent scholar with interests in archaeology of the Northeast United States and materials analysis. She studied as a special student in the Department of Anthropology, Harvard University.

PENELOPE B. DROOKER is curator of anthropology at the New York State Museum, Albany. Her research on protohistoric interaction networks in eastern North America has been recognized by a Presidential Distinguished Doctoral Dissertation Award from The University at Albany, SUNY, and the C. B. Moore Award "for excellence in archaeology by a young scholar in Southeastern studies" from the Lower Mississippi Survey.

JEFFREY D. IRWIN is the manager of the Cultural Resources Management Program at Fort Bragg, North Carolina. His current research interests include Woodland burial mounds of the Carolina coastal region and modeling prehistoric settlements through lithic raw material characterization. He holds a master's degree in anthropology from the University of Kentucky.

ROB MANN is the Southeast Regional Archaeologist for Louisiana and is based in the Museum of Natural Science at Louisiana State University. He received his Ph.D. from the State University of New York at Binghamton. His research interests include the fur trade, French colonial archaeology, political economy, ethnohistory, and culture contact. He is currently involved in research at Pointe Coupee, an eighteenth-century French colonial site in the Lower Mississippi Valley.

MICHAEL S. NASSANEY is associate professor of anthropology at Western Michigan University. His current research interests include social archaeology, ethnohistory, and the material consequences of culture contact in North America. He is the editor of the University Press of Florida's The American Experience in Archaeological Perspective series.

SEAN M. RAFFERTY is an assistant professor in the anthropology department at the University at Albany, SUNY. He received his Ph.D. from Binghamton University, SUNY, in 2001. His research interests include the archaeology of eastern North America, ritual practices in prehistory, the archaeology of smoking pipes, and residue analysis in archaeology. He is currently the editor of Northeast Anthropology.

PAUL RECKNER received his B.A. in anthropology from Temple University in 1994. He holds a master's degree from Binghamton University, SUNY. He is currently a Ph.D. candidate at Binghamton University, SUNY, and his dissertation project focuses on the interplay of solidarity, difference, and the materiality of social practice within the Ludlow Tent Colony community, Ludlow, Colorado, 1913–14.

NEAL L. TRUBOWITZ, a Registered Professional Archaeologist, currently is an independent consulting scholar. As an affiliate of the Peabody Museum of Archaeology and Ethnology at Harvard University, he is continuing his research on smoking pipes, part of his interest in the colonial era in North America.

RICHARD VEIT is an assistant professor in the Department of History and Anthropology at Monmouth University and directs the university's M.A. program in Liberal Arts. He is the author of *Digging New Jersey's Past: Historical Archaeology in the Garden State* (2002). His research interests include early American material culture, especially tobacco pipes, ceramics, and gravemarkers.

Index